The Muddy River Boys

Dakota Tales

J. David Erickson

J David Erickson
Aug 26, 2012

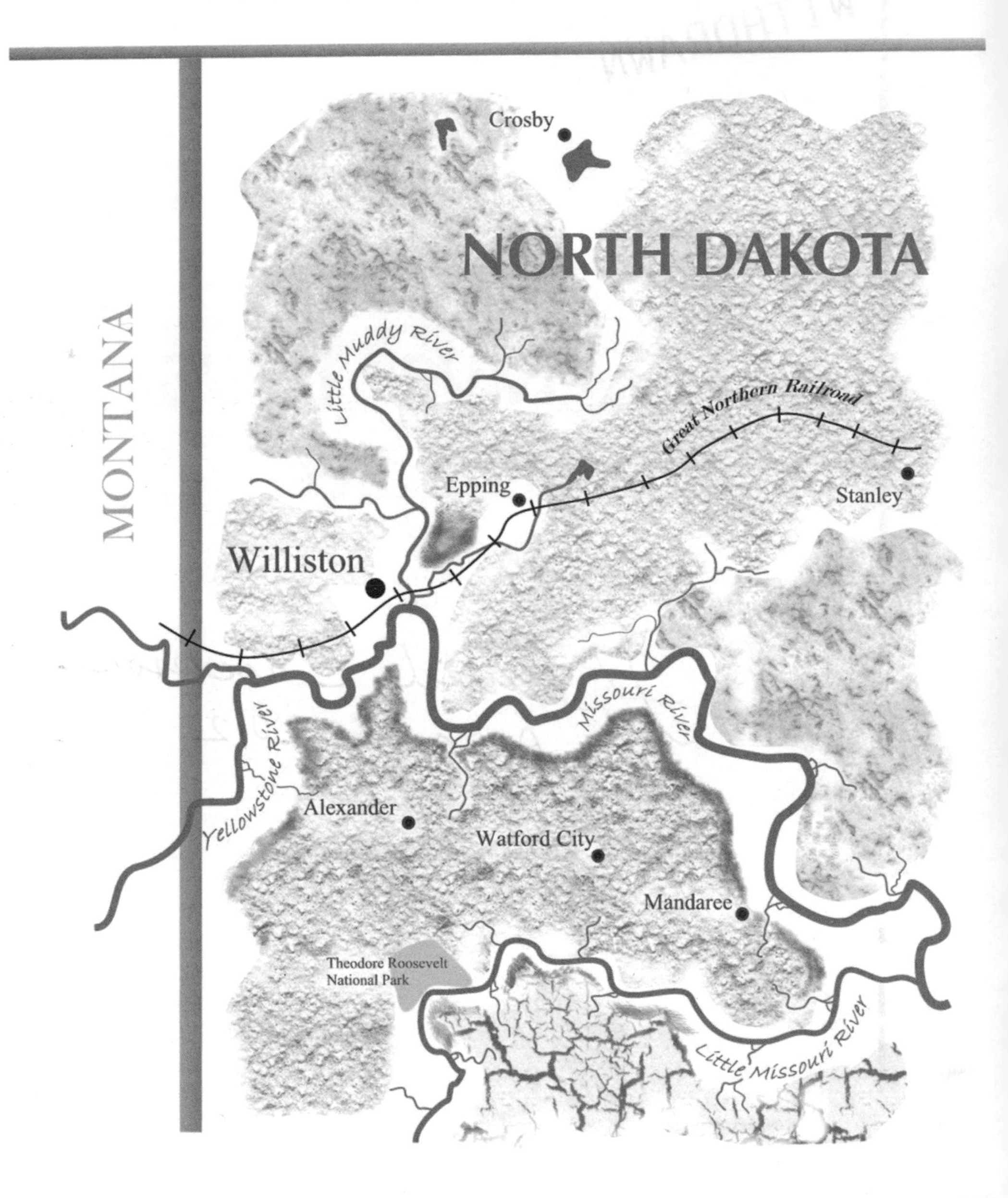
SASKATCHEWAN
MONTANA
NORTH DAKOTA
Crosby
Little Muddy River
Great Northern Railroad
Epping
Stanley
Williston
Missouri River
Yellowstone River
Alexander
Watford City
Mandaree
Theodore Roosevelt
National Park
Little Missouri River

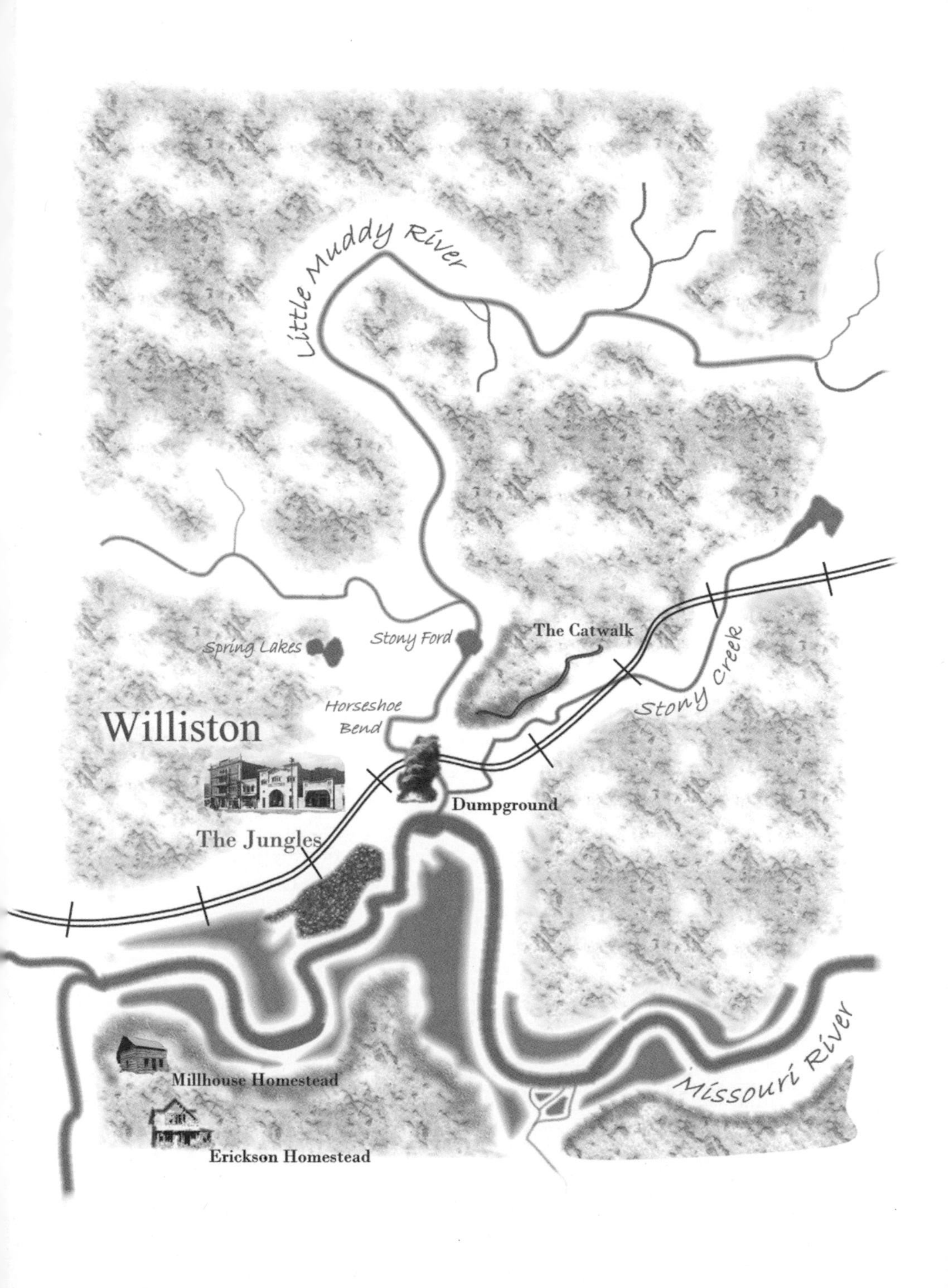
Little Muddy River
Spring Lakes
Stony Ford
The Catwalk
Horseshoe Bend
Williston
Stony Creek
Dumpground
The Jungles
Missouri River
Millhouse Homestead
Erickson Homestead

The Muddy River Boys
Dakota Tales

ISBN 978-0-9846459-0-9

Illustrations by J. David Erickson, Shena King, Jessica Erickson, Marie Erickson, Morgan Erickson.
Maps created by Ken Jones.
Book layout and design by Daryl Hunt.

Printed and bound in the United States of America.
Published by Swede Hill Publishing, LLC.

Contents

Dedication

To my brother, Jim, whose wanderlust
and Muddy River spirit reign supreme.

To the Muddy River Boys.
To all Muddy River boys and their rivers.

And for my wife, Carolyn,
wandering star, and wielder of the mighty green pen.

Author's Note

Dear Reader:

North Dakotans are inclined to foster the notion that glory reins in far off places. During my boyhood the Great Northern Railroad did its part by glamorizing outbound destinations. The Great Northern's Empire Builder streamliner, sporting its majestic mountain goat logo, could spirit North Dakotans away to the Rocky Mountains and the Pacific Ocean. Many posed Montana as the epitome of magnificence, an easy sell supported by movies, storybooks, and tales of cowboys and Indians, lumberjacks, and speckled trout swimming in ice-cold water so clear you could drink it.

Big folks presented an unfinished picture of the Far West to be filled in by youngsters like us with our fantasies and dreams. "I'm gonna live in the Rockies someday," Buck said. "Not me, I want to sail on the ocean," said Little Ergie.

North Dakotans are inclined to "open the gate, turn 'em out"—branded calves and youngsters alike. With grandiose imaginings from the adult world tucked away, we were "turned out." The Little Muddy River and its grass valley beckoned, inspired, challenged, and collected a loose tribe of boys. I named us "the Muddy River Boys."

The prairied treasures of the Muddy River countryside ran north to Canada. We had to see more: climb and explore one bluff to find another—this one transected by an Indian trail, the next sporting foxes carrying dead gophers. We'd round a river bend to discover another amber pool, prettier than the last, hiding deep mysteries.

The river was there to delight, astound, and teach. And it nurtured flying, plopping, and swimming creatures to capture and roast on sharpened sticks.

"Keep going, keep searching, there's much more," the country beckoned. "Our wise teacher the Little Muddy River will show you the way, marking the path to unfettered boyhood. Her wisdom and beauty are subtle. You'll find no shortcuts here—no compromises. Grand discoveries will come with time and persistence. Ever after, no matter where you travel, you'll carry my Muddy River spirits with you."

And so it happened with the Little Muddy River and me. I eventually headed to the West to pursue a fisheries career, packing along precious memories and some of the little river's "good medicine" too, a magic symbolized by the Muddy's musky fragrance that we called the "armpit of the turtle." It anointed me when I was five and inspires me still.

—J. David Erickson, aka Little Eric

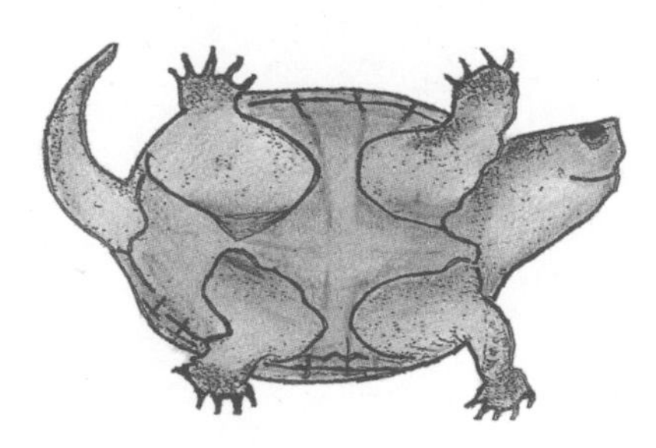

Foreword

The freedom to do creates the freedom to wonder. —C. Erickson
. . . and wonder, once untethered, races for freedom. —J. David Erickson

Perhaps God had such a vision when He rained umpteen gazillion adventuresome, freedom-loving genes on the boys of the Little Muddy River country. With fragmentary coherence our band of adventurers first wandered the mile east from Williston to a place called Horseshoe Bend, where we learned enough of the river's mysteries to want more.

Legs gained muscle, confidence grew. Our discovery trail beckoned us northward to sheltered river pools, trickling tributaries, and "Indian trails" that climbed the Muddy Valley bluffs.

With seasoning we took to bicycles and eventually—by hitchhiking—we traveled ever farther north. We suffered for our innocence: punctured by catfish and bullhead spines, poison ivied, sun-burned, and slopped with slough mud. We ran ourselves to bare-ribbed exhaustion, energized by freedom, the sweet nectar of boyhood.

The Little Muddy River, nurturing and tame, flowed into the daunting, dangerous Mighty Missouri, which curved past Williston a mile to the south. Without wings, and lacking means to overcome the obstacles of the Great Northern Railroad, and The Jungle, we were confined for a while to the Muddy River territory.

I named us 30 years later. We never called ourselves the "Muddy River Boys." We were not a club with formalities, but a band of adventurers armed with parental wisdoms, a few of which stuck crosswise instead of *"going in one ear and out the other."*

About The Characters

The adults in these stories include parents, grandparents, uncles and aunts, business people, teachers, and an important neighbor, Reed Gwin, the policeman. Folks said Mr. Gwin looked like the heavyweight champ, Jack Dempsey. Officer Gwin was big and tough—and indeed a former prizefighter; but with his high speed brain that nailed bad actors like window breakers before sunset, we boys likened him to Dick Tracy.

Our unlikely friend, Smoky Roy, the unofficial "mayor" of the dumpground squatter-village, became an important figure as well. Other adult characters will fall into place in the telling of the stories, but four of them, my parents, Bill and Ruth, and grandparents on my mom's side—May and Rollie Millhouse—deserve special introductions, and not only because my brother, Jim, and I were progeny.

Our parents and maternal grandparents were a colluding team and used all willing grown-up sympathizers, including Police Chief Olson and his right-hand enforcer, Officer Gwin, to watch over us. Parental strategy was simple. Number one: kick the kids the heck out of the house. The genius in that strategy came to me later in life—all about freedom, the wise and ennobling teacher.

As I embarked upon *Muddy River Boys,* I listened with more purpose to my 95 year old father's stories that spanned three generations of Western North Dakota pioneering. Dad's core philosophy told of meeting adversity head on, accepting risk, and celebrating success—a formula that he and Mom used full force in raising Jim and me. They loosened our tethers, let us roam; even though closer confinement would have vastly reduced child rearing worries. After all, by 1944 when our escapades extended beyond the city limits, our town of 8,000 had begun the process of civilizing children by instituting a city recreation department, Little League baseball, Boy Scouts, and 4-H, a sort of interfacing of town kids with surrounding farm life. Yet our parents and grandparents had little inclination to guide us toward overweening town organizations. The "why" of their thinking is plain to understand given the context of three predominating forces of the culture: WWI, The Great Depression, and WWII.

By the time Jim and I were old enough to ask questions, one-legged or one-armed vets provided mementos of what the future could hold for children. Fellows like Mr. Nelson were ever-present reminders. Mr. Nelson, a sad soul WWI veteran, walked jiggedy all day up and down Main Street. As far as I know, he did little else. I had seen him jitter and jump many times; a car door would slam and he'd shoot straight in the air, and land with a trembling "aaahhhg," as if bad hurt. I thought him a nitwit until one day Mom thought I should understand. "He was in the war, Davey," she said. "It's what can happen to a man when too many bombs land close. Shell-shocked they call it."

By age seven and six when my brother and I grabbed freedom that bicycles and buddies presented, WWII recruits were streaming out of North Dakota. Three of our dad's brothers went early. Indelible moments of parental angst were not always well hidden. Eavesdropping on Mom and Dad's troubles, I heard Mom crying and Dad's futile attempt to console her. "He was just a boy," she sobbed. Enough broken words followed for me to learn that Johnny Meissner from 4th Avenue West had been killed in combat. Anxieties about war motivated grown-ups to toughen us early.

Financial security was the second motivator. Before Mom and Dad were married, the Great Depression—a King Kong beast—had only recently been snared by a foot and shackled to the ground, but for how long? The Great Depression had hardscrabbled nearly everyone in the territory. Examples were everywhere. Dad's young brother, at age 13, rode a freight car to the West Coast to work on a strawberry farm. Dad was a bit luckier. He and his older brother, Dick, found jobs working for a drunken dairy farmer near Mandan. Though impossibly cantankerous, the farmer paid them both a dollar a day.

Though the Depression had officially ended when Jim and I were "turned out," Depression lessons groomed us. "Eat those potato skins," Grampa Erickson said, "they put hair on your chest." And woe unto the Erickson kid who left a bread crust on his plate.

Polite panhandlers coming to our back door were curiosities for Jim and me, but object lessons for Mom: "That's his first and only sandwich from me; can't find work, let him go hungry, and by the way—you boys get out this very minute and spade the garden." Preparing for the next Depression required cussed resilience. Allow hard reality to sober your children. "It'll do them good."

Grampa Rollie Millhouse and Grandma May lost their McKenzie County ranching enterprise in the Depression. With a couple of working sons to complement their two homemaker daughters, they might have held on. Gramp loved all things wild and un-tameable. Teaching sons Daniel- Boone sharpshooting, or Casey Tibbs bronc busting, and Gramp would have been king of the world.

Failure to sire sons during pioneering ranching days could have made a man mournful. Not Gramp though, and not Little Gram either. They moved to our town of Williston, where Grampa—R. B. to his business friends and country customers—became a traveling insurance salesman. Quite a comedown for a renowned pioneer rancher, but to his credit lasting well beyond his lifetime, nobody heard Rollie, R. B., our Gramp utter a bitter or regretful word. Instead he and Little Gram turned the bad luck side of the coin to the ground. Shining up at them were Jim and I, two grandsons to love, but love untraditionally. We were to them a new life project, and—by damn—we'd turn out to be ready for depressions, wars, and hardships. And throughout the molding process we'd learn to love life with their homesteader's exuberance. Never had a partnership carried out a more dogged and consistent mission.

Grandma May was tagged as Little Gram in deference to her frail frame. She was five foot, one inch tall and 93 pounds big. "Little," was an inside joke for many who knew her and her ranching history. All through our boyhood, she showed Jim and me her tough, no-nonsense character. I credit Little Gram with helping me discover my unquenchable fascination with fish.

Three months short of my fifth birthday, Little Gram informed me that I would learn to catch fish. "Store fish are expensive and smelly; fish we catch ourselves are fresh and sweet. Time you learn about fish, Davey. Go to the garden. We'll dig worms." She came out of the house wearing men's coveralls—too big, rolled up on her shins and belted at the waist. She looked lost in all the blue. I'd never seen her before in anything except a long dress.

With our worm can stowed and Gram's cane pole tied on the top of Gramp's black Nash, we headed north out of town. On that July morning, Gram planted us on the bank of Spring Lake. A few feet from shore a ring of musty weeds gave way to blue-black mysterious deep. Spring Lake's rich fragrance seeped into my core, embedded and grew into a pleasant myth: *When you come upon fishy smelling water—by dang—stop right there and dunk a worm.*

Gram initiated me into hook worming and cane pole slinging. Then . . . nothing happened. "We'll wait for them, and we'll be quiet," she said. While our bobber rocked on soft ripples, she sat close to me whispering, contemplating sleeping fish down there along the dark bottom. "They'll wake soon and come to eat our worm. Worms taste like licorice." I caught her sly brown-eyed twinkle, and we laughed together.

Suddenly the water before us darkened. The red-wing blackbirds, the wind, and sky—everything around us quieted. I turned back to see what frightening mystery had pushed the heated mid-morning sun from the sky. And here it came from the north, racing down from the clay hills, first a gale that bent the locust trees. Behind the wind came a gray tumbling cloud rolling upon itself like a monstrous fighting pillow.

This was my first look at a wild Canadian storm front, so thick and water laden that its continuous cloud hung tenuously to the sky, racing low, skirting the treetops. The thick of the storm reached the lake in seconds, introducing itself not with a gentle pitter patter, but with an immediate drenching clatter. I hadn't quite gained my feet to run for the car when Gram grabbed my arm. "Sit your butt back," she ordered. "You won't melt. Now, we came to fish, and we're going to fish!"

Though it was July the rain was icy. I sagged to the ground, shaking, soggy-cold. Gram ignored our discomforts. "Dig in the can, Davey," she said. "Get us a big fat, fresh worm."

While I wormed our hook, Gram hunched over, sheltering me. Then she stood and bent before the curtain of rain, all 90 pounds of her, whipping the cane pole forward to sling the yellow line, bobber, and wormed hook. "Here," she ordered, "now be ready," and she handed me the butt of the pole. She plopped down next to me—close, so our clammy hips touched. I barely heard her through the rainy din. "You get the chance . . . fish in the rain. Rain on the water makes fish hungry." She hurried her words, as if to keep pace with the driving rain: "Watch your bobber, watch it!" I strained, peering through the watery curtain. Among a million dancing rain diamonds, I made out the blur of our red and white bobber . . . there, there it was . . . then gone. Gram grabbed my arm and yelled, "Pull, pull, you've got one!" And I hauled back on the ten-foot cane pole and heaved with all my might, finally freeing the fish from the water. It came fast, arcing over our heads, a golden-yellow perch landing behind us in the sopped grass. He was not much longer than my little hand, but—by golly—he was my first fish. I pounced on him, getting a bloody spine jab that hurt, but a hurt that seemed to come from an unimportant place.

Gram stringered the first perch for me, and I helped with the rest. They came quickly and steadily, every minute new surprises pitched to the grass: perch, sunnies, and purpley iridescent bluegills that smelled indelibly wonderful—a tinge of salt, but sweet and pungent, so inexplicably good that even now I can close my eyes and smell them.

Fishin' in the rain, one of life's little-known delights, I owe to Little Gram. Also important, after insisting I stand up to the storm, she later bragged on me to Gramp and my parents, "Davey's good, a real good fisherman." *Good enough perhaps, and tough enough to one day tag along to that place called Horseshoe Bend with my older brother and his buddies,* a vision that now seemed almost real.

Little Gram was but one of countless grown-ups who filled in for absentee or overworked fathers, men either away in the war or, like my dad, doing their patriotic duty at home. Dad worked six and one-half, sometimes seven days a week for the War Effort. Mom's homemaking work paralleled Dad's in determination, no different from our buddies' moms. Moms painted, scrubbed, gardened, baked, canned, patched worn duds, made lye soap, and forever ran *kawhoosh kawhooshing* wash machines. Our town's singular mission was to get the war out of the way; then one day we'd live at a measured pace. In the meantime, the demands of war years left little time to marshal youngsters, a blessing for independent-minded Muddy River boys.

Beginning to compose our stories, my task was first driven by little more than an old guy's propensity for recollection and reflection. As I resurrected each adventure, I increasingly called on my brother, Jim, and other Muddy River characters. My work became more and more collaborative. As if my old buddies and I had each taken a "young pill," we recounted our stories, reliving joyful memories. In a sense we were back on our little river experiencing the free-wheeling high octane life of Dakota boys. I have come to understand that those extraordinary years reside at the top of my list of life experiences. My interviews with the Muddy River Boys revealed that they were like-minded. Why else would Jack Shemorry, at age 60, float the length of the Muddy, maybe the first to do so since the fur trading days of the 1800s. He launched his yellow kayak in the river's rivulet up on the northern prairie; battled blood sucking deerflies and voracious mosquitoes; lugged the kayak across boggy portages, and navigated the Muddy's entire 50 miles. I'm supposing also that he smoked a few reed stogies along the way.

Jack, two years older than I, was an experienced reed smoker when I first tagged along to the Muddy River. He watched my eyes water as I puffed my first bitter-hot smoke. I picture his angled, freckly face and hear his raucous blue heron's laugh run the octaves, go back to the beginning, and run them again. My mind stores dozens of such highlights from 60 years back.

Girls will also appear among these pages. Although we boys knew that we owned certain "superior" skills, like inscribing yellow signatures in the snow and throwing dirt clump grenades, we were aware that many of the girls were plenty scrappy, and adventuresome—like the farm girls from north of town who forayed on their ponies into the Muddy River countryside. Some mortified boys, like the rope climbing, hard punching Hicks girls and Leah Russell, next to my brother, the fastest runner in town. Williston girls have great stories to tell too.

Initially I fretted about misconstrued texture and dapplings of color added as the events were retold, first in the heart-pounding aftermath moments, and secondly, in story writing recollection. Fortunately, I tossed such concerns aside, coming to the realization that the boy story is a wild, incorrigible specie, unsuitable for a literary cage.

Offer a band of boys a goodly measure of freedom and you have gifted them a special power, one that endures over millennia. Consider a band of skin-clad boys racing into the clan's cave, wheeling about the fire, all jabbering at once. They are so adrenaline-charged they've forgotten to pee.

"It had dagger teeth, longer than a flint knife."

"No, no—longer than that, and, and . . . red!"

"Yah, blood-red, dripping with blood, and he was tall as a horse."

"No, no—taller, with huge shoulder muscles, and when he roared he shook the trees."

Such is the boy story, true at its core—like the veracity of the cave boys' saber-tooth tiger—but rippling at its edges, bursting with passion, and—like an old movie re-mastered, undiminished by new *Technicolor* and stereophonic sound.

Like cave-boys, we children of the '40s and '50s were given liberty, enough to test courage, solidify resilience, and eventually absorb good sense. Freedom was the norm of the times. As our Uncle Frank, the cow-man, liked to yell, "Open the gate, turn 'em out." Youngsters charged out of the gate, "hell bent for leather," especially the Muddy River guys, with parents so like minded that *"You have one minute to get out of this house,"* could have come from any one of them.

Adult energies poured into managing modern children are engendered by great worries over their safety. Admittedly there is much to fear in modern culture. Far-flung tragedies are publicized, and extraordinary pains are taken for child protection. But the 1940s and '50s presented opportunities for tragedy too, threats of a more primitive nature. Comparing the now and the then, the scope of the Muddy River adventures today seems almost inconceivable. Was the ice-caked river raging down out of the north prairie country as wild as I remember? After all, three of us managed to pole a raft across. My wife shook her head incredulously as I told the story. Then, two summers ago, Buck handed me confirmation of our wild raft story and a dozen other adventures that matched memories.

I located Buck Bundhund in Whitefish, Montana. Buck, Jack Shemorry, and my brother, Jim, composed the original core of "The Muddy River Boys." Buck retired in Whitefish after a career banging about the country practicing accounting for General Electric.

After hugging, laughing, back slapping, and punching out unfinished sentences, I sat down at his kitchen counter, face-on to Buck in his non-sitting mode, the better to dance and gesture. Buck's story telling raced right out of the gate, phrasing away: "Remember the time you and your brother . . ." while my cognition of immediacy began its habitual accounting: his wiry chestnut hair is grayer and thinning, face is fuller, and . . .

Suddenly a different force seized me, the unshackled one—old, yet as familiar as the back of my hand. And I see Buck as the seven year old, radiating confidence . . . the kid with famous crinkled Chesapeake dog hair that flipped skyward over his forehead, his blue laughing eyes, face-wide smile, and blocky oversized build. I couldn't erase that image, nor did I try, as 70 year old Buck grinned and animated onward: "Remember how your brother talked us into crossing the Muddy at ice-out?" I chimed in, filling spaces. As Buck and I stitched together memories and reassembled stories, our astonished wives looked on with incredulous faces.

For three days our mates tagged along with Buck and me, perhaps suspecting we'd gone bonkers, recalling memories of our Muddy River days, understandable because our conversation returned again and again to reminding each other about "the time we . . . ." I believe it is grand and organic that the river and its nestling valley continue to bless and inspire us.

Buck, Jack, the Bervigs, Jelly, Little Ergie—each carries a Muddy River spirit to this day. And my brother, Jim, continues to explore his beloved lands and rivers: the Big Missouri River and its bottomlands, the Yellowstone, the Little Missouri of the Badlands, and especially our treasured Little Muddy River country.

Over the years I've been fortunate to spend time with Jim despite 800 miles separating us. Once or twice each year I return to North Dakota to visit Jim and his family. We poke about the countryside, visiting our old haunts. We head out pheasant hunting or trailering his fishing boat, headed for walleye fishin'. As we cross the Scenic Highway Bridge a mile east of town, Jim invariably slows nearly to a stop. He gazes up the meandering Little Muddy River, and nods his head, unfolding a factoid or two: "It's still a great little river, holds a few walleye if you know the holes," and, "You can't beat those little yellow bullheads up there at Stony Ford. Remember roasting them on a stick? First chance I get, I'm going back and catch a dozen." Thusly, Jim re-opens the book of memories, and over the next twenty miles, we lose ourselves in unfettered Muddy River dialect: a language embedded since childhood, probing, wondering, and celebrating what we have learned and what we have yet to discover. Gratefully, the joyous quest to discover goes on. "As the fun-loving entertainer and philosopher, Jackie Gleason, so artfully exuded, "How sweet it is!"

Chapter One

The Footsteps of Lews-en-clar

22nd of April Monday 1805
"Capt. Lewis & my Self walked to the River which is near the Missouri four miles above its mouth, this river is 60 yards wide and contains a greater perportion of water at this time than is Common for Rivers of its Size."

—Captain William Clark (1)

Grampa Millhouse must have planned our jaunt to the bridge on the Little Muddy River for some time. He moved quicker that day. Instead of coming in our house to get us and grabbing "a spot of coffee," he tooted the horn. I climbed into the back seat of his black Nash. "Slow as a turtle," Gramp jibed with a gentle boost to my butt with his shoe.

I rode in my usual spot that afternoon, standing on the floorboards in the back seat of Gramp's four-door, where I held tight to the back of his seat. Grampa warned, "Hold on, Davey. I've got a bad clutch." I had a good view out either side window or past his shoulder to the front. Most important, I had dibs on talking under his hat brim into his meaty right ear, the good one. Jim claimed the front seat where he squatted on his knees right next to Gramp.

Gramp drove us down Main, with his window down, ready to cuss at bad drivers: "Drive it or park it you old biddy," or his favorite: "Get a horse." He never intended for anyone to hear, and seldom groused at anyone in person, yet cussing drivers came as natural as lighting his Camel cigarettes.

Today though, his Camel bobbed in his lips, unlit. He had something "up his sleeve." True, Gramp was headed for South Main and the Great Northern Depot, but we were two hours early for our routine jaunt to watch the Empire Builder streamliner come in. Sure enough, as we came to Broadway, Gramp extended his left arm, headed for a surprise. And Gramp's surprises were top of the world special.

"Where we going, Gramp?"

"Where to, where to?"

"You'll see." His going-to-the-country grin was a clue. And he wore his long tailed wool coat and winter fedora on that blustery March day. Furthermore, he'd advised Mom to put Jim and me in our winter coats too.

At the city limits Gramp took his unlit cigarette from his lips and placed it in the ash tray. Topping the hill above the Muddy River flats he shifted to third and clomped on the foot-feed, sending the Nash bucking and bounding down the hill through broken-iced potholes.

"We should have come out here earlier, boys, but I just learned at noon that the ice on both the Missouri and the Little Muddy broke up in the night. The Chinook wind came in around midnight; that's what did it."

Gramp hunched over the steering wheel, "driving like Barney Oldfield," as my dad would say. He worked the wheel to dodge potholes, and instructed Jim and me: "Now, when we get to the Muddy, you boys stay right with me. Anybody who falls in today is a goner." At the end of the mile east down the Scenic so-called highway Gramp pulled over on the west end ramp to the Little Muddy Bridge, talking the entire time. Gramp walked us out on the bridge, grasping each of us tightly by a hand. *"Lews-en-clar"*—I thought I heard him holler in the wind—"hiked out of a boat camp 140 years ago to investigate the Muddy River." I was only five and one half, my brother a year older, but already we'd heard stories about the famous explorer, *"Lews-en-clar,"* who had been invited into the lodges of mighty Indian chiefs, killed bull buffalo by the dozen, and faced down a giant grizzerly bear that took many bullets before chasing him into the Big Missouri River.

Before our trip to the Muddy River Bridge was over, Jim and I learned that the adventurer was not one hero—our mistaken *"Lews-en-clar"*—but a pair of trusting partners: Captains Meriwether Lewis and William Clark. And before the summer of '43 was over, our country education was well underway. Grampa Millhouse would have it no other way.

Gramp took my brother by one hand and me by the other and walked us to the center of the bridge. Jim raised his voice above the wind, "Gramp, those explorers Lew and who?"

"Lewis and Clark, Jimmy, and they came here after ice-out. The river was running 60 yards wide, just like today."

Wow! Gramp was right. The river raced down the valley, at least 60 yards wide, moaning like a troubled beast. We stood against the north side guard railing. Gramp looked over the top rail and Jim and I peered underneath it. A dozen more onlookers, all grown-ups, stood on the bridge looking north—naturally north, since that's where storms and water came from. Low gray clouds scooted down the valley above the roiling blue snow melt of the river. Ice cakes, as big as refrigerators, bobbed on the water, rasping, and banging together. "The Muddy is draining the north prairie country, spilling what's left of winter," Gramp said.

With so much to see, we fell silent, watching wave upon overlapping wave round the bend above the bridge. The river carried a flotilla of jostling ice cakes banging each other and tinkling toward us like giant Christmas tree ornaments. Altogether, the raging river was a fearsome thing. By the look on Gramp's face, so it was, even for him.

I felt the bridge vibrate under my feet and squeezed Gramp's hand even tighter. As if alive and troubled, the bridge creaked and shuddered. Gramp hugged Jim and me close against the bridge rail. "This won't last long, boys. The river's just shedding its winter. Two or three weeks she'll be tame. Hell, you boys could hike out here in nothing flat. Maybe catch a catfish."

At that moment I couldn't imagine coming near the Muddy River without Gramp or Dad, even though last fall Jim had hiked out once with his older friend, Jack.

Jim put his head through the bridge rail uprights, and I cautiously followed suit. Below, scarcely a yardstick away, the jostling ice cakes fought for passage through the bridge's pillars. I was reminded of our uncles' bug-eyed cattle bawling and crowding into their loading chute.

"Mornin,' Rollie," a voice hollered above the wind and the noisy river. I looked up to see a man in a gray work uniform standing alongside, his serious eyes gazing on the river. "I don't like it Rollie. That ice starts to jam, this bridge is in trouble."

With a quick sideways glance Gramp answered, "Harold, you lose this bridge, you've got a lot of explaining to do. It's only, what . . . 5 or 6 years old?"

At our level, waist high to Gramp, Jim reached across and rapped my knuckles. Out of his rascally grin came Jim's tease, "You hear that? Holy Moley, if the bridge goes down the river, we could ride it to the Missouri."

Meantime, Harold—the bridge man—seemed puzzled as to how to answer Gramp. He cussed a couple times and turned away. Gramp seemed not to notice or care. He gazed up the valley, as if trying to see into Canada. I'd seen this gaze often out in the country, where he drove with his window down, wondering what's over a hill or across a river, and stopping often so he could wonder even better. There in the middle of the Muddy Bridge, Gramp propped his elbows on the bridge rail, cradling his chin in his big hands.

"Look right up there on the bluff, boys." Gramp straightened at the rail and pointed, "Good reason for the Indian's trail. Just imagine, thousands of buffalo and elk, and deer, and antelope filled this valley. From the highest point on the bluff, the Indians had a lookout where they planned their hunts. That's the way Lewis and Clark saw it too. They wrote it all down."

Monday April 22cd 1805.
"I usscended to the top of the cutt bluff this morning, from whence I had a most Delightful view of the country, the whole of which except the vally formed by the Missouri is void of timber or underbrush, exposing to the first glance of the spectator immence herds of Buffaloe, Elk, deer, & Antelopes in one boundless pasture."

—Captain Meriwether Lewis (2)

"It's high time I read you the Lewis and Clark story," Gramp continued.

"That'd be great, Gramp," Jim said. "I want to hear the part where they explored further, way up the Muddy River."

"Well, Jimmy, they didn't do that. They headed up the Missouri and left this river for you boys to explore. And you've got years to do it."

Gramp turned away from the rail with his big arms encircling our shoulders. "We've got enough time to stop at the Luzon for a cup of coffee before the Empire Builder comes in." Jim appeared not to hear. He stood staring, fascinated by the river.

"Jimmy," Grampa barked. That's all it took. Jim turned and moved quickly. I welcomed our leaving. I imagined the commotion beneath the bridge growing louder. With Jim and me trailing, Gramp set off for the end of the bridge in his rocking amble that in time I came to recognize as an old horseman's walk, like

Randolph Scott, the cowboy movie actor, who was tall and muscled like our grandpa and firmed his jaw just the same. By the shape of his pursed-lip grin Gramp had accomplished some kind of mission.

As we neared the west bridge abutment, here came Harold, the bridge man, carrying a camera. He stopped to greet Gramp next to the wooden sign that named the river, well—according to the sign—a *creek*.

"Had to come back for a picture, Rollie," Harold said. "We may never see the Little Muddy this high again."

"Jeezus Kee-rist, Harold!" Gramp followed that with a laugh that rolled on. He pointed at the sign behind Harold. "Who the hell did up your sign? Look at it: Little Muddy *Creek! Creek?* Jeezus! It's draining enough water out of the north-west of this state to fill Lake Erie. And you call it a *creek*?"

"The Department's sign shop guys in Bismarck, Rollie. Guess we oughta bring 'em back out to see the Muddy in the spring."

"While they're at it, Harold, you might ask them to read their history. Lewis and Clark knew a river when then saw one. Come on boys," Gramp said, tromping off toward his car. He chuckled, but not a funny bone chuckle. By the side of the road a tin can caught his eye, and he booted it hard. "You saw the Muddy at ice-out boys, and you know damn well it's a river. Don't let anyone tell you any different."

I'm not sure Jim heard all of that. Gramp reached his Nash and opened the driver door and my back door. I climbed in. Jim, though, stood by the side of the road, rooted. With squinted brown eyes, he studied the valley and winding river. "Wonder how far I could hike?" Jim said, mostly to himself. He turned, ready to climb in beside Gramp, but was stopped short by eery cries in the distant sky.

Gramp's window was down, mine too; we traveled that way whenever possible. The cries—"hoowaauk, hoowaauk, hoowaauk"—came rhythmically, without let-up. Yes, I remembered from last fall, maybe before. I'd been told, Little Gram—explaining: "Sandhill cranes, Davey, they fly south exactly on time and return when it is truly springtime. You can count on them."

Gramp and I stepped out alongside Jim. The three of us stood on the road searching the southern skies. There must have been hundreds, maybe a thousand crying out from the clouds somewhere over the Big Missouri River. We watched and waited. "Here they come," Gramp said, "coming up the Muddy."

The giant vee of tiny flapping crosses swung to and fro, fighting the north wind. We watched them come on, straining necks to see. They crossed above us, flying as high as Piper Cubs. The cranes worked their giant wings frantically, without pause, no time to soar and rest.

"They sound anxious, Gramp," Jim said.

"They are indeed, Jimmy boy. They'll be in Canada before dark. Half of them are carrying eggs, and the mother cranes need to find a perfect marsh to lay them."

The sandhills passed over us wavering but purposeful against the wind, headed up the Little Muddy River. As the sandhill vee faded from sight, Gramp said, "They just passed Stony Ford . . . real good fishin' up at Stony Ford."

"Can we go there, Gramp?"

"Nope, not *we,* Jimmy. *You* can go to Stony Ford, you and Davey, soon as you learn to swim." He nodded and pointed upriver. "You'll hike out to Horseshoe Bend; follow the river north to the big pool below a washed out crossing. That's Stony Ford." Gramp gazed up the valley for a spell. Then he smiled and swatted each of us on our butts. "Get in boys. We're going for coffee, and today, chocolate ice cream too."

Chapter Two

Rarin' to Go

"Someday is not a day of the week."—Anon.

Even at age six Jim always had a venturing plan, one that couldn't wait. Following ice out on the Little Muddy River, he pestered Gramp again and again to drive us out to one of the bridges to look at the river. But these outings were more than "just lookin'." Jim used the occasions to go to bat for us. "Gramp, Dave and me are plenty old enough to be on the river. Tell Dad, will you?"

Gramp chuckled, promising, "I'll do my best." He did too. But with the Muddy still running high, Dad held firm: "Yes, I know the boys think they can swim, but they're not ready for a river."

In the meantime, Gramp proceeded to further whet our appetites for exploring rivers. Jim and I often spent nights with him and Little Gram. On one of those occasions a downpour came in the night, forcing Gramp to change his insurance selling plans. "Country roads are going to be a mess this morning. I'll wait till they dry out some." We were housebound with Gramp, a good deal as it turned out, for we were to learn all about Gramp's very own river.

First though, he launched the day with his special entertainment: a tease for our Gramma and his raucous celebration of a new day that Gramp had no inclination to hide from us. He stood in front of the bathroom mirror wearing his customary shaving outfit: his gray felt hat, round gold-rimmed glasses, and nothing else. With lathered face, he stropped his razor and danced from foot to foot, intermittently whistling "Campground Races" and singing its *doo das*. Dependably, Gram gruffed at him, "Rollie, get some clothes on. The little boys are here."

"Hell, May, they don't mind. They were born with the same equipment."

Gram went off to fix oatmeal and eggs for us, while Gramp finished his slicking up. To go with his hat, he added his on-the-road salesman's outfit: starched and pressed white shirt, blue tie, bank-teller vest, gray wool pants and suit coat to match.

"I've got something special to show you boys," Gramp said. We raced through breakfast after which he took us to his book shelf corner where he kept his old trunk with leather bindings and brass hinges. When Gramp opened the lid, out came the smell of musty coal dust. "Time you boys learned something about rivers," he said.

We gathered around Gramp, as he pulled a chair close to his trunk. His blue eyes danced while he began, digging through books, papers, and old photographs. You'd have thought it was Christmas morning. Gramp rustled papers and tossed photographs aside. Finally, he pulled out a folded yellowed paper and closed the trunk lid. A picture with mouse nibbled edges fell from the paper.

Gramp tipped back his grey fedora, which was present at every important conversation.

Gramp smiled wide, holding the picture for us to see. Two boys and the hugest fish you ever saw filled nearly the entire picture space. The boys looked to be about the same ages as Jim and me. "That's your Uncle Milt and me," Gramp said, "me on the right, your uncle Milt on the left; and that's our great northern pike."

Gramp and Uncle Milt hefted opposite ends of a pole, and from the middle of the pole hung the giant fish, long jawed and scary. In spite of the boys' proud moment of half-smile, half-grimaced lifting, the fish's tail drug the ground. I held the pike picture carefully, but Jim grabbed it away. Gramp settled the squabble by slipping it into his coat pocket.

"Never seen a bigger pike since than that one," Gramp said. "Weighed twenty five pounds at the butcher shop; seems like the whole town came to see him. Now I'll show you where we caught him."

"Here we go boys—my map. Made it myself, way back then." He carefully unfolded and smoothed the map, which covered most of the trunk lid. *What could this all mean?* We'd need all day to sort out the maze of symbols and jottings and lines running every which way.

Gramp reached for a letter opener and placed its point on a diagonal scribbling labeled *TOWN*. "My brother, Milt, and I lived right here in this little town in Minnesota called Luverne. Right past Luverne ran our very own little river. At least it seemed our own river to Milt and me. We seldom saw another soul out there."

From the smudge of Gramp's town he traced a squiggly blue ink line down the map, opposite direction from a boldly drawn arrow marked by N for north. "Right here," Gramp pointed, "is where the West Branch of Rock River joined the main river. Milt and I usually came out as far as the main river, three miles or more. Later on, after the country seasoned us, we'd sometimes travel clear off this map. We'd spend nights out there by a campfire."

Gramp straightened in his chair and chuckled about what was coming next: "Our dad loaned us five dollars to buy a worn out old white mule that we rode double. Dad's farmer friend pastured him on a trade—one that I believe favored the farmer."

Once more Gramp bent over his map, intent with his pointer. "From the farmer's barn right . . . here, we'd ride ol' Whitey through the willows on an old moose trail. Through this winding section of river we caught perch and bullheads, sometimes even hooked a pike that would mor'n likely break the line. We covered this whole territory. Found a rocky bottom to wade Whitey across the West Branch to a cedar swamp. We discovered a pond in there fed by a clear water creek. Big old mossy-backed walleyes hid out there."

Gramp tapped his pointer, ready to go on, but Jim held his arm. "You have walleye pictures too, Gramp? Maybe you could take us there."

"Can't, Jimmy. Too far; but you two will find great fishin' places of your own."

"For giant pike, Gramp?"

"Sure. I am about to tell you how to catch 'em. . . . Now, after we found the secret walleye pond—and we caught some dandies too—we had two years of heavy winter snow. Wet summers too. The river stayed high all through that second summer. By August the beaver decided to build a dam. They went to work and changed our river."

"Milt and I cussed those beaver. They built a dam here below the forks. See, I redrew it, the way their dam backed the lake into the woods, formed the shape of an hourglass. The beaver flooded our mule trail. We had to hike out to fish or hunt. But, you know, boys, Nature knows best. The river overflowed into the sloughs. The ducks, fish, and muskrats thrived in all that new water. Our granddad came along with us one time. When he saw the great number of muskrat houses he brought us out with traps and taught us how to use them. In two winters trapping we caught enough rats to buy a horse, old but still good . . . Ginger, her name was. Trapping the rats was good for us. So was hunting. We shot so many ducks and grouse and snowshoe rabbits that our mother said, *'No more.'* Good thing, too, because then we turned to selling our game to the neighbors. We filled fruit jars with coins, Milt and me."

"What about your big fish, Gramp. How'd you catch him?"

Gramp crinkled his funning grin at Jim and tipped his hat back, "We fooled him, my boy, with a foot-long river sucker. It was my little brother, Milt's, idea. You see, he had spotted the big pike hiding in the shade of a muskrat house. I marked the spot with an X, it was . . . right here in the neck of the hourglass. That old pike was ambushing every poor fish that came through the narrows."

"So, how'd you catch him?"

"I told you, we suckered him," Gramp chuckled. "Your uncle Milt saw him dart out and grab a sucker. Once we knew about his feeding habits, he was easy. We borrowed some wire telephone cable from our dad's storehouse. On the end we tied a cord with Dad's biggest hook—a 'musky hook,' he said. Then we buried the hook into the back of a live sucker. Pitched it out by the rat house and jiggled it. Out from hiding came Mr. Pike, grabbed our sucker, and the battle was on. Took both of us to haul him in. We carried our pike into town and right down Main Street of Luverne to my dad's telephone exchange. Most of the town came out to see. We all went to the butcher shop for the weighing. People filled the shop and cheered. I never had more fun in my life."

Gramp refolded the map with the pike picture tucked inside, returned them to the trunk, and closed the lid. "We'll look at my map another time boys. Right now Gramp's got to go sell some insurance."

Gramp's map and picture remained in his trunk for only a day; then out it came, in—out, in—out, until Gramp tired of retrieving his treasure for Jim and me to look at. "Gramma," he said, "we're keeping my map right here on the mantel for the little boys."

With Gramp's Rock River hundreds of miles away, the Little Muddy River would have to do. Yet, one by one our free Saturdays of spring slipped by without Dad's permission to leave the city limits. I tagged along, exploring the town with Jim. We hiked the seven blocks from our house to the animal park to slip cookies into the bear cage. Other times we'd join pocket marble games on the playground at Central School or find a game of kick the can. And Little Gram and Grampa Rollie took us to Spring Lake for cane pole fishin'. Aside from hearing more of Gramp's Rock River stories, though, our Saturday fishin' trip with him and Gram didn't pan out. A big family moved in on both sides of us, and a couple of the naughty kids threw rocks in the water, ignoring Gramp's warnings. "One more time, I'll throw you in," Gramp said. A snotty kid waited for five minutes, then tossed a stick. "Come on, boys. No fishing here today."

"I should have thrown the parents in," Gramp said on our way to his car. Our unsuccessful trip made Jim and me even more anxious for a real fishin' trip.

The month of warming May unfolded with enticing tales carried home with Jim about Jack and Buck and "bucketfuls of yellow bullheads and jumbo frog legs" taken from the Muddy River.

Jim grew more irritable by the day, especially after hearing I was his problem. We both overheard Dad and Gramp at the bridge table: "I know Rollie, Davey *can* swim a bit. Well, he dog-paddles. But I came within a whisker of drowning when I was his age and it scared the bee-jeezus out of me. Let's give him a little more time."

"What about Jim, then?"

"Nope, he stays with his brother. When it's time for them to go off fishin', they oughta be together."

After hearing that, Jim took his teasing to a new level, boosted along by the last dragging days of school before summer. Jim made me think of the ornery coyote at the animal park, pacing and biting at things, even the cage wire. Jim cranked up his needling until one day I blew up in our back yard and took a poke at his nose. Though I didn't connect, I triggered an all-out scrap.

Our fistfight amounted to a wild flurry of flailing misses until the peripheral hulk of our policeman neighbor, Mr. Gwin, appeared. Jim and I instantly halted our fisticuffs, expecting a scolding. *Wasn't his job to break up fights?*

Reed Gwin loomed above us, as tall as our lilac bush and thick as the trunk of our box elder. He started with me, I suspect because I was the littlest. He bent down and took my wrists. "Keep your dukes up high, hide your face. Here, hold your left fist next to your left eye, the right covers your nose." His plate sized hands placed everything just so. He stepped back. "You're looking good," he said. "Now tuck the elbows, protect your chest. Aim your punches, don't waste them."

Then he turned to my brother, "Now Jimmy, you saw how I set up your brother. Start by flexing your knees so you can move quick. Okay, now get those fists up and . . . ." Mr. Gwin proceeded with basics of boxing for Jim too. Finally he stepped back and smiled. "At least you men *look* like boxers now."

The big policeman clapped his hands. "Okay men, have at it. Bend those knees and keep moving. Fake and jab, fake and jab. And when you see an opening, nail your opponent low then high, belly then jaw. Keep him guessing."

Jim and I eyed each other, trying to put Mr. Gwin's instructions in order; but then, nothing . . . nothing at all. The steam had gone from us. Mr. Gwin laughed, stepped forward, spread his wide arms, and gathered Jim and me close. "You are brothers and you were fighting mad. Rule one: never fight mad with a brother. You'll need him for a friend more than you know. You want to *box* each other; that's different. Now, rule two: Don't fight *anyone* mad. Can't lick 'em that way. You gotta' fight smart, not mad." He scruffed the tops of our heads: "You got that?"

"Uh, yes sir."

"Mm—me too. Yes sir."

"Alright, next time you're scrappin', lace on those gloves that your dad keeps for you."

Mr. Gwin's boxing advice was the start to a glorious summer ahead. The first hot spell came the day Jim's first year of school ended. The cool fun of Harmon Park Pool drew us and most of Williston's kids.

On every hot day, Jim's school buddies swam, including Buck and Jack, the two who last summer passed the fearsome swim test conducted by Mr. Soine, the boss of the pool. Passing his test qualified a kid for deep end swimming, and Buck and Jack strutted proud, having done it. In short order they established themselves as popular deep end swimmers.

Jack was a fantastic deep water diver, scrounging the 10 foot bottom for Mr. Soine's salted pennies and nickels. Jack would pop up and shout, holding each coin high for all to see.

Buck showed off even more elaborately for Jim, and Bervie, and Razzie and the littler kids like me, who watched jealously from the shallow end. Buck would galumph the length of the high diving board, spring high, and launch into a swooping arc, yelling, "Ger-ON-imo." At the last instant he tucked his blocky body into a ker-whumping cannonball.

From just across the life-line divider I looked over to the excitement. The big white buoys attached to the life line could have been marked, *That side: fun; this side: non-swimmer's purgatory.* Such conflict couldn't last and it didn't. One-by-one my brother and his friends took on Mr. Soine's challenge: first five minutes of treading water, while junior lifeguards created havoc by dropping cannonballs around the kid who believed he was good enough for the deep end. Jim was wound tight when he took on the swimming test, but only his wide eyes gave any hint he was nervous. Mr. Soine blew his whistle: *Time to start.* Ducking cannon-ball-made waves and ignoring distractions, Jim finished his scary water tread, and began the long, half-mile swim. For Jim the five laps—half a mile—swim was almost a breeze, because he swam like he ran, smoothly, not effortlessly, but that's how he appeared.

By the middle of June, all of Jim's friend's had passed Coach Soine's test, leaving me to play in the shallow end with the little kids. Soine's rule said I couldn't even choose a safety buddy from the deep end. Helga in the front office assigned me Norman Jellum, a thin heinie-headed kid from Third West. I called him Jelly like everyone else. Since he couldn't even dogpaddle yet, Jelly worried me. I didn't want to watch over Jelly; I wanted deep end privileges so bad it hurt. By golly, hell or high water, I'd do it.

"Today's the day," I told Jim. I took Jelly by the arm and led him to Miss

Kinstler, the shallow end lifeguard. She agreed to watch him while I went to see Mr. Soine. I stood looking up at him on his high life guard chair—the Coyote football coach—a Charles Atlas figure. He peered down, grinning broadly. "You can try, Eric," he said. "I was expecting you. Now go see Miss Kinstler. She'll have you swim out there in front of her, give you some tips."

At four o'clock Mr. Soine blew his whistle and hollered, "Everybody out of the water." With the pool cleared of swimmers, he blew his whistle and I dove from the deep end deck. Coach Soine's junior life guards—his up and coming football players—bombed close while I alternately treaded water and floated on my back. "Just be sure to have your mouth closed before those guys hit the water," Miss Kinstler had warned. I stayed calm and sailed through the five minute test. Mr. Soine blew his whistle and I stretched out for my best stroke and leg flutters to cheers, taunts, and the last of bombing bodies falling around me.

Jack Shemorry had helped me learn the Australian crawl and a resting back stroke allowing quick gulps of air in between surging waves. I dove under the life line, headed for the shallow end. And that's all I remember of the five down and back laps. For the first time I swam without the effort of thinking swimming. Visions appeared, swirled and fought for attention: me diving gracefully from the scary 10 foot board and, other images where I ran the banks of Muddy River with Jim and Jack and Buck, all of us lugging stringers of big fish.

On the final lap I finished to a chorus of cheers from Jim and a dozen guys standing around Mr. Soine. I hoisted myself out of the pool in front of him. He stood grinning. "I've got something for you," he said, turning his fist over, unfolding his fingers. "This is yours." He placed a gleaming thing in the palm of my hand. It was a bronze coin, Mr. Soine's award imprinted with the figure of a swimming man. The precious coin was the size of a quarter, but worth—I dunno; money didn't seem to figure in to it.

"Thank you, sir," I said, preparing to step past Mr. Soine and run home with my news. He grabbed my arm.

"Hold on there David. How old are you?" I gulped, thinking he might have remembered some sort of age restriction for the deep end, causing him to take back my swimmer's coin.

"Almost six," I said, thinking four months short of six could pass by as a reasonable fudge.

I had started to breathe heavily when Mr. Soine patted my back. "I guessed you at six. Congratulations. You are my youngest deep end swimmer."

Well, that news, said in front of Jim and his friends, added luster to my medal. Jim and I ran the three blocks home. Mom might be persuaded to call Dad at the shop. If not, at least we could call Gram and Gramp with my news.

I reveled for a week with Jim and the big kids in Harmon Park Pool's deep end. I even worked up the nerve to jump from the high board. Then a Canadian front rolled in to chill our town and squash thoughts of cold water swimming. Jim and I stayed home, spending the day trying to build a blackbird trap without success. Mostly, we got on each other's nerves. Near suppertime, Jim teased, "You want to fight?" Thankfully, Jack and Buck showed up in our back yard. "We're going to Horseshoe Bend in the morning," Jack said. "See if you guys can come with."

"We'll come. Guarantee, my dad won't say no this time," Jim said. "Let's go dig worms."

Jim was right. Mom and Dad were excited about my swim test and my medal. "Sure, you two can both go," Dad said. "Just be home by supper."

Before eight o'clock the following morning, I trailed Jim and Jack, headed for Horseshoe Bend. I'd never been this excited. I had peed three times at home and felt the need again.

If I had to pick a single day in which the blinds fell away from the window on life, it would be that June day of 1944, my first day on Muddy River. My education began the moment we left Jack's house. He led out with Jim on his heels and me tagging as close as I could to overhear their jabbering. Every few minutes I broke into a trot to keep up with long-legged Jack and my quick-footed brother. We crossed 5th Avenue, passed the last solitary house on the eastern edge of town, and trotted down a grassy gully along a dirt trail and onto the apron of the Muddy River valley.

The banter ahead never stopped, but drifted on the wind to me in fragments . . . "two hooks or three?"

"No, no, two hooks, *number* three, Eagle Claw."

. . . "do you think we might catch catfish even . . . ?"

And much more I didn't hear clearly, something about Buck coming out early to claim the best place for us all.

Jack and my brother would swirl to a stop, overcome with the Muddy River's possibilities, toe to toe in imaginations. Then, abruptly ending talk, they'd twirl, running and challenging for the lead, elbow jabbing, not serious, more like something else to laugh about. Jim took the lead, then Jack again, back and forth, until finally the three of us broke and ran in a string through mounds of gopher digs and musk grass.

"It's not really a horseshoe," Grampa had said one day from the ridge top vantage. He scanned the valley with his binoculars; then handed them to me. He worked the eye spacing adjustment and taught me to roll the focus knob. "See what I mean? The legs of the shoe are nearly straight; this part of the river's not a horseshoe. It's a perfect muleshoe." *Like one of Whitey's muleshoes,* I imagined.

With eyes intent on seeing a glint of water, mine was a stumbling, tumbling run. I came to my feet muddied and cow-pied, with a half-painted picture of Horseshoe Bend in my head.

Up ahead Jim and Jack halted, pointing this way and that. I ran up beside them. With no sign of the river, I was puzzled. We topped a grassy knoll and suddenly there lay the river and Grampa's *"perfect muleshoe"* bend.

For me, Horseshoe Bend or Muleshoe—whatever the name—was like entering Barnum and Bailey's hubbub circus. Mother killdeers scattered, racing on twiggy legs, crying, and flapping what I believed to be broken wings, until Jack explained their trickery.

Blackbirds! Dozens! Out here a guy could spend days hunting redwings, yellow heads, and regular blackbirds. They bobbed on skinny willows and dabbled at the shore of the river, all squawkeling at once.

Most every fence post held a meadowlark, each competing for best singer. Their pretty melodies, though, were interrupted by raspy herons and a hundred croaks from hidden frogs, and birdsong like tinkling glass: "Cowbirds," Jack said.

Below us, the river flooded back into reeds networked by lanes like little watered highways where mother ducks led fluffy babies . . . and more: turtle heads popped up and disappeared. The critter hullabaloo would take time to sort out.

I was forced to set it all aside by another surprise: *Boys!* Up and down the river—boys—and not a single grown-up in sight. Some boys seemed as young as me, others double of me. They dotted the shoreline in clusters of threes or fours as far as I could see up the north side of the muleshoe, and down the south leg as far as the sharp bend above the Scenic Bridge.

"Holy cow," Jim said. "There's standing room only out here. No place for us to fish."

"Maybe there is." Jack nodded to the north leg of the shoe. "Up there, the horses and camels are barebacked, except for the biggest. Buck has that one."

Camels? "What camels?" I blurted. My words trailed off after Jim, who was already running with Jack toward some new strangeness.

"You'll see," whisked back on the wind.

In quick loping minutes we arrived at a collection of steep sided earthen humps and pinnacles with head-like knobs. The shapes seemed sculpted and rubbed smooth, *"bare as baby's butts,"* Gramp would have said. "They're clay animals carved by the river," Jack explained.

The strange animal figures crowded the river, like a herd going to water. Some I imagined as horses, others—yes, camels. A boy sat on the tallest one between humps of his "camel." He didn't need to turn for me to know it was Buck. His arms folded on his chest in front of those big shoulders. Kids don't do that . . . except for Buck.

"Hey Buck, how's fishin'?" Jack sent the question across the space from the high bank where we stood at the rear of the animals. Buck half-turned, enough for us to see one edge of his fishin' grin.

"No good yet," Buck said. "A school of shiners came through a while back, robbed me five times. I hope you guys brought extra worms. 'Bout time you showed. Those guys down below have been lookin' this way, anxious to squeeze in here."

We scrambled down the bank and gathered at the foot of Buck's camel, craning our necks to talk with him. Buck sat there like a king, his throne as tall as the seat of Mr. Soine's lifeguard chair. "Where's the bullhead hole, Buck?" Jack asked. With a wave, Buck blessed a swath of water below his camel. "From down there by the buffalo, past me, as far upriver as the horses. Throw out about half-way across. That's the deep channel. I think we're wasting our time, though; the bullheads must have run past, toward Stony Ford."

"Well, we'll try bullheadin' anyway, as long as we're here," Jack said. "We'll give

Little Eric the buffalo, since it's his first time at Horseshoe Bend."

"Long as he's big enough to ride him," Buck laughed.

Wow, I thought, *who needs to fish when a guy can sit up over the river on a sculpted buffalo and see far in every direction, watching ducks and mushrats and maybe the big fish with the yellow tail will roll again and . . .*

My brother boosted me onto my buffalo from where I watched him and Jack prepare throw-lines. They unwound yellow surveyor cord from stick holders, making neat coils on the edge of the water; they wormed the hooks, and pushed the ends of their holder sticks deep into the mud. Jack retrieved a heavy rock and braced it on the river side of his stick holder, advising Jim to do the same. "Big carp in this part of the river. I saw one run off with a guy's outfit."

This was my first chance to watch throw-line fishin'. The fishers, Jim and Jack, had tied machine nuts to the ends of their lines for sinkers, and above them two wormied hooks. They grabbed their lines a foot above the uppermost hook and whirled them like lasso throwers: one, two, and they let 'em go whizzing on the third whirl. Jack cast first. His heavy sinker straightened the line coils and his twin baits plopped on the water. He sung out: "That's it, on the money; caught a two-pounder there last time."

Jim came easily to the routine: his rhythmic cast, rub of hands, an offering of good medicine: "Ahh! That looks really, really good." He and Jack grabbed hand-holds and foot-holds on their clay camels and climbed aboard, leaving their throw-lines to fish unattended.

I wanted to learn throw-line fishin', yet I wondered why it was better than Gram and Gramp's cane poles and bobbers. What could be better than watching the bobber dink, dink, and disappear—pulled under by who knows what?

I had never felt so proud, astride my buffalo, among older boys, and all of us perched on solid clay animals, sitting right over the water so close I could spit in it. *Next time I'll be ready. I'll build a throw-line. I'll learn to cast in our back yard.*

Dad's words from the breakfast table returned: "Bring home as many bullheads as you can." And Mom, the money-worrier: "They'll help cut our grocery bill."

The river whisked and gurgled. A cock pheasant across the river crowed, and a pair of meadowlarks sang back and forth from fence post perches. Otherwise our place was quiet and peaceful; but then the yakking began. When fish don't bite, that's what happens.

"Let's go up to Stony Ford and try it," Jim said. He got no takers. Jack and Buck were content to just sit and talk fishin' strategy, waiting for some mystery fish to grab on.

Buck started: "Catfish love this part of the river . . . lots of frogs along here. Cats love frogs."

Jack added his two cents about cats being "Next to walleye, the best eating."

"Well, don't expect any catfish action," Buck opined. "Cats ain't in here 'till later, my Dad says. A bullhead run is due though . . . they start biting, we'll need to get down on the water to work the lines."

My brother threw in again too: "Next time we'll go upriver, all the way to Stony Ford."

"Yah, Stony Ford," Jack agreed, "We'll go at sunup, stay till dark."

That's the gist of what I remember, distracted as I was. I gazed up the valley, beyond the river to the bluff, the lookout place that Gramp had showed us at ice-out time, the lookout from where Lewis and Clark surveyed the valley covered with buffaloes and elk. Indians walked the high ridge trail too, where they could plan buffalo hunts and watch for enemies.

Back then, two months ago with Gramp, I wanted away from the wild, ice-grinding river. Now it glided gently, whispering and lapping—barely wider than a city street, the color of cream soda, just dark enough to hide fish by the millions: wonderful fish I had heard talk of but never seen, like walleyed pike and catfish. I had galores of questions, but without a single grown-up to ask, and unsure that these older boys would allow bother from me.

It was Buck who broke my day dreaming. "Jim, I've got an extra throw-line in my pack for your brother. How about it, Little Eric?" Yes and no flickered in me, settled in favor of doubt—the tricky twirl and cast of the line that I'd never done.

"I'll . . . just watch you guys," I said.

Down river I counted thirteen boys scattered along the shore at the inside of the Bend. A few held cane poles, but most had no visible gear at all . . . throw-line fishermen, like my guys. During the hour I watched, three times one of them hollered and scrambled to his line. Others gathered round each time, while the kid pulled a huge flopping yellow fish ashore. "Another slimy carp," Buck or Jack would remark. After watching carp landed from a distance, I couldn't stand it. I'd never seen fish so big. I climbed off my buffalo and headed downriver.

I started along the reedy shoreline with hurry on my mind, but hurry couldn't work here. Every few steps I surprised a hidden frog. He'd plop and dive into the shallows and I'd stop and wait to spot his head popping up. Then a waddling snapping turtle on the sandy path turned to face me. He glared with angry, piercing eyes. I stepped around, giving him the path and some to spare. A pair of muskrats swam the river edge trailing water grass from their mouths. Intent on them, I nearly stepped on a bull snake fat as my arm. He had a lump in his throat and a gray stringy thing hanging from his jaw. Looking closer, I recognized it as a mouse's tail.

Except for the snake, Horseshoe Bend felt friendly with its crawling, swimming, flying things close and all around. Unlike the gargantuan Big Missouri that frothed and foamed and trembled its banks, the Muddy River in the month of June ran gently, and small enough to throw a stone across. I know, because I set my legs good and skipped a smooth flat stone right over to the far bank.

At the back curve of the bend, I came upon some boys I recognized from town. Three of them sat together on the bank with throw-line sticks stuck in the mud and cord lines running into the river. A dark haired, smiley kid called "Razzie" rolled from his butt to his knees and began hauling in his line. He tumbled backward and scrambled to his feet. "Gol-damn, I got a big one," he hollered. He dragged his fish through the sand, away from the river. It was a monster fish, a foot and a half long carp. I watched Razzie kneel on the poor fish and finagle the hook out. I walked up close to look at Razzie's carp. He was stupendous, thick-bodied and golden. Sad too, how he gazed up at me with a big bulging eye, desperately looking for help. He bridged his body frantically and ker-whumped the earth as he flopped his way a few inches at a time toward the water's edge, picking up patches of sand and mud over his nickel-sized scales. Razzie noticed me admiring his fish and came over. "You want him?" he asked.

"No thank you. My grandpa says carp have too many bones."

"Who's he?"

"My grandpa. Grandpa Millhouse."

"How would *he* know?"

"Because he's the smartest man in town, that's how."

Razzie eyed me with intense brown eyes, grinning a tease, one like my brother's. He nudged the carp with his foot. The big fish was pooped, but managed another flop toward the river, gaping his mouth like crazy. *He needs water real bad,* I thought. I knelt and put my hands under his cold, muddy belly and rolled him: once, twice, and again, nudging him into the mucky shallows of the river.

Razzie stood next to me, now a bit more interested in the fish. Our carp lay on his side with only his bottom side under water. He pumped his mouth and flared a red gill. Finally the carp swiped his wide tail against the mud and shot into the depths. "Next time I catch him, he'll be *really* big," Razzie said. He pushed on my shoulder. "So, you fishin' with Buck up on the camels?" Razzie asked it in a funny way, swaying from foot to foot like he wished he'd been invited to the camels.

"Yeah, Buck's up there . . . my brother too, and Jack Shemorry."

"They ketch any bullheads?"

"No, not yet. But they're talking about a place upriver that has lots of them, Stony something, they said."

"Yup, that's Stony Ford. I know all about it. Bervie's been up there. He's goin' to Stony Ford soon as the bullheads get there, maybe next Saturday. *I'm* going with. Ain't I, Bervie?"

The curly headed kid, Big Bervie, had come alongside. I recognized him, the oldest Bervig, the boy I'd seen riding around town on a fancy red Monarch bike with two beam lights and an electric horn.

Bervie sniffed, "Razzie, I'm bettin' you won't be out of bed in time to go to Stony Ford." Razzie pumped himself taller. "Oh yeah?" he said. He pulled a paper matchbook from one shirt pocket and a cigar from the other. Except it wasn't a real cigar. It was a piece of cut reed about the same size as a real one. "It's a *stogy,*" Razzie bragged, striking a match. He held the match under the stogy and sucked hard. The end glowed red like Gramp's cigarette. Razzie blew smoke out over my head, *a little smart-alecky,* I'm thinkin'. He could have been a swaggering movie cowboy, the kind who talks too much and gets beat up for it.

"You want a cigar?"

I had no answer, shocked that anyone would offer a little kid a smoking thing.

"What grade you in?" he asked.

"Ain't in school yet."

"That's what I thought. You're too young to smoke." True enough, and supposedly too young to get the joke. Razzie was a second grader, "old enough" to smoke. After he said something about moving up river and riding the big buffalo next to Buck, I left in a hurry.

"Who was that down there?" Buck asked.
"The one I talked to was a kid named Razzie."
"Big or little?"
"What?"
"Big Razzie or Little Razzie?"
"The second grade one," I said. "The wiseacre one."
"That's gotta be Little Razzie," Buck said. "His brother's a fifth grader. He say anything about Stony Ford?"
"Yup. He said he and Big Bervie are going there next Saturday, and the other kid too . . . Tommy something."
"Must be Tommy Stahl," Buck said.
"Well they might be thinkin' Stony Ford; but they won't beat us there," Jack said.
"Wouldn't make a nickel's difference," Buck laughed. "They don't know the bullhead hole."
I felt like a spy snitcher standing there, looking up at the questioning generals.
"You want a boost onto your buffalo?" my brother asked.
I didn't answer right off, and didn't know why . . . finally: "Uh, no. I guess I'll just sit down here by the water." I spied a grassy shelf tucked in between my brother's camel and the river. It was a cozy place, as if someone had carved a nook in the bank. Curled at the back was a small clay animal. I imagined him to be a grinning lion cub. I plopped down in the mud grass next to my lion and listened to the lapping water, waiting to hear another cackle from the rooster pheasant across the river.

The clay animals blocked my upriver view of the country that my guys were talking about. They were excited about a place called Stony Ford and the northern run of the Little Muddy where Buck went with his dad to catch walleye pike in "water that runs crystal clear."

The west wind had blown gusty all day until this very moment. A new breeze drifted over me, a softer one. It flowed steadily, floating down over the river from the north, warm and fragrant, like the air coming out of Mom's oven. Except it smelled nothing like her baked bread. It smelled of a mix of river things: the one bullhead Jim had caught and held close for me to sniff and see; Razzie's carp; frogs; swamp grass; and, Gramp's mallards laid out for feather picking . . .

The Muddy's cream soda water whisked softly past my special nook. Across the river, swaying reeds turned to green haze. Dreamy visions faded out and in until one settled: a big white mule carrying me across the river. My brother, chest deep in the water, led the mule. Off to the side I peered deep into clear water and its bouldered bottom. A long gray shadow bellied across the deep—a huge fish and long like Gramp's pike from Rock River.

My monster fish searched with golden beamed eyes. He rushed forward, opening his jaws. Minnows flushed; but they were too late. The pike's jaws opened wide and chomped. The pike swam 10 feet deep against the bottom; still, I heard his jaws snap shut. Dreams can do such miraculous things. And unlike serial movies, Muddy River dreams don't have THE END.

Chapter Three

Stony Ford

Stony Ford days: wonderfully stupid and stupendous.

A week after my first adventure at Horseshoe Bend, we came back, this time hiking past our clay animal steeds. We headed north, hiking on a cow trail that followed each bend of the Little Muddy River. Our destination was Stony Ford, but not without diversions. First Jack, then Buck or Jim would lead us down branching trails where cattle had gone to drink or cross the river. After a couple of such forays, I had to know why. "What are we looking for?"

I took Buck's deadpan stare to mean, *You should know; anyone should know.*

Jack offered little help, only, "We're just lookin', that's all."

Such was the beginning of the Muddy River lesson, where *just lookin'* is reason enough, leading to the new and unexpected, like Jim running 'round the bend to the next pool and racing back even faster. "Hey guys, there's a mink on the bank up there. He's got a fish, a big catfish."

Around the next bend, came Buck's turn. "Good gravel in here, looks like a walleye hole. We'll come back later in the year and fish for 'em."

Jack pitched in too, telling how his uncle fishes walleye. "You gotta' sneak in quiet. Stomp on the bank and they're gone. Uncle Bill makes me crawl."

Usually it was Buck who claimed the last word. He'd been taught by his dad on the north Muddy. We had come to a rocky riffle that dropped into a deep, amber-green pool. "Too bad about this hole," Buck said, pointing at a pair of turtle heads . . . "Snappers. They'll gobble most of the minnows and ruin this pool for walleyes."

Our *just lookin'* detours didn't last long with Buck and Jack nervously looking back to check on the progress of a far off trio of boys coming up the east bank. We didn't need binoculars. Jim, "Eagle Eyes," announced, "I can tell by the way they're traveling—Big Bervie, Razzie, and Tommy Stahl coming."

When Jack said, "We're movin' out," my patrol took off like a pack of striped-ass apes. I shouldn't have wasted time trying to catch the biggest frog I'd ever seen.

Though I ran my fastest, I never saw my guys again until I topped the drift of black sand bordering the south end of the Stony Ford pool. My guys were already planted in the curve of the western shore with their lines out. Buck glanced quickly at me and back to his line. He said, "Little Eric, you're late. Move in below me. We want this whole beach claimed before those other guys get here."

I fumbled in my pack and pulled out my worm can and throw-line. But that's as far as I got. I just stood and stared, hardly breathing. This famous place was better than the picture I had stored in my brain. The hidden pool was bordered by a black sand beach and nestled into a cozy cove, sheltered from the winds of the flat, treeless valley. Best of all, a wide rumbling, whooshing waterfall tumbled into the pool.

The waterfall was fantastic. It cascaded over a rock ledge, plunging white and frothing into boulders that lined the entire northern expanse of Stony's pool, a distance nearly as wide as a football field. Our loud talk rose barely above the rumble of water. "First waterfall I've ever seen," I said.

"It's not a real waterfall," Buck said. "Real ones in the Rocky Mountains are as tall as pine trees. I've seen 'em. They roar like freight trains."

From his knees, tending his throw-line, Jack took up my cause. "It's a waterfall, Buck, just a small one."

"Nope. Gotta be higher and louder, with more spray—enough to drench us sitting here," Buck insisted.

"How high then?" I needed to know.

"So if you fell in from the top, the undertow would pull you down and hold you. They'd need dragger hooks to find your body. That's what my dad said when we were in Montana."

"Like Niagara Falls," Jack said. "I have a book with pictures of it. This one here, you'd need twenty hundred thousand Stonys to add up to one Niagara."

"This one does the job though," Jim said, nudging me. "Thousands of fish stack up in here. Not all of them stay, though. Look over there; halfway across, there's a chute between those white boulders."

"There he goes," as Mom would say, "Jimmy's one ear on the conversation and the rest of him gone somewhere else."

"A big strong fish like a walleye could swim right up the chute," Jim said, defining part of his plan intended for my ears. "Up over the top, just above the falls, that's where wagons used to ford the river. We'll catch our bullheads; then I'll show you."

I followed Jim's search across the breadth of Stony's falls—yes a *falls,* even if a walleye *could* climb it. "Between the biggest boulders, is that the chute?"

"Yeah, and I'm gonna find a way out there sometime and catch me a walleye," Jim said. "Maybe we'll build a raft."

"I dunno, Jim. The water runs swift out there."

"Worth a try, though."

The Little Muddy whooshed and rumbled over the fall's crest, not pine tree tall, but maybe half a pine tree. The plunge of the Muddy had to be a real waterfall, and Jim would back me on that when we told Gram and Gramp and our parents.

We rested on our knees, spacing ourselves along the curve of the pool's west shore. The whole place moved: foam and driftwood, mud ducks, and muskrats. Everything swam and swirled this way and that about the pool, which had to be the hugest one on the river, as far as Canada or wherever the Little Muddy River came from. Even big kids like Buck or Jack wouldn't be able to throw a rock across Stony Ford Pool.

I wasn't much of a fisherman in my condition, so distracted by new wonders, including the dark pungent sand where I sat. I used a pretty bronze-hued clam shell to dig in the sand. In one scoop I found black snail shells and white ones and miniature pearly clam shells—and fish bones, "Left behind by the mink," Jack explained. I dug deeper.

"Hey Jack, what are these?" I cupped the five brown nuggets in my hand, which caused Jack to shriek his cackling laugh.

"Great discovery, Little Eric," Jack laughed. You uncovered coon poops."

"Well, they don't stink," I countered. Fact is, all the interesting animal shits and bones and scales and shells came together in that sand to make a fragrant mix, one that moved in and stayed with me.

But where were the bullheads? Mid-day now and nobody had caught one. Regardless, Stony's pool was too nice to leave. A cool breeze drifted down upon us from the waterfall, or if Buck was to have his way, the rapids. The drift and swirl of air brought us a strange, tingly fragrance, not unpleasant, but pungent. Jack said, "Stony Ford smells like the armpit of a turtle." By strange coincidence, a minute later here came a fiercesomely huge snapper, the king of all turtles. He lumbered unafraid along the beach, threatening us with reptiled eyes and mean snapping jaws. We teased him with sticks, but nobody was brave enough to turn him over and sniff his armpits.

Stony Ford was a joyous place, constantly celebrated by birds: cowbirds, meadowlarks, and redwings trying to be heard over wind and water. Stony overwhelmed, enthralled, and adopted me. A kid would never be the same after coming here.

When Buck hollered, "I got one," he snapped me back to fishing, remembering what Jack had said about the "mother lode" of bullheads at Stony Ford. Hand over quick hand Buck pulled a fat, long whiskered bullhead onto the sand.

"Me too, a big one," Jim yelled, as he jumped to his feet, hauling in his jumbo.

"Yah-hoo! The bullhead run is on," Jack hollered. With frequent glances at his own throw-line, Jack scootched over on his knees next to me. He worked his quick practiced fingers while he talked. "Cover the entire hook; but be sure to leave a tail of your worm dangling, like this . . . and worm the entire hook shank. These bullheads like to mouth your worm first, and they don't like the feel of a steel hook. Now let's see your cast. Land it in the current right along that foam line." I whirled the end of the weighted line three times, like a lasso, and let fly. "Yah, good job, Davey," Jack said.

Jack stayed with me until I understood his bite teller trick. He pulled the line into a tiny limp circle at the water's edge. "When the line moves, it means the bullhead is lipping the worm. But don't go yankin' until your circle closes." With Jack's advice no sooner out of his mouth, the line in my bite teller circle moved, then closed. I yanked; the fish pulled back, and I quickly hauled my first slick, steely-skinned, yellow-bellied bullhead ashore. My heart pounded double time. Jack clapped his hands, every bit as excited as I. Buck, too, was excited. From his spot up the shore, he yelled, "Hey, Little Eric got one," as if my catching a bullhead was an unlikely but pleasant surprise.

I grabbed my stringer, ready to thread my prize bullhead, but Jack held my arm. "Hold it—don't you know he's got stinger spines? They have a poison in them." He pointed without touching: "Lookie here, two spines on the sides and the big one on top." I watched my bullhead squirmy his fat little tummy into the sand, then rest in his fish-made nest. He looked up at me with his beady black eyes shining, his wide whisker-framed mouth grinning. He gaped his mouth slowly, as if he could nestle there all day. He's thinking, *"Come on, try me, I dare you."* We fooled him, rather Jack did. His hand came in quick as a rattlesnake and pinched the bullhead, thumb and forefinger an inch behind his side spines and in front of the spiky dagger on his back. Jack's grip paralyzed the little devil. Jigger-quick, Jack threaded my bullhead on my stringer. He drove the stringer's spike deep into the sand and tossed my tethered captive into the water to keep him fresh and alive. At least that bully-head didn't spine me. A few others did, until I got the hang of it. Still, I finished the day with 20 bullheads on my stringer, only about a dozen short of Jim and the other guys. I figure I had 10 pounds of bullheads to lug home.

Mom and Dad cheered us for our bullheadin'. In the midst of helping us skin and fillet, Dad repeated, "Cornmeal fried bullheads—yessiree! They fry up better'n anything."

"They'll cut our grocery bill too," Mom added.

Over the course of that bullhead spring and the next one, me and the guys must have taken a thousand fat bullheads home for family, and to share with neighbors, and the bald eagles at the animal park. The eagles got the leftovers, the littlest ones, or even jumbos when Dad, Jim and I ran out of skinning and cutting time.

Jim and I hoofed it to the animal park until our second Stony Ford summer when we biked the six blocks on our blue Hawthornes. In order to balance our bikes we learned to even the count of bullheads onto paired stringers tied swinging from both handlebars.

At the park we snuck our bullheads in on stringers hidden behind our legs, creeping past several *DON'T FEED THE ANIMALS* signs. Fish-by-fish we poked our bullheads through the cage wire, all the while keeping an eye out for Knute Odegard, the animal keeper. The pair of fierce-eyed bald eagles watched us cautiously before sailing from their perches to claim their bullheads. They'd screech, squabble, and spar with flapping wings before ripping into the fish with talons and beaks. We never tired of watching them gorge on bullheads.

With each trip the pair of eagles greeted Jim and me less cautiously. Finally, they trusted us enough to hop down from their perches without hesitation, like a couple of overgrown chickens. We were happy for them. The eagles liked our bullheads way better than the half-rotten meat Mr. Odegard provided them.

Again and again we returned to Stony Ford, as long as the bullhead run lasted. Thousands gathered in the pool. Other fish too. We hooked an occasional powerful carp that raced off zinging the line, burning our fingers before finally tiring. Carp, the homely and bony devils, were granted their freedom, and sometimes the tiniest bullheads too, but never prized channel cats or rare walleyes so hungry or bored with a steady diet of minnows that they fell for lowly worms. Our main target, though, was bullheads. They were plentiful. We were good at catching them, and proud of our success in supplying bullhead fillets for Gram and Gramp, Mom and Dad, and sometimes Uncle Milt and Aunt Jane.

An hour into my first day at Stony Ford, Razzie, Big Bervie, and Tommy Stahl managed to hop rocks across the top of the falls, landing on our side. Buck and Jack gave them 20 feet of shoreline space on the beach downstream. Stony Ford proved so generous in giving up its bullheads, that its pool was big enough for the few ambitious kids willing to travel three miles.

Stony Ford kids were easy to spot. Take Buck, for instance. His mom bought him durable cotton drill fishin' pants from the Monkey Ward's catalog. She bought brown ones that wouldn't show dirt. Didn't work. Buck's cotton pants, our blue denim ones, they all showed permanent dark butt stains from Stony's collection of poops, and rotted bugs and animals. "Dust to dust," they say. I say, "mud to mud" better describes life and death on the river.

Stony Ford went home with us. Mom always caught us at the back door. "As soon as you clean your fish, it's in the tub with you." Baths couldn't erase the essence of Stony's black sand beach. It seeped through pants, into skin, into my brain. And I could conjure its musty aroma anytime I wanted, even in the dead of winter.

Not bragging, but after three years of providing neighbors, relatives, and Mom and Dad's friends with "a mess of bullhead fillets," Jim and I felt a tad uppity about our fishin'. Talk of our fishing savvy found its way to our great uncle Milt. He called, teasing, "I want to move up on your bullhead customer list."

Uncle Milt was Gramp's brother, and like Gramp, shared his great love of animals. Milt believed the whole world should know and respect animals, and acted on his belief. He served on the city parks board and used his position to successfully stump for the building of Williston's zoo park—except he wouldn't call it that. "Not a zoo," Uncle Milt said. "We're gonna make it better, natural—an animal park where critters have room to dig and play, and they'll have better food than any cottonpickin' zoo." I guess that's why we rarely caught a glimpse of the badger. His underground lair was designed to perfect badger specifications and given away only by a round hole in a slab of concrete. Sneaking quietly to his cage, we'd sometimes see his fierce dark face, and black eyes glaring out the hole.

Uncle Milt was a great joker. He socked away a supply of teasing ammunition gathered from people about the town and countryside. Wherever possible, he'd pick up tidbits on Jim and me; then, he'd boomerang us with our own shenanigans. He did so again when Jim and I brought him a mess of bullheads.

Uncle Milt and Aunt Jane were most pleased with our ready-to-fry bullhead fillets. They invited us to sit at their kitchen table and enjoy Uncle Milt's incredible chocolate malt milk shakes. A tease was in the works. His twinkling blue eyes said so. Jim and I slurped our shakes as he started in, "So boys, how's fishin' been? I hear tell you're fishin' the Little Muddy pretty hard."

"Yah, we're doin' real good, too, catching gobs of jumbo bullheads," Jim said. "We'll bring you some more, anytime you want."

"Well, much obliged," Uncle Milt laughed, "but on one condition. You've got to take care of my eagles first. My animal park manager has been watching you come and go over the past two years. Nobody fools old Knute."

Jim's jaw dropped. I suppose mine did too. Jeepers-creepers, big trouble—we'd been caught red-handed sneaking fish to the eagles. Yet, Uncle Milt still grinned.

"Go ahead. Tell the boys the rest," Aunt Jane said.

"Reckon I will. I don't think they'll spend more than a month in jail." But Uncle Milt couldn't tease with a straight face.

"My park manager says . . ." Uncle Milt stopped, unable to contain his laughter. "Knute says his eagles come out of winter looking scrawny. Your snuck-in fish fatten them and put a sheen on their feathers."

What? . . . We'd been so sneaky careful. Jim was speechless for a full minute, squirming in his chair. He was able to give back only: "Heck, Uncle Milt, we know eagles need fish."

"Well, I hope you know that now you've started my eagles on fish, you can't quit. And don't short 'em." Uncle Milt filled our tall malted milk glasses once more from his shiny metal canister. "Be sure to tell Knute hello for me next Saturday," he laughed.

After two years of carefree country days spent at Stony Ford, we knew the spring, summer, and fall of our magical place, now as familiar as our backyards. I pestered my brother, "Who discovered Stony Ford for fishin'?" I needed to know.

"Buck's dad. He figured out the bullhead run," Jim said. "He taught Buck, and Buck brought Jack to Stony two years ago. They don't want us braggin' up the fishin' there, though. It's our private hole for bullheads."

Jack and Buck were the two we looked to as leaders with savvy to semi-organize the rest of us. The two of them were an intriguing pair of opposites, Jack the freewheeler and Buck, like 'Sergeant Preston' of the Royal Canadian Mounted Police: thoughtful, confident, always in the right place at the right time.

Buck mastered challenges well before others his age. Be it bike jumping or racing, BB gun shooting, or bullhead fishing, Buck was a master. Watching him move you'd judge slow and lazy, but I say his way was smart, exactly how a big kid with a blocky frame carried on oversized feet should go about things, succeeding without wasted motion or fanfare, intent blue eyes analyzing before setting to the challenge of the moment. Chances were, whatever big escapade we had in mind, Buck had already done it or been halfway there.

If I had to name Buck like the Indians did their boy warriors, I'd call him Plodder. I'll bet as a toddler he plodded across the floor, big sturdy feet going "*phlat . . . phlat . . . phlat . . . phlat,*" marching slowly, but relentlessly. Had his mom opened the door, Buck would have plodded his way around the block, returning home just before dark with two friends and a puppy.

Buck's solid bike traveling style served him well, too. He rode slow to middling, but did so more resolutely than anyone. *Crank . . . crank . . . crank,* he'd pump for hours, whatever needed to get himself far up into the north Muddy country, even as far as the Nine Mile Bridge. The Plodder walked the banks of the river with the same constant determination, carrying his big boned, wide shouldered frame like a plowhorse. From the day I first met Buck he seemed out of place, carrying more confidence than others his age. Come to think about it, so did Jack.

While Buck went about country escapades masterfully and calmly, Jack accomplished the same things in wild celebration, shrieking with laughter and romping about as if he had ants in his pants. With every fish landed, save the tiny throwbacks, Jack waltzed the sands of Stony Ford in celebration. He was lighthearted about everything but bikes, throw-lines, shoes, or BB guns. Jack cared full time about cleaning, polishing, and organizing them. I took the chain guard off my bike, which sure irritated Jack. "It always rattles," I said.

"Then put it back, and keep it tightened," Jack said.

Jack was known as a fun guy, a good whistler and popular joke teller, always quick to cheer his friends, as he did for me when I won my freestyle blue ribbon at Harmon Park Pool. He threw so much energy into having fun, he could bring a crowd to watch a game of alley basketball or entice 30 kids into a game of *pump-pump, pull-away.*

Of course, Jack could come out of a rough game of *pump-pump, pull-away* looking ready for Sunday school. He was neat and groomed, the sort of guy girls and grown-ups called good looking, nearly always wearing a clean shirt and pants with ironed creases, as if ready to be photographed. He was the only kid I'd seen ride a bike in a long-sleeved shirt buttoned at the neck. Even on fishin' trips, Jack looked as if he'd come out of the barber shop. Never wore a hat or cap—none of us did; but Jack was the only kid whose hair stayed in place. He wore his sandy hair long, neatly slanted above the left temple down and across his forehead. After each gust of wind his miraculous hair homed back into place, something only Jack and Gary Cooper managed to do.

Jack's knack was instigation, nurturing ideas and serving them with perfect timing so he could sit back and enjoy the outcomes, fiascos and all. He connived with Buck to arrange us according to abilities. Tommy Stahl, for instance, was one of their projects. Tommy showed little interest in fishing, hadn't patience for it. On one of his first trips to Stony, Tommy sat most of the morning on the shore between Jack and Buck. Tommy mostly whittled sticks, smoked reed "cigars" and tended our campfire. With time-outs for catching, stringering, and re-baiting, Jack and Buck questioned Tommy about his experiences grilling at the Barrel Drive Inn alongside his manager dad. "So, you've done okay cookin' hotdogs and burgers you say?"

"Damn tootin.'"

"Yah, too bad that's all he knows about cookin," Buck teased.

"*Ha!* I know lots more, French fries and everything."

"Bet you can't do fish or frogs."

"Bet I can."

"Hey, I got an idea, Tommy," Jack said, as if it just popped into his head. "None of us brought a good lunch. Buck will pot us some frogs. Big Eric will help. He's a good shot, and he can borrow my new BB gun. Then, Tommy, you and Razzie can cook us a batch of frog legs. How about it? While we hunt firewood, Buck and Jim will hunt jumbo frogs."

"Won't take us long," Buck said.

An hour later Buck and Jim proudly dumped a couple dozen dead frogs from their canvas pack. Tommy went to his cooking and shortly thereafter we feasted on brown-roasted frog legs plucked from Tommy's sharpened willow sticks.

That was an easy beginning to a tradition of game and fish lunches cooked on Stony Ford's beach, though *"game and fish"* may be an exaggeration considering the menu: poke-on-a-stick frog legs and bullhead fillets seasoned with dustings of ash. The cooker, Tommy, was helped along by Jack, or Big Bervie—who augmented standard fare with Bervie's Indian lore items like blackbird—each providing a pair of quarter-sized roasted breasts and the bird's tiny drumsticks worth arguing over.

Wily crows were fair game too, although Buck and Jim managed to kill only a few with their plinking Red Ryder BB guns.

Tommy Stahl considered himself a real chef, like his dad, who wore a tall white cookin' hat at the Barrel Drive Inn. Tommy was not satisfied with poke-on-a-stick, and came up with the idea of roasting our bullheads, frog legs, and baby cattail shoots over beds of wetted willow fronds.

The cattail shoots were Bervie's idea. He was a book reader from way back forever. He could have been dropped on earth from the last century, using expressions like *"out yonder,"* and when bike riding: *"Don't spare the horses."* Bervie kept a notebook full of important facts, like using cattail shoots as vegetables and other livin'-off-the-land ideas he lifted from his Mandan Indian book. He learned from his Indian book—and another called *Lore of the Northwood*—helpful knowledge about killing water germs, for instance. He'd filter Muddy River water through a contraption made of reeds and grass and boil it in a tin can over a driftwood fire. "The book says five minutes," Bervie said. "We'll go ten." Little Bervie assisted in the cooling process, handling the hot can with his scavenged pliers and nestling the can in wet river sand. Long as the Bervigs were around, we didn't bother with canteens. Just mention how hot and dry we were and they'd hop to boiling water.

The Bervig boys epitomized summer life in North Dakota. Flashing back, trying to remember and describe the look of the Muddy River characters, the Bervigs are the easiest. Picture a pair of grinning, sunburned Opies from the "Andy Griffith Show." Give them short, kinky hair that held firm against the wind . . . short sleeved checkered cotton shirts, the right pant legs of cotton drill rolled up to keep them clear of bike chains. That's it: carefree North Dakota "Opies," off fishin' with buddies, their world of big people forgotten.

The Bervig boys loved projects, worked like a pair of beavers, even reminded me of roly-poly beavers, grinning on the job, working top speed. They spent most of a Saturday afternoon surveying, analyzing, and drawing plans in the sand next to a boulder strewn, broken concrete jumble, all that remained of the washed out crossing known as Stony Ford. "Has to be fixed," Big Bervie declared. "Come on, Allen. We'll make a walkway bridge," and the Bervig boys headed out across the flats to the north, to the abandoned farm site that's "gotta have some good boards left." All afternoon they toiled, trekking to the farm for boards, and heaving rocks at the crossing to build supports for bridging. Jim and I left our lines with Buck and Jack and hiked up to the crossing to watch and heave a few rocks. Big Bervie toted a board on his head, wading to the middle of the crossing. "Get with it, Bervie," Jim hollered. "Tomorrow we need to cross over and go upriver. Stony's bullheads have either been caught or wised up."

At mid-morning the next day, Jim got his wish. Big Bervie stood in the middle of his rickety bridge and announced, "She's ready. It'll cost each of you a nickel to cross."

Jim rose to his feet and wound up his throw line. "I'm opening a charge account with you," he yelled back. "I'm gonna cross over and hike up to the east bank of the Fishhook Hole. Who's going with?"

Off went the entire gang of older guys, leaving me with Little Bervie to tend lines.

Jim, the *Pied Piper,* was responsible for dozens of such adventures. I suspect the Muddy River Boys would have gone stale and turned back to town mischief without Jim's incessant wanderlust.

With his soft, coppery tan that held over through winters and deepened through summers, I likened Jim to Natty Bumppo loping tirelessly across the prairie, swimming swift creeks, and traveling for a hundred miles just to see new country. Our Grandma Erickson started me thinking of him as part Indian. She said he was a throwback to the Cree Indians from her side of the family up in Ontario. She had him pegged: long, lean muscles that never tired and brown squinty eyes forever searching horizons. Most telling, Jim refused to recognize obstacles to adventure, judging objectives as never too far, too difficult, or too anything.

Jim's wanderlust was embedded in him by the time we began exploring the Muddy River country. While the rest of us quibbled about how far we could hike, the relative wisdom of heading out in a spring snow storm, or hiking to far off destinations, Jim stayed out of conversations, content to sit back and wait until arguments croaked of natural causes. Then in the unsettled vacuum he'd simply announce: "I don't know about the rest of you, but I'm going." I have no idea why his Pied Piperness worked on us.

On a blustery March Saturday Jim, Buck, and I rode our bikes north. Our plan was to leave our bikes at Stony Ford and cross there to hunt gophers on the sunny slopes of the eastern ridge. Racing down the country road to Stony, we heard the moan of the river, the cracking of ice. "Oh, oh," Buck said. "She's breaking up." We rode to Stony crossing, today a falls for sure. Whooshing water ran fast and furious, carrying refrigerator sized ice blocks to the crest, where they piled high in a broken jumble. One at a time, the ice blocks tipped and fell, crashing down, sending showers of water skyward. Underneath the mass of ice the Bervig's bridge built last summer would be smashed and gone. There'd be no crossing of the Muddy today . . . or would there? Jim stood apart, wearing that *look,* gazing upriver.

"Let's hike up to the wide stretch of river above Fishhook Bend," he said. "The ice will still be sound up there." His voice portrayed exaggerated hope. But Buck's skeptical glance at me and my return shrug didn't stop us . . . curiosity, I suppose. We trudged off behind Jim toward Fishhook Bend.

No luck upriver either. Though the river ice was still intact, every few seconds it snapped and cracked like the report of a .22 rifle. The spooky mass shifted eerily east and settled back west.

We were right about prime time for gopher hunting. We watched them on the far side, beyond the Muddy's heaving and cracking ice, gophers by the dozen scampering about the winter-dead prairie grass.

A beautiful red fox ghosted down the hill toward the gophers' spring frolic. At that distance the fox appeared to float legless above the ground. Suddenly, she stopped and went to her belly, then arc'd high, gracefully leaping and landing forepaws and snout on a luckless gopher. We watched her toss the gopher into the air, grab its dead body and trot up the hill. "Goin' to her den with it," Buck said. "She's got babies."

"It'd be fun to find that den and bring her some more dead gophers," Jim said.

"Should have come out last Saturday," Buck said. "The ice was solid and safe."

We turned for home that Saturday afternoon discouraged but not defeated. On our bike ride home, Jim conjured another way. "Guys, we'll come back tomorrow. We'll hike up to the S-turn and cross over on the ice jams. And from what I saw, we better bring plenty of ammo."

At nine o'clock Sunday morning we dropped our bikes by the side of Stony Ford road and hiked north to the sharp river bends, the place where Jim predicted: "The ice will jam, making a bridge. We'll crawl across on the ice cakes." We carried only BB guns and BB cartons tucked deep into pants pockets. I anticipated a competition hunt, belly creeping, chin ducked to the earth—Daniel Boone style—sneaking close to the gophers for fatal head shots. Jim would likely win out with his eagle eyes and wiry, athletic body, and slinking belly crawl; maybe, though, I could out-hunt Buck.

Buck trotted in front of me and gradually picked up his pace to a lumbering lope.

Still, we fell far behind Jim. Arriving at the knoll overlooking the first S-turn of the river, we found Jim leaning against the corner post of a falling-down corral, surveying the half-mile stretch of river below. He shook his head. "*Dang!* We need a new plan. No crossing here. The doggone ice jams have gone down the river." Indeed, the river ran free, out of its banks, as wide as a football field, carrying a flotilla of baby icebergs that sailed downriver like little aircraft carriers. One of them carried a pair of hopping, pecking magpies feasting on the remains of a winter-white jackrabbit.

"New plan, you say? Heck, what we need is a boat," was a joke Buck should have kept to himself.

Wishes like that didn't go unnoticed. Jim rapped on the corral post. "How about a raft? Look, these posts are perfect . . . and there in the junk pile is a whole bundle of wire to hold 'em together. All we need, perfect makings for a raft."

Buck covered his face with his hands and shook his head. "Jeez, Jim, the Muddy's flooding, for criminy sakes. Ain't a place for a two-bit raft."

"Prob-ly right. But, let's just build it and see."

Like me, Buck bought into Jim's overall scheme, because raft building sounded like fun. We loved the Huck Finn story about running the Mississippi on a log raft. I'd day dreamed about setting off on a similar adventure. So easy, just let the river take us down and away, winding through deep wooded bottomlands—far south, where the water is always warm and big fish never quit biting.

"Jim, you're nuts," Buck declared. "Sure, we can put a raft together. Maybe by July the river will be tame enough to use it."

Jim didn't answer. He busied himself loosening and pushing over the few posts still standing. "Come on guys, we'll haul those posts to the river," Jim said. Buck shrugged, and we went to work dragging the best of the posts—the *half* rotted ones.

I sat on the river bank watching, while Jim and Buck laid out the posts—our raft "logs"—in a six by eight foot rectangle. Then we pulled the jumble of twisted, rusty wire next to our raft and went to work untangling. We straightened the wire best we could, then lashed it over and under, over and under, until the raft held in a flexible platform. Jim jumped onto it, declaring it "perfect, ready to go." *"Perfect"* was Jim's favorite word. How many times in our history did "perfect" lead to trouble and *"kowabunga,"* one of Buck's favorite Indian words, meaning big, big trouble. Nevertheless, Jim arranged three skinny corral rails by the shore. He picked up the longest one, "This one will fit you, Buck."

Buck stared at Jim, shaking his head in disbelief. "Uh-uh! I said we'd *build* the raft, not use it. Not today."

"Buck's right, Jim," I said. "I'm not about to go swimmin' in an ice river."

Jim shrugged and sat down on our raft, while Buck and I piled together all the logical reasons we shouldn't try crossing the flooding Muddy on a raft built of rotting wood posts and rusty wire.

"Don't think it'll float the three of us," Buck said.

"Those doggone icebergs are getting thicker by the minute, can't risk it," I said. "Give her two weeks, Jim. The Muddy will be ready for a raft . . ."

With the best argument of all, Buck added what should have been the clincher: "My dad told me never mess with a river at ice-out."

Buck and I made perfect sense. Yet, Jim sat lost in his own world, while Buck and I exhausted every good reason we should forget about rafting. We should have turned and walked away from the river; we didn't because the Muddy's magic had us in its hold, especially Jim: "You guys gotta' see the crazy mallards. They've flown by here twice already." On cue, here they came, flying faster than any ducks I'd ever seen—a female followed by two bright greenheads, dodging closely behind her, rocking wings like Jap Zeroes.

The three of us sat on the edge of our raft basking in springtime. Between gusts of wind the river's musty fragrance, the *armpit of the turtle,* rose from the grass and mud, tinting the air. This was a pivotal moment, when *armpit of the turtle,* rich with inseparable memories, had been unleashed from its winter ice entrapment . . . as were the critters, all on the go: muskrats and a pair of snappers dodging ice cakes along the river's flooded margin in the grass. Out of that grass a garter snake came slithering, another trailing behind. Killdeers ran the shore piping noisily, competing with herons, blackbirds, and meadowlarks. The critters, like us, were infected with *river mood,* when spring can't be held back a minute longer. I'll blame *river mood* for what happened next.

Jim stood and laid his BB gun crossways on the front of the raft. "Come on guys. We built the raft, let's use it. Help me get it in the water." Jim didn't wait for us, but dropped to his knees in the mud and began heaving against the heavy raft. Buck and I joined in the pushing until, save for one corner, our raft floated free.

"Dave can ride in front and keep the guns safe. Buck, you and I will pole us across." Buck shrugged his shoulders and scooted his Red Ryder over next to Jim's. This time he accepted Jim's offer of the pole and boarded with a laugh: "I christen her Queen of the Muddy."

I hesitated, stuck on defending my record: no "chicken outs." It had been a year since my first Muddy River trip to Horseshoe Bend. "You keep up, you can go along," Buck had said. I rode my bike hard, swam hard, and ran fast. I had good "keeping up" legs. I'd been allowed to go along on Muddy River trips for a year. Now 6, going on 7, I'd keep my record intact. So, I made the only logical choice. I hopped aboard as Jim pushed with his pole to separate our raft from the shore.

I knelt at the front of the raft holding our three BB guns and my pole crosswise at my knees. Our raft floated softly, like a magic carpet; but it flexed a little too freely, I thought. The two logs I knelt upon bobbed independently under my knees. Ice water surged up between them, drenching my legs.

"Ho . . . ly cow! Hold on!" Jim hollered. *"Here comes a big one!"* He leaned against me as "the big one," a "baby iceberg," swirled and rammed a corner of its piano-sized hulk against our raft. The impact spun us sideways. Buck and Jim braced legs, holding their poles parallel for balance, like circus high wire performers. The water came over their ankles with the ice collision, and the raft tipped back, leaving Buck and Jim high and dry and me submerged down to my hunkered butt. Finally our raft leveled, softening my panic to simple helplessness, a condition that had come about too quickly to comprehend. Had I more time to

think, I'm afraid hot pee would have flooded my crotch. I felt as important as an ant out there, and about as smart too. I held tight to the raft, dizzied by the motion of humming water and bobbing, rasping ice cakes.

We could not have known how uncontrollable our ride would be. We were of no more consequence than the river's "icebergs" that Jim and Buck worked at fending away with their poles. My original vision of crossing was ridiculous. No such thing as simply poling across. The Muddy had another idea, to take whatever rode its swirling, racing currents as fast as possible, caroming the four miles down its valley into the Big Missouri River. To make matters worse, a covey of quick hitting clouds scurried across the valley, opened, and spilled wet spring snow on us.

"Push off on the ice, Buck," Jim yelled. "It's too deep out here to reach bottom." With half the river crossed, its swift current had taken us a quarter mile downriver. I saw Fishhook Bend coming up. Another quarter mile south lay the Stony Ford rapids—no, now a *falls* for sure. *Doggone it, Buck, will we have to plunge over to prove it is a real waterfall?*

I looked hopefully at Buck for re-assurance. But his fun-loving face had turned pale. A thin ledge of snow crusted his frizzle hair. He shivered and shook like a wet dog trying to shed the snow. "Kowabunga, Jim," Buck hollered. "Give 'er heck! We don't want to mess with the Fishhook Bend." Buck, big eyed with determination, thrust hard with his pole. Jim picked up the pace too, and I felt our raft surge forward, thinking we might make it after all. The gophers thought so too; as we moved closer to shore, they scurried and ducked into burrows.

We reached shore just short of the Fishhook. I grabbed the BB guns and jumped. The second my feet hit the ground I felt brave and important. *After all, didn't Washington do this on the Delaware?*

"I told you guys, nothin' to it," Jim said. Maybe so, but why did a fearless guy like Buck plop on a rock and just sit there staring at the river?

From his knees Jim cocked his lever action and waved his BB gun like John Wayne charging the Chiricahuas. "Come on, guys. I'm bettin' you a dime on the first gopher." Buck paid him no mind. He shook his head at the river and blasted it with a really bad cuss word. Finally Buck turned his back on the river and shivered it away, scattering the snow gathered around his collar.

The black cloud drifted off and, on cue with the sun, little brown gopher heads popped out of burrows. Buck nodded up the hill. "Your brother is getting a head start. I'm betting you an extra nickel just between us."

Hunting gophers turned out to be more difficult than we imagined. Their sharp-eyed sentries stood tall, ready to chitter alarms. We used hillocks and buckbrush for cover to sneak within range. Still, each stalk required 10 minutes of belly-skinnying. Each time, hearing the pop of a gun, the gophers neatly ducked under the BB's and dropped into their burrows quicker'n striped-ass weasels. Besides, after slinking through the musty grass close enough to see twitching whiskers, nibbly little lips, and glinty black eyes, I wasn't so unhappy they got away.

After an hour of stalking, Jim finally killed a gopher with a head shot. We took it up the hill to the fox den and dropped it on the fresh dirt mound amidst splintered bones, hair, and baby fox footprints. I was on my knees peeking in the hole when Jim warned, "Here she comes. Let's get out of here." High on the eastern hillside following the Indian trail, Mrs. Fox walked along sniffing right and sniffing left. She was an unforgettable sight, part of the pay-off for risking the river crossing. Days, weeks—even years later—when Jim, Buck, and I recounted our rafting escapade, the story had to have a destination. We called the long curve in the bluff the Fox Walk.

The Fox Walk trail lay under the crest of the bluff. Up there, 140 years ago Meriwether Lewis and William Clark stood gazing across the prairied landscape of the Muddy River Valley. Jim would have fit in perfectly with their expedition. Buck too. In fact, the pair of them complemented each other in the same way as the two famous explorers: Jim impulsive, Buck knowledgeable and steadfast.

Quickly we vacated her den area, heading for the shore of the Muddy. A minute later Missuz Fox arrived home. She sat on the mound by her den watching us ready our raft for departure from "Gopher Town."

"We'll push off and let the current carry us over," Jim said. "Should make it easy."

Good thing for all of us that Buck brought along his reserve of outdoor expertise. As things turned out we needed his special nugget of wisdom on our return trip across the wild, icy Muddy River. Buck had gleaned valuable knowledge from days spent with his dad, some of them on the Muddy further to the north of Stony Ford. Mr. Bundhund was known as Ernie to townfolk and his farmer customers who bought his farm machinery. He somehow saved precious time for Buck, to take him fishing and hunting. Ernie had even taken Buck twice to the Montana Rockies to fish trout, where they had watched a log drive on the Kootenai River. As it turned out, Buck's experience witnessing those timberjacks riding logs down a wild, swift river possibly saved us.

Jim had done some good thinking, too. Had it not been for poor raft building materials, his plan may have worked. "We'll lay the guns in the grooves between the logs. That way Dave can pole there from the back. Buck, you and I will push from the sides so we can keep her straight. We'll scoot right across, no problem."

Jim had it figured alright. We laughed out loud at how easily we poled our raft to mid-river. And we hadn't lost enough downriver drift to account for much. But then, I gasped, feeling a dreadful something go wrong. My left leg went left, my right went further right. "OOOHH, SHIIIIT!" Leg splits right there in the swiftest part of the wild Muddy River. Our raft was separating, like a splitting zipper. The binding wire had busted, the gol-durned rusty wire that had been in Jim's overwrought optimism, *"guaranteed plenty strong if we use a lot of it." 'Plenty strong'* took us as far as the middle of the river, where the fatigued wire gave out and our raft logs began to go their separate ways.

I've never been worth a dang at the leg splits and was about to topple into the river when Buck grabbed me by my jacket collar, steadying me upright, trying to stay balanced. But the two of us were too much for half a raft, and top-heavy to boot. Our precarious platform listed one way, then the other. Its downside lurches took us underwater to the shins before bobbing upright. We struggled desperately to stand against the lurches, using our poles for balance. From his one-half raft Jim extended his pole to me, hollering, "Grab on." I grabbed ahold, which sent the whole caboodle of us spinning out of control. Then, just as I worked up gumption for a swim, Buck pulled off his miracle.

Like a timberjack dancing on river logs, Buck calmly stepped off onto an ice cake. It was about twice the size of my grandpa's desk and held Buck's weight better than the raft itself. Jim took Buck's cue and stepped off onto an ice boat of his own. "You keep the guns with you, Dave," he said. "You've got enough raft left for one guy."

"Come on, Jim, follow me," Buck hollered. He frantically poled his ice boat, pushing hard, first from one side, then the other. I dared a second glance from my fragile balance to see yet another miracle, an ice shelf projecting out from the west shore, reducing the river's width by a third. Jim reached the ice shelf first and did so in dramatic fashion. He leapt head first, belly flopped, and skidded onto the smooth blue ice. Buck landed beside him, somehow having the foresight to first toss his pole ashore. I came riding the current behind them, but was caught up in a faster run that commanded and controlled my three by eight foot platform of weakly bound logs. I pushed against ice cakes with my pole. My awkward, skinny raft wavered, but refused to move closer.

"I think I better swim for it," I hollered.

"No Davey, no! It's ice water, way too cold. Stay with your raft," Jim yelled, as he and Buck ran the ice shelf alongside.

On shore, Buck was his old self, calm and reassuring. He directed: "Dave, toss the guns." My fleeting thought was, *Who cares about the dang guns?* Nevertheless, I reached down and pitched the BB guns across to the ice. "Now pole that raft in here, Dave," Buck said.

All I could think of was the roar and rumbling of Stony Ford Falls growing louder, and Jim and Buck rescuing my battered and bloody body from the swirling pool below the falls.

Jim and Buck sensed my shock, whatever had me bound. They shouted frantically: "Get with it, Davey. . . . Come on, pole that raft—move it in here." They ran the ice from not 10 feet away, yelling all the way.

Had not their voices broken through, I might have ridden over the falls in a stupid trance. I braced my legs and pushed into my pole against ice cakes like I'd watched Buck do. Pulled by the fast water, I gained a yard or two closer to safety, but not enough. Out of the corner of my right eye I saw moving figures and Buck's pole, the end of it thrust forward just close enough to grab. Then Buck's calm voice . . .

"Grab a-hold, both hands, and hang on with all your might." I dropped my pole and clamped onto his with every ounce of my strength. Buck and Jim trotted together at the same pace as my raft, holding their end of the pole, maneuvering like synchronized dancers.

I searched the purposeful blue eyes of Buck, the timberjack. "We're gonna pull the same time as you jump. You ready?"

"Yeah, ready," I said.

"Okay, we'll go on three," Buck said.

Together then, we sang out, "One—two—three," and my mates pulled mightily and yanked me from the raft. I flew over the water and crashed on top of my rescuers. We lay in a tangled heap of soggy, shivering bodies, laughing, celebrating, lost in the sillies.

The pile of us smelled like wet muskrats. The stinkin' jumble of us untangled just as the sun found a hole in the clouds. We sat dumfounded on the ice, relishing our victory over the river. Wisps of steam rose from Jim and Buck's wool jackets the same as it does from fresh horse turds in the snow. The three crazy mallards flew over quacking in double-time, a welcome addition to Stony's waterfall rumble.

"There she goes," Buck said, nodding down river. Our remnant of a raft slid into the maw of the falls. We watched silently. Our "raft's" rear end rose high like the ass end of a bucking bronc. It tipped and disappeared with a slam and snap. "So much for your so-called raft," the river seemed to say.

"You lost her, Dave," Jim laughed. "She was a perfectly good raft, and you lost her."

"Perfectly good? Didn't last even one day. Buck and I tried to tell you . . ."

I couldn't go on with my teeth chattering so. I shivered, and not from damp cold alone.

We sat on our butts, watching the beastly falls batter and break the baby icebergs. Stony Ford had just had the final word on its spring upheaval.

Just as I began to feel betrayed by my favorite place on earth, Buck cuffed Jim on the shoulder. "Hey Jim, we've got matches. Bervie's rock cache . . . remember? Let's go."

We tromped down, past the noisy falls to our fishing pool, now a giant frothy swirl of things collected from upriver: ice cakes, sticks and snags, old boards, and—of course—raft logs. But a welcoming strip of black sand beach remained above high water. "Find some dry tinder and sticks, Dave," Jim ordered. "Buck and I will check out our 'cupboard.' "

I waited long enough to watch Buck roll back the rock hiding our cache, reach in and pull out a box of wooden matches. He reached deeper and pulled out a can of pork and beans, the can opener, and our hand-carved wooden spoons.

After ten minutes of wood gathering and fire building, we hunched around our fire, cozied close to drive away the chill. Then we passed the can and slurped hot beans. We pitched our thoughts over the racket of the falls and the ice-flowing river, just a stone's throw away.

"Whew!" Buck shuddered. He spewed a mighty "son-ama-BITCH!"—a cussword I hadn't heard from Buck before. "Dang you, Jim!—you and your plans."

"She's quite the river this time of year, ain't she?" Jim said.

Buck allowed a grin and a weak laugh.

"It could have drownded us, you know," I said.

"Nah, coulda swum for it," Jim countered. "Besides, you had it easy poling that little raft." That statement neatly sums up my brother, doggone his hide. Bless him too for our rare adventure, an unforgettable scare that we overcame with Jim's fearlessness and Buck's knowhow. Plenty of luck helped too, speaking of which: Little Ergie was in deep Dutch at home and couldn't come along on the gopher hunt. With another kid on the raft, who knows what would have happened?

"Sure glad Little Ergie couldn't come today," I said. "We couldn't have kept him from riding the raft across—"

Buck cut me off. "I don't want to think about it."

"Me neither," Jim said.

Jim and Buck were right. Better not to think on it, because, given the chance, Ergie'd have surely come along. I reached in my pocket and pulled out my lucky charm, the one inscribed with the eagle. I licked my charm and polished it on my jacket sleeve. Buck laughed. "Little Eric, you run around with your brother, you're gonna need that. If you bring Little Ergie along, you'll need a pocket full of them."

I hadn't come to the river believing in lucky charms, but since my cousin "Twinkie" Pederson gave me the eagle charm, I felt obligated to carry it. Now that none of us had drowned in the ice river, I'd have Gramp drill a hole so I could put the eagle on a chain and carry it around my neck.

Chapter Four

Jimmy the Box Man, and Little Ergie

"Character is Destiny." —Heraclitus, (540-475? B.C.)

Our town was blessed with a pair of omnipresent personalities. They wheeled about town on separate and personal missions. Jimmy Bruegger rode his ancient rattletrap bike with a cargo rack over the back wheel piled high with cardboard boxes. Little Ergie pedaled his balloon-tired, deluxe tricycle to the pool, the Eastside Army's clubhouse, or wherever there was big boy action. Ergie was complex, funny, and unwilling to settle for little boyhood. By contrast, Jimmy Bruegger, though boylike in some ways, was a young adult when my brother and I were six and five. Jimmy often stopped by our curbside delivering Major League baseball reports. A man on a bike in scruffy man-worker clothes should have looked out of place. Jimmy Bruegger didn't. He was eternally at ease and welcomed in every neighborhood.

In modern terminology Jimmy Bruegger would be labeled "limited." Sure he was simple, but he was also steady and seemingly satisfied with his station in life. And if you befriended Jimmy, as did many dozens of townfolk, you had a friend for keeps.

Jimmy Bruegger could be seen anywhere in town, tirelessly pedaling his old bicycle. Jimmy carried out two missions on a daily basis. He was a "box man," a collector and purveyor of cardboard boxes, and he was the "Town Crier" of sports. To any willing listener, Jimmy reported on big league baseball and the Williston Coyote teams. Ask Williston natives from the 1940s and '50s about mayors or bigwig business people and you may get a shrug or a dull stare. Yet we old timers light up with mention of Jimmy Bruegger or Little Ergie. Those two, so vastly different, shared the trait of dogged persistence. They were equally celebrated by hundreds of Willistonites.

Jimmy Bruegger, being about 16 years older than Ergie, came first to the role of town icon. He biked the streets year 'round, shut down only by the worst of blizzards. His paint-peeled old bicycle must have carried him 100,000 miles. I remember when he went down with appendicitis. By the following day our whole town knew, and people all over town cheered him when he recovered.

Jimmy's first love was sports. He listened to every possible radio play-by-play, absorbing player news and statistics that he shared with as many people as possible. As dependably as the milkman, he made his scheduled rounds delivering his products: sports news reported reliably, with comic style.

Bruegger was about 20 when my brother and I first became aware of him, an unchanging daily presence in faded blue coveralls and plaid red or blue flannel shirt. I suppose his mother washed his clothes nightly, because Jimmy never appeared unkempt, except for his dark hair. His hair draped beyond his ears and flew in every direction, like hay falling from the stack.

Jimmy wasn't a big man, more like an eighth grader who quit growing. His dark whiskers and stout build indicated early adulthood. We believed Jimmy to be tough, too. A story made the rounds about a big kid from Webster School who teased Jimmy into a wrestling match. In a matter of seconds Jimmy had the guy in a hammerlock. It took a passel of kids to release the Webster kid.

Jimmy Bruegger was easy to spot. Without traffic, which was most of the time in residential neighborhoods, Jimmy rode steadily up the exact center of the street. Never did he rise from his seat to stand on the pedals. Jimmy's news was there for the asking, even if you weren't a regular sports customer. Shout him down and Jimmy'd ride over and visit. He never smiled, but reported each game as if it was the last thrilling game in the World Series. His dark eyes darted and danced among listeners. He talked fast, and moved on. With his sports reporting and box business, Jimmy had lots of ground to cover.

Jimmy had not only "wegulars," who were simply sports fans, but also "wegular faverts," all Yankee fans. Because of Dad's Yankee loyalty, my brother and I were automatically bestowed longer visits with extra game details. Weeding the garden or playing basketball at our back alley hoop, we'd hear Bruegger coming, singing his tuneless tune, *"Oklahoma hills where I was born, Oklahoma hills where I was born."* He'd swivel his head, looking for us. We'd holler, "Hey, Jimmy?" and he'd jam his brakes, swerve, and head for us, yelling "Yankees won, Yankees won." If the Yanks lost, we'd know it by Jimmy's silence and downcast eyes. Regardless, Jimmy would ride over. Without moving from his bike seat he'd prop a foot and report.

We relished his enthusiasm when the Yanks won. His report went like this: "Yankees won 4 ta 1, 4 ta 1, Rizzuto got three hits, three hits, Yanks clobbered the Dodgers. Don't like 'em, bigmouth Dodgers. Bums, bums, bigmouth bums."

Jimmy talked of a few other players, like Stan Musial. But mostly it was his beloved Yankees and the hated Dodgers that held his interest. He knew those two teams thoroughly, player statistics, RBI's, ERA's, homers, stolen bases, even bits about players' personal lives. As for the Williston Coyotes: he knew the players and bragged on them all. A town never had a better fan and a publicist to boot.

Jimmy collected every sports fan along the way. Age had no bearing. Jim and I were just tykes when we became "wegular favert" customers. I should say customer, because Jimmy regarded Jim and me as a single entity. He'd stare smack dab between us and address us as "Erickson."

"Jimmy isn't right," my dad explained.

Mom was keen to remind us, "You boys be nice to Jimmy. He can't help how he is." Not that we had to be told. To his credit, there wasn't a nicer fellow in town. Furthermore, nobody ran a more responsible business than Jimmy, "The Box Man."

Jimmy's persistence, day after day, year after year, supplied Borrud's Bakery with cardboard boxes he collected from downtown businesses. Borrud's needed boxes to pack with fresh baked bread for delivery to stores in northwestern North Dakota and eastern Montana. Each morning the bakery crew filled specific shipping orders; for example: a small box or two of fresh bread for the store in tiny Froid, Montana, and larger boxfuls for Plentywood, Montana and Grenora, North Dakota. Bruegger kept Borrud's truck bay heaped high with boxes, working six days a week to stay ahead of the bakery's needs.

Since we lived on a direct line between Borrud's Bakery on the West Side and the downtown business district, we often visited with Bruegger on his outward bound trip, when he spewed scores and tidbits from yesterday's games. If we happened to be in our back yard in the afternoon, we'd see him return with his bounty of boxes gathered up from the alleyways and backdoors of downtown businesses.

The keen-eared, barking fool collie across the alley announced Jimmy Bruegger's return travel up First Avenue. Jimmy and his contraption were blocked from view by the large Catholic church down the block, but the dim-witted collie heard the scraping slide of cardboard on pavement, the "dragon monster" coming. As his contraption emerged, Jimmy still couldn't be seen. He walked, pushing his bike from the far side. His bike and its cargo rack were piled high with boxes, and his makeshift rope harness—the tail of the "dragon"—drug a dozen or so more boxes behind. Jimmy strained against his handlebars, legs churning like a plow horse. In his peculiar way, Jimmy Bruegger set a standard for impressive, unfailing determination and style.

At the same time, in the making was another irrepressible personality, another standard setter: Ronnie Erdmann, the considerably younger brother of Richard. Ronnie was not quite five when Jim and I met him. By coincidence, Jimmy Bruegger showed up at our first encounter with Ronnie, the boy known about town as Little Ergie.

At mid-morning with a hot June day building, Jim and I were about to mount our bikes on the boulevard in front of our house, headed for Harmon Park Pool, if possible to be first into the water. But here came Jimmy Bruegger, and an unavoidable delay. He yelled out his catch-all greeting, meant to snare Jim and me as one: "Hey Erickson, wait up."

At that time, in 1944, Jim and I cared little about major league baseball. We took our cue from Dad, who'd lost interest because his baseball heroes had gone off to war. Even Jimmy Bruegger had changed the thrust of his reporting by changing allegiance to the National League and Marty Marion.

Jimmy nosed his bike in between Jim's and mine: "You hear about Marty Marion?" Jimmy paused to catch his breath, then: "Marty Marion's played . . ." I remember mostly Jimmy's excitement, jabbering about a zillion or so games Marion played without an error. Whatever the number, I failed to pack it away for safe keeping, because we were interrupted by a yell from up the block: "Haaaay, look out below." Hurtling toward us came a white headed kid on a tricycle. He apparently had us targeted. He careened down the sloped sidewalk with his feet thrust up against his handlebars. The trike's wheels spun ever faster, out of control. Yet the boy shrieked with laughter, ignoring his likelihood of a crash. I recognized him from Harmon Pool, the kid called Little Ergie. My brother jumped from his bike, preparing for some sort of body block rescue. He was too late.

Little Ergie jammed his feet into the trike's spinning pedals. His front tire smacked the concrete retainer in front of our house, and the back of his trike and his butt went airborne. Ergie and his machine came down beside us, still upright—perfect luck! He laughed nonchalantly, as if such a stop were routine, but then abruptly changed demeanor, demanding to know: "Where you guys going?" He furrowed his blond eyebrows, and sucked in his lips. He peered through narrowed eyelids, a look that was far too serious for a little kid. His baggy hand-me-down swim trunks were hiked up, showing solid muscles around his knees. His little arms were muscled, too. All in all, Ergie was a comical-looking, white-headed kid with a freckly face and a stubborn, hard-set jaw.

Jimmy Bruegger backed his bike away. I saw him as puzzled and confused. He took one more wild-eyed look and rode away without saying goodbye.

Ergie pedaled up tight to us. "Come on, where you guys goin' to?"

"Swimmin'," Jim answered.

"I'm goin' with then," Ergie insisted.

"How old are you, Ergie?"

"I'm gonna be five pretty quick."

Jim mounted his bike and waved Ergie off. "We're leaving, Ergie. You need to go home."

"I'm going with you guys."

"No, you can't," Jim said.

"I can *swim!*" Ergie argued. Jim and I maneuvered our bikes around the little pesk and pushed off, heading up First Avenue West toward Harmon Park and the city pool. After gaining cruising speed, Jim and I glanced back. Little Ergie came, furiously pedaling, dead center up the street. "Go home," Jim shouted back.

As we turned east toward Main Street, I could see that we had gained a block on the tricycler in spite of his fast churning little legs. I thought, *That's the last we'll see of Ergie today.*

As always, Jim and I raced the four blocks north to Harmon Pool, with the same kind of hurry-up in our locker room change into swim trunks. Immediately, we dropped a couple of cannonballs from the low board. I was climbing out of the pool, halfway up the ladder, when tiny tanned feet appeared on the concrete deck in front of me. I looked up into the determined blue eyes of Little Ergie, pleading: "Can I swim with you guys?"

Before I could speak to deny him, Mr. Soine, the pool director, blew his whistle and pointed sternly. Ergie peered across the pool to Mr. Soine's lifeguard chair. The big, husky man bellowed, "Ergie, you get your butt down to the shallow end. Next time I catch you around the deep end, I'll send you home for good."

"Well, I can swim; I can swim good enough," Little Ergie muttered. He turned and race-walked toward the shallow end. Nearing the life line, which officially separated the deep, swimmers' area from the shallow, non-swimmers' section, Ergie quickened his steps and dove out across the life-line into the shallow end, emerged, and dogpaddled across the pool. At the pool's far edge he hoisted himself up the climb-out ladder and looked to the lifeguard chair to see if Mr. Soine had seen him "swim."

Certainly he *believed* himself to be a swimmer. After all, Little Ergie stayed afloat and covered a lot of water with his furious dog-paddle. With such energy he was a natural curiosity. I took time out that day to spot him "swimming" across the shallow end. Days and days of sun and chlorine had tinted his white heinie head lime-green, a beacon in the crowd of kids. Back and forth across the pool he paddled, occasionally diving quickly and re-emerging like a dipping bobbly-headed duck. Seldom, though, did I see Ergie cavorting with the other little kids, not even Johnny Lund, his safety buddy. When Ergie caught me looking, I returned his wave and rejoined my deep-end fun, where Jim and I and our gang cannonballed from the high board, and dove 10 feet down for pennies, and dumped cold water on sunbathing girls.

We reveled in non-stop fun that day, with occasional time outs for skin broiling rests on the deck. We toasted back sides, rolled over to toast front sides, then back sides—front and back, deep heated pleasure. All energied by sun magic, we'd go right back for more water games.

At 4 PM closing time, exhaustion left us with light headed exuberance, enough to extend the day a couple hours somewhere else, quickly deciding on an impromptu destination for our *patrol*. After all, these were war times, which called for patrols.

The Muddy River patrol checked out, and headed for the bike rack. And there sat Little Ergie on his tread-worn Hawthorne tricycle tucked tight to our cluster of bikes. He sat poised with his ragged little blue Keds readied on the pedals. He had rolled up a denim pant-leg—the right leg—the same style preferred by experienced bike riders like the rest of us, who rode free without rattling chain guards.

Little Ergie sat on his trike with sturdy little arms folded, an aspiring bike rider, but sized and muscled perfectly for his balloon-tired tricycle. He demanded to know, "Where we goin' now?"

"Don't have a plan, Ergie," I said. "But you can't keep up on your trike anyhow."

"What about swimmin' tomorrow then?" Part of me wanted to ignore him or scold him, but something inside said no, the kid needed a friend. He searched the faces of my patrol. The guys just grinned, shook heads, and climbed on their bikes.

"Not swimmin' tomorrow, Ergie," I said. "We're goin' fishin'." I mounted my bike to chase after my guys. I swung through the park driveway and turned to wave goodbye. Ergie didn't wave back. He was already on his machine, shoulders hunched forward, pumping after us. Ergie didn't know our destination, nor did we; it could be a choose-up baseball game, bike jumps at the gravel pit, a scouting incursion into the territory of the West Side Army, or a ride out to Horseshoe Bend on Muddy River to—best as I can explain—*"check the water."*

After on-the-go bickering, we settled on patrolling out to Horseshoe Bend. To get there we raced through the East Side, zigging up alleys and zagging through vacant lots, enough to shake Little Ergie or kraut spies from the West Side Army.

If Little Ergie had been a normal kid, our ditching would have been enough to be shed of him for good; but he wasn't "normal." So Jim and I weren't surprised the following morning digging worms in our garden to see Ergie chugging his trike down the alley.

Ergie jumped from his trike. "Can I help you guys?" Without an answer he dropped to his knees in the dirt. Jim turned spades full of wormy dirt, while Ergie and I broke clumps and picked out the biggest worms. We had just finished worm collection and tied the can into the rag-bag on Jim's bike when Buck, Big Bervie, and Jack rode up.

"We're going to Spring Lake," Buck announced. "Horseshoe Bend didn't look so good and, besides, my dad says Spring Lake has jumbo perch."

"Yah, and if it doesn't pan out, we can ride on over to Stony Ford," Jack added. He led out, yelling, "Heeeyaah." As I swung onto my bike to join the charge after Jack, Little Ergie yelled, "Hold up. I'm coming with." In hindsight, Jim and I should have put Ergie down hard, but there seemed to be no reason to do so. The kid was too comical, and for his determination, admirable.

Heading up First Avenue, I raced Jim, both of us trying to catch our patrol. At the north end of First Avenue we caught up with Jack, who was engaged in his goin' fishin', roostering celebration. As Dad said, "Jack gets a big kick out of life." He did, far more than anyone, finding something to hoot about 20 times a day, even the ridiculous kid a block and a half behind, trying to catch us on a tricycle. Jack jerked his thumb over his shoulder. "Little Eric, your buddy's gonna need a motor on that thing. He wouldn't try to follow us out on the highway, would he?"

"Naw, he'll be tuckered before he gets to the city limits. He'll never keep up that pace pumping a danged trike."

"Well, take a gander behind. He's making pretty good time," Buck said.

On North Main at the city limits sign I checked again. If Little Ergie was back there, I couldn't know, because a few cars in the half-mile stretch behind us blocked my view. I concluded discouragement won, and he headed for home.

Beyond the city limits, North Main became U. S. Highway 2, at that time the transcontinental route from Boston to Seattle. Drivers with minds on faraway destinations sped the narrow two-lane at 60–70 miles an hour. Nevertheless, we traveled this two-mile stretch to Spring Lake Park often. Cars bearing down from the rear were especially scary. We gauged their coming by the pitch of whining tires. "Ditch," Buck or Jack would holler, and we'd head our bikes off the highway into the ditch, where we waited for the "all clear." Miraculously, grown-ups or policemen never came to kick us off Highway 2.

In 30 minutes we reached the turnoff to the park, banked through the stone arch gate, and raced down the steep gravel road to the lake. Minutes later we were casting our five throw-lines across the weed beds to the deep, this time fixed with stick floats to avoid snagging weeds. An hour later, after landing only a few dinky throw-back bluegills, Jim proposed swimming, an idea quickly nixed by Buck's recounting the guy who "got his legs tangled in the weeds in Spring Lake and drowned."

Jim, forever itchy to travel, offered: "How about Stony Ford? If the bullheads aren't biting, we can swim over there. No weeds at Stony." Nobody objected, except Bervie, who messed around by the old splintered diving board trying to figure how to fix it. With no tools, Bervie agreed to abandon the diving board, Spring Lake, and head to Stony Ford.

We rolled up our lines and stowed them, ready to mount our bikes and attack the steep hill and road to Highway 2. I heard wheels on gravel and glanced up the hill. *What do you know? Holy Moley!* I blinked three times. Here came Little Ergie rocketing down the rutted gravel road, legs extended for balance. He swerved crazily, dodging potholes. He didn't miss them all. His trike bounced high and came back to earth, careening toward us. "Look out below," Ergie hollered.

I remembered the lake. *We'd better be ready to rescue Ergie from the lake.* Instead, he saved himself. Ergie jerked his handlebars abruptly, and flew off, landing "ker-bop" onto his back in the sand. *Jeez,* I was thinking, *how are we going to explain to his folks how their kid broke his back?* Amazingly, Ergie rolled over and sat up, big-eyed and distressed, but not from his crash. . . .

"Hey, where we goin' from here?" Ergie pointed at Buck and Jack, both poised on their bikes. Neither managed an answer, only speechless, head-shaking amazement.

"Ergie, dang your hide," Bervie said. "You need a kid to play with. Go to town, find my little brother. He's at home, probably in his sand-box." Bervie picked up the trike and pointed it up the hill. He grabbed Ergie by the back of his belt, pushing him to his trike. "You little rascal, get on this machine and head for town."

"Yah, Ergie, your dad finds out you came out here, he'll tan your hide," Jack added.

Ergie sucked his lips into his mouth to hide their quivering. He climbed on his trike, but couldn't resist talking back, "Okay then, but where are you guys going?"

I wasn't smart enough to lie. As last in the line of departing riders, I answered over my shoulder, "We're going to Stony Ford over on the Muddy. You go home." Ergie swiped away a tear. As far as I know, that was the one and only time a tear escaped him.

From halfway up the hill, I heard Ergie's wail, "Wait for me." I was at once torn—my patrol was leaving me, but a forlorn little boy was a long way from home.

Down the highway a half-mile south of the park, my guys took a left turn onto a farm road. I followed, finding pedaling tough in the grabby sand. Honestly, though, I didn't work particularly hard to catch the guys, thinking of the little kid two miles from town with tired legs and only a tricycle to take him home. I worried he might again try to tag us. Yet, despite being scolded to head for home, I hoped Little Ergie would follow us and turn off the dangerous highway. Over and over I looked back to see. Should I go back or catch up to my patrol? Worried and uneasy, I decided on the patrol.

My guys were nowhere in sight. I headed east toward the ridgeline above the Muddy River Valley. I crossed the hump, and there was my patrol standing at the crossroads. I was happy, yet surprised. Never had they waited for me before. In fact, when I first got my bike, I was not a welcome member of the gang until I learned to keep up.

As I rode up to them, I saw serious faces. “Maybe you should go back and check on Little Ergie,” Buck said.

“You should,” Jim added. “He’s a stubborn little bugger. I bet he’ll turn off the highway to follow us. I hope he does. He shouldn’t be riding a doggone trike on a highway. But, if he *does* come this way and turns down the hill toward the Muddy, he could take the wrong trail and get lost.” Jim nodded west toward Highway 2. “He’ll try to follow us. I’m betting on it.”

“Your brother is right, Davey,” Jack said. “Ergie is your little buddy. Go back. Find him. Take him down the ridge road to town.” I took that as a directive, being that four older guys stared hard at me, before each adding his own two-bit’s worth.

Jack conjured a joke as he swung onto his bike. He struggled getting it out over his giggling . . . “Little Eric, we’re going to the Muddy. Take Ergie to town, and try to keep up with him”—a poke at me that, even for me, was funny. Yah, I’d keep up all right. First, though, I had to find him.

I rode halfway down the farm road toward its intersection with Highway 2, almost ready to believe Ergie had ridden the highway to town. But on the horizon a little blob appeared, moving slowly. I got off my bike and waited. Soon I saw a light colored top and a dark part low to the ground, recognizable as Ergie’s trike, pumping body, and whitey head on top. His exertion moving the trike through the sand became audible, the steady beat of his breathing synchronized with his piston pumping legs. Finally Ergie chugged up to me and stopped, short of breath. He all but ignored me, gazing down the road, “Where are the other guys?”

“They turned down the hill at the crossroads, another mile. They’re goin’ to the Muddy. They said to take you to town.”

“How come?”

Fed up with his stubbornness, I didn’t answer. Ergie stared down the road. “Well, at least you can show me where they turned off,” he said. I chuckled to myself, *Ergie’s not in the mood to listen. Is he ever?*

I pedaled along beside him, fighting to balance with his snail’s pace. Ergie pumped along furiously, needing five or six pedals for each turn of mine. Amazed, I watched his short legs churning, to the sound of his “chuff . . . chuff . . . chuff.”

We arrived at the crossroads 30 minutes later. Ergie stood over his trike, extending his arms, hands clutching handlebars. “They took off down that road,” I said. Ergie stared at the bike tracks in the mud. “It’s a long way down to the Muddy, Ergie. It’s a bad road, lots of mud holes. The guys will be walking their bikes some. The worst thing, though, is that it’s uphill coming out. If we go, I don't think we'll make home before dark. We better take the road to town."

Ergie scowled at that and turned to gaze into the valley. "Can't see the river," he said.

"I know. The river bends all the way to the far side, by the long ridge on the east. The Fox Walk, we call it." Ergie made a face, wrinkling his nose dead-skunky like.

He studied the expanse of ridge and valley. "Let's go down a ways, just to look," he said. A stubborner kid I'd never known. Trouble was, he was too little to fight and too big for a butt blistering.

I pointed south to the road toward town, and with my biggest grown-upy voice, I ordered, "You're coming with me, Ergie. We're going to town."

Ergie's answer was a sour glare. Time to test him, I decided. I shoved off for town. Finally, from a long stone's throw behind, I heard him wail, "Wait up then, dang it. I'm coming." As Ergie pulled alongside me, he declared: "Next time, I get to go with you to the river."

We rode side-by-side south toward town, two miles to go. Ergie pedaled and argued his case at the same time: "If I ... wasn't ... so far ... behind ... to start ... this morning ... I coulda ... kept up. I can go ... fishin' ... with you ... next time."

"Keeping up is one thing, Ergie. But you'd have to learn to swim, too," I said.

"I can *swim!*" he hollered. With that he hunched forward and pedaled harder.

"No, you can't, Ergie. I've seen you. You need to know real swimming. Floating and dogpaddling aren't enough. Kids can't be out on the Muddy River unless they can swim. That's what my dad says. You have to pass Mr. Soine's swimming test."

"Then ... I ... will ... I can ... pass it." With a sideways glare at me, he surged ahead.

I saw the curve of the road coming up, remembering how the gravel turned to pavement. We'd round the curve on pavement and have a nice easy coast down past Gauthier's Dairy. Little Ergie spotted the pavement too and worked his little piston legs furiously to gain momentum. There he went, flying over the crest and down the hill with his feet up on his handlebars. With the wind watering my eyes, I used just enough braking to stay alongside. For the second time that day, Ergie raced out of control, yelling, "Look out below." At the bottom of the hill, Helen Gauthier and four of her friends riding Shetlands came onto the road. Ergie hadn't time to jam his spinning pedals. With skittering ponies and squealing girls dead ahead, he swerved sharply to his right and flew from the road into the road-side ditch. He tumbled over his front wheel and piled with a *thunk* into the ditch.

I dropped my bike and jumped the ditch, thinking: *broken arm, broken leg, broken something.* But Ergie was already up on his knees, laughing, and waving at the girls.

Ergie's fun with the wreck lasted all of one minute. As I helped him and his trike back onto the road, he asked, "How many laps in Mr. Soine's test?"

"Ergie, he has pooped it up to eight laps, three quarters of a mile. And that's after five minutes of treading water while his junior lifeguards cannonball, trying to sink you. Before you take the test, you should join Miss Kinstler's swimming class and learn the Australian crawl. I don't think you can swim three quarters of a mile your way."

"Nope," he said. "I've watched that little kid's class. They're too scared to learn. They cry even. I'll learn everything on my own before they do in that class."

We biked across the north end of town to the intersection of the farm road and First Avenue East, Ergie's street, where I left him with some advice: "I'll see ya' at the pool tomorrow, Ergie, and I want you to ask Jack for help. He's the best swimmer I know."

Ergie turned around on his trike seat, jutted his lower jaw, and said, "Well I'm ready right now. I'll pass Soine's test. Tomorrow I'll do it." He headed off down the street, winding his machine up as fast as a tricycle could go: "chuff chuff chuff chuff." I laughed right out loud. Little Ergie had just pedaled six miles on a tricycle. If I hadn't seen it, I'd never believe it my ownself.

The next morning turned hot even before the 9:30 AM check-in at the pool. The Muddy River guys arrived early to avoid the long line. We believed being first in the water bestowed some kind of honor.

Little Ergie arrived early too and caught me at the bike rack. He tagged along to the check in line. "I didn't see your trike," I said.

Ergie shook his head, disgusted. "My dad took it away. I wasn't supposed to be on the highway. Somebody told on me." Ergie jostled in between Jim and me in the check-in line. He tugged on my swim trunks. "Can I be your safety buddy today?"

"Uh-uh, can't, Ergie . . . against the rules. You'd have to be a deep end swimmer."

"Well I'm gonna be one," Ergie said. He craned his neck to look around me, back down the line at Buck, Jack, and the Bervig brothers. He drew himself up taller and announced, "I'm passing my test today." Spotting Allen Bervig, he hollered, "Hey, Little Bervie, how about bein' my safety buddy?"

Little Bervie didn't wait, but came and butted in line with Ergie. "I want you on my side for water tag," Bervie said.

I spent just enough time standing in line with Jim to grow some worry. I wished Ergie would wait to take his swim test, take lessons from Miss Kinstler, like I did. Mr. Soine, strict as an army general about deep end swimmers, would most certainly flunk Little Ergie, break his heart. Ergie was brim full of hope, no—more than that—belief, *false* belief. I walked with Jim from the check-in office across the deck toward the pool and past the NO RUNNING ALLOWED sign.

"Ergie's nuts," Jim said.

"You don't think he has a chance?"

Jim stopped and shook his head. "Naw, no four year old dog paddler is going to pass Soine's test. You better tell him that."

"I already did."

"Better tell him again." Jim turned and dove in the deep, where Buck and the others had begun a game of "bean 'em" with a tennis ball. Jim was right. I should put it to Ergie, have him take up playing with kids his own age and forget Mr. Soine's impossible test. He could start with Little Bervie, a pistol of a kid, lots of fun. Little Bervie stood with Ergie on the deck adjacent to the lifeline that divided the deep from the shallow. Their toes were legal, placed not across, but directly on the red words painted on the deck: SWIMMERS ONLY. I laughed. They looked silly and comical.

"Ergie, I don't think you . . ." I started to say—

"Eric, you gotta talk to Mr. Soine for me," Ergie pleaded. "Come on, he won't even let me go down there." Ergie glared across the pool to Mr. Soine, sitting high on his head life guard chair. "Go tell him, Eric," Ergie said. "Tell him I'm ready for my test."

I grabbed Ergie by the arm. "You talk to your folks about this?"

"Naw, I'm gonna surprise 'em. Now I need you to go tell Mr. Soine."

I didn't budge and didn't plan to. Little Bervie put his hand on my hip, pushing me to go,

"Yah, Eric, you tell him Ergie's ready," Bervie said.

I never saw bigger expectations on faces, or heard better begging: *"Puleeeeaase,"* and, *"Come on, give him a chance, at least."*

What could I do? I found myself saying, "Well, okay," in a voice that didn't sound like mine. I put a finger on Ergie's chest. "Okay, but Ergie, you're coming with me."

I grabbed Ergie's wrist and led him, following another rule: No Unescorted Shallow-enders. We walked to the deep end, circled behind the low diving board, and the high one, and around to Mr. Soine's lifeguard chair. A pod of water treaders gathered beneath Soine's chair. It was Jim and the guys from yesterday's Stony Ford patrol, plus a few others who'd gotten word of Little Ergie's far-fetched plan to pass his swim test.

Mr. Soine sat on guard on his 10 foot perch, looking out over the pool as if he owned it. With his Tarzan muscles and glistening golden-haired chest, he continued his glinty-eyed survey of the deep end.

Meanwhile, jittering from foot to foot, Ergie was about to pee in his trunks. He pushed on my arm. "Tell him," he said.

"Just wait, Ergie," I said. "Mr. Soine will talk to us when he is good and ready."

This was a peak of the season day, 300 kids—laughing, crying, yelling, and splashing all at once. Jim and I swam on nearly every hot day. Occasionally, when we stayed home to help Mom in the garden, we heard the Harmon Pool hubbub from four blocks away. The frenetic pool caused the pool guardians a lot of worry. "You kids and your buddies help all you can," Dad said.

Mr. Soine and Miss Kinstler, perched down there on her shallow end chair, wouldn't allow distractions from their duties. To ease their worry on busy days like today, Mr. Soine appointed three of his junior life guards to mingle with swimmers and keep watch. They were burly guys Soine toughened for his Coyote football team.

"Stannard, I need you," Mr. Soine shouted. The big hairy chested high schooler swam swiftly, and hoisted himself out of the pool.

"Stand right there, under my chair, Tommy. You're on duty for the deep end watch, until I say otherwise."

"I got it, Coach," Tom Stannard said.

Finally, Mr. Soine looked down with a wisp of grin. Ergie and I craned our necks, looking expectantly up at him, like a pair of baby storks. Mr. Soine dropped his gaze on me, the spokesman. He nodded. "What can I do for you gentlemen?"

Before I could answer, Little Ergie stepped past me. "Mr. Soine, I'm ready to take your test."

Mr. Soine furrowed his blond eyebrows, "Hmm—*my deep end test?*" He pursed his lips and squinted at this funny little believer. But he wasn't annoyed, I knew, because I'd never known Mr. Soine to put up with annoyances more than two seconds. There he sat, rubbing his chin.

Mr. Soine's smile broke big and all out, as if a big lummox farm boy had just turned out for football. "You know what my test entails?"

"Yes sir."

"You know I don't give special breaks for little kids like you?"

"Yes sir. Don't need a break, either."

"Okay, Ronnie, you'll tread water for five minutes; then you'll need to complete eight laps. My assistants are free to bomb cannonballs, make it rough treading." Mr. Soine paused, holding Ergie's gaze. "You still saying yes?"

"Yes sir, I am." Ergie rubbed his palms together and jiggied his feet. "When do I get to?"

Mr. Soine turned back to eyeballing his deep end. Raising his chin, he boomed his announcement down the way to Miss Kinstler: "Ronnie Erdmann, swim test today at four o'clock." Back to Ergie, Soine said, "Be back here at four. I suggest you take it easy until then."

Ergie raised his arms like a prizefight winner. He turned away, yelling, "Yay! yay!" I grabbed his arm to keep him from running.

The deep end water-treaders managed minor celebration cheers, expecting at least one heck of a try out of a stubborn kid. Jack pumped his legs double time, as if riding a unicycle, and lifted his chest halfway from the water, shouting, "Go Ergie!"

For those of us waiting and wondering, the middle of the day dragged on. Water games were spotty and undisciplined. Jack left twice for the shallow end, where he pulled Little Ergie aside and put him flat out on the water, moving his arms and legs, then on his back to practice a resting back float.

At a quarter to four Mr. Soine's double whistle toot signaled a safety check. "Everybody out," he hollered. A minute later, at the second whistle, you'd *better* be out; and we were, grabbing safety buddies by the wrists, holding 'em high. After Soine's triple whistle that signaled all accounted for, Little Bervie and Ergie went off, jabbering along on a race walk for the rest room. Ergie was crazy nervous, I knew, because ten minutes later he and Bervie legged it back to pee a second time. Shortly, Mr. Soine blew his whistle again. Miss Kinstler blew hers, and they dismissed all shallow-enders from the pool, excepting Little Ergie, who was now my responsibility.

Nearing *the time,* Little Ergie stood by me with his toes on the red line. He stared down the way to the big round clock mounted on the wall by the pool office. "Three minutes more," he said. My heart raced just like last year when I took my own test. This was just too important, and not just for Ergie, but for me too. I had to admit I was his friend now, noticing things that friends do: like all the people behind the fence rooting for him.

On any given day a few onlookers stood behind the 10 foot woven wire fence surrounding the pool, including a few parents, grandmas and grandpas, and others maybe just taking a break from gardening. But today was different. Three or four dozen parents and a big batch of friends and neighbors gathered behind the fence. I spotted Ergie's big brother, Richard, and I knew: word had spread from Harmon Park Pool to the north side blocks and from there to the Erdmanns' neighborhood.

At straight up four o'clock Mr. Soine stood on the steps of his high perch and blew his whistle. "Deep-enders out of the water," he hollered, "all except junior life-guards."

As Miss Kinstler conducted a final pool check, Mr. Soine came down the guard ladder. He put one huge hand on my shoulder, the other on Ergie's. "Okay, Ergie," he said. "In a minute I'll get you started. Give it your best."

Mr. Soine and Miss Kinstler gathered their team of junior lifeguards for instructions. The pool guardians looked as stern as preachers. I tried to not think of them as enemies, because I knew better. They did what they had to do to keep us safe.

Mr. Soine gestured us to our meeting place at the corner of the deep. His blue eyes smiled on Little Ergie. He'd add up to four of the little peanut kid. He leaned over and grabbed Ergie's wrists. "Now Ronnie," he said, "if you play out, if you can't make it, just raise a hand. Miss Kinstler, here, will throw you a life ring." He patted Ergie on the shoulder. "Let's get started, son. Good luck." Ergie faced the pool and wind-milled his arms like a racer, and voices joined in a rumble from behind the fence. Deep-enders gathered in a pod behind the lifeguards, clapping hands and cheering: "You can do it, Ergie!" and "Go, *Ergie!*"

A lady's piercing voice rose above the others: "Come on *Ronnie,* come on *Ronnie.*" The lady standing next to Big Ergie was undoubtedly his mother.

Mr. Soine knelt to even his gaze with Ergie's. He grasped Ergie by his wrists. "Remember, Ronnie, you'll tread water for five minutes; then I'll blow my whistle, and you'll swim eight laps."

Ergie tiptoed to the very edge of the pool, his face hardened, eyes squinting, mouth tight. "Go when you're ready," Mr. Soine said. Ergie waited, staring at the 80 yards of water. I saw the trembles start in his knees. Perhaps he worried Mr. Soine would notice, because he quickly crouched low and leaped high from the deck with his arms stretched to the sky. Just before he hit the water, I caught his grin. I knew the feeling: at last, his first jump into long-forbidden water.

Ergie's leap from the concrete deck above the pool took him deep, so deep that his white head appeared blue underwater. He came up with a gasp and began immediate frantic pumping of legs and fluttering of arms. I watched for a minute or so, worrying. Then I began my sidle past the junior lifeguards and Mr. Soine, toward the very edge where Ergie could hear me. Surprisingly, Mr. Soine nudged me along. "Eric, slow him down," he said.

I leaned down. "You're treading too fast, Ergie. Save your energy." Ergie spun my way to look, blue eyes flashing. He nodded and immediately slowed his leg pumps and arm flutters just enough to keep his chin above water. I knew right there that if Ergie had a chance, it would be because of smarts that matched his stubbornness.

Quite a scene it was: about 30 kids like me standing around the deep end. Mr. Soine, Miss Kinstler, and their junior lifeguards, and with Ergie's supporters behind the fence, all of us focused on a little boy treading water in the very corner of the huge pool, and for the present breathing quite easily. I felt better watching him pump his legs with the same rhythm as his trike riding. The crowd relaxed, too, reduced to murmurings, punctuated by an occasional cheer: "Keep it up, Ergie," and "Atta' boy, Ergie."

After the first minute, Ergie's water tread struck me as an oddly peaceful time. Even his supporters quieted. I imagine a few of them prayed. The loudest voices came from arguing crows in the cottonwood across the fence.

I remembered my test last year, how Mr. Soine had planned an early interlude. Now, with Ergie, he allowing a similar time of adjustment, you might say trickery—no other swimmers, no shouting, hubbub, divers, or choppy water. Make it easy at first, and then launch furious disruption to see if the kid panics or survives.

With a minute left to go in Ergie's required five minute water tread, Mr. Soine called in the dogs. I saw them coming. "Get ready, Ergie," I yelled.

The husky Stannard brothers climbed the high board ladder. An even bigger guy, Fougner—the fullback—came behind them. I caught Ergie's eye and pointed. He wisely spun around to face the onslaught.

Jim Stannard came first, striding down the long board, 14 feet over the water. At the end of three graceful high steps his 200 pound muscled body sprung and the board launched him high—I'll bet he was up there 20 feet at the top of his arc. When his shoulders tipped forward, his butt followed. He didn't flip, rather spun gracefully in a slow motion lay-out tumble . . . until the very end. Ten feet above the water, Jim tucked into a ball, a hurtling human boulder. Ergie looked up, wide-eyed, gulped air, and ducked. Stannard landed a scant six feet away, sending a few hundred gallons of water washing over Ergie and up onto the deck. He had just enough time to grab a mouthful of air before Tom Stannard came, hurtling down in his famous "howitzer jackknife." With a leg tucked up under his chin and the lower leg (the knife) extended, he rocketed into the water, foot and rump first. He landed with an awesome *"kerwhunk,"* disappearing within his own deep crater, which lifted Ergie in an up-surge that rolled over him.

Fougner came bombing next, then Jim, and Tom making their second rounds, having fun, showing off, but at the same time trusted by Mr. Soine to not hurt the little guy, only scare the beejeezus out of him. Such shenanigans would never, ever be permitted during regular swimming hours. Dad had explained it all: Mr. Soine and Miss Kinstler had come on the job the year after a boy drowned at Harmon Pool. They added laps and harassment to their swimming test to ensure that nobody would swim in deep water until battle tested and ready.

So far, so good; Ergie sputtered some, but he treaded water successfully though the bomb attack. And I was encouraged to see the same determined face I saw yesterday. Now he set his eyes on the far end of the pool. After a glance at his stopwatch, Mr. Soine blew his whistle and motioned for Ergie to start swimming. Ergie pushed off against the end wall. Yes, the bombers had turned the deep end into ocean waves, but there went Ergie dogpaddling straight through the chop. He paddled away fast, down the inside racing lane. I yelled loud to be heard above the others, "Slower, Ergie. You've got a long way to go."

From behind, I heard Mr. Soine: "He's gonna try to dogpaddle it, Kins. I want you to walk him all the way. He could go under without any warning." Soine spread his arms. "The rest of you stay put."

Miss Kinstler hustled down the deck carrying her life ring. I noticed her leaning, and I knew she was coaching and encouraging, just as she'd done for me. Ergie would need every bit of her help. The dogpaddle . . . heck, it wears out dogs in no time at all.

It's true, we all called it the dogpaddle, but the back of a dog shows above water. Ergie, on the other hand, rode lower, showing only his crew-cut limey-green head, moving steadily and a little jerky from all his leg commotion going on below.

The Muddy River guys gathered at the head of the inside swimmer's lane to watch Ergie's progress . . . spending the time jabbering, speculating, and sometimes laughing. "Jeez, he's part muskrat," Jack said. Ergie had just dived under the life-line and emerged neatly and quickly on the other side, shaking the water from his head.

"Yah," Buck said, "too bad he can't swim like one."

"I bet he'll keep goin' though," I said.

Jim elbowed me. "Maybe, but you know we gotta be home for supper."

Jim's wising off made me wonder: did Soine have a time limit? Ergie's trial could be a marathon. When his steady beat brought him back under the life line, more than five minutes had passed.

I stood amongst the pod of deep end swimmers, waiting for Ergie's approach at the end of lap one, looking for a sign, something to hope for. Ergie came on at the same slugging one-gear speed, staring straight ahead, concentrating. But at the end wall he raised his head slightly and grinned before flipping a kick-away turn. "Gotta admit, he's a damn tough little guy," I heard Mr. Soine say in a curious way, like an uncle. I guessed he'd let Ergie paddle on till dark, if necessary.

Off Ergie went, 80 yards down, 80 back on lap two, same steady pace, same strategy, though he did briefly experiment with Jack's face-in-the-water crawl, broken with periodic head up, dogpaddled breathing. But such unpracticed technique proved awkward and tiring; back he went to his trusted dogpaddle.

Killing time, the Muddy River guys milled about, talking fishin': where we'd go next, what to fish for, and who wanted to go. "How about Little Ergie?" Jack posed.

"What about him?" Buck said.

"About Ergie going with us. Little Eric has held him off so far; told him he'd need to pass his swimming test. What if he passes?"

Jim and Big Bervie chimed in then, and me too. With eyes on Ergie struggling through lap three, we mostly agreed his chances were slim. Razzie poked in, too, wanting to bet quarters one way and—with odds—the other way, all without a single taker. Betting for Ergie didn't seem smart, but betting against him just wasn't right.

As Ergie started off on lap four, Mr. Soine checked his stopwatch. I didn't have to peek to know Ergie had slowed considerably. Some of that, though, was strategy. On lap three Miss Kinstler had signaled, flipping her hand and talking at Ergie. Immediately, he turned over, laid back with his face to the sun. He sculled with his hands like an upside down turtle, resting. Then later, on lap four, he again flipped over twice to turtle-rest.

"So, what if he passes today? Who's gonna wait for him tomorrow?" Buck said to no one in particular.

"I don't think anyone has to," Jack said. "He can find his way out to Stony on his own, even if he does take an extra hour."

"Ergie can't make the White Bridge Hole, though . . . too far," Jim said. "We gotta try for the White Bridge, Lindvig's too. I'm goin'. I don't know about anyone else."

"Me . . . You can count me in, darn tootin'," Big Bervie said. Our banter ran on: the lower Muddy for catfish, Bervie's plan to supercharge our BB guns for the Fox Walk, and the rumor of a trench battle coming with the West Side Army.

On lap six I noticed Ergie's worrisome change. His chin periodically slipped below water level causing him to splutter and gasp for air. Miss Kinstler jiggled her life ring, like she wanted to toss it, pull him in, and end his suffering. We heard his troubled huffing, all the way from the other end—the shallow end of his lap. Someone behind the east fence yelled, "Get him out! Get him out!" I searched the crowd, unable to spot the yeller. Big Ergie and his friends had the yeller circled. No doubt, another word and there'd be a fight, with Big Ergie's crowd against one loudmouth doubter.

"We could leave Little Ergie and my brother at Stony, pick them up on the way home," Big Bervie continued.

"Nope, not until Allen passes his test too," Jack said. "And Ergie's not looking so good, either. He's outa gas and he has another lap."

So close, so close; somehow he's gotta make it. Now Miss Kinstler bent low, coaching Ergie, who rested on his back by the lifeline, gasping for air. I sidled near her to listen and watch. "Paddle, move on your back for a while," Miss Kinstler said.

Tired as he was, Ergie couldn't stand his slow-turtle back swim. He flipped back over to dogpaddle and labored on toward us at the end wall, "huff, huff, huff," huffing. I know the crowd across the fence heard his laboring, because their cheers came louder and oftener, "Keep it up, Ergie."

"Steady. Be steady."

"Come on, one more lap."

"You can do it, Ergie."

Jim and I and the guys were kneeling on the deck with Mr. Soine when Ergie came in for his final turn. He looked up, wide-eyed, as Mr. Soine declared, "You're gonna make it, Ergie." Ergie flashed a smile, turned and levered his tricycler piston legs against the end wall and froggied a smooth launch away. Wow! Amazing! This time, no back rests, just up-and-go dogpaddle, beaver paddle; don't care what you call it. He was incredible. He chugged down and back in about four minutes, coming at us with a grin I'd never before seen.

Mr. Soine leaned far out, reaching, grabbing wrists, hauling Ergie up and out. As he lifted Ergie to his great muscular chest, a volley of cheers rose above Harmon Park Pool. I know the entire north end of town heard us. Mr. Soine put Ergie down in the center of our circle of swimmers. We were delirious; we'd been part of Little Ergie's miracle. Guys rubbed his heinie head, shook him by the shoulders, and slapped him on the butt. Miss Kinstler pushed through the crowd with a beach towel. Ergie fluffed it on himself, but refused her attempt to wrap it around him.

Mr. Soine smiled, rubbed his balding head, bent over the little tyke and shook Ergie's hand. "Ergie, you've passed my test," he said. "Welcome to the deep end." Mr. Soine turned his palm up showing a swimmer's medal. "You have a pocket in your swim trunks for this?"

Ergie shook his head, gasping for air.

Mr. Soine nodded across the way. "Then take this medal over to your mom."

"Okay . . . but first . . . first can I go off the high board? Eric can hold my medal."

Mr. Soine grinned, considering. "Make you a deal, Ergie. You swam so slow that it's past closing time. But, I'll allow you on the high board on one condition: You'll have to take an intermediate class from Miss Kinstler . . . Deal?"

"Uh . . . okay, okay. Can I go now?"

On rubbery legs Ergie climbed the 10 foot ladder with the Stannard brothers standing below at the ready. Ergie crept to the end of the scary, narrow board, where he turned in the direction of his mom and brother. He raised his arms, hollering, "Yaaaay!" Then he crouched, tipped forward, and leaped, arms to the sky, hollering, "Ger-ON-im-o!"

Ergie knifed into the water feet first and, by a few seconds, delayed popping out of the deep, I suspect relishing his first deep water visit to the bottom of the pool. At my side, Miss Kinstler edged forward, watching bubbles rise from Ergie's crater. As she crouched, ready to leap, Ergie popped up and dogpaddled for the climb-out ladder. I stood, listening to every kind of hoorah and cheer. I found myself jigging my feet and hollering too: "Way to go, Ergie! Way to go!"

Ergie climbed out of the pool, pumping his fists. I handed over his prize medal. He took it, hurried to the fence, and handed it through to his mom. Then, among the chorus of cheers I heard a voice—flat, penetrating, and unmistakable: "Yay Erdmann." I followed the voice to the far end of the long pool. There sat Jimmy Bruegger on his bike, braced against the fence.

"Way to go, Erdmann," Jimmy cheered again, not *Little* Ergie, but *"Erdmann."* Oddly, it was Jimmy Bruegger, supposedly dim, who gave Ergie his due. From one town "celebrity" to another: Little Ergie, barely five, wasn't so *little,* and he'd broken my record as the youngest deep end swimmer.

Ergie tagged along with us the rest of the summer, out to Stony Ford and beyond. He triked, hiked, ran, swam, fished, and climbed the bluffs, meeting every challenge. We learned not to bother telling Ronnie Erdmann he couldn't do something.

I figure mind-numbing cold and
winter boredom turned kids stupid . . .
Who can explain the fun of our crazy ice water swim?—
maybe a fancy, highfalutin' sickologist.

Chapter Five

Frozen Nuts

"What are we looking for?" —Buck Bundhund

"I dunno. We'll know it when we see it." —Jim Erickson

In early March, 1944, Jim was the lucky one to spot the first spring robin. He came storming in our back door, yelling, "Spring is here everybody! I saw a robin." Jim's robin must have been an addle-brained bird, because she'd flown into town in early March with snowdrifts still banked in the hedges and bugs and worms deep in hibernation. Jim's premature spring fever, like most clinical cases infecting Williston folk, ignored all facts confirming winter's tenacious hold. By March some kids had lost whatever sense they had. 1944 was not unique in this way. Every year we heard kids bragging about plans to run away from home. A few actually tried. More of running away later, but first on to explaining *frozen nuts,* like the robin's, an addled episode requiring no more good sense than running away from home.

The robin had lit Jim's fuse. He ran off to school announcing to anyone who'd listen, "I saw a robin; spring is here." His audience was more than ready. Like firecrackers in a string, Jim and his buddies—Buck, Jack, Razzie and Stahl, Big Bervie and others—whumped up reasons for a premature spring trip to Stony Ford, bolstered by Jim's ever-optimistic weather forecast: "I feel a Chinook coming on." Buck helped with, "I heard the bullheads are movin," and Jack with the biggest whopper of all: "I heard Joe *whatszizname* caught a tub-full of bullheads." Ninety-nine percent of their reports could be discounted, hope disguised as reality. Yet, there lay that one percent in hope-swizzled brains. Yes, *what if* the bullheads came early to Stony Ford? *What if* for some mysterious reason they decided to shake their winter doldrums early and go on a feeding binge? Possibilities lived. We had to go see.

On Saturday morning we awoke in high spirits. Then Jim opened the blinds. *"Crap!"* There lay a blanket of new snow. No matter—Jim and I hurried through morning readiness and left home with spirits wired together by last year's bullheadin' memories.

We met up with the guys in the alley behind our Gramma Erickson's garden. She had a reputation for harboring the biggest, fattest angle-worms in town. We started after them with a pair of spades, digging in shifts: Jim and I, Jack, Buck, both Bervigs, and Little Ergie. Furiously we dug down through the snow cover and into the stiff earth below. Finally, two spade lengths deep, we found our quarry lying in refrigerator earth, motionless, and stiff as yesterday's bubble gum. Sad as those worms were, we shoulda warmed the poor critters and put them back. But no, Stony Ford and that one percent chance beckoned. Off we went, all except Razzie and Tommy Stahl, who planned another meeting in their secret clubhouse (that was not so secret). They talked endlessly of their scheme to run away to the Rocky Mountains, always followed with the warning: "Don't tell anyone." Laughable. They, themselves, blabbed their far-fetched plan far and wide.

Jack talked us out of bikes for that first spring trip. His Schwinn was new and polished, and unlike our bikes, Jack's sported fenders, perfect for packing with gumbo. "I'll help you take 'em off, so we can go on bikes," Buck offered.

"Nope, my bike keeps her fenders," Jack said. "I'm hiking. We'll all hike. We need to protect our wheel bearings."

"My bearings are already shot, Jack. I'm riding." Jim didn't mean that, had no intention of riding. Jabbing at Jack was part of the game. And, hiking it was.

Ice glazed snowbanks, gumbo mud, and floodwater trash slowed our travel. Then, coming around the last bend the rumble of Stony's falls beckoned. Our foot race was on, won—naturally—by my brother, who'd never been beat. We tumbled onto the sand, scrambled out of our knapsacks, and dug into them with awkward winter-stiff fingers. Out came worm cans and throw-lines.

We spread ourselves along the shore, tending lines, full of expectant energy buzzing like electric wires. Two hours later the electricity sputtered and shorted out. Our banter dwindled to murmurs, three guys sitting by a smoky willow fire and the other four of us cutting and trimming reeds to build make-do cigars. Lines lay unattended, their business ends baited with frigid, limp-noodled worms. Yet, not one word about pulling out, though I'm sure I wasn't the only one thinking it.

A guy couldn't give up on Stony Ford. Finally, about noon the sun broke from behind the clouds long enough for us to shed wool jackets. After the fire sitters let their flames die, Jim announced another plan: "Why don't we go swimmin' then?"

The rest of us could muster only "What?" "Huh?" and "You crazy?"

We human boys sat mute below the roaring blue ice-water of Stony Ford Falls. Finally one guy, Little Bervie, worked up enough chicken to object right out loud, which goes to show you never know. Because in time he turned out to be as courageous as they come, a sparkplug of a football player, a relentless rah-rah leader on the field of battle. On this occasion, though—I'll lay it to the fact that he was only six, a year older than Little Ergie—when Little Bervie said, "Not me. I'm not that stupid."

One by one we rolled up useless throw-lines, stowed them away. With hopeless fishin' done, we'd do something, but surely not swim. Yet, Jim had removed his shoes and socks. He tested Stony Ford Pool with a toe dip. "Not bad," he said. "Come on, swimmin' time."

I glanced down the line at puzzled faces. We watched Jim toss his denim jacket and red-checkered flannel shirt to the sand. He kicked out of his fishin' corduroys. *Jeez, he means it.* As Jim shed his white under shorts, Jack laughed and held his palm up: "Hold on, Jim, I'm coming with." Then Buck, with a shake of his wiry head: "All right, what the heck." In rapid succession the rest of us caved, and began to peel, including Little Bervie.

Jim waited, bare-assed, grinning, and happy to see his stupid plan take hold. Finally all seven of us lined out, shoulder to shoulder at the water's edge, buck naked in front of seven piles of clothes. Our teasing sun had again returned to hiding behind the clouds. I felt the snow-chilled breeze out of Canada ice my blood and freeze the sap in my body. Big Bervie declared our condition with his one and only known cuss word: "DAG-NABBIT, it's *cold* out here." *Come on, somebody,* I'm thinking, *chicken out so we can fold up this stupid idea.* But no, not a one had the guts to chicken out. Like nutty Finlanders, the line of us danced from one foot to the other on the icy sand . . . except for Jim.

Jim stood in the center of our line-up, heels on the sand and toes in the water, slapping his chest. "Okay, the deal is: we all go at once."

Buck shook his head. "Nope, Eric, this was your idea. You go in to your knees and test the water."

"Feet," Jim said.

"Shins," Buck countered.

"Ankles."

"Bull pucky," Jack said. "We gonna talk or swim? It's too dang cold to stand here."

Jim, in line at my left, inched forward. "Okay, everybody together," he said. I looked left and right, across the bare-butt line. The whole gang studied Jim. He moved and we moved, matching exactly his inch-by-inch creep into deeper ice water. Skin turned blue, pain numbed toes, ankles, and shins. Pain penetrated deep into muscle and bone, knifing into knees, numbing into thighs. Whatever blood was left down there became useless red slush.

Talk amounted to only "criminy sakes, craps, cripes, and holy moleys." We stood at the moment of truth, an inch short of nut deep in Stony Ford's frigid pool. We paused, tormented lemmings at the edge of fate.

Jim smidgeoned ahead, while three of us watched from his right and three at his left. Just an inch deeper and *"AAAAHHHHHHH,"* our mighty screams joined as one, piercing the sky. The ice water clamped, vise-like, around seven pairs of testicuts: *"AAAAAAAAAAAHHHHHHHHHH."*

Jim took a deep breath, hollered, "GER-ON-I-MO," and dove under. In the next second we all dove after him.

We came up sputtering and gasping for air, scrambling for the shore, and laughing uncontrollably. Who can explain the fun of our crazy ice water swim?—maybe a fancy, highfalutin' sickologist. For my money, our nutty behavior had something to do with spring-fevered brains, as addled as the crazy robin's.

We should have forgotten *frozen nuts* like you kick a bad dream. But North Dakota's strain of spring fever is incurable. I know this because the following spring we did *frozen nuts* for an encore. Episode number two of frozen nuts helped mold the concept of metaphor.

Our opportunity came a year later, same place, same conditions. This time the Bervig brothers, known for smarts, opted out. Razzie and Stahl had yet to make good on their annual spring boast to hop a Great Northern freight train for the Rocky Mountains. They opted in. So did Jelly, my school buddy. And again we went through the motions of bullheadin' without an ounce of confidence in bullheads cooperating in such frigid water. We managed to land only three bony goldeyes.

"Everyone gather driftwood," Jack ordered. "A big fire will be merciful handy. It's frozen nuts time." This time our wade to nut depth took but a minute. We knew we were going in.

Frozen nuts had rooted itself in a tribal sort of way that we couldn't explain to parents, even if in an unguarded moment we were to own up to such foolishness. Yet foolishness misses the point too, because nine months after swim number two, amid a background of winter gloom and jailhouse school rooms, we discovered the power of metaphor and usefulness of *frozen nuts.*

Winter of 1945–46 gloomered us into desperately foolish measures. Razzie "borrowed" his uncle's key to the Odd Fellows hall so he and Tommy Stahl could sneak in to play pool. They hookied from school and played pool all day long. The Odd Fellows never caught on, but Principal Wilkinson had school spies and town spies. One of them ratted on Razzie and Stahl. Miss Wilkinson brought the culprits for sentencing, penalizing them with 20 hours after school detention for playing hooky. Then she called Razzie's uncle, who sentenced Razzie and Stahl to two Saturdays of scrubbing floors and spittoon cleaning in the Odd Fellows hall.

Winter brought six foot snow banks and bitter blue northers 20, 30, and 40 below with 30 mile per hour winds to boot. Kids like Jim and me, living within a few blocks of Harmon Park skating rink, put skates on at home and skated the ice-covered streets to the park.

I figure mind-numbing cold and winter boredom turned kids stupid, even "A" students like my friend, Norman (Jelly) Jellum. Who would have thought he'd try to lick a steel rail? Unfortunately, Jelly's temptation for tongue-on-steel came at a very bad time.

Jelly liked to be first at everything. At four o'clock dismissal on a 30 below afternoon, Jelly was first to reach Central School's double door exit. He pushed open the one unfrozen door, leaped to the bottom of the concrete staircase, and turned to wait for me. I saw him lean for the rail with his tongue out. "No, no, Jelly, don't," I hollered. Too late. Jelly stuck his tongue on the rail as the long string of kids streamed though the door, down the stairs, stampeding past like a herd of black-snaked steers.

"Jelly, don't move," I said, again too late. "Let the heat of your tongue melt . . ."

"Gaahh, uhngh, gugh, gahhhhhh!" Jelly answered, pulling back. The first to pile into him was Stretch Johnson, who never missed a set-up victim. Jelly fell away to the side, squealing like a piglet.

"Hey Jelly, you left your tongue on the rail here," Stretch laughed. He'd lied, of course; I knew that because I had been an early casualty of an irresistible steel rail. The frozen rail claims no more than a thin strip of tongue skin and a few drops of blood. I managed to sympathize with Jelly and did so without laughing out loud.

Despite Jelly's weakness for frozen steel, he was one of the great thinkers of our time. He concocted a plan to join 4-H, to take advantage of the club's gym privileges at the National Guard Armory. He signed us up. Then we brought the other Muddy River guys aboard. We lasted only three weeks. Mr. Hotchkiss, the County Agent, booted our whole caboodle for failing to attend his Saturday pig and chicken farming classes. Jelly, though, seemed unfazed. He was already working on his next plan to get us inside a gym to play basketball.

Jelly came to our house early Saturday morning. I loved Jelly's morning visits. He was a fun kid, full of nervous energy. Besides, he brought a bonus to our house. His dad was a baker for Borrud's Bakery, and the owner provided the Jellums a nice apartment upstairs. The fragrance of baking bread wafted throughout Borrud's bread factory and seeped into the Jellums' upstairs apartment. And Jelly brought essence of baked bread to our house, diluting Dad's harsh Old Spice.

Mom, as usual, kicked us out of the house. No matter that a blizzard was a-building. "Go find something to do," she said. For a month we had been building our snow fort—more accurately, an ice fort—at the side of our house. On this blizzard Saturday Jelly and I and Jim went to work packing snow, pouring water to ice the walls, adding height. Jim and I worked on the outside, Jelly inside.

"Hey guys. I gotta talk to you. Come over the wall," Jelly said. "I have a plan."

"You can talk to us right here," Jim said. "Here—reach over, take the water bucket."

"That can wait. Now get in here. I've got a secret deal."

Jim and I crawled into our ice fort through the back "Eskimo tunnel." Jelly rubbed his mittened hands together, his voice conveying a big deal in the making. "You guys aren't gonna b-believe this. I c-can get us into the j-junior high g-gym." Jelly wasn't a stutterer, except when super excited.

Even tucked in behind our fort's six foot walls, Jelly felt the need to whisper: "I c-can sneak us in to play b-basketball." Jelly reminded me of James Cagney, planning a bank heist.

"Jelly, the gym is tighter than Fort Knox," I said.

"No, no, l-listen. I've worked up a g-great plan. The j-junior high gym is empty every S-Saturday. Mr. Pederson s-stokes the furnace early, b-before eight o'clock. Then, the other janitor, Nelson—name's Nelson, comes in and the t-two of them go through the hallway, pass through the gym, and up the stairs to the th-third floor."

"Hold on," Jim said. "How do you know so much about grumpy ol' Pederson and his buddy?"

"Just a second, Jim; I-I'm getting there. Like I s-said, they s-s-start on the third floor and work down to the gym."

Down to business then, Jelly steadied himself, outlining his plan to fool the guardian janitors of the junior high gym. "They s-spend two solid hours cleaning classrooms. Up on the third floor, I doubt they could hear us; but later, when they move lower, especially on the first floor right above us, we'll need to be extra quiet. We'll pull out before noon, 'cuz they'll move down before lunch to work on the gym floor. Don't ask me why. The danged gym floor hardly ever gets used."

"How do you know so much, Jelly?"

"Well, Miss Wilkinson made me her honors assistant, you know. I get to run notes from the elementary wing through the connector hall to the junior high principal. On the way back I detour through the gym and the furnace room. I know the layout inside out."

"Great, Jelly, but how do you have grumpy ol' Pederson figured?" Jim countered. "He's big and ornery, and you know Miss Wilkinson lets him use a hickory paddle on kids."

"Aw, don't worry about him. Last Saturday I snuck in ten minutes after Pederson opened the back door to the furnace room. Figured he doesn't lock after himself, and he doesn't. I hid behind a partition, listening to him stoke the furnace. He banged about, singing some caruuping cadooping Norwegian song. That's the key to Mr. Pederson. You always know where he is. When he isn't singin' in Norskydiddle, he's hollering at Nelson. Ol' Pederson's a Paul Bunyan walker with those clod-hopper boots. He creaks the floors so's we can hear him comin'. But he can't hear good himself, even though he wears two hearing aids."

"Jelly, you're forgetting Nelson," Jim said. Jim wore his tease grin that Jelly—in his eagerness—didn't notice.

"What do you mean?"

"Nelson can hear good, can't he?"

"Jimmy, you gotta trust me. I know these janitors. Sure, Nelson can hear; but he won't want to catch us. He has a kid in fifth grade who wants to play ball. If Nelson had his way, he'd let us all in. Anyways, we'll always know where he is, 'cuz he sticks to his boss like glue."

Jelly held his palms up and looked skyward, as if to say, "Lord, these guys are hopeless." Jelly put it to Jim, "So, are you in?"

"Maybe. Gotta think about it," Jim said. . . . *Funny thing,* I thought . . . *Everybody goes for Jim's crazy plans, while he skepticizes ours.*

"Come on," Jelly pleaded. "All we gotta do is play quiet basketball. We work this right and we can play basketball every Saturday."

As we huddled in our snow fort, the blizzard winds "whoooed," pitching up and down the music scale. A sideways curtain of snow blanked out Gwin's house, 30 feet away. Blizzards add urgency to whatever you're doing, like planning hare-brained schemes.

Jelly shouted to be heard: "Just think. Every Saturday, real basketball in a real gym."

We huddled like snow-bound husky dogs. "Jeez, Jelly, that would be fantastic," I said. "Short scrimmages, huh?"

Jelly cuffed me. "Hey, when I said basketball, I meant real basketball—only with special rules."

"Special rules? What special rules? For the risk we're takin', I want a real game," Jim said.

"It can be a regular game, sort of," Jelly said. He climbed on the upturned bucket, checking for possible big people listeners. Jelly rubbed his hands together, overcome by another wave of excitement, stuttering again: "L-like I s-said, we'll need to p-play quiet ball. We need to ch-change the rules some. No dribbling or hollering. And n-no rattle-rim long shots."

"Oh, come on Jelly, no dribbling? That won't be a real game," Jim countered.

"Yah, but let's try," I argued."

"Well, I wanna' hear more first."

"Little Eric wants to, Jim," Jelly pleaded. "What's wrong with you? Tell you what: You can be one captain and Dave the other. And I figure you guys can get enough players for regular teams or at least four on four. So, whadda ya think, Jim?"

"Not sure yet. What about these 'special rules?'"

"They're in my head. I'll show you captains and then we'll teach the other guys. The special rules for quiet basketball need to be enforced. If we get caught, I'll be the one in the biggest Dutch, 'cuz sneakin' in is my idea."

"Okay Jelly, but keep it simple," I said.

"Easy," Jelly said. "First, no hollering and no dribbling."

"Hold it, Jelly," Jim protested. "I can go with no hollering. But how the heck is it basketball if we can't dribble?"

"Easy. You pretend it. Now watch how it's done." Jelly vaulted the ice wall, landing in a foot of drifting snow. Jim and I climbed up onto the ice wall to watch. Jelly eyed us. "Watch this now." Jelly high-stepped through the drifts in his buckled rubber overshoes, yo-yoing his hand over a mythical basketball. "Just like this, a silent dribble," he said. "The ball never touches the floor. If the ball bongs the floor, Pederson will come clomping on the run."

"Well, I don't know," Jim said. "Doesn't look like basketball to me. Do that again, Jelly. I'm trying to imagine." Jim elbowed me, holding back a laugh.

"It's easy," Jelly said. He trudged through the snow, "dribbling."

"I don't know, Jelly," Jim laughed. "We'd need to practice that. Show us one more time."

On the serious side, Jim had been collared once by Mr. Pederson, barely talking his way out of a butt paddling. "Hey, how about goin' out to the Muddy for ice fishin'. Gramp has a crow bar. We can chip a hole."

"Jim, we can fish anytime. This will be a game in a real gym with regular ten foot baskets. We gotta do it," Jelly insisted.

Flabbergasted wouldn't do to explain how I felt. I knew Jelly was smart, a straight "A" student. But this was A+ + + brilliant. On the far side of my brain, though, Mr. Pederson stood glaring, slapping his huge hand against the paddle.

"Okay, Jelly, you got a deal, but you're in charge of rules," Jim laughed.

"Don't worry," Jelly said. "You bring the players. I'll get us in."

With Jelly's plan so well organized, convincing our guys was easy. Basketball, basketball—everybody was nuts about basketball, including every single Muddy River kid. For every high school game, our town filled the crackerbox school gym to overflowing. Our revered Williston Coyotes were in the middle of an exciting season, set for winning the state finals. All of us little kids wanted to be players, but rarely had opportunities to play in a real gym.

Our secret game was on: Jelly, Jim and me, the Bervig boys, Jack, Buck, and Little Ergie. Saturday couldn't come soon enough. If the school guardians of their Fort Knox gym had been sharper they'd have known something was cooking. Our players huddled at recesses while Jelly, the perpetrator, jabbered intensely and quietly, as if spies could hear us from across the playground. "Remember, men: only tennis shoes. They're quieter and won't leave black heel marks. If we get caught, black heel marks would mean double trouble."

"Thought you said your plan is foolproof," Big Bervie said.

"It is. But just in case . . ."

Jelly's optimism and, Jim—with his captainship, well . . . they fizzed like shaken bottles of Coca-Cola. Our secret plot was too exciting, creating an attitude that should have been visible. Jelly, in Miss Brynjolfsen's class with me, acted outright chirpy, like it was his last day of school.

I credit our teachers and Mr. Pederson with winter drowseys. On Saturday morning at nine o'clock they left the school unguarded, as Jelly had predicted. We slipped and skidded on ice, playing "no dribble" basketball, shooting at the wimpy seven foot playground basket with no net, all the while watching for signs of adult activity around the school. There was none, no signs of anybody, only the pair of janitors' junky pickups parked as usual, in the alcove behind the school. We wandered nonchalantly across the playground and assembled by the coal chute. Jelly went to try the door. He tested it, and looked back with a nod and a grin. "Unlocked," he whispered. "I'm goin' in to case the place."

Jack chortled, "Jelly's seen too many cops and robbers movies." We all laughed nervously at Jack's tidy little joke. *It's easy to laugh standing out here,* I thought. Unlike Jelly, we stood ready to escape by running across the snowy playground.

The door opened, and out poked Jelly's blond, heinie cut head, "Come on!

Hurry." He put his finger to his lips, "Ssshhh." We gathered inside the door, Jelly whispering, "T-they're on either the second or third floor. I heard the f-floor creaking."

We single-filed in through the coal room, passed the janitor's cubicle lunchroom, and followed the darkened hallway to the gym. Aside from a few giggles, we were sly as weasels, pattering after the faint blob ahead that was Jelly, already stripped down to his white t-shirt.

With the ball under his arm, Jelly ran out to the gym's center-circle. He stood in the spare light that penetrated from the end windows. "Okay," Jelly whispered, "you guys heard that door bang up there. I think they're on the third floor. But we're stickin' to the rules; like we said: no dribbling and no long shots. It's too dark in here to see the bucket more'n ten feet out anyway."

After a quick whispered choose-up, Jack, Jelly, Little Ergie, and I stripped jackets and shirts. This was one time I was happy to be on a skin's team. I had enough hold-over summer tan so I could hide in the shadows and get open for passes. Jelly called "heads," and deftly flipped a nickel onto the back of his hand. "Heads it is," he whispered. Jelly stepped to the side with the ball for the inbounds. "Let's go to twenty, and then change teams." Jelly found me with a lob pass, and our game was on.

Little Ergie skittered around me, headed down court. I passed off to him and he took the ball at full speed. For six or seven short-legged strides he honored Jelly's no dribble rule, pumping his hand and the ball with a realistic mimic of a real dribble. Then he spied Buck planted at the free throw line, ready to cut him off. Buck was big enough to make two of the little white-headed tyke, who charged ahead with the ball under his arm, fullback style—barreling past Buck. Ergie bored in on the basket, lurching forward, staggering on legs unable to keep up with expectations. In the middle of a glorious dive to the hardwood he desperately thrust both hands upward under the ball, heaving it skyward. The ball launched high to the top of the backboard, teetered there, then dropped—incredibly . . . straight down through the net. From his back on the floor Ergie cried out, "Yaay, I scored, I scored!"

Jelly was over Ergie in a second, pulling him to his feet. "Great shot, Ergie, but you can't yell. Don't forget again."

Ergie's miraculous play was the last good one of that Saturday's no-dribble game. From there on out, fake dribbles were forgotten and passes were rare. Ergie's opening play became the order of the day as players ran wild and woolly, football style, colliding and ending in five or six player dog-piles. The game was fun, but it wasn't basketball. Even arguments were bogus, whispered and punchless; they wouldn't impress a soul. After twenty minutes, with the score six to four, Jelly's patience just exploded. *"HEY!"* he hollered. Jelly's outburst bounced from the walls and echoed up the stairs toward the enemy janitors. The effect shocked the other seven of us to stunned silence. Jelly grabbed the ball and walked to center court. We followed without a whisper and stood waiting, ready to run should Mr. Pederson come stomping down the steps with blood in his eye. Frozen in place, like hunted rooster pheasants, we stared at the stairs, our ears tuned for trouble coming.

Finally, "Coast is clear, I guess," Jelly whispered. "Now look guys, we'll get caught for sure if we don't follow the rules. Two things: Buck, for criminy sakes, no more long shots. You're boiy-yoi-ing the rim loud enough to carry clear up to the third floor. Besides, they might even be down to the second by now." Jelly stood stiff and important, ball under his arm, eyes sweeping players like an official striped-shirt referee. "And we gotta play with the no-dribble, like I explained before."

"Okay, Jelly," Buck laughed a little too loudly. "Your game is nuts, but let's get on with it. It's our ball." Buck reached for the ball that Jelly pulled away. Jelly looked the part of a Navy guy with his blond nubbin'd head, short cut pants, and white socks . . . and a ranked Navy man, too, boasting a swagger, too swaggery for a skinny third grader. Jelly rubbed his jaw, as if he had whiskers to rub. He held a palm up for silence.

"Now listen up, guys." In his excitement Jelly forgot to whisper. "Now, we're doing okay on the no-bounce part of the dribble," he said right out loud. "But you're all traveling. Here, I'll demonstrate." With slow-motioned steps, Jelly pumped the ball toward the floor without an actual dribble. He set his jaw and narrowed his blue eyes to show he meant business: "I *know* the ball doesn't actually hit the floor, but you've got to *pretend* it. You don't, you're traveling. It's like this." He continued around the circle of us, pantomiming his pumped up and down phantom dribble. Jelly was ridiculous and incredibly comical. Right there his fragile hold on command began to crumble, starting with a chorus of muffled giggles. Jack could no longer contain his famous cackling laugh, made better by repeated failures to contain it. In short order we players, including Jelly, erupted in un-suppressable laughter.

Amidst the distraction, Jack walked over and grabbed the ball from Jelly. Then in his normal, oldest kid voice, he spoke full out, "You all remember *frozen nuts*. It's time for a decision. Let's play basketball, real basketball. First score wins, *sudden death*—or whenever Pederson shows." *Yeah,* I'm thinking. *Sudden death could be a perfect description.*

"Okay, everybody, *frozen nuts* time." Buck boomed it out, and the game was on: real dribbles, cussing, squeaking shoes, and caroming balls rattling the rim. At last, honest-to-goodness basketball lasted all of two minutes before the arrival of *sudden death* himself, Mr. Pederson, lumbering, cursing, and crashing down the staircase and onto the floor, followed by his sidekick Nelson.

"*Yeeow,* let's get out of here," Jack hollered, and we skedaddled like bee-stung monkeys, grabbing shirts and jackets on the go.

"Skins won, six to four, skins won." Jelly's boast echoed throughout the gym as he scrambled down the tunneled hallway. I couldn't resist a look back for Pederson. I wasn't the only one. We must have looked like little Spaniard runners escaping the bulls. From behind, Mr. Pederson's clompings and raging echoed and amplified down the long, dim passageway to the coal room: "Git back 'har you leetul basturs. Honyauks! I ketchya, I'm a gon' bleestur hyur butts."

On the run, out the door, and half way across the playground—I glanced back and saw Mr. Pederson and Nelson puffing out onto the landing. I joined the guys at the corner of the playground where we roostered about, gloryifying our escape. "Cover your faces with your jackets, like this," Jelly said. "Otherwise, they might identify us." I pulled my jacket up and peeked through a pokey hole. There stood Pederson on the landing with his hands on his coverall hips, and his smoking glare, a certainty—though too far to see. And Nelson, janitor and school guardian, most certainly was smiling.

We ambled away then, splitting into natural joinings of two's and three's. Jelly pounded on my back and yelled loud for the losers to hear, "Skins won. Skins won."

"Hey, who's the skins?" Jimmy the Box Man hollered. He stood beside his bike with its train of cardboard boxes. Jimmy turned his bike and box train our way, obligated to investigate and report a "sports" score, any sports score. "Who won?" he had to know.

"Little Eric and me," Jelly said. "And we had Shemorry and Little Ergie."

"What was the score?"

"It was close; but we got 'em, six to four—a real game."

"Not exactly true, Jelly," I said to myself; but we did hold that lead when *frozen nuts* ended our game.

Years later in ninth grade English class my teacher devoted most of an hour explaining metaphor. I smiled, and a laugh came right out with the memory of our metaphor spawned at Stony Ford. *Frozen Nuts:* When a decision is called for, make it, even for a phantom basketball game.

Chapter Six

The Catwalk

Life is what happens when we forget to make plans.
—Adapted from Woody Allen.

"Little Eric, you'll be the lookout right here." With that, Razzie pushed me down behind the right wing of our snow fort. "Give us plenty of warning as soon as you spot them coming," he ordered. Razzie was our squad leader, assigned to command his five men in ambushing the West Side krauts. Our set-up was perfect. We'd camouflaged our snow fort with dead tree limbs and built a stash of hard packed ice-ball hand grenades.

With a dozen grenades stacked in a pyramid at my feet, I carved a peeky window in the wall of snow. I knelt to wait and—son-of-a gun!—here came a target, not the kraut patrol, but a doggone fun one. "The milk truck is comin'," I whispered to Razzie.

Wow!—Motoring up 4th Street, tantalizingly vulnerable, came the Coop milk truck. Bessie, the Holstein, adorned the steel paneled side of the white panel truck. Her silly grin made her an irresistible target, and her huge pink tit-bag a perfect bulls-eye. Though Bessie was not a target authorized by our East Side Army officers, Razzie laughed, stood, and cocked his arm. "Get her," he hollered needlessly. His troops, five of us, simultaneously let fly our first volley, and snow balls smashed into the side of the milk truck, immediately followed with a second "Bonzai!" We clobbered her good, our dead hits reverberating—*Ker-boing, ker-boing, boing, boing, boing, ker-boing!* We sang out in victory—

"Yaaaah!"

"I got her twice," Bervie yelled.

"Yah, but I dented her tit-bag," Razzie bragged.

For such risky behavior Razzie was a good leader. He wasn't disciplined enough to command, "Hold fire." When word got back, he could argue with Commander Korwin, "General, we just used the truck for practice, 'cuz the West Side bike patrol didn't show." True enough, but only last Saturday the dirty rat krauts pedaled up this very street on their way to stink-bombing our dugout headquarters in the vacant lot on Fifth Avenue. And they could still show up today.

On a great March snowball day like this one, the milk truck driver didn't bother to stop and scold us. He knew Bessie would be targeted all along his route. Our risk was overdoing, using Razzie's snow fort ambush two days in a row, in which case the driver might have Officer Gwin or Chief Olson tailing a block behind, ready to nab us. Today, with no signs of them, we settled back behind the wall, feeling smugly victorious, hoping for the West Side patrol, ready to blast them.

Razzie manned our snow fort's center lookout hole, still giggling long after Bessie had gone. Yet, Razzie attempted seriousness, too, barking out new orders: "Build more ammo, men; use bare hands, better for ice balls." Razzie strutted too big for his lieutenant's rank and too big for the occasion. After all, he didn't command the most important outfit. Only a skirmish was expected. Jim and I and Big Bervie had agreed to join his squad for the fun of a good snowball fight that favored our side tucked in behind the wall with plenty of snow grenades stashed and ready.

Joining Razzie's army patrol was our best option for the day. What else to do? Countryside bike travel through ice-water and mud was impossible; besides, even if we hiked out there, the Muddy was still frozen in.

Patrol skirmishes with the West Side krauts were more fun than the big trench warfare battles. Patrol soldiers kept tempers in check, especially when we knew the guys on the other side. Prisoners were exchanged before supper time, whereas the commanders of big battles sometimes kept prisoners until after dark. Last summer the West-siders captured Jelly and Nordell. They were blindfolded, held as prisoners in a dugout, and released by moonlight. Mr. Nordell raised some hell with parents after that episode; thereupon, officers from both armies met in a sort of Geneva Convention. Jack was a delegate. He said the generals couldn't agree on prisoner treatment, but decided to outlaw BB guns and cherry bombs. "Signed the agreement in candle wax," Jack said. The BB guns I understood. Only a couple of times did a stupid kid sneak one into battle, risking a blinding eye shot. But no cherry bombs? How could we hold a decent war without explosions?

After three years of recruiting, training, and the occasional battle, our East Side leaders lacked enthusiasm, incapable of mustering much rah-rah, "go get 'em," stuff. Time and circumstances had dampened hatred for the West Side krauts. Some of us had become arm's-length acquainted with West Side Army guys from Webster School. That was Floyd Clausen's doing. He was the forever spirited radio personality, the Voice of Agriculture on KGCX. Mom, an English teacher and big time book reader, was the smartest thinker I knew. Mom said Clausen was "hyper"and "drank too much strong coffee."

"Floyd Clausen would invite pigs to the dinner table, long as they were champion pigs," Gramp joked. Anything agriculture—anytime, anywhere, all the time ag—that was Floyd Clausen. In winter with farms frozen in, Mr. Clausen volunteered to be the 4-H recreation director. Clausen was smart and ambitious. He secured the Armory gymnasium as a recruiting tool. It worked. Honest-to-goodness indoor basketball enticed most of our East Side soldiers to join 4-H. When we and the enemy West-siders arrived in separate groups for after school 4-H basketball, Mr. Clausen purposely mixed the teams, giving us opportunities to snipe from close up about the other side's woeful army. One remark hit dead center: "Who cares?" Larry—"The Stew"—Stewart said. Being that Larry was a West Side lieutenant, I concluded that their army, like ours, had become bored with the war. Larry argued that East-siders were the real krauts and West-siders Yanks. But Stewart, I could see, was no more willing to fight about it than I. He got a kick out of our little war of words. His on-going, likeable laugh scattered seeds of friendship. Before long I began calling him "Stew" like his West Side friends.

Imagine that: enemy soldiers as friends, growing soft on both sides. New recruits, however, were different critters. They joined up with gung-ho in them. "Piss and vinegared," as Gramp would say, and our new inductees, Little Ergie and Johnny Lund, came full up.

Ergie and Johnny had only seen the Grand Theatre newsreels, had never been in their own war battle, and were anxious for action. Building ice grenades with me behind Razzie's snow fort wall, Ergie agitated for action: "Hope the chicken krauts show. We're gonna clobber 'em."

"Yeah," little Johnny Lund said, "and then we'll run for my hide-out."

Lieutenant Shemorry recruited the little guys, quite illogically, I thought: five and six year olds, too little for a big important army of old guys of 7, 8, 9, even 10. I wouldn't have understood if not for Jack's laughing and carrying on. I pressed him for an explanation. "After the train wreck we have to recruit them," Jack said. "The West-siders have nobody famous like Johnny Lund—and they have nobody as much fun as Little Ergie."

Jack saw opportunity in Johnny Lund's exaggerated reputation for heroism in the aftermath of the train wreck. In January, Dr. Lund had taken Johnny along on the train to a medical convention in Minneapolis. West of Grand Forks the Empire Builder derailed in an ice storm, accounting for a few passenger injuries. Naturally Dr. Lund—a good Samaritan man—carried along his emergency bag. He went to work on the injured, using Johnny as his assistant to hand over doctoring tools and bandages, and running for blankets. Give little Johnny Lund his due. He was a smart and gutsy six year old. So after the *Herald* ran a special feature on Johnny, his doctor dad, and the train wreck, the kid had to be recruited. So did his fearless buddy, Little Ergie. "No piddly private status for them," Jack said. "We'll make them captains."

Jack took me along to my first Headquarter's meeting and introduced me to General Korwin. To me, he seemed big enough and smart enough for high school. The general was a wide-shouldered sixth grader. He wore a nifty black heinie cut, and a constant smile.

Jack knocked on the timber frame entrance to the East Side Army's headquarters dugout. "Captain Shemorry with Private Erickson, sir."

"Enter!"

Down we went into the musty, candle lit room of dirt. General Korwin, sucking on a dead cigar butt, paced the center of the dugout, while four of his officers worked on a rubber sling tommy gun on a sawhorse table. Jack pushed me to the front. "One of your newest soldiers here, sir: Private Erickson, Little Eric." I saluted. General Korwin returned my salute and shook my hand.

"General, I've come with a proposal," Jack said. Jack struggled, trying to keep from laughing. "I'm proposing to enlist Johnny Lund and Ronnie Erdmann. We should bring them in as captains."

Jack and Korwin were two peas in a pod in the fun department, knowing what the war needed was levity. General Korwin searched the eyes of his officers around the perimeter of the dugout. "Any objections?" Hearing none, the general assigned Corporal Bervig to burn C's in poker chips for captain's medals.

By happenstance, on their very first army assignment, only minutes after clobbering the Coop truck, Johnny and Ergie found themselves in the midst of a serious skirmish. The little guys could have been captured and punished by this new enemy—well, not really *enemy.* They were only a gang of girls, tempting targets and defenseless . . . or so we believed.

"We're gonna bust 'em good; everybody ready," Razzie said. A little voice in my head said, "Nah." The girls stopped momentarily, worrying about a patch of ice, too tempting, and giving me time to build a respectable, soft snowball. Ergie knelt at my side too low to see. "Make soft snowballs, Ergie," I said. "Girls coming." They came pedaling gingerly, five long-legged, giggling, eighth grade girls. Fortunately, today, Jack wasn't in our squad, because his big sister rode second in the string.

When Razzie stood to fire, the rest of us joined, unloading a mighty volley that smacked them good. Razzie's grenade, an ice-ball, nailed their blond leader on her butt. I know it hurt, 'cuz just before I took off running, I saw her angry face as she dropped her bike. "You little shits," she yelled. I remembered who she was . . . Lorna Jones. I had watched Lorna win every track event in junior high, the thought of which put fire to my legs, running close behind Jim.

I glanced back to see the girl gang running for us. Lorna in the middle vaulted the middle of our snow fort wall, screaming, "Get 'em!" When I saw her grab for stumbling Razzie, I kicked into high gear. Each to his own, Razzie's squad scattered over snowy hedges, through alleys, to the safety of friendly garages and hide-out forts.

Our attacks on Bessie and the girl gang I chalked up to small 't" trouble, excused by boredom from a tardy spring. Hopefully, Officer Gwin had a burglary investigation or something more important on his mind than mostly harmless snowball shenanigans. My instincts proved correct; otherwise, just after suppertime Mr. Gwin would have come barging in our back door.

Headed off for school on Monday morning, Jim volunteered his exciting, conjuring plans. "Buck and I are setting up a snaring line for rabbits."

Jim volunteered, "We can sell rabbit meat, you know, and make mittens outa their fur. You want in?"

"Doggone right. What do I need to do?"

"For now, just keep quiet. We're gonna sneak across the railroad to the willow jungles." With rabbit hunting plans, last Saturday's skirmishes with Bessie and the mad girls flew off to history . . . or so I thought.

Jelly caught me in the cloakroom at school, knuckling me on the arm to get my attention: "You know what happened to Razzie?"

"You mean on Saturday?"

"Yah, Saturday, after you escaped. I've got the whole story." Jelly always had the "whole story."

"You missed the fun part," Jelly laughed. "Razzie shouldn't have ice-balled those eighth grade girls. Lorna Jones caught Razzie and held him down for the other girls. They de-pantsed him and threw his pants up on a telephone wire. Razzie ran home in his under-shorts. I heard a half-dozen East Side ladies called the cops on him."

With that news our laughing attracted a crowd in the cloakroom that had to hear Jelly's story told a second time. I joined in the fun, my enjoyment slightly dampened by a pang of guilt for disloyalty to my squad leader for not staying behind to fight the girls off. Still, the grin on my face lasted all day.

Razzie wisely played hooky that morning. Our school was abuzz with his embarrassing capture and de-pantsing by girls. By second hour, Miss Brynjolfsen, my third grade teacher, was about to pop her bloomers with curiosity. She took me to the corner of the classroom next to the American flag, the sacred place where fibs could not be told. And before you ask: yes, she was that smart, maybe the smartest teacher I ever had. Fortunately for me, she didn't have tough to go along with smart. *"David, David, DAVID,"* she said in teacher talk. "Just what is this misbehaving commotion about?"

"Nothing important, really. I don't . . ." My fumbling answer didn't seem a real lie, only a half-fib or a *Shorty.* With her hand on my shoulder, Miss Brynjolfsen lowered her gray eyes, studying me from top to bottom. She was a tall and skinny lady, the kind who gnashes green lettuce and wrinkles her nose at juicy beef steak. She was forever serious. I knew the fun of Razzie's de-pantsing would be wasted on her. So, I just held her long stare and waited.

I appreciated Miss Brynjolfsen. Her job managing tough kids like Stretch Johnson and rascals like the rest of us was near impossible. She wore the pain of it on her long face with the droopy mouth. But Saturday had been official army business. I was duty-bound to reveal nothing. I was tempted to give her name, rank, and serial number, deciding instead to keep that my private joke.

"You must tell me," she said.

"Just a little snowball fight, ma'am," I said.

"Then what's so funny, David?"

I held my ground, furrowing my eyebrows to appear serious, while my gut ached from holding a giant laugh. Summer goofies lay only weeks ahead, but already I felt them trying to escape. Just as I was about to bust a gut, Miss Brynjolfsen gave up, nodding for me to take my seat. Had she been down on Main Street, instead of stuck teaching third grade, Miss Brynjolfsen wouldn't need me to tell her about Razzie and the eighth grade girls. Heck, outside the school, maybe even Miss Brynjolfsen could laugh.

During classroom daydreaming time, I practiced drawing snowshoe rabbits, and toyed with the idea of telling Dad the whole story about Razzie, deciding yes, I would—that very evening. Dad enjoyed hearing a good story as much as he did telling one.

How dumb of me to think a story so good would need me to tell it. Dad wore a grin when he walked in the door at five minutes to six. Either he'd sold a tractor or he'd heard the Razzie Rassmusen story. I guessed right. It was Razzie.

"That scoundrel Razzie; serves him right," Dad laughed. At five minutes after six at the supper table, the fun ended.

The phone rang at precisely the wrong time: in the middle of Dad's dinner. He hated that. Dad commanded the phone in our house. It hung on the wall by his table place. As usual, he picked it up before the second ring: "Bill here" . . . "Yeah?" . . . "Yeah?" . . . Dad swiveled his glinted blue eyes to Jim, then to me: his stone-killer stare. "Yup, they're sittin' right here." . . . "Yup, you got it. I'll lay down the law." . . . "Yup. West Side. I'll see to it. OK. Thanks. You can count on it, Chief."

CLANK!—lucky the phone receiver didn't break apart.

"What's wrong Bill?" Mom worried. "Who was it?"

"Chief Olson."

"Are the boys in trouble?"

"Some. He wouldn't say how much, something about some snowballing getting out of hand, plastering girls on bikes—Saturday."

"Now, here's the deal." Dad turned to Jim and me, pointing his crooked old football player finger at Jim, me, back at Jim, me again. "Chief Olson says he doesn't want to see either one of you on the east side of Main until further notice. He says it'll simplify his job."

Dad targeted Jim first. "You know what he means?"

"Yeah, I think so," Jim said.

"Me too," I said. I went back to digging into Mom's burger-roni-mato.

Dad fought back his grin. Still, he had to side with the law. "You knew better. Pickin' on those girls will get you in trouble every time."

Chief Olson's decree on Jim and me was certain to cramp plans for spring. No going past Main. Though we lived on First Avenue West, we considered ourselves East Side guys. Excepting Jelly, our friends lived east of Main and the stranger kids lived blocks to our west and attended Webster School, a sort of a foreign nation populated by tough characters. A few like Pete Reed and Denny Ferrell were dirt wrestlers. Let them inside your fists and they took you down, locked you in a half-nelson, a leg-nelson, or a complete nelson nelson. I'd seen them do it.

Jim and I were now restricted to "no man's land," pinned against the west side of Main Street, unable to visit our East Side army headquarters, the gravel pit bike jumps, or buddies' back yard forts. Add to that the usual spring fever school day antsies and we were headed for some kind of pent-up, bust-out. And it wasn't only kids. Big folks seemed out of sorts too. Even Gramp allowed a grump or two, one of them reserved for his Stony Creek friend, Jess Eastland, the "Chicken Man."

"Told the stubborn old coot—stubborner than that black mule he used to mine lignite with—told him to fix decent chicken pens. 'Got a new watchdog,' Jess told me, and he says, 'Jardo Kelley's comin' out to hunt down the foxes and coyotes.' Hell! No lazy mutt or gov'mint trapper will save chickens if your fencing ain't good. Now Jess has cut me off his egg delivery. The thievin' predators have taken so many hens that he has barely enough eggs to cover the top of his customer list. And a man needs to be a mayor or somebody's cousin to move up on his list."

Long winter had wearied Gramp, like everybody else. Just last year he'd won the Elks Club ice-out pool. But this year ice-out on the Missouri came so insanely late that Olaf, the garbage man, won with his "stupid" April 24th prediction.

By the sound of things, Gramp and Dad felt unusually cramped. More than once Jim and I had picked up on what seemed to be strange jealousy with comments like: "Damn, just to be young again like the Riley Boys. They'll have all summer . . . no worries. They'll go hell bent for leather." True; and summer freedom couldn't come soon enough.

We did have April and May Saturdays to muck about Horseshoe Bend and the lower end of the Muddy. But they weren't even full Saturdays, what with chores of lawn mowing, garden spading, and plinking young blackbirds that otherwise would grow up to be garden thieves. The ansties seemed to rule my life. Jim's too. He used spare time to craft dumb tricks like tying my shoelaces together when I was napping on the lawn, then turning the hose on me, laughing crazy when I fell over.

Frustrations had been building since Chief Olson's March decree shut down our army escapades or biking into the East Side, where we could visit Jack's latest garage project. We had seen only the start of his building a derby car with a real gas motor.

I remembered exactly the same kind of antsy-dancy feeling from last spring. Something big was destined to happen the day after our escape from school: the *Great Catwalk Adventure,* so called now that Jack's sideways humor is stuck in my brain. The *Catwalk* was a goofy escapade, starting out as kid-silly and ending up with the town gone silly too.

When the last day of school came on Friday the 31st of May, Jim and I and the Muddy River gang had reached a dangerous edge. Like jailbirds about to be let out after 10 years in the hoosegow, we should have been assigned parole officers.

My last day in third grade was a real doozie, though it started out calm and boringly normal. After the Pledge of Allegiance, Miss Brynjolfsen promptly reminded my third grade class, "We're going to make the best of our last day, children," followed by her warning that she had not yet completed scoring us on conduct. She stood by her desk holding her stack of yellow report cards, fluttering them like a deck of canasta cards. "I will be handing out report cards this afternoon, just before dismissal. But I do need to remind you: if Miss Wilkinson serves you with after school detention, you'll not get a report card until you finish your summer detention." *Summer detention!* I shuddered. Just the sound of those two words would gag a maggot.

Our teacher's show of force had little immediate effect. She was of secondary concern. Yes, she did own the right to boss us in her classroom. But detention kind of trouble usually happened in the hallways or on the playground, and those were under Principal Wilkinson's command. Classroom whispering resumed, and Miss Brynjolfsen was too nice to do much about it.

Miss Brynjolfsen had scored me "good" on conduct, which was nothing special. Since few boys scored higher than "good," I believe she meant I was okay, but a long way short of angelhood, and that was reserved for girls anyway. Today,

I'd sit out the last day of school with my mouth shut, let the girls' dutiful enthusiasm keep Miss Brynjolfsen happy. I sat at a school desk, but I was already gone off fishing.

I hunkered down, hiding behind big ol' Dale Williamson, with my tablet and colored pencils, drawing goldies (or, officially—according to my fish book—"goldeyes"). Gold glows out of their big eyes and shines from their bright scales. Goldies are the prettiest fish that swim . . . except for speckled trout, of course. I imagined a wild glittering school of goldies like I saw last summer . . . 50, maybe a hundred, some jumping high out of the water, playing. They were ready to run west up the Yellowstone for spawning. That's what Buck's dad said goldies do.

I imagined, drew, erased, drew and colored, started over, imagined again. On this particular day I found it impossible to sneak in a decent drawing in our jittered classroom. Even normally obedient girls whispered. Listening in, I discovered they had missed two answers in a row—a rarity. Miss Brynjolfsen stood and paced, pursing her painted lips. Deciding on fresh air, she turned and tottered on her high heels to the street side of the classroom, where she went about raising the bottom halves of the four tall windows. She wasn't thinking right. For Pete's sake, it was distinctly *summer* air she'd let in, torturously fresh, carrying along smells of lilac and fresh cut grass, the chirrups of robins, and blackbird chatters.

The class rustled, and from the back row, Stretch Johnson growled, "I'm gittin' outa here."

Miss Brynjolfsen put her finger to her lips, and walked urgently down the aisle toward him, fluttering her hands. "Kenneth, please calm down," she pleaded. Fortunately for her and Stretch also, the buzzer bell rang for recess. She'd nursed him all year, had only a few more hours of him . . . maybe.

This was Kenneth "Stretch" Johnson's second year in the third grade, and if nothing drastic happened on this last day, the rumor said he might pass this time. If he didn't make it, and she had Stretch in her class again, Miss Brynjolfsen could land in the loony bin.

Stretch's failing again would make Razzie's nasty joke come true: "Stretch will do three in the third." Razzie, you see, had been whipped bad by Stretch, same as a couple dozen other kids.

Stretch angled constantly for a fight, just as he did now with me, elbowing me in the ribs as we ran down the steps, headed for morning recess on the playground. I stepped aside, not anxious to fight him. Heck, let's face it. I was afraid of him. We both ran for the game of pump-pump pullaway, where about 50 players lessened my odds of tangling with Stretch Johnson.

Jack volunteered to be "IT." From the middle of the field he challenged the body of Central School's boys and a few of its tom-boys, "Pump-pump pullaway. Come, come, or I'll pull you away." He pointed at Jim and me on the line. His challenge meant we had to run next, try to out-maneuver him on our race to the far side goal.

"Be ready," Jim said. "We'll do the crossover," meaning we'd run full bore at Jack and cross sharp in front of him. "Jack will miss tagging one of us, maybe both," Jim said. "When the next gust of wind blows dust, we'll go."

"Now!" Jim yelled, and we took off side-by-side, sprinting dead on to laughing Jack. He crouched, ready to move on us. He never got the chance. A monstrous blow hit me in the back, bowling me over. I went down hard just like last September in Grandpa Erickson's sorting pen, when a yearling bull ran over me. Whoever flattened me on the playground was big. Picking my face out of the dirt, it dawned on me the tackler was Stretch Johnson, who forever smelled like a bacon grease camp fire. I rolled over and pushed him off. He laughed and popped to his feet, landing in his practiced boxing stance with fists clinched, eyes glaring, taunting.

I jammed Stretch on the shoulder as I scrambled to my feet. "Watch it, Stretch," I said.

"Make me," Stretch said, sneering over the tops of his fists. One dark eye challenged me, the other mostly hidden by his slant of shiny black hair. His was a peculiar face, intelligent from the cheekbones up, but set in anger across his off-set jaws and mouth. He shuffled in a circle, like a coyote toying with a wounded rabbit. I'd watched his boxing dance more than once, just before he bloodied his challenger. I'd dreamed far-fetched glory of some day whipping Stretch. And once again I sized him up, not because I was ready to take him on, but because it seemed I had no other choice.

Stretch Johnson wore holey Levis, tight and too short, showing raggy socks above his black ankle high work boots. Stretch's Western shirt bulged with chest muscles; his rolled-up sleeves showed off thick biceps. He pranced and circled me on thick, bowed legs. His dark eyes glinted and bored into me through squinted eyelids. His knowing grin challenged, "You'd be stupid to try me, but a coward not to." Because of the presence of the throng of yelling schoolkids, I took a half-step toward him.

I remember seeing a flash of movement, that's all—no sound of Stretch's sledgehammer fist smacking my right jaw and no feeling going down hard in the dirt. From my back on the ground I peered through fog. I saw a fuzzy gang of guys grabbing and hammer-locking Stretch. Beyond the ringing in my ears I heard voices: Jim, Jack, and Jimmy Schwartz cussing on Stretch. Big Bervie pulled me to my feet and held me by the shoulders. He checked my eyes and pronounced, "You're alright, Eric."

Clearly, Stretch had no more interest in me. The guys released him and he danced away, throwing pretend punches at the air. A crazy guy, Stretch; he'd just cold-cocked one enemy, but he was already imagining another. His all-the-time anger was something I had yet to sort out. I needed Jelly, a peace making guy, to put Stretch in perspective. Jelly hated turmoil. If he had a dislike for a person, he'd never admit it. We were spectators once at a good fight at Harmon Park. Jelly walked away, couldn't stand to watch.

Jelly walked me toward the school door. "We'll get you a cold rag and Miss Brynjolfsen will give you an aspirin. Stretch has a rough life, you know. One thing is his nickname. We shouldn't call him that just because he was born with his mouth stretched off kilter. My mom says there could be an operation to fix it."

"He doesn't seem to care," I said. "His older buddy, Goslin, calls him Stretch. Everybody does. How about little Shorty Roberts? *Shorty*—he never complains about it. And Sheridan Baxter? I don't care how many dumbbells he lifts in his basement. He'll be a sissy as long as we call him 'Sherry,' like his mom and daddy do." I'd spoken the words, even as I was unsure of them. Still, since Johnson went out of his way to pick on me, I could hardly be the one to start calling him Kenneth.

Stretch Johnson lifted weights and boxed for the National Guard team. I'd seen his picture in the paper, hoisting trophies. He was by far the toughest kid in elementary school. I heard he took on junior high boys, too. Heck, age-wise Johnson was nearly ready for junior high anyway. Unless he straightened out, he'd never get to junior high. He'd flunked two grades already.

After whipping me, Stretch ambled over to the junior high side, where he and Goslin cuffed each other about. Jelly brought me the cold rag for my jaw, and I went back to the game trying to look unhurt.

I lined up next to Jack who had tagged someone and earned the right to run from the sidelines. "He coulda broke your nose if he wanted to," Jack said.

"Probably," I said. I rubbed my puffy jaw. It was numb and hurting at the same time. Sure, a sore jaw and the shame of getting whipped, undeniable. But mostly I was troubled by a dark thought: the image of Miss Wilkinson and Mr. Pederson, her enforcer. They'd be standing at their lookout windows in the third floor foyer of Central School. I stole a guilty look across the playground and up to the tall windows hoping I was wrong. I wasn't. There they stood in side-by-side windows. They had seen the scrap between Stretch and me. If Miss Wilkinson decided to sentence me to detention for fighting, I would spend the first week of summer, maybe two, in schoolhouse jail.

Miss Wilkinson filled the expanse of the bottom third of the floor to ceiling window on Central School's third floor. From where I stood looking up, our elementary grades were to the right of her lookout and the junior high wing on the left, that half of the building with its own principal. But the entire building, Central School, was really Miss Wilkinson's. When Officer Gwin came to Central to check up on truants or troublemakers—even junior high boys—he came to her office first.

From her lookout window, with beefy arms crossed under her big bosom, Miss Wilkinson commanded the entire block of playground. She never missed a noon time or recess, and she spotted not only big rule breakers like fist fighters, but also girl teasers and gum wrapper droppers. Furthermore, her huge janitor and rules enforcer, Mr. Pederson, stood on her left, watching from a companion window. The Battle of the Bulge had General Eisenhower and General Patton. Central School had Wilkinson and Pederson, a six-four Paul Bunyan Norwegian, who enjoyed whacking butts with his hickory paddle.

I returned to class after recess escorted by Jim, Jack, and Buck, all peppering me with half-baked advice. Strangely enough, the only suggestion of any comfort was Jim's stupid joke, a backwards kind of morale booster. He said, "Pederson's gonna blister your butt. If I was you I'd run home at noon and put on four extra pairs of under-shorts."

I returned to Miss Brynjolfsen's class dreading a message coming from Miss Wilkinson. It would be delivered by Jelly, the student messenger, granted the big deal job because he was a straight-A student and a friendly sort with grown-ups. Anyway, that's how I believed he was chosen.

On his first step into the classroom, Jelly caught my eyes and stuck out his tongue at me. His code meant: you're in big, big trouble. The bottom dropped out of my stomach. Jeez, Stretch Johnson and now Miss Wilkinson. How could my last day in third grade be worse? Jelly brought a folded note paper to Miss Brynjolfsen. She took it, quickly scanned it, folded it back, and handed it to Jelly. She nodded in my direction, and Jelly brought my death sentence down the aisle. For the time being Miss Brynjolfsen forgot about teaching, just as my classmates forgot about learning.

I opened the note, and cupped my hands so only I could see. Whispering grew stronger, while Miss Brynjolfsen rapped her ruler on her desk. Finally a *girl,* crazy as it sounds, spoke right out loud. But then, on the last day of school, anything can happen. In sing-songy fashion, lilting, missing only the sad violin, Judy said, *"What does the note say?"* That was ridiculous. She knew; they all knew.

Miss Wilkinson had no patience with playground fighters. Even guys who fought back against the fight-starter caught heck. The instigator had no chance. In fact, Stretch Johnson was already gone. Jelly had the dope on him. He whispered, "Wilkinson turned him into juvenile court . . . too many fights." In his excitement Jelly said right out loud. "Officer Gwin came and took Johnson away in his police car."

Some boys murmured, girls clapped, and Terry said, "Hope they keep him in jail."

Being rid of Stretch, even for a short time, was a small victory. But I still had to face Miss Wilkinson. I was stunned by her simple note, so beautifully written. Her perfectly crafted words were done in ink pen. She looped her large letters smoothly, like one of the signers of the Constitution. She wrote: "David, You will please come to my office promptly at five past twelve today. Be prepared to discuss your playground behavior." Below that she signed her name artistically, and three times larger than the sentence before it. Her "Miss Lily Wilkinson" deserved an A++ in penmanship, especially for its finish, which continued on from the "n," looping back to underline her name. Below her name she printed, large and bold: PRINCIPAL, meaning: *"I have the authority to keep you in school all summer, if I decide to."*

At noon dismissal I hurried to the central staircase, where I stopped to map my strategy. A few of my friends piled in around me, including Jelly. "Good luck, Eric," he said. "Just tell her your side. She's not as mean as she looks." Jelly, a dependable good buddy, was trying to buck me up.

Jim, though—*How could he enjoy teasing a guy in my predicament?* He squinched me his joker's grin and whispered, "Nothin' to it. Relax your butt muscles so's the paddle doesn't make blisters."

I took a deep breath, and started the climb, regretting I hadn't gone to pee first. The stairs creaked and scuffed with fifth and sixth graders coming down. I jostled past them, laughing teasers and twittering girls, all knowing full well my predicament: anyone going up at noon was headed for purgatory or worse. I turned the loop for the third floor flight with its shinier, polished stair-steps. They were un-trafficked steps, mostly used by Miss Wilkinson and Mr. Pederson to get to their lookout windows in the third floor foyer, and—somewhere up there, her command room—her principal's office.

At the top of the stairs, I stopped to study the terrain. I was scared; yet, I savored this small and secret victory, like sneaking into enemy headquarters. I allowed a quick fantasy: if I could just cross the room and stand at Miss Wilkinson's outpost.

The foyer room was almost as tall as wide . . . a hollow, empty place that magnified sound, including seconds to doom ticking from the official wall clock. The clock was big as a truck tire. It said two minutes after 12—three more minutes . . .

A thick rope hung from the corner next to the clock. This afternoon Miss Wilkinson would nod, and Mr. Pederson would pull three glorious times, ringing the "Liberty Bell" mounted on the roof of Central School. *You children are free, free, free,* the bell would ring . . . except for Stretch, the dirty rat, and me. In minutes I would know for sure.

On my left Miss Wilkinson's door stood open. Because of the creaky stairs, she would know I had arrived. I stood back around the door-jam, thinking of peeking around the corner. Maybe she's waiting for me to pee my pants here in the hallway instead of at her desk. Should I wait for the minute hand to spell exactly 12:05 as she instructed?

I dawdled, arranging my thoughts. Finally, time to go; I took a step and looked in. Miss Wilkinson dwarfed her wooden desk. She examined a sheet of paper, elbows propped, her hands forming a tent in front of her big bosom. A huge golden brooch rested there at the top of that big pink valley. She studied the paper through small wire-rimmed spectacles. I took a deep breath and knocked on the door frame.

Miss Wilkinson didn't answer right off, but plucked her glasses, letting them fall and hang from gold chain tethers. She looked up and peered into my eyes. She beckoned with flicking fingers and one word, "Come." I sidled forward, slowly, on shaky legs. I stood before her with my hands in front of my belly like a perfect choir boy. While I waited for her to start grilling, I moved my eyes left and right beyond her desk looking for Mr. Pederson's notorious paddle.

Before this moment, I saw her a few times walking the main floor hallway, where everyone gave her a wide berth. Mostly, though, I saw her from below, on the playground. Day after day she posed regally high up at her command post, looking down on her subjects.

From the distant playground below, Miss Wilkinson appeared as an orange-red figure. Now, close up, I learned why. Her color blasted: silky orange dress, red-orange hair, and the pinky-red skin of her face, neck, and shoulders. Her eyelids slanted, drooping across her rusty eyes, spooky eyes. Why, I can't explain, maybe because I'd never seen a human person like her.

"David," she said, tapping the paper on her desk, "did you provoke Kenneth?"

"No ma'am," I said.

Miss Wilkinson pursed her lips and surveyed me up and down, finally targeting my eyes. When she spoke, her overgrown eyelids drooped even more. I thought of her as a lumpy orange wizard who knew everything about everybody. She was perfectly at ease, in no hurry to sentence me. I stood waiting forever, thinking of confessing how sorry I was. *Let's get it over,* I was thinking. *Bring in ol' Pederson to whack on me. I can't stand the suspense.*

Finally, licking her plain lips, Miss Wilkinson hinted a decision was on its way. She pinched her glasses tighter onto her nose and glanced at her note paper, which gave me relief from her ambered eyes. I noticed a single long white hair growing from a mole poking from the corner of her dimpled chin.

She tapped her pen, then pointed it at me. "Did you tease him?" she asked. The white mole hair bobbed when she talked. Later, I thought it over, wondering: *Dang her hide, she saw me staring. Does she grow the hair on purpose?*

"No ma'am, I didn't tease him," I said. She waited, staring at me with—surprisingly—a hint of a smile. Fortunately I didn't need to fib. If I'd been forced to, it wouldn't have worked, not with her. I shook my head and repeated: "No ma'am, I haven't any reason to tease him."

Miss Wilkinson paused, studying her notes, upside down words too small for me to make out. Her notes were sparse, but contained important words she'd underlined.

She let her glasses fall again and stared right into my brain. I tried to look tough and innocent at the same time. Instead, the only thing I pulled off was scared. I shuffled my feet so she wouldn't notice my knees quivering. Miss Wilkinson ran her tongue across her lower lip. She bobbed her head three times, a sign like my mom's that says, "I have decided."

Miss Wilkinson raised her eyes to mine. She lifted her index finger; it seemed a gentle finger. I believed her eyes to be smiling. Then incredibly, "I'm pleased to hear, David, in your own words, that you didn't tease Mr. Johnson. You are dismissed."

"Uh," I began, edging toward saying, "Thank you," but I couldn't put words together with a jillion summer possibilities suddenly running wild: Stony Ford tomorrow? . . . And the next day and the day after that?—gopher hunting at the Fox Walk; arrowhead hunting; building a new raft for the Fishhook Bend . . .

As I turned to leave, Miss Wilkinson picked up her pen and wrote on her note paper, possibly, "David Erickson, tells the truth; he's a good boy." Well, I hoped it anyway. I left her room confused. I'd confirmed what everyone thought about her fearsomeness; yet, she'd maintained a glint of smile throughout. She'd spoken softly. Try as I might, I couldn't put my finger on mean-ness.

I walked out and across the foyer, reaching the top of the staircase as fast as the law allowed. Halfway down the first flight I said *to heck with the law* and leaped a few steps. As I turned the corner to the next flight, I heard Mr. Pederson's clomps coming up. He glared at me in passing. "Slow down 'dere; you cud brek a lek." Heeding his warning, I reached the bottom in six seconds instead of three. The light of noontime freedom glanced through the front entrance windows. Holding back until the second I reached the threshold of the wide double doors, which Mr. Pederson had locked open, I raced through the doorway, jumped the outdoor staircase, and ran for the playground. I . . . had surprised them all. No, on second thought, Miss Wilkinson—bless her—had done the surprising.

Even fifth and sixth graders crowded around, wanting to know. I felt heroic, even though I didn't deserve it. Stretch had whipped me with one blow. Nevertheless, I relished the questions: "What happened?"—"You get one week or two?"—"You and Stretch git paddled?" Stretch and me in the same sentence! The idea put me in the league of tough guys. My chest felt bigger, and my legs swaggered all on their own.

After a short noon time game of pump, pump pullaway, I gobbled a peanut butter sandwich and returned to class, where I spent much of the time trying to see the minute hand move. We'd be dismissed early today, at three o'clock, celebrated by the "Liberty Bell" ringing its three big bongs from the roof of Central School.

Miss Brynjolfsen used the afternoon hours to glorify us, but deep down I suspect she was relishing her own summer freedom, too. "Children, I will pass out your report cards now. First, I'm pleased to announce that everyone in this room will pass to fourth grade. Your classmate, Mr. Johnson, you must know, has behavior problems, so he must successfully complete two weeks of summer detention." I wanted to yell out, "Yeah!" and the extra pain from my swollen jaw would have been worth it. I'm sure Jelly, and a few others who'd been banged up by Stretch, silently celebrated too. Still, what was the point of being mean about it? Summer detention should be reserved for thieves and robbers. Gladness for his troubles mixed with regret summed up my feelings for Stretch Johnson. Some worry, too. If he passed out of detention, I'd have more of him in my fourth grade classroom, as well as on the playground.

At five minutes before three, Miss Brynjolfsen gave up, nothing left for the fight. The guys and I sat squirming, with one-half of our butt cheeks hanging in the aisle, ready to run. Miss Brynjolfsen raised her eyes to the ceiling, waiting . . .

Two floors directly overhead, ol' Pete would clamp his huge hands on "da bell rope." He'd soon be rid of "da leetul basturs." Miss Wilkinson, standing at her lookout, with eyes on the giant wall clock, would give the command, Mr. Pederson would yank the rope, and a minute later we'd stream out of the doors and race across the playground. Miss Wilkinson would still be standing at her window, on duty even then, still searching for bad actors.

When the second hand swept to 12, Principal Wilkinson would nod, and . . . *holy cow! She did it!* "BONG, BONG, BONG." Pederson must have hung his 250 pounds on "da rope." The huge bell, "Liberty Crack" and all, rattled windows from its roof perch four stories above us.

On the second "BONG," I jumped to my feet and bolted for the door, joining the kids stampeding through the hallways, like calves zapped by electric prods. In the background I heard Miss Brynjolfsen plead, "No running, please! Stop! No running!"

As we reached the twin doors opening onto the school yard, Mr. Pederson rang the bell one more time, for good luck or good riddance. We boiled out across the playground, running the streets, yelling for the whole town to hear, "Yaaay, school's out, school's out!" Central School's Liberty Bell had never gonged so sweet and pure. I never looked back. *Muddy River, here we come!*

Somehow I had escaped school exactly on time, but not without cost. I was left frizzle-frazzled by that last day. And I had a feeling that the rest of the Muddy River guys were off-kilter too, what with the long winter, spring that never arrived, crabby teachers, and endless days of school.

When Jim jerked me out of bed on Saturday morning, we had no packsacks ready and no plans. Nobody had taken charge this time. Jack said we'd try for Metzer's Lake, 11 miles out. Buck had argued for the Lindvig holes . . . "I heard they're full of walleyes," he said.

We'd fly out of town, that's all I knew. Probably decide on our final destination on the beach at Stony Ford. "I poured you some Wheaties," Jim said. "We're leaving in 20 minutes."

"What about 4-H?" I reminded Jim. "Floyd Clausen said anyone who doesn't show up today for the bus trip won't play on his 4-H basketball team next winter."

"Clausen! He takes the cake, tryin' to make farmers out of us on the first day of summer."

"We're still on the 4-H rolls. I saw our names."

"Yah, but ride a bus? Where the heck is he going?" Jim asked the question haphazardly, his brain locked on some faraway place. My answer wouldn't amount to a hill of beans.

Jim scurried about, while I strategized how we could play 4-H basketball without being loyal 4-H'ers. As Jim dug about in the bottom of his fishin' gear drawer, I negotiated for his cooperation, though I noticed the lack of *want to* in my voice. "Clausen has us programmed for the Madsen Ranch. We're supposed to learn how to judge beef cattle. It could be fun."

"Huh! Sounds like more school to me. If you're goin' with me, get your stuff; while you're at it, grab some extra hooks for me." Jim strapped his BB gun across his handlebars and we headed out. Our backpacks held two cans of pork and beans, oatmeal cookies, worms, Hershey Bars, and throw-lines.

We stood on our pedals, racing up 11th Street and through Chief Olson's forbidden East Side. We stopped to wait for our guys next to the CITY LIMITS sign, where disconnected souls milled about on the street. The Lundby brothers, off their bikes, edged toward a fist fight. A pod of West-siders rode their bikes in a circle, eyeing Jim and me, making us nervous. Fortunately, Buck and Jack rode up, and the West-siders took off down the hill toward Horseshoe Bend. Other kids filtered onto the Muddy River Road. They wore blank, numbskull faces, and wandered like motherless lambs.

Jeez, it ain't just me, I thought. They've all got cooties on the brain. Summer freedom, it can cause the crazies.

Without a word, Buck swung onto his bike and started north. Jim and I, Jack, and the Bervigs followed. Next to the last house on the north edge of town we found Jack waiting by the roadside, perched on his polished blue Schwinn, close to a pair of jackrabbits nibbling lawn grass. The rabbits were so tame and citified that Jack ignored them even though he carried a Red Ryder BB gun retrofitted with double powerful spring pistons, enough to cold cock a rabbit at close range.

"I told Buck we'd meet up here," Jack said.

"Besides that promise," I said to myself, "Jack is having too much fun wising-off here."

"Look at 'em," Jack laughed, "a bunch of Oklahomers." He'd been to the same matinee as Jim and me, where frantic land rushers raced for free land. They'd lost their senses, bending under heavy packsacks, pushing wheelbarrows, and racing lathered horses harnessed to bouncing wagons. Similarly, the road to Muddy River was strung with hikers, bikers, and a kid putting along on a homemade motorbike—the kind with a wash machine motor bolted to the cargo rack of a bent-framed bicycle (I'd seen several like it, every one bent crooked from wrecks). A pair of bigger guys, Bob Craven and Larry Gaudreau, stood arguing by the gravel pit crossroads, Craven pointing north, and Gaudreau east.

I recognized the fractured mood and its randomness: young and old kids in twos, threes, fours, and a loner kid weaving to and fro on a bike with a 10 foot cane pole over his shoulder.

"Gol dang, the whole town's headed out," Jim said. "If we don't get going, Stony Ford's gonna be overrun."

"Hah, they don't know how to fish, Eric. We'll take over when they give up." Not that Jack cared so much. We could always move up to Fishhook bend or to Lindvig's. But Jack liked nothing better than to spar with Jim. Before the two of them could settle their argument, here came the whackiest deal of all: Johnny Lund and Little Ergie trying to ride girl bikes, a cousin's and a sister's. I say *trying*, because they were crappy bike riders. This may have been Ergie's first ride. He wobbled two ways, three, then crashed into the ditch. He recovered quickly and ran his sister's bike in amongst us, furrowing his blond eyebrows, pressing for an answer, "Where we going today?" Buck and Jack allowed only sideways glances, inasmuch as they were locked in an intellectual discussion about bikes and girls.

"Why is it, Buck?" Jack asked, "Girls get bikes without the nut busting cross bar when they don't have nuts?"

"I dunno. Why don't you ask your sister? Maybe girls have a secret doo-jingy that hurts as bad as crushed nuts." But I knew Jack wouldn't ask his sister. She was grown up beyond her years, no-nonsense, one in the gang that de-pantsed Razzie for his ice-ball attack.

Jim didn't wait to learn intriguing facts about girls. He pedaled away up Muddy River Road. "I'm going to Stony Ford," he called back over his shoulder.

The rest of us shoved off after him. You'd have thought a race starter had fired his gun. We stood our pedals, pumping to gain the first rise of hill. We topped the rise and there below, in the road's swale, rode the Shetland riders of the Northside Girl Posse—that was our private name for them. They broke into a jiggedy trot, but not fast enough to keep us from passing them—except for Ergie and Johnny, far behind, and—as for getting to Stony—they'd make it eventually.

On this first warm day of summer every dependable bug, bird, and critter let fly with crazy happiness: chirping, buzzing, warbling, croaking, and whizzing wings up and down the valley. We'd waited all winter and through week after week of icy spring winds for a day like this.

Jim still held the lead coming off the western ridge at top speed. Stony crossing lay dead ahead, a quarter mile down the prairie road.

Tradition powered our race. In a string of bikes, we flew down the road and peeled right, in front of the falls, our bikes airborne off the road-bank, then skidding and sliding through the black sand beach. We dropped our bikes and ran to the shore, stood gazing, mesmerized again, inhaling the Muddy's special fragrance, the "armpit of the turtle."

We'd made the trip from town in 30 minutes, a record. Now it was time to breathe river air and look. As always, Stony's waterfall and its broad pool intrigued and beckoned: swift swirling currents, deep and gentler walleye water, back eddies, and a favorite pocket rounding the curve of beach that could school 500 yellow bullheads bellied to the sand bottom.

We dug into pockets and packsacks for gear and dropped to our knees, anxious for "bullheading" . . . except for Jim; he didn't claim a spot on the shore, but stood gazing southeast to the ridge bordering the valley. His glazed-over expression told me Stony Ford wouldn't hold him that day. "You fishin' today?" I asked. Jim didn't answer; I doubt he heard.

Our mother, the English teacher, knew the insides of Jim and doubtless had a match from one of her literary characters. "Jim has gathered in the biology of Grandma Erickson's Cree ancestry," she said. In time I came to comprehend her insight into people. Unlike Mom, my understanding surfaced after years of thrashing about, trying to discover what made Jim tick.

Well before Stony Ford of 1945 and many times after, I witnessed Jim's unquenchable curiosity, his wanderlust, and keen expectations. Like our Grampa Erickson, Jim has always been driven by far off dreams. The two of them could have been "blood brothers," despite 55 years difference. Their kinship showed clearly on a fishing trip to northern Canada.

In June of 1950, Jim and I and Grampa Erickson were crossing Manitoba's giant Lake Athapapuskow in an 18 foot wooden boat with a weakling outboard. Northern pike, lake trout, walleyes . . . Gramp would find them all before our trip was over. Early June felt more like February up there with the Arctic Circle just over the brow of the globe. Five miles out we emerged from the shelter of pine topped rock islands into the full force of a cold front streaming out of the Arctic. "We'll cross over to Lost Bay where we can duck out of the wind," Grampa said.

Slanting, wind driven snow turned worse: to sloppy bone-chilling sleet. At the tiller, Grampa drove us head on into the sleet, bucking three foot swells. Jim perched on the board seat in front of Gramp. Though he had the option of facing rearward with his back to the icy spray, he didn't. Jim faced ahead, playing a ducking game with each sheet of spray breaking from the bow, soaking him.

I sat on the bow seat facing to the rear, shivering ever deeper into my mackinaw and heavy windbreaker. I allowed a faint hope that forlorn misery upon my unwhiskered 12 year old face would convince Grampa he should turn the boat downwind and head for the warm cabin. Yet, I knew better. Grampa sat steady, blue eyes intent on the distant green line of pine trees, his countenance like Teddy Roosevelt's rock face on Mount Rushmore. Same confident grin, too.

As our boat crested and plunged with each new wave, I ducked low, under the spray. Gramp, though, was so intent on knifing the boat perfectly through the next dangerous wave, that he couldn't be bothered with drenching ice water. He tucked his chin slightly, with his straw hat brim flopped over his forehead, his sole protection from misery. Water streamed from his reddish Swede face. What were Grampa's intense blue eyes smiling about?—and likewise, Jim's brown ones? I needed most of my growing up years to fully understand.

You know what they say about a picture and a thousand words. I saw Grampa Erickson as the Viking sailor and Jim the Cree scout. They never twitched or squirmed throughout the hour's frightening voyage across Athapapuskow. They canted forward on their plank seats, looking for the entrance to Lost Bay, or perhaps imagining its three foot long pike coasting through the reeds, and golden walleyes finning deep among shadowed rocks.

They were *leaners*—Gramp and Jim—leaning into the world of possibilities. Whatever the transportation, be it boat, tractor, or wheeling a truck, they leaned anxiously forward. Even on horseback. I know John Wayne sat regally in the saddle, straight as a corral post. But Grampa in his own way looked every bit as noble, tilting forward, chin over the saddle horn, surveying wooded coulees to spot the cagy snag-horned bull. Just like Jim at Stony Ford on the first day of summer, 1945, leaning forward, seeking new adventures.

Jim's fevered antsies ran only a degree or two higher than ours on our first day of summer freedom. Not even our favorite fishing place could hold us for long. Well, there were exceptions. The Bervig brothers and a pair of recruits teamed up to rebuild the ford part of Stony Ford. Oh, and not to forget Razzie and Stahl, as dependable as thin clouds in a drought. One day those two rascals were on board as regular Muddy River guys, the next not. Today they were not. They showed up with two stolen bottles of beer. They sat next to the water without fishing, clinking beer bottles, laughing, and blowing smoke from reed stogies. "We're gonna get drunk to celebrate the end of school," Razzie said.

"I'm climbing for the Fox Walk trail," Jim said. "Who wants to go?" Stony had lost its appeal, tainted by nasty stolen beer, and a noisy crowd of kids tangling throw lines, horning in on each other for a spot on the shores. Even Jim's favorite getaway nook on the east bank was occupied. Over there, across the pool, the Stewart brothers and their cousin waded waist deep in their underwear, probing under the cut bank for snapping turtles to bring home for the family's famous turtle soup. We watched the Stewart boys reach deeper, feeling for turtle dens under the bank. They laughed to hide their fears: feeling, hoping the cold, pointy thing deep under the bank was the snapper's tail, not the beak with horny jaws that could snap off a finger.

Since Bervig's bridge building was far from finished, Jim declared his plan to cross the swift channel below Stony Ford pool. He waded in first, followed by Jack and Buck in front of me, with their BB guns across their shoulders and high-topped shoes necklaced around their necks, like Marines in the Grande Theatre newsreels.

Ergie arrived just in time to tag onto our expedition. In tennis shoes, he waded behind me, but in midstream he lost his footing and went down and under. Ergie surfaced downstream, dogpaddling, cheered on by Jack and Buck: "Go, Ergie, go!"

"A white headed beaver," Jim said. "All he needs is a stick in his mouth." As if to prove the point, Ergie crawled out on the bank, shaking water from his heinie head. Buck gave him little time to catch up.

"Hurry it up, Ergie," Buck admonished. "You're holding back our patrol."

"And wring those socks or you'll get blisters," Jack ordered—*officers* instructing and *privates* nodding heads—we naturally fell into army "patrol" mode. Before the day was over, we'd be something different, explorers having more fun.

Our patrol clamored up the slope, found the Fox Walk trail, and scattered . . . scavenged about looking for arrowheads, rabbits to shoot at, and looking for . . . I don't know; I found Jack sitting on a flat-topped rock, gazing north. "Before summer's gone, I want to see into Canada," he said.

"Yeah, well Jim's headed the wrong direction," I said.

"That's him, Wrong Way Corrigan," Jack laughed. We scrambled to our feet, and ran to catch Jim and the guys lined out on the Fox Walk trail, headed southeast.

Jim was squirrelly impatient. Only long-legged Jack could keep up with him walking fast. The rest of us mostly trotted. Our hurried travel felt good, probably did us some good too, like Gramp roaring his Nash's motor "getting the gunk out."

A few hundred feet above us, scattered white clouds scooted along in the breeze, going our way along the ridge. Wild rose in its full bloom flooded the ridge with its potion. From the high bluffs we had an eagle's view of the Little Muddy valley, and its meandering river and sheltered coves, where the river promised lunker fish of every sort. Our trail dipped and squiggled through rocks, prickled-pear cactus, and Brer Rabbit buffalo-berry patches that forced us to scuttle through on hands and knees.

Over-the-shoulder stories flew about willy-nilly on our hurry up and get somewhere hike: Lewis and Clark paddling canoes, Jim Bridger's run from the Indians, Gramp's horseback trip across Montana. With such talk, the faint path soon became an "Indian trail" going south to who-knows-where. Instead of bare heads, we should have worn coonskin caps.

Jim had one destination tucked away all along. An hour after crossing the river, we gathered around him, where he posed on a point of bluff. Jim waved the air like a priest or medicine man consecrating the blessedness of the wide countryside below. "This is it!" he shouted, "Lewis and Clark's lookout." The Mighty Missouri curved away in the distant south, and the delicate Little Muddy River wandered every whichaways across its grassy valley, in no hurry to join the Missouri.

None of us had been up on the promontory before, though Jim and I knew of its significance. Three years ago, when Gramp took us to the Scenic Highway Bridge he had pointed out this very lookout on the bluff, telling us of Lewis and Clark standing up there gazing upon thousands of buffalo and antelope, herd upon herd, as far as they could see.

No wonder Lewis and Clark wrote of this place. Wow! This lookout gave us the biggest view in the territory. What we knew of life's playground stretched out before us: the gray jumble of town across the valley, and more importantly—everything surrounding town. North of town, Spring Lakes Park showed deep green against the prairie. Beyond the park, steep hills opened to reveal the Little Muddy River curling south, then tumbling at Stony Ford and snaking southward. The Muddy seemed to lose its way at Horseshoe Bend, abruptly turning west, before looping east, headed for the Scenic Highway bridge.

Horseshoe Bend, so close to town, running wide and quietly, was known as a tame place for kids, and also marked our southern limit. Below Horseshoe lay the bad stuff, water bloodied by the packing plant and—worse yet—the city dumpground.

"Someday let's go downriver from Horseshoe," Jim said. "We can hike to the mouth of the Muddy, maybe fish in the Missouri."

"We'll never get permission," Jack said. "Not with the filthy dumpground and the Big Missouri so close . . . too dangerous."

"We can always ask," Jim said. "You're the oldest, Jack. You try first."

"Ya, Jack. You try," Buck said. "You're the best talker. We've just gotta go see the Missouri."

"The Jungle, too," Jim added. "I can see it from here." A glint of sun showed the Missouri's wide bend where the Little Muddy joined the big river, and upriver from there: the long green sweep of willows and swamps—a wilderness called the Jungle.

Luck had given us a perfect day for the Lookout. Last night's drencher sweetened the air. And now a mellow breeze came over us, returning good memories from last summer. We plopped down around the diggings mound of a badger hole, all except for Jim with "ants in his pants." Jim turned this way and that, gazing far and wide, searching.

Conversation turned easily backward, into history, with Buck and Jack ever ready to imagine. Jack wondered aloud: "Buck, do they call it buffalo grass because buffalo ate it?"

"Heck no. It's about the smell. At the Minot Zoo I could have reached through the wire and scratched a big bull buffalo. He smelled just like this buffalo grass." Buck pulled a handful of gnarly buffalo grass entangled with shriveled Indian potatoes. "Last year's crop," Buck said. He thrust the pungent stuff into Jack's face and Jack quickly returned a fistful. A short fracas. Even small fights had no chance on a perfect day like this one.

Far below, along the bend of the Muddy's Horseshoe, tiny specks moved about—had to be bullhead fishers lounging the shore. From up on the Lookout, feeling superior to them came easy. Though they could have traveled on, further from the drab confines of civilized town, the suckers chose to put up with their own crowding. Yet, if they knew better, well—we wouldn't like the consequences. Too many like us would ruin the country.

Ten minutes of Lookout time was enough to transform us. No more army patrol. Rather, the infectious jargon of Indians and explorers set in. We yapped away, pretending we knew their ways: Buck with his big arms crossed like a chief, "The Yellowstone two moon travel." Jack added the white man trader's version, borrowing expressions like "out yonder." Little Ergie spoke of "griz and wooves."

"We should travel up into the Stony Creek country sometime, spend a few days exploring," Jim expounded. He'd turned to face the prairied hills rolling off to the east, for want of something impressive, exaggerated as "high country." You'd have thought Jim was smiling upon the foothills of the Rockies.

The Stony Creek highlands rose only 300 feet or so above the valley of the Missouri River; yet, they promised untrammeled spring-greened hills that cradled secretive little Stony Creek. "We could stay out in those hills all summer," Jim said. "We've got matches, guns, and fishin' lines . . . all we need."

"Don't know about all summer," Buck said, "but I'd sure like to check out the deep holes up there on Stony Creek. My dad says walleyes go over the spillway at Springbrook Dam. He says in high water years they probably scatter all the way down the creek."

Jack shook his head and turned, ready to go back the way we'd come. "Stony Creek will have to wait. My brand new Schwinn is stashed at the Ford. If it gets swiped, my dad will disown me."

Jim beckoned him. "Hold on, Jack; just a little farther. We'll hike to the bluffs where we can look up into Stony Creek Coulee. The rail line goes through there, but no roads. It doesn't get explored. When we get past Eastland's chicken farm, well . . . that's the end of civilization."

Jim's ploy hit familiar notes of bare-bones exaggeration: simplistic, stupid, but somehow workable. I can't explain why, but we fell for his game time and again: "Just a bit farther, then we'll turn around," until a "bit farther" found us 10 miles from town in a snowstorm or lost in the willow jungles.

"Well, I'm going. Who's coming with?" Jim said, adding his clincher: "We've come this far, we ought to just hike to the spring holes."

"Well, that's where the walleye would be," Buck agreed.

If not for the unlikely event that came next, we could have laughed Jim's far-fetched visions away in the wind. Call it fate, or—if we could total more than a nickel's worth of Indian blood in the bunch of us—we could lay it to "good medicine."

"Look, it's plain to see. This trail leads over the hill, headed for Stony Creek and . . ." Jim began. Suddenly, he dropped to his knees on the path, "Whoa, whoa." He spread his arms like protective wings, sheltering his prize. He plucked a glassy black shard from the sand: "Holy moley! Look what I found!—an obsidimum arrowhead, just like the one in Gramp's collection. Obsidimum arrowheads are from the Rocky Mountains. They got traded out to the plains tribes. And this one was pointed right up the trail toward Stony Creek Valley."

We gathered close while Jim passed his prized arrowhead around, following the chain of command, lastly to Little Ergie, who put it in his pocket and feinted running away, until Jack collared him.

Jack handed the treasure back to Jim, then Jim to me for safe keeping. I spit on it, polished it on my pants. It was delicate, just a smidge longer than my thumbnail, but skinnier. I tested the edge. With a bit of pressure it could have cut my finger deep. The arrowhead was perfectly beautiful, damaged only by a nick in its shoulder.

Because I know what happened next, and then after that: how Jim and Buck became famous and Jack, Ergie, and I half-famous just for being with them . . . because I know all of that, I'm declaring Jim's obsidimum arrowhead an omen, 'cuz omens can happen to white kids too, not only Indians. Besides, omens aren't like Indian good medicine that needs asking for. Omens just drop on people for no reason that people understand, like how we happened to end up there at the Lookout, and practically everything else about this day that was becoming more exciting by the minute.

We trotted out behind Jim, eastward, following a faint trail in the buffalo grass. Though now only printed here and there by jackrabbits and deer, the path must have been used first by Indians. It rode the crest of the hills separating the Muddy River Valley and the Stony Creek drainage. Gramp had said, "Indian trails followed ridgelines, where they could watch for enemies in two valleys at once." Jim waved us onward toward Stony Creek. "Trail go to green grass hills," said Jim, the Indian scout . . . "un plenty good water."

Within fast-traveled minutes we crossed the high plain east of the Lookout, crossed the gentle divide, and walked a bluff that faced the valley of Stony Creek. The bluff was steep and high, maybe 300 feet; not really a bluff. I say it qualified as a cliff—not a coyote-roadrunner cliff, where the coyote falls, whistling like a rocket, faster, faster to 200 miles an hour, enough to splat a five foot deep spread-eagled coyote crater in the desert. The cliff above Stony Creek wasn't like that; but, if you slipped and fell from it, your ten fingers gouging furrows into the hard baked clay wouldn't save you. You'd tumble backwards and bounce, roll, go airborne, and bam against the cliffside again and again, breaking legs, and go "umph" and be dead as a doornail at the bottom.

In other words, the cliff—I'm declaring it a cliff—became another exciting place. Yet, I saw disappointment on scowly faces, scouring at Eastland's daggone chicken farm laid out down there across the creek from this very cliff and only a holler away. Old Jess Eastland, the "Chicken Man," had spotted us, cupped his hands around his mouth, and hollered big enough we heard his words reverberate up the cliffside ravines, "You boys . . . get down . . . offa' there. Yur' on . . . *MY* . . . properdy. I don't allow . . . *NOBODY* . . . up there. You could git yerselfs . . . *KILT!*" Eastland stood in the middle of his scattered buildings and rickety chicken pens with his hands on hips, glowering; had to be glowering, though his face was too distant to see. The big man hollered on, an angry finger jabbing his mad words.

"Jim, you fibbed," Jack said. "You said Stony Creek wasn't spoilt."

"It ain't. We just gotta get around Eastland's place. Besides, chickens gotta live someplace." Jim waved cheerfully across the distance to Mr. Eastland, who stood yelling amongst hundreds of white chickens, some clustered in pens, others running free.

The Chicken Man cupped his hands around his mouth and hollered, louder than before, "I said git the *HELL*—down offa' there."

"We're comin'," Jim hollered back. "We're lookin' for a way down."

Jim motioned us onward, "Let's go guys," he whispered, as if Eastland could hear us from way down there. Jim had no intention of surrendering to no grumpy ol' Chicken Man. He nimbled his way along the cliffside trail; Buck too, one big slow foot at a time, scared, even though he'd claimed to have climbed to the top of a real Montana mountain once. The last three of us strung out behind, creeping along the narrow trail. The trail was covered in greasy, wet clay. If not for looking stupid, I would have crawled.

Up ahead, Jim rounded a jut-out in the cliff and stopped. He crouched, gripping his BB gun. Without turning around, he waved for Buck to come alongside. He fluttered his hand faster, meaning, *"Hurry Buck."* Buck edged forward on hands and knees, tight to the bank. He joined Jim, where they crouched together, hip-to-hip, with no room to spare. They stared ahead, mesmerized by something. Then they raised their guns, and the simultaneous firing of their customized BB guns "punged" as one. "Got him," Buck hollered.

Jack crept forward, and I followed on his heels. Ergie bumped me, wanting to push past to see, but a-scared of the edge. Jim and Buck crawled forward, out of sight, around the bend, and their excitement whisked back at us. "I hit him, I hit him," Jim yelled.

"I got him, too," Buck declared.

"He's hurt bad," Jim said—the overblown claim I'd heard before, when I watched him hunt. I knew full well a copper BB has a slim chance of downing a thickly feathered pheasant or a fur-coated jackrabbit.

Our commotion and hollering seemed to make Eastland madder than ever. Now that we'd rounded the easterly curve in his creekside bluff, he couldn't see us. I heard faintly, "What . . . the goddam hell's . . . goin' on . . . up there?"

"Don't know any more than you do, you old coot," I wanted to yell. Instead, I hollered up ahead, to the disappeared Jim and Buck, "What the heck did you shoot?"

Another few feet of scootching around the bend and . . . there, Jim and Buck on their knees, were peering down a black hole in the vertical bank. The narrowed hole, guarded by jutting timbers, was an old mine shaft. "All right, what happened?" Jack demanded.

Jim and Buck pulled back then, so we could join them, sitting in a row, our backs against the vertical bank, legs stretched across the trail. Jim gulped and blew air as if he'd been holding his breath all this time. As he talked, he never took his eyes from the hole. "It's his den . . . BOBCAT! HUGE! Not even scared of us. We . . . we wounded him bad, though."

"Not him . . . a her, and she's got kittens," Buck said. "Look over there. See those tiny cat tracks? White feathers, too, strung right down into her den."

"We need a volunteer to go and tell Eastland we found his chicken killer," Jack said.

Jim crawled over to the hole again. He held his hand up for silence. "Listen, I can hear her breathing."

I crawled in close to Jim. Ergie pushed past me. "I wanna' see." That's when Buck crawled forward. He pulled on back pockets, jerking us back.

"She comes charging out of there, she'll knock you guys right off the cliff. I say we leave her alone. Now I'm hopin' we didn't hurt her bad. Her kittens will starve without her." Buck backed against the side of the ledge bank, pursed his lips and blew, too dry to whistle. "She was gonna charge, wasn't she, Jim?"

"Dang right. She crouched just like a panther, ready to spring. Probably thought we were going after her babies.

"Jeez, wait till the Chicken Man finds out," I offered. "Maybe he'll give you guys a reward."

"He's not gonna find out," Jim said. "I agree with Buck. Eastland can afford a chicken now and then for a cat family."

Jack surveyed faces. His own face seemed suddenly older, without a smile or one of his easy-to-come cackling laughs. "Bobcats are nothin' to fool with, you guys. They can carry rabies. Still, in case this one doesn't, she deserves a chance to raise her kittens up."

"You're right, Jack," Jim said. "We're not telling anybody; otherwise, word might get back to Eastland."

Buck spoke up, knowing this business, more like an eighth grader instead of fifth. "No, we're not saying a word. Once the govermint trapper gets told, he'll come out and trap the whole family of bobcats. The dadgum Chicken Man would call him if he knew."

Speaking of whom, around the bump in the cliff spewed his madness: "I'm dun dun . . . foolin' foolin' . . . with ya ya ya," came his echo. "I'm call'n 'n . . . the sher iff iff iff," bounced up to us.

Jim put his fingers to his lips, and pointed down the trail. "We'll sneak around into that ravine. Eastland will never see us go."

Silently we went, unseen, whispering—conniving our way into a hidden tuck, up and over the bluff-cliff which had grown to "at least 500 feet" in our non-stop storying. By the time we crossed the divide to the Muddy River side, the cat had grown too, now weighing "80 pounds of huge muscle" and not a bobcat at all but, according to Jim, a Canadian lynx that wandered south. "I swear, I saw big ear tufts. Didn't you Buck?"

Jim took the lead again, trotting along, yelling back loud enough that Ergie and I, last in line, could hear: "That trail we were on. It's a regular catwalk. Bet the bobcats and lynxes have used it ever since Indian moccasins wore it into a trail."

And what of the secret spring holes of Stony Creek? . . . Completely—and I mean *completely*—forgotten. Without explaining, Jim swung westward at the top of the bluffs. He broke into a trot, then a lope. We lined out behind him and ran without let-up for 30 minutes. When we came down off the Fox Walk Trail, Bervig's bridge was ready for crossing Stony Ford. I was disappointed to find that the Bervig boys and the Stony Ford crowd had already pulled out for town. The Catwalk story needed telling. Wow! What a day!

Biking home, banter flew steadily, replaying our adventure from every angle. Buck, Jack, and Jim peppered the conversation with reminders about our pledge to protect the chicken thief. What a joke that was! Never was a pledge more quickly and completely abandoned.

How could we expect Little Ergie not to talk about the most exciting adventure of his life? Or, Jim and me? On our way home we detoured to Gram and Gramp's house. The minute we walked in the door, Gramp sensed we carried a big story along with us, and it tickled him, too. He looked us over, took note of pants smeared with Stony bluff clay. "Looks like you Riley boys been out Riley-in,'" Gramp laughed. He hollered into the kitchen, "Gramma, you start the coffee. I'll dish the ice-cream."

As Jim fiddled his spoon in his sugared coffee and cream, he skirted the edge of our story, "Gramp, how do you tell a big bobcat from a lynx?"

By the time Jim drew his next breath, Gramp deciphered the birth of the question. He leaned close to Jim's face. "So, where'd you see one?"

To Gramp's delight we spilled the story then and there, heroically so, in light of Gramp's wisdom about predators and Jess Eastland's ignorance. "Been tellin' Jess for years, the old fool: 'Don't put 'em in decent pens and your chickens will be taken faster than you can raise 'em.'"

Gramp urged us onward, wanting every detail of the Catwalk story. The telling was fun, too (so much for our pledge of secrecy). At home, we told Mom and Dad the full version at suppertime, then Reed Gwin in our backyard, and Grampa Erickson on the telephone. Buck's cousin called, wanting more of what Buck left out. By bedtime probably half our dang town knew about wildcats stealing Eastland's chickens. Just before lights out, Buck called Jim and brought him up to date.

"Wish we hadn't said anything," Jim said from his twin bed next to mine. "They say Jardo Kelley's the best trapper in the country, and . . . ." Before sleep took me, Jim had more worrisome things to say, enough to spawn an awful nightmare about Jardo Kelley's steel traps littering the Catwalk and motherless baby lynxes huddled on a cliff as high as the sky.

By Monday morning the Catwalk story was moving. Neighbors, telephoners, kid friends at the pool, everybody wanted the story. Then, just before supper, a *Herald* reporter called, asking for an interview with Jim.

The reporter met with Buck and Jim at the Luzon Cafe on Tuesday morning—son-of-a-gun, only them, cuz' they were the cat shooters. I went along, took a counter seat where I could watch and maybe hear, too. The reporter put the guys in a cushioned corner booth, treated them to chocolate-marshmallow shakes. What I did hear was mostly Buck's laughing. He and Jim tucked down, whispering, mimicking their hunters' stalk. Jim humped his back like a bobcat or his lynx. Then they both raised pretend guns. The reporter, a skinny gray haired man in a suit and tie, fought to keep up with the action: watch, scribble, and laugh; watch, scribble, and laugh.

The *Herald's* article on Jim and Buck and the Catwalk came out on Sunday, a big hit and partly true. Then Floyd Clausen made his move. The story for him, naturally, was about chicken farming. He invited Jim and Buck to come onto his agriculture radio show for a live interview.

Just before 10 AM on Saturday, Mom tuned her kitchen Philco to the "Floyd Clausen Farm and Ranch Show." Gram and Gramp had come to listen and join the fun. Gramp saved a spot for me next to him at our big, round kitchen table. He poured me coffee, said it would "put hair on my chest," even if I did add sugar and cream.

Only Floyd Clausen, with the exact opposite in mind, could turn the Catwalk Story into comedy. After introducing the boys, Clausen began with Jim. "So, James, you and your friend here, Buck Bundhund, did the right thing. But, when you took on a bobcat with air guns, did you know just how vicious he could be?"

"Naw, not really, and it wasn't a he-cat. She was just a mother cat doing what mother cats do. She took her babies down a dirty ol' coal mine to keep them safe. Sort of wish I hadn't shot at her."

At our kitchen table, Dad nudged Mom. "Jimmy's wearin' his stubborn hat."

"Sshh," Mom said.

Clausen probed patiently, "Well, James, don't feel bad. Don't you know how many valuable farm animals bobcats kill?" *James* again. Mr. Clausen must have picked that up from Jim's 4-H application form.

"Yah, bobcats might get a few. But this cat is a lynx, and my grampa says lynxes won't bother farm chickens for long. They like prairie chickens much better."

"But you said you caught her in the act of slaughtering one of Mr. Eastland's chickens."

"No, I said she might have hunted down a stray one. She had a white feather on her chin whiskers . . . isn't that right, Buck? I s'pose she got close enough to the farm to be tempted and, uh . . . probably grabbed a no-good crippled chicken." With that, Dad began laughing and couldn't quit.

Mom banged the table. "Shush, Bill, I want to hear."

Mr. Clausen came back, persistent: "And perhaps the bobcat, 'er lynx, took many more valuable hens, too, wouldn't you agree James?" The radio crackled, and someone rustled papers. We heard Buck speak, but faintly, not intended for radio transmission. What I believe I heard was, "Mr. Clausen, Jim likes to be called Jim." We waited.

"Ma, turn up the volume," Dad said.

Finally, Clausen came on: "Uh, well, hold on here, boys. Folks, we're going to a commercial," Mr. Clausen's tinny, professional voice announced through the radio. "Back in a minute to learn how two brave young boys came to the rescue of Eastland's Chicken Farm."

We listened to a Bessie the Cow creamery commercial and an ad for Savings Bonds; then came Buck's turn. Mr. Clausen cleared his voice, managed to make even that sound important. "So, young Mr. Bundhund, were you, uh, were you . . . *scared?*"

"Nope, not scared; maybe a mite nervous. Never shot at anything before that growled and had big fangs. But there was two of us and one of her, and we were shooting super-charged BB guns. We put oversized springs in them."

"So, you wounded the predator cat, maybe even killed her?

"Well, she flinched, didn't she Jim? We hit her, but Jim and I think she'll be okay. And she has at least one chicken down in her den for food."

Jim jumped in then, volunteering his belief that for sure it was a Canadian lynx. "She's probably already on her way, taking her kittens back to Canada."

Jim must have had the mike in his hands then because he came in loud over the radio. He said, "Canada is so doggone overrun with snowshoe rabbits that the Stony Creek lynx has no reason to come back here, especially after we stung her pretty good." Of course, that was pure horsepucky. Jim had about a nickel's worth of lynxy knowledge. Clausen had even less, and he was plumb out of ideas. Those of us listening at home thought the radio had gone dead.

Jim came to the rescue (Buck told us later that Jim reached over and took charge of the microphone). Jim said, "Lynxes ain't a farmer's problem, not like bobcats, and foxes are the worstest of all."

Listening to my brother, I puffed up proud. Even when he didn't have professional answers, he sounded professional on radio; having fun too, exaggerating away: "Lynxes are wilder, won't spend much time around farms or people." At home a passing neighbor might have thought a pack of laughing hyenas had taken over our house.

Jim talked over the radio as if he'd done it for years. He loved his chosen subject, too . . . "My Grampa Erickson homesteaded in Canada. He says lynxes live in the wilderness and hunt snowshoe rabbits."

Grampa Millhouse leaned his good ear close to the radio. "Atta' boy, Jimmy," he said.

Floyd Clausen had run out of appropriate academic ammunition. In desperation, he turned to a statistical lecture about 10,000 defenseless baby calves taken—and chickens, ducks, goats, sheep lost—all numbered and accounted for, attributed to culprits ranging from hawks to coyotes and bobcats. At the end of his obituaried accounting, Clausen ad-libbed his guess about the cost of allowing Canadian lynxes to roam free in North Dakota: "Many thousands of dollars, we'll never know for sure. And if Canada doesn't control their lynxes, next we'll have their wolves to contend with. Now, out there in farm country, be sure to call your county agent when you have predators about."

Before he signed off, Mr. Clausen thanked Jim and Buck twice more, and put the audience at ease with the news that Jardo Kelley had been notified and was already on the trail of the dangerous lynx.

Later at home, for all their laughing, Buck and Jim struggled to explain what happened, how a frazzled Floyd Clausen desperately flipped through his farmer's predator book. He found not one word about lynxes. "I thought he was going to cry," Buck said.

In the days to come Jim and Buck faced the inconsistency of the *Herald* story versus Floyd Clausen's reporting. Townfolk blabbered on about the adventuresome tale in the *Herald* and the entertaining radio interview, a sparring match, touching on cantankerous and full of holes. Dad had a simple answer, chuckling as he explained: "Jim and Buck are just plain contrary. If you don't care so much, you'll get the straight story. You push on them, they'll stiff you."

Despite contrariness, the radio interview provided good Main Street fodder. Coffeeing at the Luzon with Gramp, Mr. Snyder didn't bother to hide his thoughts. He nodded at Jim. "Rollie, this grandson of yours . . . I suppose you taught him how to invent looney stories."

"Nope, he comes by it naturally enough." At that, Mr. Snyder's belly laugh nearly shook the Luzon's soda glasses from their shelves. The last laugh, though, was on Mr. Snyder and the doubters up and down Main. As luck would have it, Jardo Kelley walked into the Luzon and came right to our table. I smelled horse manure on his boots, a ranch perfume I'd always strangely appreciated, even in cafés.

"Found your cat, Jimmy," Jardo said with his gap-toothed grin. "At least I know where she's headed." I grimaced, afraid of what was coming next. Jardo had sign; now he'd set traps. Jardo chuckled, grinning proudly . . . "I cut her tracks, two-three days old, three kittens too, found the prints in the mud bank on Stony Creek, headed upstream."

With that, Jim's long face brightened, "Well, that's what I thought," he said. "She's a smart lynx and she's headed northeast to the end of Stony Creek, up and out over the prairie to Canada."

"Jimmy boy, you have quite the imagination," Mr. Snyder said. Across the table from him, Gramp clanked his coffee cup on its saucer, and tilted his head at Jim to deliver his nod, wink, and growly laugh, Gramp's signature approval. In that Luzon moment Jim sat tall. Despite his rascally behavior, or maybe *because* of it, Gramp's wordless pronouncement meant, "He's my grandboy. Ain't he somethin'?" I was only a 7 year old tyke, but I knew Gramp and Jim were two peas in a pod. Two years later Gramp bestowed Jim with his beloved whoopee cushion.

Our discovery of the Catwalk on June first, 1945 brought the Muddy River boys a comical sort of fame, what you get when a pent-up town, desperate for summer, takes the first good story that comes along, grabs it and pitches it far and wide. Besides good timing, the story had optimism—even wandering town kids can help with farmer problems. Folks liked how we happened to set the stubborn Chicken Man straight. Eastland did "eat some crow," Gramp told Jim and me: "He's repairing his pens. And because I'm your grandpa, he moved me up his customer list for fresh eggs."

I needed time and seasoning to piece together the significance of the Catwalk adventure. For the story to happen, it needed a magical place invaded by piss and vinegared boys, who a day earlier had fled schoolhouse jail. The story needed Jim, the "horizon gazer," and most of all—the hungry momma cat. Finally, flavoring the stew was Floyd Clausen, a very earnest and excitable publicist to bless and nurture the tale by putting a couple of Muddy River "heroes" on the radio. Clausen, in his peculiar way, provided talking fodder, pulling townfolk out of their doldrums and starting them into summer. As for the Muddy River boys, the Catwalk was a great beginning to the most wonderful summer ever.

Chapter Seven

Rats, Cats, and Sex Education

. . . and a little mystery to boot, as Dad would say.

After our Catwalk adventure, the Muddy River boys couldn't drink excitement fast enough and not only because of ferocious lynxes and radio notoriety. We ran fast and hard, fueled by the high octane spirit of the adult world as well as our own. If we needed a motto, we could have chosen between "As If There's No Tomorrow" or "Hell Bent For Leather." We youngsters had a vague understanding that without our parents' "Hell Bent For Leather" grit during war times, tomorrow was a worrisome proposition. Tenacity and optimism ruled the times and defined language. Gramp's friends in the Luzon talked of profitable durum wheat and beef on the hoof—"good for the country." And by the optimistic tone of the Grande Theatre's newsreel narrators, the war could be over any day now.

Main Street's expert on the war—Shorty, the funny, hairless barber—enjoyed talking loud over his electric hair clipper: "Tojo's days are numbered (they were numbered during last month's haircut too). "Tojo can't hide forever. My brother's in the Pacific; he's in an outfit that could get Tojo, you know."

Shorty was but a molecule in the national stew called the *"War Effort,"* a phenomenon accounting for our town's frenetic energies. I know that I haven't seen such flurry and determination since. Men left at home—either too old to enlist, or with sons in the war—seemed driven to walk tall. Mr. Snyder was a good example.

Mr. Snyder was the proud owner of the elegant Grande Theatre. "Grande" indeed, with purple velvet curtains, a wide curved stage, fluted white marble side columns, and rich purple carpeted aisles. Besides the fragrance of real buttered popcorn, warm aromas of leather and cigar smoke floated down from the entourage in box seats at the rear, where the plump Mr. Snyder—dressed in vest, coat, and tie—smoked fat cigars and entertained Main Street businessmen and anyone wearing a military uniform. Earlier, throughout the day and prior to his afternoon matinee, Mr. Snyder strolled along Main or lounged about the Luzon Cafe, imploring people to not miss his previewed newsreels. For those without means, Mr. Snyder carried a pocketful of free tickets.

The Grande featured "status of the War" films, always accompanied by an official newsreel optimist in the background putting voice to launchings of new battleships or squadrons of silver fighter planes wheeling out of factories.

Main Street was a striving place for business people and kids too, where we earned money sweeping floors, shining shoes, or setting pins at the raucous Playmore Lanes. Jimmy Bruegger worked the alleys on both sides of Main collecting boxes. Collecting milk bottles, Little Ergie rode his tricycle south on the Main Street sidewalk as far as Walt's Corner Market. Walt gave Ergie a Tootsie Roll or a "Superman" comic for each returned milk bottle.

One of my favorite places was the brilliantly neon-lighted Luzon Café. Our Grampa Rollie Millhouse often took Jim and me to the popular Luzon for coffee, and—I suspect—to show off his grandsons. Jim and I sipped coffee dosed with sugar and thick cream. Waitresses in white, nursey uniforms laughed and fussed over us and brought us doughnuts to dip in our coffees. The Luzon was of another world, where elaborate neon tubes glowed pink, lime-green, and "planetary orange."

The Luzon, the Grande, the Great Northern Hotel, Greengard's Clothing, and the few dozen other stores on Main, including sidewalks, hummed with activity. Having seen no other time or place to compare, I could not have known the source of Williston's inspiration. I thought it normal that my grandmother would not allow a single weed in her garden and that every car on our street was washed weekly. Or, that my friend Karen's dad, Mr. Kinstler, worked 7 days a week, just like many dads. Or, that the city street cleaner drove his machine fast, relentlessly, the song of his beating brushes heard halfway across town.

I supposed because men in uniform had to be neat and clean, towns had to be too. Even kids were spotless. To paraphrase Garrison Keillor: Williston children were all above average in cleanliness—at least in summer. Harmon Park Pool opened at 9:30 each morning, welcoming the flotilla of kids who raised the water level a foot. We were swimming pool bleached all summer.

The pool's stern manager, Helga Sorensen, made us shower before we entered the pool. She'd pop her head into the doorway of the boy's dressing room and sing out, "If I don't hear you in that shower, I'm coming in." The dressing room floor's strong disinfectant removed the dirt as well as a layer of skin, leaving us with two-toned feet, brown tops and white bottoms. The pool itself, heavily dosed with Helga's chlorine prescription, sanitized the rest of us. After the first two weeks of summer swimming, fair-haired girls turned Marilyn Monroe blonde and formerly whitey-heads, like my buddy, Little Ergie, sported lime-green heinie hair. Kids came home from swimming smelling like freshly Chloroxed laundry.

All of these nice things are easy to smile about. Strangely, though, images from the opposite end of the spectrum—the city dumpground—also rest easy on my psyche. The dump was ugly, smoky, and frightening; yet, poignant memories thrive. Weirder still, I remember the incessant, sicky-sweet smell of burning garbage, the stench that wafted too much mystery to be thought of as simply stinky and hostile.

The rat infested dump lay east of town on a point of land at the joining of the Little Muddy River and the Big Missouri. The dumpground was bad by itself; but, it was neighbored by other horrible, messy stuff. Upstream from the Little Muddy Bridge a meat packing plant perched on the east bank, from where it periodically spilled blood and guts into the water. And hard by the northern slope of the dump lay a ramshackle wrecking operation that scattered its shards of sheet metal and glass hither and yon among mazes of crumpled car and truck bodies. Around the bend from the wrecking yard, the city sewer pipe spewed into our Little Muddy River. Fortunately, the Muddy promptly spit out the sewer poisons near its confluence with the Mighty Missouri, itself the most dangerous of all: fast running, half a mile wide, full of swirling currents and roaring whirlpools. As if all of that wasn't enough, the dump was home to a squatter village fostering grimy, downtrodden characters of unknown origins.

"The Depression is over; the city ought to run those bums out," Dad opined to Gramp.

"I don't agree, Bill. Better to keep those derelicts there, where the sheriff can keep an eye on them." Gramp and Dad made no effort to keep such conversations from Jim and me.

Jim and I were accustomed to hard facts laid upon us, like talk of a bank robber with a stash of loot living in the dumpground squatter village. What a place!—Criminals, a blood-and-gut-strewn river, rats and filth, bordered by the huge, scary Missouri River. The territory east of town reeked of *danger*—in other words, a fascinating attraction for Muddy River boys.

Jim and I first laid eyes on the city dumpground in the summer of 1945 when Gramp took us there to hunt rats. As Gramp's Nash rolled down the Scenic Highway and onto the flats east of town, we saw gray-black smoke rising from the dumpground hill.

Gramp turned south in front of the Muddy River Bridge and followed a rough road to a dirt ramp, where he shifted to low gear and climbed to the top of the dump hill. The flat top of the hill was as big as a football field. We parked next to a rusty bulldozer, the machine used to flatten refuse and push heavy junk like car bodies and worn out appliances off the edge of the hill. A row of rotting, bloated cows, dead horses, cats, and dogs lay on the eastern perimeter of the dump. "They should have buried them," Gramp said. "But as long as the wind is steady out of the west, we'll be upwind of the stink. We'll shoot some rats, but we won't get out of the car."

Gramp sat behind the wheel, Jim on his knees next to him. I commanded watch from the back seat. "Roll your windows down," Gramp whispered. "Be quiet and sit perfectly still. Move your eyes to look, not your head. Rats are smart and they're spooky. Davey," he said, "if you spot one, tap me on the shoulder and I'll hand the gun back."

We waited and waited for the first rat to show. Finally, a twitchy rat nose poked out, the rest of him hidden in the shadow of a crumpled wash machine. "Stay still," Gramp whispered. "He'll come out."

He did. *Bang, splat!* Jim plugged him.

"You got him, you got him," Gramp yelled, for the moment forgetting his own warning about quietness.

"Pretty good shot, huh Gramp?" Jim bragged.

"Shssh," Gramp whispered. "Shots don't bother them, voices do." We waited some more. "Be patient and don't move," Gramp said. Gramp watched left and

Jim right. Jim's eyes were exceptionally good, but he missed the next rat. I spotted him at close range, skittering under the bulldozer. I tapped Gramp and he very slowly passed me the .22. I pumped in a round and lined the peep sight on the rat. He moved to the open and stuck his head in a tin can. Bam! The impact knocked him backward a foot. Gramp again put aside his quiet hunting rule and whooped as if I had bagged a pheasant or prairie chicken.

With our wait, shoot, and wait again routine, Jim and I shot a dozen fat rats. Before and after each exchange of his pump .22, Gramp made Jim and me inspect the chamber to be double sure it didn't hold a live round. He was always a stickler about gun safety, and about not shooting animals we didn't eat, rats excepted. "It's good to get rid of them. They carry disease," he said.

After an hour of rat hunting, no matter how patiently we sat, the rats refused to show even a nose tip. "That's it boys. We thinned them out," Gramp said. "Climb in the front, Davey. Let's get you boys home."

"Gotta pee first, Gramp," Jim said.

"Me too," I said. I stepped out alongside the Nash with Jim. While we pizzled on tin cans, Jim whispered, "Let's see if Gramp will take us to see the mouth of the Muddy. You back me up."

Jim stuck his head in the window. "Gramp, Dave and I been talking. How about we all hike down to the mouth of the Muddy an' have a look, find a place to fish. I've heard all kinds of big fish move out of the Missouri into the Muddy."

"Yah, Gramp, even big sturgeons. We might spot one," I added.

Gramp didn't say no right off, thinking seriously about the idea, I could tell. But then—"Nope, better stay in the car. Over the hill there . . ." Gramp nodded: "the squatter town. Can't trust those bums as far as you can spit. Besides, the dump is a filthy place. We'd get gunk on our shoes. If the wind changes, the smoke smell will get in our clothes and we'll catch hell at home." Jim and I were disappointed, of course. But I liked Gramp's slanting way of saying no. It didn't matter that he was 50 years older; he fit with us like the famous swashbuckled guys, *"all for one, and one for all."*

Looking back, I'm grateful for Gramp's teaching valuable hunting skills and rules for gun safety. But what he tempted us with was exciting, too: tales about a wild and funny man, Jardo Kelley, living upriver from the dump on the edge of the Jungle . . . and a giant buck across the river on the Madsen Ranch, and buckbrush loaded with cock pheasants, and a hollowed beehive tree—all of those treasures hidden in the bottoms beyond the dump. If not for the unfortunate location of the dump, Gramp would take us to the mouth of the Muddy, where we could look over the Mighty Missouri and its bottomlands. Gramp was a good measuring stick. If *he* wouldn't help us visit the confluence of the rivers, Mom and Dad would absolutely, for certain, say no. Even to ask would be risky. A trip there would be unapproved, unsupervised, and dangerous—in other words, an adventure made to order for Jim and me, and the Muddy guys.

As Gramp U-turned, heading out of the dump, I noticed Jim staring east, toward the Muddy. I knew he was conniving some plan to pull off a kid's trip out here to explore the territory. Buck would go, except the lucky dog was in

Montana fishing trout with his dad. And Little Ergie had been recruited to play baseball for a new league called Pee Wee. Jelly had his paper route, besides covering for a neighbor kid's route. Little Bervie—naw, too *little*. Big Bervie or Jack were most likely, and Jack questionable. Jack was game for absolutely everything except dirt and grime. But then, about halfway to the Little Muddy Bridge, we saw something that could possibly turn Jack our way.

"Holy cow, look at that," Jim hollered. "Hey Gramp, slow down! Look at the size of that monster catfish." Gramp coasted and braked to a stop. There, on a slanting trail coming from the Muddy, stood three Carns brothers, two waving, while the other hefted a huge catfish on a rope.

Gramp whistled, not the pretty girl whistle, the big fish one. "Wow, hell of a fish, boys," he shouted. We stared, hoping the Carns boys would come close so we could see their lunker catfish better; and maybe tell us the how and the where. The biggest Carns brother, Richard, slung the rope and catfish over his shoulder. The fish hung down his back, below his butt.

"They ain't coming to talk," Gramp said. "I wouldn't either. I keep good fishin' holes to myself."

"Nice one," Jim hollered. As Gramp pulled away, Jim turned and winked at me. "Wait till Jack hears about this," he said. As luck would have it, Jack heard our story only a half hour later.

As Gramp dropped us at home, here came Jack racing his Schwinn up our driveway and around the house to our backyard. He had a big golden fish strung from his handlebar. "Wow, Jack has a huge walleye," Jim said. We ran through the house yelling, "We're home, Mom," and straight out the back door. Jack had stepped off his bike, jackknife at the ready. I ran and fetched Dad's cutting board.

Jack grinned and did a little dance. Even at six o'clock in the afternoon his motor ran fast. "Uncle Bill and I found a hotspot for walleye. We brought three home, and I saved one for your folks." Jack held his knife over the walleye while regaling us with his story about a secret deep hole his uncle found at the confluence of Cow Creek and the Little Muddy.

As his walleye story petered out, Jack went to work filleting. Jim, the salesman, stepped close, lowering his voice as if the neighborhood held spies. "Jack, you won't believe what we saw today. Bet you've never seen one like it—the biggest catfish ever. The Carns boys pulled him out of the Muddy, by the dump."

Jim spread his hands three feet wide. "This long, Jack. A channel cat: forked tail and black spots. And I saw six inch whiskers hanging down. You can ask my Gramp."

"He saw it?"

"Yup, from close up. Tell him, Dave, what Gramp said. On second thought, forget that. Jack won't believe it," Jim teased.

"I will," Jack said. "Your grandpa never fibs."

Jim dawdled, squinching on his lips—"Fifteen pounds, Jack. Maybe more. That's what Gramp said."

Jack, with ghosty eyes, blubbered . . . "Uhhh, Davey . . . run these fillets in to your mom."

I returned in seconds to catch Jack's swooping celebration dance, skittering, bobbing up and down. He stopped momentarily. "Man alive, a *MONSTER* cat!" Then whooping and cackling, Jack danced again. Maybe he'd seen too many Indian movies. That dance was trademark Jack.

His hands flew. His voice rose and carried half-way around the block, "Ho-o-o-ly cow! Cats! Cats! I knew it." Jack punched Jim on the shoulder and clapped his hands. "I heard about those big cats; now I know it's true." No big people listeners were in sight; yet, Jack gathered Jim and me in, arms around shoulders, like a football huddle. "You see, the Scenic Packing Plant dumps ground guts and livers. The stuff floats down the river and settles—perfect food for cats. The Big Missouri cats pick up the smell and follow it up the Muddy. Now they're lying in the deep holes like German subs. Those cats will gain a pound a week."

Always thinking things out that no one else would have imagined—that was Jack. And, once started, he couldn't stop.

"Dang, there's nothing like cats, especially the big ones. I love 'em even better'n walleye. They're smart too. You land a big cat! Holey Moley! Now, you've *done* something!"

Now, we had a chance to not only catch cats, but monster cats. I pictured my cat tug-of-war ending as a wide, menacing head emerges, and I slide his slick-skinned body onto the shore, where I whomp his noggin with a heavy stick.

They were cats, according to Jack—just cats, never catfish. That made sense though, just as we would never say troutfish. Trout, in fact, were considered only slightly nobler than cats. I learned that from Jack when I caught my first cat above Stony Ford just a month before—a silvery two-pounder. Jack had pounded me on the back like a real hero and showed me the fish's trout-like forked tail and black spots.

But would Jack go near the awful dump? Well, after his ceremonial dance, I thought so, despite his Dutchman dad's insistence on eternal neatness. Heck, Jack even wore clean pants on fishin' trips. This time though, Jack's dutiful, tidy nature would lose its struggle with visions of magnificent cats.

Jack cocked his head. "Say, does your gramma have an unplanted spot in her garden where we could dig some of her jumbo worms?" Right then, I knew the trip was on. Once you plan worm diggin', there's no turning back. Well, at that point, you're already in quicksand to the knees. Jack moved away from our back door, and we followed him around behind the fallen cottonwood, well beyond even Mom's birdy ears. Jack whispered, "Here's the deal. We're goin' out to the *Muddy* fishin.' Right? We'll leave it at that."

"Yup, the *Muddy*, just the *Muddy*," Jim said with a grin. I was four months short of 8, but already well-versed in the guys' strategy (about a year later, when Jim tried it one time too many, Dad named it Shorty). Shorty, Truth's poor cousin, is—in fact—truthful, but conveniently *short* of full detail. Yes, we were bound for the Muddy, but a despicable part of it not needing mention.

"You guys remember to test your throw-lines for strength. 15 pound cats—your lines better be good," Jack said as he pedaled away. "The *Muddy*, remember: the *Muddy*."

Supper conversation that evening went smoothly. Dad was chipper. He'd sold a Farmall M tractor and Jack's walleye fillets would make a Sunday dinner. Dad got a kick out of our rat hunting stories, and Mom was pleased that we killed "those awful, dirty things." We never mentioned the Carns' cat, though, because that could have tipped off tomorrow's destination. Still, we weren't necessarily out of the woods. Evening supper talk was always on that day's events. But at breakfast Dad would nail us down about our day's destination.

Next morning we tried to sleep late and fuss around in the bathroom, hoping Dad would eat breakfast quickly and leave for work. Unfortunately he seemed in no hurry. Finally, as he got up from the table, I had a sinking feeling; Dad's serious blue eyes met Jim's, then mine: "Well, boys, where you galavantin' off to today?"

I was glad Jim, being a year older, was expected to answer. "We're goin' fishin' with Jack," he said. That was a good answer with bonus points: Our folks liked us running with an older kid, especially a polite one like Jack, who had just last evening brought Dad a walleye, and who said,"Yes, sir," and "Yes, ma'am." Still, despite Jack's credibility, Dad held our feet to the fire.

"And just where are you going fishing?"

"The . . . the Muddy," I stammered, hoping for the inquisition to die quickly—not likely, though. Dad's brow wrinkles deepened.

"And, *whereabouts* on the Muddy?"

Jim glared at me, meaning: *"I'll handle this!"*

"We're gonna start out at Horseshoe Bend," Jim said.

When Jim said this, I ducked my head and took another bite of Juneberry jam toast. His answer was perfectly brilliant, and now I know a superb Shorty. Dad knew we roamed up and down the Muddy, in line with Jim's admission that we wouldn't stay all day at any one place like Horseshoe Bend. He would never imagine us traveling south of Scenic Highway to the awful dumpground. Nobody went there but garbage haulers or rat shooters. Dad turned to go out the door with the same send off as always: "Be home before supper." Mom sterned her eyes upon us, demanding confirmation.

"Don't worry, Mom. We'll be home by six," Jim said.

In my little Cub Scout backpack Jim and I packed four sets of new surveyor cord throw-lines, worm cans, and stringers. We left in too big a hurry. In our excitement we'd biked to the alley behind Jack's house before realizing we had forgotten to pack a lunch. And our cooking-out stuff was in our cache at Stony Ford. Still, we couldn't risk going back home and facing more questions.

We found Jack waiting for us in his backyard with his war-bag tied on his bike handle bars. "I went over early to your Gramma's, dug plenty of worms for all of us," he said, patting his canvas bag. "Let's go."

Jack carried only a canteen and no lunch, because—as he said—"My folks know Horseshoe Bend is only a mile out and I can easily ride home for lunch. Let's get outa' here." He took off fast with Jim and me trailing out the alley, east up 7th Street along the edge of town. Man, Jack was fast on his Schwinn. Up ahead, he swung out and passed a dawdling car driver. Jim pumped hard to keep the gap from widening. I pedaled fast as possible to keep the two of them in sight. I regretted not taking Jack's advice to overinflate my tires to make them run fast.

I expected Jack to turn down the hill to the flat in front of Horseshoe Bend. In 10 minutes we could hike through the marsh grass to the edge of the river so we could say we went to Horseshoe Bend as promised. Instead, Jack leaned into a quick right turn at the top of the hill above the Bend. Suddenly, he braked and skidded to a stop. We pulled alongside, and Jack took a couple of deep breaths, before hunching forward, ready to go. "Morning is best for big cats," he said. "Let's get to the dump and set up. We'll stop by Horseshoe Bend on the way home just to make it official."

Jack jumped hard on his pedals and raced off, whizzing south on 5th Avenue, opening a sizeable lead on Jim and me.

This was the delicious part of fishin' trips, traveling fast, anxiously savoring thoughts of fish waiting to be hooked—bigger ones, exotic ones we had yet to catch, like 15-pound cats. Today, though, my mind muddled, spoiling the daydream. Tonight, at the supper table, when Dad had time for questions, we could face trouble, maybe double Dutch.

I imagined Dad's grilling, Jim's dodging, perfecting his "shorty" . . .

"How was fishing at Horseshoe Bend?" Dad was certain to ask.

"Well, it didn't *look* too good there at the Bend."

"What the hell you mean, it didn't *look* good. You didn't *fish* there? You told me that's where you were going."

"We went *by* there."

Ready to blow, Dad would melt us with his glare. Jim would go for the full confession—well, 90 percent full confession.

"Well, we went further down, down there by the dump, but we were real careful and . . ."

Suddenly, Jack yelled frantically from the Broadway intersection ahead: "The *dog!* The *dog!* Pull your legs up." Goslin's mean Chesapeake came running at us, lips curled, snarling, ready to jump on a fallen rider and chew him up. Jim had the lead on me, thank goodness. He stood on his pedals, pumped hard, and swerved directly at the dog. The stupid dog jumped sideways, and Jim and I lifted our feet to our handlebars, avoiding his snapping jaws. We banked into the downhill curve, pushed by a good wind.

Halfway down the hill, speeding at 30 miles an hour, my heavy steel bike vibrated and wobbled. With watery eyes I made out the sign announcing the end of East Broadway and beginning of Scenic Highway. Yah, sure, a "highway," graveled and potholed. I blinked hard to see the potholes in time to dodge disaster. Crash now and I'd be a meat sandwich for the ferocious Chesapeake. I dared a look back. The bristle-haired dog stood in the center of the road staring after us. *I'll get them on their return,* he seemed to be thinking.

We set a speed record covering that mile to the dumpground road. By the Muddy Bridge, Jack sat waiting. He waved us to the front. "Lead out, Jim," he yelled. "Show me the trail where you saw the Carns brothers. We'll fish just an hour, long enough to . . . catch one big one," Jack said from behind.

A quarter mile south of the Muddy River Bridge, we turned off the road embankment onto a narrow path. The path took us weaving among wrecked car bodies, skirting the banging metal hubbub of the Strand brothers' wrecking yard. We threaded our way through sandy hillocks and snagging brush. As the path neared the slope of the dump, it twisted through hulks of rusted metal, finally becoming too narrow for bikes. We stashed our bikes, grabbed our gear, and took off running, anxious to sink worms to the cats.

This place, so jammed with awkward obstacles and sharp things, should have held us to a walk; but, like the rest of the Muddy River country, we took it at a run, jumping barrels and clattering over mounds of flattened cans. Jim ran in front, next Jack, then me.

Suddenly we gasped, sucking putrid air. I remembered our rat hunt and the rotting animal carcasses at the dump. We held our breaths and sprinted. Beyond the drift of stench, we spit and blew and sucked in the regular smoke-flavored air from the dump, by comparison, almost decent.

"Any more of that, and I'm turning back," Jack said.

Our trail merged with the remnants of an old weedy road on the bank of Muddy River. Jack stopped us. "Hold up, men. Whew! Look at those holes. There's gotta' be big cats hangin' up in those eddies and—that stuff." Protruding from the water, the "stuff" was a scattering of broken boulders, huge rooted tree stumps, and a wrecked pickup truck. I stopped to unwind my throw-line, but Jim pulled me along. "We can always come back here later," he said. "Let's head for the confluence."

Jack brightened. "You're right, Jim. The clean Missouri. That's what we need."

We trotted three abreast now, filled with goin' fishin' anticipation—thoughts of monster catfish lying deep, waiting for worms—enough to make our hearts pump double fast.

Jack waved us onward. "Missouri River, here we come." We traveled easily down an old weedy road. The Muddy ran on our left, a spit shot away, while on the right the garbaged slope of the dump hill loomed: the mountainous heap made of year upon year of collected, compacted garbage and junk. Here, though, out of the wind, with the Muddy rippling gently along, well—the place held some promise. The air was fresher here, too, since a steady west wind carried the burning garbage smoke over our heads.

The dump hill loomed ever taller and intriguing enough to call another halt. A few items were identifiable, like broken tree trunks poking out of glommed together refuse. In place of mountainside boulders, smashed ice boxes and wash machines gripped the slope.

The hill was composed of glass, rusted metal, worn out machines, shredded tires, grease cans, discarded clothing, bathtubs, greasy dirt, ashes, and shards of bones, much of it crushed, mixed and burned. Nothing grew, not even weeds. "It's a gol-durned mountain of *glunck*," Jack said.

We strolled along, gawking at the strange landscape and the final run of our treasured Little Muddy escaping past the dump mountain. Then, near the top of the hill directly above us, the billows of smoke shifted, and we saw two dark human shapes, ghost-like shambling ones. A pair of garbage crows circled over them.

The dark figures traveled methodically, trudging down the slope. Did you ever see something unfold that your brain fails to register? When you wake from your stupid trance, blood pounds your temples, as it did when I realized these were real men, scary ones, and they were coming in our direction. I shuddered. "Chunk, ka-chunk, chunk, ka-chunk, chunk, ka-chunk," came sounds of stiff and heavy boots, the kind that crunch glass and pack dirt smooth. Their purposeful clomps grew louder, like marching soldiers, Germans soldiers. I desperately wanted to run, but wouldn't unless Jack and my brother ran first. And they didn't. We closed in a huddle to watch.

As if hiking into a thicket, the dark men disappeared among jumbles of battered appliances, charred tree stumps, and rolls of rusty barbed wire. In minutes they re-appeared lower on the hill, moving fast along a switch-backed trail.

We three stood rooted, mesmerized by the improbable forms now coming into plain view. They turned east on the final switch-back, close enough to reveal faces that smothered light, faces so dark they could have been Negroes. Could have been men, could have been boys.

They were skinny, like boys, but with rounded shoulders used to lifting, like worker men. On the other hand, hatless and hair gone wild, they weren't like men at all, at least not men with pride. They moved nimbly, yet dirt-darkened faces and coveralls stiff with grime confounded explaining them.

Their trail and our old river road merged at a Y just ahead. Jim stepped forward to get a better look. I was glad Jack grabbed a back pocket to stop him. "They're dump people," Jack whispered. "Stay away from them."

The dark men emerged from behind a mangled car body and stopped to face us. I braced my legs, ready to run. They carried wire baskets crammed with scavenged stuff. I made out checkered red and white paper holding a smashed loaf of bread, half-black bananas, and a lumpy package wrapped in dirty butcher paper.

The men were skinny, but not stooped like the railroad bums we'd seen on South Main. They were hatless with hair longer than Jesus's, only mangier, and clothes raggedy, as if they'd run a long way, through barbed wire.

In unison they stepped toward us. They stopped 20 feet away and glowered dark eyes at us. The bigger one nudged the other. Out of his whiskers, came a yellow-toothed, sneering grin. He was pleased to see our fright. I admit being scared by what they might do to us, scared also by what they were. I shivered. They were sparsely whiskered men, young men, gone only a year or two from boyhood. Finally, without a word, they turned and trudged away, leaving an image, one that would last, one that could wake a guy with nightmares.

They were sort of animal-men, with dismal, leathery, gaunt faces—old ones—old faces on young bodies, and so alike they had to be brothers, maybe twins. A thought ran through me that chilled me then and chills me still: people, young ones, looking strangely seasoned to the dumpground, as permanent as prairie dogs in burrowed towns of dirt.

I had believed bums were old loners, a sad understanding, but not half as bad as the truth of brothers living poor, miserable lives and rapidly growing old. The old-young men shocked my buddies too. Jack and Jim waited silently, a rarity for them.

At last, when the fearsome brothers were nearly out of sight, Jack shuddered like a dog shaking dust. He nodded in the direction of our river's confluence with the Big Missouri, "Let's go, men. They're out of our way." His voice wavered. I had hoped for confidence.

Up ahead the dark forms of the old-young bums turned abruptly from the road toward the steep bluff of the dumpground hill. A few steps and . . . *they simply disappeared into the side of the dump, like a pair of Houdinis.* Without a word, the three of us ran forward to the place where the men had turned from the trail.

We stood gaping at the near vertical slope. I blinked my eyes, and spied a narrow door, and in that instant Jack declared, "For criminy sakes, they *live* in there." The unpainted door with a single pane of smoky glass and a stove pipe sticking out of the overburden of "glunck" were the only outward signs of a dwelling.

"You think they dug a cave there?" Jim asked.

"No, it looks like they built a shack, and the junk from up on the dump slid down and buried it," Jack said. The door provided no clues. And we weren't about to knock on it to find out. We watched in stunned silence, the quiet finally broken by a rat moving tinkling cans. Then a shadow moved behind the square glass pane at the top of the door. Its muffled voice sounded like, "Get the *HELL* out of here."

We didn't wait to be told twice. Hard on Jack's and Jim's heels, I raced down the slope toward the Muddy, panicked by a pair of awful worries: *Don't fall in the broken glass*—and worse—*Had the mean brothers come out their door to chase us?* The thought prickled the back of my neck.

Jim and Jack stopped on the bank of the Muddy and turned back. Had they dived in the Muddy and swum across, I wouldn't have hesitated; but, like the end of a scary movie, Jim laughed, "Those guys are all bluff. Let's go fishin'."

Our relief lasted only a minute. Another door banged from beyond the brothers' place.

A man appeared on a different path that slanted downward toward the river. Carrying a tapered pail, like a milk pail, he wore blue striped farmer coveralls with suspender straps. A gimping white mongrel trailed behind. The man gimped slightly, too. He occasionally placed a walking stick for balance. Beyond the man and dog, several thin columns of smoke rose. "Son-of-a-gun, there's a whole dang town out here," Jim said.

The farmer-looking man paused to glance at us before continuing along the bank of the river. He disappeared between two car bodies, and moments later returned, retracing his route with the water sloshing over the sides of his bucket and his dog close at his heels. The man clumped up the slope toward the edge of the dump escarpment from which rose a column of smoke, the apparent site of his squatter house.

We must have been stupid-struck, standing there with our backs to the Muddy, looking for more signs of dump bums, trying to breathe easily. Finally, Jack broke the trance.

"Hey, guys, look at that—a perfect place to fish." He pointed at a wrecked flat-bed truck, its front wheels clinging to the bank and the back half partly sunk in the Muddy. The truck hadn't a trace of paint remaining; but, there on its nose, looking at us, was an oval blue glass Ford emblem. The Ford sat broken-backed with rubber-less rims half buried in the bank and its flat bed sitting like a dock in the river. The truck was anchored on the down-river side by an angled trunk of a bark-less cottonwood. "We can sit in the back of that old truck without having to mess with the greasy mud," Jack said.

"Yeah," Jim said. "And there's bound to be cats holed up under that log—looks perfect."

Jack crawled out over the crumpled cab. "Hey, hot diggity. There's dried worms here on the flat bed. This must be where Carns caught his big one." Jack crawled to the end of the truck bed and Jim followed. They both claimed stake holes to hold their throw-line sticks. I jammed mine in a stake hole by the cab. I felt good about my place close to the shore. If the truck moved, I wanted off quick without a swim in the Muddy's dumpground murk.

We unwound our lines and coiled them in small circles on the wooden bed of the truck. "Big worm gobs, now," Jack said. "Big cats want a mouthful." He finished baiting first, and we ducked while he twirled and slung a weighted trio of wormed hooks. Jim picked a spot further out and plopped his tripled baits perfectly. I dropped mine in behind the log. At last we settled in, absorbed in warm anticipation of throw-line fishin', waiting for that first delightful tug.

We had lucked onto Carn's spot. I visioned my yellow cord line tightening and zinging rapidly off upriver with a big cat churning up a plume of mud. I held my line tight in my fist, same as Jack and Jim. I stared at the water, wondering. We waited a half-hour, changed to fresh worms, and waited some more. No talk of any importance, only, "What gives?" and "Any minute now."

I had second thoughts. This was a poor place to *not* catch fish—stinky air, broken glass, and sharp metal everywhere, and rats, and scary dump people. Still, we had connived to pull off the trip. We were bound to stick it out for a while.

The first jerk on the line: would it be a slimy carp, ugly sucker, worm stealing shiner, or a bragging size catfish? Maybe even a sturgeon capable of pulling a guy right into the Muddy. But dreams need food, and ours were starving. Finally, Jack broke the boredom—"You guys hear about the bank robber living out here?"

"I heard," Jim said. "Hope it's true. We'll capture him and claim the reward."

"No, I'm serious," Jack said. "We gotta be careful."

"You got a whole pocket of money, Jack?"

"You know I don't."

"Me neither. So why would a robber bother with us?"

"Uh, maybe because . . . heck, I don't know," Jack laughed.

Periodically the friendly sun broke through, enough to lift our spirits; but, just as often, a shift of wind blew dumpground smoke over us, darkening the sky, stink swirling into nostrils. The smoke also carried intriguing smells, a specific mix that identified the dump. Yes, it had a stink to it, but interesting stink, albeit not downright appealing like the smells of the rich fishy sands of Stony Ford and the marsh grass of Horseshoe Bend. Those were pleasant, close-up reminders of clams, bullheads, goldeyes, suckers, and froggy water weeds. And up there on the untainted Muddy you could enjoy new fragrances and scenes simply by moving around the next bend of the river. Not so in this territory.

The dumpground's weird aroma was all the time and everywhere, rising, mixing with the breeze above the fires, where it hitched rides to far off places. It had tickled noses when we left the Scenic Highway. Now the smell penetrated our clothes, our skin, hair, and far up the nostrils, into brains. The garbage smells teased for discovery. Flavors landed and stuck on the tongue, some crispied like bacon grease, toast, and fried potatoes—familiar things reminding me of forgotten lunch and my sucked-in belly.

"How long we staying today?"

No answer. Instead, the guys bantered about bullheads mouthing the worm as compared to cats swallowing it deep and running. They were so engrossed they didn't hear the man's approach.

I caught his movement and turned to see the bum man in the blue-striped coveralls standing close behind with his white dog sitting by his leg. He was the same fellow we'd seen come to the river for water. He looked at me with a bit of a grin that looked good as gold. I judged him friendly. I wasn't so sure of his wild-eyed dog, though. The man saw my concern and poked his walking stick at the dog. Without so much as a tail-wag, he dropped to his belly alongside his master. He flattened his ears and pinned his nose between his paws, brown eyes glued on mine.

"Good morning, sir," I said.

"It is at that," the squatter man said. He appeared to be old enough to be a dad, but not old enough to be a grampa, and so . . . so *normal,* and amazingly clean. Not town clean, but more like bachelor farmer clean, where the guy might wash his hands and face every day, but save the rest of himself and his clothes for Saturday when a week's grime could be gotten rid of all at once. He was stocky, about six feet tall, like my dad. He had a stubby gray beard, a reddish Scandahoovian-looking face, and blue eyes—the same intelligent, Swedish eyes as our Grampa Erickson.

The fellow looked like a farmer man; reminded me of our uncles, Frank, Dick, and Bus—purposeful, always with the next farm job in mind. The man wore a heavy blue cotton shirt that showed beneath the straps of his coveralls, and a straw hat with a hole on the crown from bumping on things. After our encounter with the brothers, this guy was a welcomed sight, especially since he stood blocking our escape route. I liked his wisp of a grin and friendly eyes that suggested, "I don't mind you boys being here." I wondered: *Could a bank robber be this polite and friendly?*

My partners stood, wearing worried faces. Jack glanced at the river, as if ready to swim.

"I hope we're not fishin' too close to your place," Jack said.

The squatter man placed both hands on top of his walking stick, one of those varnished, hand-polished diamond willow sticks. “My place is a little ways down the river there,” he said with a jerk of his head. “And I don’t own the river.” The man talked well, like Dad’s business friends. He jabbed his thumb over his shoulder, toward the brothers’ shack. “Those two up there can be a little grumpy. I don’t think they’ll bother you, though. I’ll see to it they don’t.”

“We’d sure appreciate that, mister,” Jim said.

“My name’s Roy,” the man said.

“Glad to meet you, sir. This here’s Jack, and that’s my brother, Dave.”

“I’m happy to meet you boys,” Roy said. “I don’t get many visitors out this way. Now if you fellas are after catfish, you need to know they’re fussy about the kind of bait they’ll take.” Roy nodded at our lines. “I suppose you’re fishing with worms?”

“Yes, sir, we’ve got jumbo worms,” Jack said.

“Three young fellas came here yesterday; fished from this old truck.” Roy took a seat on an old pail. His dog used his single hinder leg to hop up on Roy’s lap. Roy studied the river for a spell before continuing, “The boys had no luck with worms. I helped them out, got them some good bait. If you boys are still around when I get back, I’ll have some bait that has enough stink to interest catfish. By the way, I wouldn’t go any further downriver to fish. The sewer dumps in there. And it wouldn’t be smart to go as far as the big river. She’s running high and dangerous.”

Roy’s dog jumped down and trotted a few steps, as if to leave. “Okay, Malta,” Roy laughed. “I know it’s time for your bone. Let’s go find you one.” Roy started after his dog, Malta, but stopped and smiled. He tipped the brim of his straw hat like a lonesome farmer riding a tractor, one who sees maybe two passers-by in a week.

We watched Roy and Malta walk the inclined trail toward the base of the dump hill. A door banged shut. Shortly Roy re-appeared carrying a wire basket. He and his dog turned upriver, headed for the trail the brothers had used, the route that would take him to the flattened top of the dump. He seemed to be headed for a time of scavenging, walking briskly, cheerfully—if I read him right. Malta too, bouncing behind on two front legs and one hind.

“Maybe Roy will come back with a skinned rat,” Jim laughed.

Jack and I settled back to wait, watching our lines. Not Jim, though. He stood and gazed upriver, then downriver. Then he did it again, like an undecided dog turning in its bed. Never ever could Jim stay put long without action. For the second time he proposed, “How about if we move on, go and see the Missouri?”

“Naw, naw, forget it,” Jack said, his eyes steady on his throw-line. Jim waited, thinking. His impasse with Jack was setting in. I’d seen it happen before.

Jim tried again: “I heard big fish hold up at the confluence, before they decide which way to go. We might even hook a sturgeon.”

“How about tryin’ that another time, Eric?” Jack said. “I think we ought to stick it out here. That Roy guy seemed serious about bringin’ us special bait.”

“Maybe, but what if we just go have a look, check out the Missouri?”

"Well, you want to go, then go; but I'm waiting for Roy," Jack said. "You better take Little Eric, though. That's not a good place to go alone."

"Watch our sets then, Jack. We've got a couple spare lines we can set in at the confluence," Jim said. "We'll give it a try there—for just a little bit."

Jim took off in his easy long trot. I followed, close at his heels, eyes out for trouble. At the top of the hill Jim took the left fork of the trail.

We stopped to face the slope of the dump hill. "That Roy guy slammed a door right along here someplace," Jim said. "I think I see it." He had spotted a door all right, but one broken at the hinges. "That cave-house is abandoned," he said. "The next one isn't."

A large wicker chair woven from willows tipped off the entrance to Roy's cave-house. The chair sat a step away from a bleached wooden plank door. A tiny tin shanty perched on the far side of Roy's door. We stood back. Jim, same as me, was uneasy with snooping.

I admit we did move some closer, close enough to figure out the sheet metal shanty. It was Roy's outhouse, a three sided shelter without a door. Inside, a barrel poked from the ground with a couple of narrow boards strapped over to keep the crapper from falling in. I was near to deciding that Roy was hopeless when I noticed that beyond the outhouse he had assembled the makings of a wood cutting operation, an arrangement similar to those we'd seen with Gramp and Dad at Missouri River ranches: a pole saw horse, double bit axe, a crosscut saw, some old corral poles for workings, and a stack of firewood.

On the far side and to the right of Roy's door sat a dented washing machine with a gas motor; next to that, a bathtub perched with its claw feet resting on flat stones. A pair of broken bicycles leaned against the back of the tub. Roy used one for a towel rack. His front "yard"—if I could call it that—seemed to be the making of a halfway civilized man. His house, though, from what little we could see of it, was little better than a bear's den.

Only the low door, a log front, and a timber framed and darkened picture window showed. Oh, and a skinny smoke pipe poked out of the dirt. That was the extent of Roy's intriguing house, a front no wider than a chicken coop and everything else tucked back under the dump. I imagined awfulness in there. Sad, I thought. If Roy likes living alone, he should live in a nice cabin in a forest.

Beyond Roy's place, we traveled fast, anxious to see the Missouri. . . . "Kowabunga!"—Standing in our way was a village of flat-roofed shanties spaced along a wide, baked-dirt path. We stood well back and stared.

Six shacks lined the right side of the path or "street," and at the end one stood alone. These thin board and tarpaper shacks weren't built much better than the West Side Army's rickety clubhouse that was knocked down by a windstorm. The dumpground squatters had propped their shacks against the side of the dump's slope for support. The few windows in sight had broken glass or cracked glass taped over. And there wasn't a squatch of paint in sight.

The village was trapped between the dump hill and the Little Muddy. We'd have to pass through, but not before checking for inhabitants. Besides, we wanted one curious look, even though Dad had said, "They shouldn't have let those squatters out of the hoosegow." Still, Jim was a lightning fast runner, and I wasn't slow. First sign of trouble, we'd be gone.

From the far end of the street came an eerie drumbeat . . . sounded like a tom tom. I tugged on Jim's shirt, thinking we should go back. "You think there are Indians out here?"

"Naw, Indians wouldn't live here, not real ones. Let's go on." We strolled forward, on alert, like the sheriff and deputy coming into Deadwood. In the same instant Jim and I caught movement by the fourth shack, the biggest one made of three square shanties jammed together. Men emerged from the shadow of a sagging porch roof. Four men stood on the porch, two more moved out the door. A pair of squatter-bums shambled to the edge of the street. "We'll ignore them; go right on past," Jim said. The men were soot dark, faces and clothes alike. Like rail hobos, these guys had gnarly beards woolly enough to hide mice.

"Hey," the tall, stooped man said. As he tottered toward us, Jim and I swerved away to the far side of the "street." The bony man was skinnier than Ichabod Crane and just as scary. "Boys, come here," he croaked. I noticed the sign behind him, over his right ear. It hung on a tilt from the porch's crosswise pole. In yellow-white paint someone had scrawled, OFFICE.

"Keep moving," Jim said, as if I had to be told. Looking sideways, I saw a jumble of white dented appliances, and broken down bikes piled between the shacks. The men stepped that way, gesturing at their "goods." We moved even with them, but stayed to the river side of their "street."

Another guy piped up, a husky Negro or half-Negro. "I see you come from Smoky's. I got better deals than that ol' codger." 'Smoky,' I gathered, was his nickname for Roy, the friendly squatter with the dog.

"Let's get outa here," Jim whispered. We scurried past the last shack in the string, toward the creepy drumbeat. I know that even Jim was fearful; yet, he couldn't resist teasing: "There might be a war party," he said. "Watch for flying arrows."

"BUMP, bump, bump. BUMP, bump, bump," the tom tom continued without let-up.

The drummer hunched on a stool under a willow switch porch roof. Behind him was a tiny shanty of thin boards and tin. A crumpled car body held up the near side wall. The man was strangely irresistible. I remembered an Indian movie, where the medicine man wielded mystical powers. We moved closer, to about 20 feet. Long strings of black hair framed his face. His shirt, pants, and drooped cowboy hat were the color of greasy dirt. He sat staring straight ahead with a tom tom braced between his knees. Using the palms of his hands, the man beat out the same monotonous drum song, the one heard in every movie where white-man settlers hear war-path drums and pee their pants. "BUMP, bump, bump. BUMP, bump, bump." The man thumped intently, as if his drumming needed great concentration. An upright pole supporting a porch roof blocked part of his face. He made no effort to move his head to look past the pole, and never once let on that he saw us, though we were close enough to see a fly on his nose.

We scurried past the man, whatever he was—Indian or maybe a crazy derelict white man with a grimy face.

The path narrowed, pinched between the edge of the dump hill and the Little Muddy. We had no choice; we had to pass by the spill of the awful sewer pipe spewing into our river. The spilling sewer would gag a maggot, its gray swirl of muck so ugly that one quick glance was plenty and best forgotten. Yet, as bad as the rotten sewer was, it marked the end of ugly and beginning of magnificence. Our path turned around a scrub willow tree, and there lay the Mighty Missouri, sending its clean, tangy breeze full into our faces.

Jim ran for the river looking like he'd dive right in. I caught him on a pretty little peninsula of rippled sand at the joining of our Little Muddy and the Big Missouri. "Wow—look at that," Jim said. He ran down the sand spit to the lapping water. He shouted out across the great noisy river, soprano voiced and giddy: "Heeyaaa!" And to me: "Yaaah!—what a great place! Not a soul out here!"

Jim and I stood together, enthralled and captivated by this grand world. Minutes passed without words. Across the half-mile of rolling river, a forest of tall cottonwoods stretched away to the McKenzie County bluffs. Upriver and down lay a vast and complicated scene: the wide, brown river allowing strips of island: green willowed and bare sandy islands . . . the river bordered by willow jungles stretching toward east and west horizons . . . channels wandering away from the river and returning . . . noise: beavers slapping tails, the river droning, whirlpools gulping . . . and—the river and bottomlands there for Jim and me, for us alone.

Over the summer, little by little, I'd learned. I hadn't come all the way to gutsy, but I wasn't a chicken either. Still, a lot of worry lay between here and home. "Maybe we better go back," I said. I might as well have been a tree. Jim didn't answer, lost in his explorer's mood.

"I don't think we're supposed to be out here," I said. I'd come part way to Jim's way . . . imagine, then charge ahead. But I wasn't ready for the big, scary Missouri River and its vast bottomlands.

As if staking out the territory, Jim pushed on the back of my shoulder, directing, "Right there, you fish the Muddy's eddy at the confluence. I'll see what's around the bend." He stared off to the northwest, squinty-eyed against the sun's glare on the river. He mumbled quietly, as if to himself, "Be back, maybe an hour. I need to check out the watercourse up there that runs out of the Jungle." Without saying goodbye, he trotted up the sand shore with the Big Missouri's gentle waves wetting his high topped shoes. In too short a time he disappeared into the willows, leaving only his trail of footprints in the sand.

My brother had left me very, very alone there on the sand spit. To my left ran a backward running eddy, the Muddy's last gasp, where its little waters were bullied by the surge of the big river coiling into its mouth, coloring it Missouri brown, and by Jim's assessment: "clean enough to fish."

"Drop a line in the eddy," Jim had directed. I went about baiting my hooks. In a daze, I found my line strung into the Little Muddy's final pool, fishing away, and I hardly remembered doing anything.

My little river was a trickle compared to the Big Missouri. "Mighty Mo," the river was called in one of Gramp's books. Gramp never ran out of stories of explorers and trappers living with Indians, learning to winter in bearskins, and building their own canoes to travel the Missouri.

I walked the few paces across the sand spit and plopped my butt in the warm sand to face Mighty Mo and its stupendous valley. Nowhere could I see evidence that a man had ever set foot in this wild place.

Despite Gramp's book and the map's designated *Missouri River,* folks just added Big in front of Missouri and let it go at that. Maybe "Big" was meant to separate our river from its southern tributary, the Little Missouri. Anyway, Big was a natural fit. The Missouri's magnitude overwhelmed me. I felt big as an ant. Though worry ached my gut, I also felt a strange new power welling in me: the idea that nobody but me was responsible for me.

I gazed upon miles of the great river rolling out of the west under a curtain of low, dark clouds drifting in from the Montana line. Beneath the clouds, the brown river and its gray-green flanking of bottomland wildness stretched as far as I could see. Lewis and Clark would have been just as excited standing in my special place. And possibly they did just that.

The river raced frantically out of the west, coming downhill as I judged by waves lapping over smaller waves. Logs twisted and bobbed like broncos; currents pushed against currents, spluttered, gurgled, and slanted away in new directions. Altogether the chorus of waters droned like a squadron of far off bomber planes.

The wild Missouri was frenetic and impatient, the master of its kingdom of willowed islands and bare, sandy islands where squawking gulls wheeled about and gangly herons stood tall, like sentries. I imagined the river wilderness stretching all the way to the Rockies, with enough excitement to fill many books with stories. Upriver and downriver, as far as I could see: water and greenery and wandering channels flowing into and out of willow jungles and cottonwood forests.

Across the wide bend of the Missouri, a summer-red whitetail stood drinking. The deer looked tiny and spindly in the distance. Behind the deer, a lane in the forest of giant-armed cottonwoods revealed a velvety green and sun dappled meadow. I envisioned a shady Sherwood Forest threaded with winding horse trails to be traveled at full gallop. Someday I'd find a way over there. Someday I'd go see.

My daydream would have surely gone on. But the deer raised its head from drinking. No glint of antler, a doe. With one brief look across the river, I suspect wary of me, she turned for the forest. The treetop canopy instantly shaded her, and in another step she magically disappeared, as if blotted away. Did she hide a nursing fawn? Or, was it taken by coyotes? That happened often, Gramp said. In the midst of wondering, I jolted upright at the sound of a kerwhumping crash and splash from downriver. I turned just in time to watch part of a tall bank cave and tumble, carrying a tree into the river.

The snow melt high among the Rockies had swollen the river, creating the annual event known as the June Rise. No matter that this year's cool summer had brought it late, well into July, folks still called it the June Rise, same as you wouldn't rename a child. Everyone knew of the June Rise, even children who were never permitted near the dangerous river . . . Sand Creek, yes, and Stony Creek, and of course the Little Muddy River. Only with supervision could children go near the Mighty Mo. Even then, nervous parents sometimes harnessed and tethered their tykes like unruly puppies.

I sat on the shore, fighting nagging guilt of yet another broken parental rule. Fortunately the river's fascination overruled. My throw-line was forgotten during that hour before Jim's return. The river's wild goings-on held me spellbound. Its sandy-tan water moved at the pace of a fast walk as I judged by watching the river's passengers: driftwood and strange objects floating past—things flushed out of Montana. A dark blob twisted about in the swirl. When the blob passed before me, I saw that it was a black cow carried by its bloated belly life raft. And gargantuan cottonwood logs came, too. Loch Ness monsters of the Big Missouri, they bobbed and dipped on waves.

Strangely, the river's deep drone soothed. I began to think of the Missouri as wild but tolerable. I'd enjoy the river's magnificence, lie back and listen to its symphony. My brother wouldn't be long now. My little sand spit haven here, so close to my Little Muddy, was safe and peaceful . . .

I bolted upright at the sound of a creepy whoosh—a whirlpool, one of the big ones. I traced its whir and gurgle downriver to a spinning dish with shallow edges. It swirled faster and faster, deepening in the middle. The monster's mouth widened . . . scary no matter how many times you watch it happen. This one was only a stone's throw downriver and near to shore where it could suck in a wading heron or a careless kid.

I'd seen whirlpools before, while Dad or Gramp stood by to leverage the event with yet another warning about the dangerous Missouri. And I had been thoroughly scared, watching the whirlpool's animal-like rhythm: gentle at first, then whirring faster, then spates and spasms of eerie gurgles. With a little imagination, you could hear it belch.

The one before me had captured a beaver-slicked limb the size of a jumbo Louisville Slugger. The limb stood straight on end, its big end grasped in the whirlpool's maw. Down went the limb and the water smoothed over like dirt on a grave. I waited a long minute, hoping for the beaver limb's escape. What if it was me down there, pinned against the bottom, trying to hold my breath until the monster threw up? An odd comparison, I know—me and the beaver limb. Yet, I breathed a sigh of relief when the limb bobbed to the surface. I sat back, remembering to breathe. "You're safe here," I tried to convince myself. I searched the maze of willow bars and channels where my brother had gone. No sign of him. He should have been back by now.

The Montana storm had moved east and south. Now it thundered over the Little Missouri Badlands. My spot had been cooled by the edge of the storm, leaving me in sun-dappled comfort, touched by a soft, cottonwood-scented breeze. I dug in the dry sand, carved a shallow nest for my back and butt. Heck, I could get used to this mighty place, even nap on the sand. Unfortunately, peace hadn't a chance to settle.

Another thunderous splash came from downriver, as if a truck had flown from the high bank into the river. Again, I jerked upright in time to watch a few tons of bank earth sink like a dying whale, sending a two foot wave surging toward the middle of the river. A big bank had caved off. I had seen these too, while in the protective care of Dad and Gramp.

Later in life I learned how the river transforms. Like a glacier's calving, in due time the high banks must tumble. With the waning of spring floods and the June Rise, the banks on the outside river bends lose their river's bracing support. Piece-by-piece, one-by-one, the water-sogged high banks fracture and fall. And they could tumble a cow or unwary person along.

I had just resettled, when an even bigger cave-off tumbled, and crashed, many tons by the sound of its whomp into the river; I thought how lucky that Jim had chosen to go upriver along low and gentle banks. Still, the thought of him gone off to an unexplored place made me shiver. I rose from my sandy nest and stood tall on the knob of the sand spit. No sign of Jim. I had never been this alone. Fishing, that's what I'd do. Get my mind off of lonesomeness.

I returned the few paces across the sand spit to check on my Muddy River throw-line. I found it bare-hooked, robbed—probably by shiners. At that moment, though, my fishless line mattered little. Here at its mouth, my little river was about to be swallowed by the Big Missouri. The Little Muddy River's final eddy pool was wide and roily. Still, on my second try, I skipped a flat stone across. Skipping another stone across, I supposed I wasn't ready to love the Missouri like I loved the Little Muddy River.

The Muddy's gatherings caught in its final big eddy could not easily escape. From my west bank perch I watched its backward swirling waters. A dead carp came past twice before a swirl of current finally took it into the Missouri. Bottles, boards, and driftwood circled by. Then I caught sight of two white somethings lodged against the muddy shoreline. They had no reason to be there. If I'd have found gold nuggets, I couldn't have been more surprised. I picked up a stick and fished them out. Holy Moley!—two jumbo sized white balloons. They would cost me a nickel apiece at Nelson's News and Cigars, which is why I'd never buy them. I might buy a tiny thumb-sized one cent balloon, a nickel "Crime Fighter" comic, and a penny bubble gum, but never five cent balloons. Across the street at the Orpheum I could watch battleships blasting Japanese islands, then a Bugs Bunny cartoon, a Tarzan serial, and a full feature Hopalong Cassidy or Lash LaRue, all for nine cents. So, after Nelson's and the Orpheum, I'd still have nine or ten cents left out of my 25 cent allowance. And today, my lucky day, I had two nickel balloons for free.

I took my prize balloons across the sand spit and washed the dumpground germs away in the brown Missouri. Like Jim always said, "The Missouri's mud is clean mud." I turned away from the river and my washing job, and—*boy-oh-boy*—here he came down the shore, on the run. I was so happy to see my brother

I allowed myself to be generous. I called out, "Jim, get over here. I'm giving you a special prize."

He'd run the quarter mile from the willows like a Sioux boy, arriving calmly and breathing easy. I extended my gift. "I found two of these here in the Little Muddy."

"Wow! Amazing you found them out here," Jim said. He stuffed his balloon in a pocket and turned to point upriver. "Boy! Is that ever wild country up there! I found some log jams and beaver houses around the bend. I'll bet that's where the big cats spawn. We've gotta come back when we have more time, maybe next Saturday. Buck will be home from Montana by then. And we can come in from the west next time and blaze a trail through the Jungle. We'll cross over to this side on the beaver dams."

"Yah, but we better get back, Jim. Jack will worry. He said it's dangerous out here on the Missouri. It is. I saw a huge whirlpool right down there."

"Can't get us here on the shore, can it? . . . Where are your fish?"

"Didn't catch any . . . there were huge banks caving off, crashing almost like bombs, and . . ." Jim didn't hear, didn't want to hear—

"Come on, Dave. Let's go check on Jack. He's the one in danger. We can't trust those creepy derelicts in the dump." Jim waved his hand across the river and over the maze of Jungle channels. "This is the place to fish."

We were off then, eager to tell Jack of our discoveries. We circled nervously past the Indian's hut, then the trader's junk-town. The scraggly salesmen sat on old kegs in front of a shack, sharing sips of something from a big brown bottle. Jim pushed me to the front. "Get going. Pay them no attention."

The men didn't notice us until we'd come even with them. The Negro fellow stood and ranted something about Smoky Roy. We stopped to listen, curious to learn more about Roy, the one squatter bum we thought was okay. "Don't let Smoky sell you nothin'," the dark man gruffed. "Our stuff is better." Then, the skinny hawk-nosed man staggered a few steps toward us, moving his lips but unable to form words to match his beckoning gestures.

"Let's get outa here," Jim said. We loped on toward Roy's place. Roy was no doubt the same fellow the junk-dealer bums called Smoky or Smoky Roy. Compared with the junk-town bums, Roy was a beacon of safety.

As we approached, his dog woofed, and Roy stood from his wicker easy chair. He poked the end of his fancy walking stick at his dog: "Stay, Malta, stay."

Roy grinned, "Paid a visit to Treasure Village, huh?" Then, without our answering: "Say, I helped your buddy bait your hooks. Holler if you hook one of those big catfish. I know how to land them."

"Hey, that's great, Roy," Jim said. "Maybe we can catch one for your dinner."

He waved us off. "Take 'em all home, boys. Tell the truth, I'm getting a bit tired of catfish."

"Change your mind, let us know," Jim said, and we started away.

"Hold on, boys," Roy said. "I wanted to tell you. The big river, she's runnin' fast and mean; if it rains up in the Rockies, she'll get higher yet. If it was me, I'd be damn careful."

"We will, sir," Jim said.

Off we went, running Smoky Roy's trail down to the Little Muddy, hoping to see Jack with a couple of cats roped to our fishin' Ford.

Jack sat with his back to us, tending his line, sitting amongst white feathers, blood, and a rotten stink. He was too concentrated to notice us. He was startled as Jim hollered out: "Hey, Jack . . . you should have come. You oughta see the Missouri. It's really rolling. And up on the next bend I found a fantastic channel with beaver dams holding deep water, almost clear water. Next time we'll hike in from the Jungle side."

Jack jumped to his feet all twitter-pated, "Chicken meat, men—that's the ticket. Roy got us stinkin' chicken meat for bait. I'm not sure a big cat is worth it . . . fishin' with this crap. But he says it works every time."

"Wow, that's perfect," Jim said. "That Roy must be a pretty nice guy. Not so sure about the rest out here, though. We met some squatter bums downriver. I think they were drunk."

"Crazy, too," I added.

I fished out my prize balloon and dangled it in front of Jack. "Lookie here, what I found. Lucky me, I found two of these big babies down at the confluence." As I raised the balloon to my lips to blow it up, I caught a frowny grimace on Jack's face, then an all out frown. With two strides and a leap he flew from the truck.

In a flash Jack grabbed my balloon away and sternly shook it at me. Then he threw it in the river. I was stunned and mad. "Jeez, Jack! Why the heck did you do that? Big balloons like that are worth a nickel apiece."

Jack ignored my pleading. He bowed low to dance a little Indian hoppy step. Then, frown gone, he straightened up, howling with laughter. On and on he went, while Jim and I watched, never more puzzled. Jack would have continued, but he ran out of breath, petering out like a balky engine. By the time he'd regained his breath for his second volley of laughter, I knew that I'd said something or done something incredibly stupid, though I couldn't imagine what.

When Jack finally finished laughing, his all-out wide grin evaporated. He looked Jim and me over and over, inspecting like someone's wise uncle. He returned to his throw-line and sat. We did the same in front of ours. Jack shook his head slowly, sad like. "Can't believe you guys don't know what that is! It's a *rubber,* for criminy sakes."

"Well, doggone it, Jack," I said. "I *know* it was rubber and danged strong rubber, too. I tested it. It would have lasted a long time. You owe me a nickel."

At that, Jack cackled some more and punched Jim on the shoulder. "And, you don't know either?"

Jim shrugged, "Looked like a rubber balloon to me."

Jack drew a deep breath and blew it out, letting his exhaled air blubber his lips like a Stooge brother. "Okay, men, listen carefully. You guys need to know about some things." Boy, after what was to come, *did we ever!*

We sat tending lines. Jack started his big person's lecture, while I hoped for a bite to turn him away from serious talk that could spoil our fishin' trip.

Jack started from the beginning, what women and men do after they get married and how it's done. I'd heard bits and pieces before. But I wasn't sure how much was true and how much exaggeration, which Jack was good at. Heck, he could pull a walleye from the Nine Mile Hole and grow it two pounds on the way to town. But, like Buck, Jack had an older sister. I'd heard both go on about them, as if having sisters made them smarter, which—I have to admit—it did. *My sister says this or my sister says that,* Buck and Jack parlayed sistery wisdom like professional experts, just like now, Jack sounding so believable that men and women wrestling plumb naked no longer seemed as unbelievable as space ships—except for the part about men putting balloons on their dinkies—I mean dinks. As Jack pointed out, dinkies eventually grow into dinks. In case Jack wasn't joking around with this strange lesson, Jim took his balloon—'er rubber—out of his pocket and tossed it into the Muddy.

Luckily, Roy didn't come down to the river until after Jack's lesson. We sure didn't need an adult in on such a conversation.

"What's all the commotion?" Roy asked from the front fender of our fishin' Ford. "I heard enough caterwauling to think you might have hooked a catfish." Malta wanted answers too, it seemed, with his chin jutted out and dog questions in his brown eyes.

"Nope. No bites yet," Jack said. Jack was steadfast that way, never one to mess up a fishin' trip by serious talk with a big person.

"You better come up to my house," Roy said. "It's well past noon, and I noticed you boys didn't bring a lunch."

By habit, Jim and I hung back, waiting for Jack, the oldest, to answer. But he hesitated, finally stammering, "Wha . . . what about our lines?"

Roy waved over the patch of water below our Ford. "I've fished two lines here myself . . . worked out okay. I'd pull one line out . . . keep from tangling the others. Leave the other two spaced apart. You've got good heavy line. It'll hold. And catfish take ripened chicken bait in deep and hook themselves."

Jim nodded at me, rolled to his knees, and stood. Though exposed to countless hypothetical parental do's and don'ts, we had heard nothing like, "When you are invited into a hermit bum's cave under a rat infested mountain of garbage, it is okay to turn him down." On the other hand, we'd been invited to dozens of farm and ranch homes and shabby rancher line shacks with Dad and Gramp. Jack had too, with his car-dealing dad. Some, especially the bachelor places, had sticky oilcloth covered kitchen tables and smelled of mold and sour milk. But it was unthinkable to turn down an invite, even to a home in the dump. Besides, Roy stood there grinning, swinging his walking stick. "Sure Roy. Thanks," Jim said. "We'll be right along."

Roy left us, and shortly after, with some convincing, Jack agreed to honor the invitation. "Smoky—Smoky Roy, the other bums call him," Jim informed Jack. "They don't seem to like him much. But I think you'll see he's a pretty good bum. He's workin' on his place, trying to make it nice."

Jack drew a big breath. "Dadgum it, Jim! How do you get us into these messes? For all we know he could be a bad guy, maybe even the bank robber. You said you heard about the bank robber."

"Yah, but it's not him, not Smoky Roy. Can't believe he is. Besides, we just have to get a look inside his cave house."

Jim and Jack jabbered back and forth on the path up the hill to Roy's place. Jack had the final word. "Guess it wouldn't hurt to have a look; but, I'm not touching any grub."

Roy stood waiting, grinning, and holding his screen door. We stepped in—Jim, Jack, and I—in that order. My brother and Jack said nothing, like me straining to see something familiar. Dark shapes and a dim shaft of light from a shaded window, that's all—nothing familiar except smells of soot and kerosene and a tinge of fried bacon.

We stood just inside the door, peering into the dimness. I turned and saw Roy grinning broadly as he passed through the shaft of doorway light. We waited for Roy to guide us. "Don't try to pet Malta here, just yet," he said, as he reached to scratch ears. "Malta was beaten before I got him. He's slow to accept strangers. Same goes for my mousers—three of them in here somewhere."

Roy moved past us toward a low rectangular shape against the far wall. We followed until Jim stepped on a cat's tail, causing a mighty *screetch*. "Don't worry, boys. That's just how Blackie gets attention. Step over here."

Roy's clanking and chunking of wood on iron told of a wood-burning stove. "I'll warm up the coffee, boys," he said. Roy crumpled paper and clunked kindling into the stove. Then he "zipped" a match on the stove. Flame flared and Roy clanked the iron lid. His second match lit a large candle housed in a coffee can. "Sit tight, boys. Be back in a jiffy."

We huddled like frightened triplet fawns. Nobody moved or made a sound, except a rat digging behind a wall. In Roy's cave-house our fright wasn't about Roy or even darkness so much, but about strange unknowns: sounds of tisking, whisking creatures overhead, and creaking timbers, and unseen dripping water.

Roy tromped a few steps to the back of the room, where he squeaked hinges and rustled for something. We waited silently by the stove, listening to the soft whoosh of fire heating iron, a rising chorus of creaking, snapping, "talking" iron.

Roy returned to our circle carrying a kerosene lantern, the squatty kind used by railroad switchmen. He placed the lantern on the cool end of his stove. Roy's voice was like our Uncle Dick's, kind and soothing. Roy sensed uneasiness. He said, "My eyes are better'n most in the dark. I'm used to it; but, a bit more light wouldn't hurt."

The moment seemed right to say something polite. Jim should be the one, since fancy things like big cars and brick houses didn't interest him. He could say, "Nice place you have here," and mean it. Upon reflection, though, how could he? Like Jack and me, Jim no doubt wondered when those million tons of glunck overhead would flatten us under this so-called house, the inside of which we couldn't make out, even though the day was sunny-bright outside. "Thanks for inviting us," Jim said, and that was about right for the situation.

I was close to offering a lame excuse for leaving, when Roy zipped another wooden match. His lantern sputtered and flared to life. Nothing could have improved spirits better. From some of my earliest memories I knew well the same pleasant whizzing of burning kerosene, its penetrating smell, and its soft light. Roy's place began to lose its frightening.

"I'll show you around," Roy said. He led us closer to his cracked and taped picture window and pulled some gunny sack curtains. The stream of light lit up the room's east wall made of flattened metal things, including a STANDARD OIL sign. The sign was riddled with .22 holes concentrated around the bulls-eye "O."

I tried not to gawk, but I know I didn't pull it off any better than Jack or Jim. They wandered about, offering compliments. Jim slapped his palm against an upright timber. It was as big as a telephone post, and it supported ceiling timbers. "You sure got her well built, Roy," Jim said. I chuckled to myself at my brother's performance, sounding like a big-shot house builder.

Roy's house was tiny, only about six or seven steps across and about the same deep. But he'd done a clever job making free stuff work, like the floors made of scraps of planking and walls of metal that had been pounded flat, like license plates and highway signs. Roy flooded his lantern light upon a few items he was proud of, first his deluxe Monarch stove. "She's a beauty. They're easy to come by now that the country has natural gas." We toured onward, Roy bragging on his stuffed chair with carved wooden arms—"In darned good shape, even before I fixed it up."

Roy thrust his lantern behind the chair to a shelf with framed photographs. The largest photograph showed off a white-painted house sitting on a prairie hill. The house was small, but its peaked roof was covered with real house shingles. "My farmhouse," Roy said. "The corner of my barn shows in the back."

Roy held his lantern high while we looked over his farmhouse and more framed photographs. "That's Mack and Charlie, best workhorses in the country," Roy said with a sad shake of his head. "They helped me work my farm, years ago. I . . . I, well it was tough times then, and . . ." Roy's voice trailed off. He lit up, though, when Jim asked him about the army man photograph. The man wore a uniform and one of those boat-shaped caps soldiers wear when they come home from the war. The young soldier was saluting something above him, but not in the picture—I guessed the American flag. "The Army gave me a promotion and a dollar a day." Roy stiffened taller—"Then they took my picture."

Roy turned, holding his lantern at the opening to an alcove. Guess you could call it a bedroom. A mattress with no legs under it jammed the space with a foot to spare on the near side and none on the other. Against the outside wall stood a floor to ceiling plank bookcase holding dozens of garbaged books, most with torn covers or none at all, and some blackened by soot. We moved in close to see, even Jack, always enticed by books. He'd been hanging back, suspicious of everything about Roy's cave-house.

"People throw out good books," Roy said. "It's a shame. Some people, though, understand the importance of keeping your mind occupied: Olaf Stensrud, for instance. He delivers garbage out here . . . leaves me a *Williston Herald* up top every day, where I have my own mail box."

Curiously, Roy never mentioned the door. The door caught my eye back there in a dim corner where his bed was pushed against it. It was narrow and short, like a midget's door. I was tempted to ask, but didn't want to be nosy. A door to another room? But why the padlock? Jim didn't ask, either, and Roy led us away from the alcove—too quickly, I thought. Or did I imagine it?

Roy took us back to the center of the big room. He said, "I'm always surprised what people get rid of, when all they need is a little repair. Now that I've finished with my house, I'm going into the business of putting things back into use."

"Like the traders down the river?" Jim asked.

"Naw, I've seen their work, all of it shoddy. I'll do it right or I won't do it. Say, I have a good bike ready if you boys know anyone needs one." Roy hesitated, giving us a chance before moving on.

"I know a kid who's lookin'," I said . . . "saving money from his paper route, riding his sister's bike now."

"Bring him out, then. Tell him five bucks will get him a good bike. Over here, boys," Roy said, guiding us to an oilcloth table. "Sorry I can't offer you all chairs. I'm one short at the moment."

"That's okay, Roy. We're used to standing," Jim said. "Say, is it okay to call you Smoky? That's what those trader men call you."

"Don't mind," Roy chuckled. "Truth be known, that's what I am most of the time since the city sanitation boys started burning up top. An' I'm used to it now."

Smoky Roy's wood fire rumbled and his coffee pot tinked a dance on the cast iron. I marveled at his coffee vapors, as appealing as the Luzon Café's. I knew his water had come from the Muddy River, and had bad stuff in it; but, Roy had boiled the coffee long to kill the germs, just as our grandpa Rollie had taught us and just as Big Bervie had studied up on. I hadn't a tinker's damn of fear, nor did Jim. I smiled back at Smoky Roy, pouring his Muddy River coffee into glass jars. Even Jack took a glass of Roy's coffee, though he reached for it hesitantly.

"It'll be a bit hot for sippin' just yet," Smoky said. "I'll bring us some lunch." He crossed the room to a bench and fiddled with the twanging wire of his tote basket. He returned with a flat cardboard tray, followed by a pair of fat yellow cats and a shadow of a black cat. He held the tray close by the lantern on the table. Dust dingles and flies danced in the light. In the cellophane-wrapped tray were a dozen—minus one—red, jellied doughnuts. In the torn corner of the package, where a single doughnut had been removed, three flies had gone in and stuck to the sugary cellophane.

"I had one of these doughnuts this morning with my breakfast," Smoky said. He jabbed the tray toward us. "They're nice and fresh; I just got them yesterday. Go ahead, boys, I've got to use them up."

Jack rocked from one foot to the other with hands in his pockets. "I . . . I'll go check the lines," he said, going for the door. Smoky took a step after him—

"Here, take one with you . . . ." But Jack was gone. When our host turned back to us, his smile was gone too.

The next few seconds seemed like long minutes. Smoky needed an answer and a kind one. A litany of credos begged for attention, mottos practiced by Swedes like my grandpa Erickson before the Boy Scouts were even invented.—THRIFT: *Never let food go to waste.*—MANNERS: *Always eat what the neighbors offer, and be sure to say thank you* . . . and, DUTY. Duty had weighed heavily on me at the Lutheran lutefisk fundraiser. Gotta *dutifully* buy the ticket (children 12 and under—25 cents). Do your part, help raise the money to reach the goal. Raise more money than last year. The jellied fish on my plate reeked and jiggled at me. I used ketchup and pepper to kill it. Then I ate the awful stuff, *dutifully.*

Jim broke my trance, reaching for one of Smoky's scavenged jellied doughnuts, and my hand reflexively followed. I had my doughnut in hand, but I froze. Time stopped, as I remembered the scariest movie ever. The beautiful, blonde queen of the brown Pygmies offers Tarzan the silver chalice brim-filled with poison, and the hundred kids in the Orpheum Theatre scream, *"No, no, Tarzan, don't do it."* But, he did. He raised the chalice to his lips, and the fact that he lived to appear in the next serial episode helped me risk my life for a germy doughnut.

"Hey, thanks Smoky. These are great," Jim said, taking a second bite.

"Yes sir, Smoky, thank you," I said, and chomped a big bite from mine.

After the first bite, reason took over, including the truth of my hollow belly. Besides, I knew a little about germs. It only takes one of the deadly buggers. If he likes his new home in your gut he'll multiply into a billion. So, if the first bite had a bad germ, enjoying the whole delicious doughnut wouldn't kill me any deader.

We stayed a while with Smoky Roy, munching doughnuts and sipping his gritty coffee. Malta became a friend too, after licking our sugary fingers. We begged off when offered doughnut fourths. "Heck, Smoky, you keep them," Jim said. "Our mom has half an apple pie left over at home."

"Better take one for your friend Jack, then," he said.

"I know he'd like that, Smoky," Jim said. "But he isn't feelin' well today. Dave and I better go check up on him. Thanks again, Smoky. You sure have an interesting house."

"Yah, thanks for everything," I added.

Smoky smiled. "Come back and see me. You're welcome anytime."

We started down the path with Smoky hollering after us, "I'll hike down there in a while. I've got a hunch there'll be a run of cats comin' this afternoon."

Jim and I magpie-d our way down the trail, ticking off the fascinating details within Smoky's cave-house, including *THE DOOR,* the door to *who-knows-what.*

"He's got another room, you know," Jim said.

"I know, I saw the door in the corner."

"I'd sure like to know what's back there," Jim said. "Got me thinkin' about the bank robber and the stash of money."

"Me too; but, do you really believe that story?"

"Jack says it's true. Jack's dad knows Chief Olson real well. He says the Chief may have some evidence against somebody living out here."

"So, you thinkin' Smoky's the robber?"

Jim didn't answer, but he strolled instead of loping. Before we came within earshot of Jack, he stopped and squinted at me. "What do you think?"

"I can't believe he is. I sure hope not. How about you?"

"I dunno. But he doesn't act like a crook. He reads books and the newspaper every day. The deal is, though, he trusts us. We're not talkin' about the hidden room or what we think about it; wouldn't be right."

"No, no. I promise. Just between you and me," I said.

Jim and I had just emerged from the path through the scattering of junked car bodies, when Jack yelled. Like an ice wagon teamster, he stood balanced and braced on the Ford's flattened cab with a line in each hand. "Fish on, fish on," he hollered. Then louder, "Get down here, we've got *two* on, and they're huge!"

"Hold 'em, Jack, don't let them tangle." In his wild dash to join Jack, Jim nearly skidded into the river.

The lines crossed back and forth below the log as the fish sent up rooster tails of bottom mud. "Come on Jim, hurry. Take one of these lines," Jack yelled.

Jim ran and hopped onto the truck, and in that moment Smoky Roy yelled from behind, "They're big 'uns, boys, let them run, work 'em." He came up beside me. No straw hat this time, but a crumply blue cotton cap. Without taking his eyes from the action, he tugged on his blue cap. "Put on my lucky fishin' cap . . . works every time."

The picture of Jack and Jim I'll never forget: side by side on the cab of the fishin' Ford, each gripping a line by both hands, and jabbering like monkeys, back and forth: "We're gonna tangle," Jack complained.

"Then move yours away, Jack."

"I can't. Whoa, whoa, baby. Dang, he's huge. I can't turn mine," Jack hollered.

Smoky pranced back and forth on the bank, whapping his lucky cap on his leg. "Don't horse them too much; let them tire. I knew it. I knew you'd get 'em, just gotta be patient." I stood at Smoky's side. He placed his hand on my shoulder like Gramp does when he has something important to tell me. "The big ones move up the river in pairs, you know," Smoky said. "Still, you need luck. And by-golly, we've got luck."

The guys were off the Ford now, shortening the fish runs, tiring them, working them close. Smoky pointed to the cupped shoreline below. "Now guide them down, into this pocket."

As I moved to the water's edge, Jim scrambled from the truck. At my side, he bent forward over his line . . . "There's mine. Wow! You see him?" At first, all I could see was a gray-blue shadow, undulating, like a python. He was as long as my leg, spooky.

Smoky came to Jim's elbow and peered into the water. "Doin' good. Doin' good. Now when you get his head turned, slide him up onto the beach." Jim waited until his fish made a half-turn up river. Then he drew back and slid the beast onto the sand. The cat lay still, stunned. His wide mouth appeared locked in a scowl, meaning: "Okay, you got me; now what?" Malta moved in on his belly, dog nose to fish nose and stared into the cat's shiny black eyes, growling.

Jim and I stayed back. To grab the cat now would mean a punctured hand from one of his stinging spines, spines as long as my pointy finger. Smoky, though, was ready. He had laid tools by for handling dangerous cats.

Like a matador lancing a bull, Smoky raised both hands high and drove the sharpened Y forks of a lance into the sand behind the cat's head. Then he picked up his three foot long dispatch pipe and cracked the fish on his head.

With Smoky's mighty splat, the cat croaked like only a catfish can croak. I had heard that mournful sound before, and didn't like it then either. Like no other fish, more like a dog with a broken leg—a catfish seems to understand.

Jim's cat quivered once and lay still. Smoky dropped to his knees and spread his thumb and index finger wide to pinch the fish's jaws. The big mouth gaped open and Smoky poked his long-nosed pliers deep and pulled the hook.

Jim and I had only seconds to admire his trophy cat before Roy booted him aside, prepared for landing Jack's fish.

"He's under the log. I can't turn him," Jack said.

"He'll come," Smoky said. "He's seen us; he's hiding out. Yank a little, let him feel the hook. . . . Moving yet?"

"Yeah. Yeah, he's coming out."

"Okay, now lead him down here. When his head turns toward you, slide him up on the bank."

"Jeez, he's huge, biggest fish of my life. I gotta get him in," Jack said.

"Stay calm, son. He's about tuckered."

A few seconds later Jack recognized his moment, and hauled his prize cat onto the sand. Smoky efficiently dispatched Jack's cat exactly as with Jim's.

"Holy cow! Look at him. Man alive, a monster cat!" Jack exulted.

"Wow, as big as Carns's," Jim said.

Jack dropped to his knees and meticulously lined up the pair of cats for admiration. He swept wet sand from their glossy heads. I never saw a happier guy. "Wow, look at them! Dang, I've never seen prettier cats." And they were . . . long and muscled, but football deep in the belly, and slick, steely skin remindful of the sheen on Gramp's lever action .300 Savage.

The four of us stood by the fishin' Ford and, over and over, replayed the fight with the big cats. But then, with the afternoon waning, town beckoned with so many people who'd want to hear our story. "We've gotta be getting home, Mr. Roy," Jack said. "You better take one of these cats."

"No, no thanks. I can get one anytime," Roy said.

We protested, all of us joining: "You had us for lunch," and "You brought us the chicken bait," and "We want you to have one."

Smoky Roy spread his wide grin upon us. In that instant, I felt like I'd known him for a very long time. He stood with hands in his coverall pockets looking up the river trail from where we'd first come into his territory. "You boys come back anytime. Can't overfish this river you know. . . . Say, I guess I will take one of your catfish. I'll take him to the brothers. They can't catch anything, won't even try. You can carry my fish up to the house if you please." He started for his homeward trail, but stopped. "Bring your fish along too. I'll help you get him ready for traveling."

With that, Smoky hunched forward and started for his house, walking nimbly. "Funny thing," I said to myself, "He's carrying his walking stick, but he isn't using it. And Malta—he's gimping, but with a hoppity gimp."

Jack and Jim threaded cords through the fishes' gills and hoisted them over their shoulders, and the three of us trooped up the trail to Smoky's place. He stood out front beside a makeshift sawhorse table. "The one you're haulin' home; put him on the table," Smoky directed.

As if he'd done it a hundred times, Smoky clipped the cat's spines, burlap-wrapped, and twined him, all done in a minute. "This'll keep him from drying out," he said, as he dumped water onto the burlap. "It won't hurt if he slimes your back some," Smoky joked. Being as Jack caught the big fish, he was obligated to carry it. He slung the roped cat over his shoulder, scowling as he did so.

We said our goodbyes, even Malta did, wagging his white tail, nosing legs, and accepting head pats. But, Smoky Roy hung back, hesitating before shaking our hands. His eyes had lost their blue twinkle, gone lonesome; maybe believing we wouldn't be coming back. "Hope you boys make it back sometime soon," was all he said.

From the trail, we turned back to wave. But Smoky was already at work tying Jim's cat to a nail on his house front. He held a knife, ready to skin the fish. He didn't watch our departure. The spooky brothers did though. They stood by their door, close enough for us to see that they still didn't smile. We waved, but the brothers kept their hands in their pockets.

Jim led out, trotting the old road on the bank of the Muddy. Jack brought up the rear, from where he could jaw us. "Next time you guys be more patient; guys like Smoky Roy, livin' on the river, they know their stuff."

In ten minutes we arrived and mounted our bikes. With all he had to do, Jack could no longer boss us. He steered his bike with one hand and held the rope over his shoulder with the other. With each bump in the trail, the slimy burlapped cat made a nice whomping thump on Jack's back, a pleasant reminder of our big braggin' fish. "Who wants a turn with this cat?" Jack asked.

Jim laughed, "He's yours, Jack. It's your duty to carry him."

All the way down the trail and the road to the Scenic Highway, the three of us bantered about plans to get past Goslin's mean Chesapeake. He'd be waiting to grab ankles on our pump up the hill on Broadway. With nothing settled about the dog, talk edged to parental questionings and what to do about them. And with no certain plans there, either, Jack simply picked up the pace.

"We'll all line up and run our bikes straight at the dog," Jim hollered as we approached the city limits. I didn't like it, nor did Jack, who chickened out a block before Goslin's and turned into an alley going north. Jim and I closed in tight to his back wheel.

Good, the Chesapeake hadn't spotted us. And now I was relieved further in believing that Jack would turn on the gravel pit road that would take us close by Horseshoe Bend, our alibi. I guessed wrong. Jack turned left on the hill road leading up to 5th Avenue.

Jack's big cat, like an elixir, had changed everything. He headed right for Grandma Millhouse's house and her trusty camera. Jim knocked, then stuck his head in the door and hollered, "Gramma, you gotta see our fish." He motioned to Jack, "Bring him here."

Little Gram came quickly, eyes bright. As Jack hoisted his cat, Gram's mouth opened, "My goodness boys, what a mighty catfish. Now, you boys don't move. I'll get my Kodak." She shocked me. I knew well her scurrying ways. But, I'd never seen her run. Gram was back in seconds, snapping pictures of us showing off Jack's fish.

We'd cut twine and removed the burlap for Gram's pictures, and now Jack's cat swung free for the whole town to see. Jack led us racing down 7th Street. He ignored the feel of the wet fish sliming the back of his western, pearl-buttoned shirt. How could that be? He laughed, steering with his knees, so he could wave at honking drivers as we crossed Main. This is perfect, I thought. *Everybody* loves the big cat. Dad will too. We'll celebrate with him. Where we spent the day will be lost in the excitement.

As always, we rode up our sloped driveway and around to the back of our house. "I want to give my big cat to your dad," Jack said. He was generous and smart that way, taking care of his buddy's dad and, at the same time, avoiding a confrontation with his own Dutchman dad about his fish-slimed shirt, and bringing home a stinking fish from the dirty waters flowing next to the city dump.

By the time we had our trophy hanging from a branch of our box elder, Mr. Gwin had wandered over to join in the excitement and hear the stories. Jack stood ready to work on the cat; but, he wouldn't skin it until Dad got home. He'd never, ever do that. A skinned cat can't be properly admired.

Our neighbor from the other side, Mr. Leiseth—the Texaco man—appeared next. Mom started with the questioning, "What in the world is that stink on you boys?"

"We were downwind from a fire."

"A fire, what fire?" Mr. Gwin asked, a natural question from the inquisitive policeman, who Dad said was the smartest cop he'd ever known.

"Down by the Muddy," Jim said.

Thankfully, a reprieve of sorts showed up in the persons of Gramp and Dad. Without inventing anything, we drug out our fish catching story as long as possible. However, the *how* part was bound to run aground to make room for the *where.* "He's a dandy," Dad said. "Where'd you catch him?"

"The Muddy," Jim said.

Dad stepped back, steeling his blue eyes on each one of us, "So did you boys pick up that stink on the Muddy?"

"We were down wind from some fires out there."

"Where's 'there'? You said you were going to Horseshoe Bend."

"Well, we planned to, but then we went further downriver," Jim said, "below the packing plant. The big cats move in there, feed on the animal guts."

"I'd better skin him," Jack said nervously. "I need to get home."

To end the awkward moment, Mr. Leiseth stepped forward with his fish scale. I wanted to cheer. We had learned to depend on Mr. Leiseth's kindness. I think because he didn't have a kid of his own, he came down on our side. "Wait a minute, Jack," he said. "Before you go, let's weigh your big fish." As Mr. Leiseth hooked the scale hook into the cat's gill and lifted, he asked the standard question, "What did you catch him on?"

"Chicken meat" came Jim's swift reply, happy to talk of fishin' and nothing more. "We found out worms aren't so good. Chicken's the answer, the rottener—the better—and . . ." Jim jabbered along, hoping to interest the big folks in anything but our day's travels.

I would have preferred more questions, indicating that Jim's technique was still in play. Instead, the circle of adults around us tightened and went silent. Fortunately, Mr. Leiseth, ever the gentle man, chose a good moment to announce his finding: "Twelve pounds even," he said. "Biggest catfish I've ever weighed."

Naturally, Jim and I, and Jack whooped at the news. But, except for Mr. Leiseth, the big folks seemed on another track. Jack rocked from heel to heel, collecting ideas.

"See, there was a man, lives down there," Jack started. "He knows the river. He was the one who gave us the half-rotten chicken for bait."

Dad stepped forward, turned his back to Jack and his hanging cat, and aimed his pointy finger at the bridge of Jim's nose, then at mine. His chin dropped low so's his eyes could bore holes in us. "Nobody lives down there." I knew what he meant. Squatter bums don't count as real people. "There's nothin' below the damned packing plant but the dumpground," Dad said. "So far, none of this adds up."

Now, at the conclusion of our dumpground escapade we faced mad parents, a police bull trained on the streets of Minneapolis, and Mr. Leiseth, our kindly neighbor who'd help us if possible, but was now retreating through the hedgerow. That left Gramp, certain to remain nervously neutral since he had taken us to the dump in the first place.

Piercing eyes returned to Jim.

"Well, uh, here's how it happened. We uh, we . . ."

Jim's brain wheels spun, I could almost hear them. And suddenly a change came over him. His eyes lit up. Here it came: "FROZEN NUTS." With freezing water lapping at his testicuts, Jim dove in: "You see we met a nice man living down there. Mr. Roy something, his name is. He built a house, sort of, on the side of the dump, well—kind of *in* it really . . . but, but—he boils his water good." Jim shifted to second gear and let 'er rip: "His house is nicer than you might think, real well built, and Mr. Roy found us the perfect rotten chicken to fish with."

What? *Mr.* Roy? I laughed inside, hoping it wouldn't show on the outside.

"And boy, we fished from a swell dock made from an old truck box." Jim rattled on, faster:

"Dave and I headed for the Missouri; crazy Indian down there . . . Missouri—you oughta see it running wild logs and dead cows comin' down, but we never put a toe in the Missouri, did we Dave? Then, when we came back, Jack and Mr. Roy had our hooks baited and after he showed us inside his house two huge cats grabbed a-hold, and . . ."

Jim spilled the works, going long between breaths . . . . "Went by Horseshoe Bend twice, didn't have time to stop, the Carns brothers caught a monster cat we saw when Gramp took us rat hunting, so we went down there looking, some spooky brothers live there in the, uh . . . the dumpground, and Roy's an old farmer, nice guy."

Jim let it all go: his fabulous discovery of a hidden channel in the Jungle, the makings of Roy's house, landing the cats, and everything else . . . well, most everything except the rubbers and the jellied doughnuts and . . . Smoky Roy's secret door.

All the while, I watched faces, hopeful that Jim's frozen nuts confession was enough, at least entertaining enough to soften them. All I saw: crossed arms, shaking heads, open mouths, no smiles, and squinted eyes. And on Mom, the biggest worry face I'd ever seen. Only Gramp offered a flicker of hope. Yessiree! I caught the quick grin he couldn't help.

Dad hunched his shoulders, mad as a chained bulldog. Reed Gwin, however, stood quietly listening, expressionless, and unreadable. Now in the chilling, silent aftermath of Jim's confession, all eyes were on Mr. Gwin, a man who people counted on for sound thinking and useful answers.

Reed backed away and rested his butt against our downed cottonwood, the "Thinking Tree" and sometimes—like now—the "Courtroom." After hours Mr. Gwin went hatless, showing his neat reddish-black crew cut. He had deep brown inquisitive eyes and heavy Dick Tracy jaws. "Irish-Indian" my dad said, the Indian part accounting for barrel chest and bow legs. He stood slightly taller than my dad's six feet and bigger in every bone and muscle. He was built like Jack Dempsey; in fact, Dad said he'd boxed professionally before taking up police work. He seldom wore the full blue uniform, mostly just the blue shirt and badge. On days spent on investigative work, like apparently today, he wore clean, plain civilian clothes: a white cotton shirt, gray bus driver pants, and high topped work boots. The uniform wouldn't have changed anything. The whole town knew him and his no-nonsense integrity. He was the cop nobody would mess with, the one Chief Olson would send to South Main to break up bad men fights, drunks who Dad said sometimes carried knives.

Despite Reed Gwin's tough guy reputation, he had a way with kids about town. He was acquainted with dozens and he could talk with kids without getting into our small time shenanigans. But, any straight thinking kid knew better than to mess with serious trouble-making in Mr. Gwin's jurisdiction, which apparently he believed we had done.

"I'll tell you what we should do folks," Reed said. He nodded at Dad, "Bill, let's call it a day. "I'd rather talk to the boys when they're rested. If you don't mind, I'll come over in the morning for a cup of coffee."

Jack moved away, about to mount his bike, but not without Mr. Gwin's "Hold on Jack. I'd like you here too, say about 7:30 in the morning." He said that while winking at Dad. "Or should I call your father and . . . come by your house?"

"No, no," Jack said quickly. "You won't need to call my dad. I'll be here."

This turn of events was far worse than expected, especially the waiting. Dad would postpone his sentence on us until he knew the full meaning of Mr. Gwin's interest in the matter. Now we'd have a restless night of worry about Dad's pending punishment and the curious nature of Mr. Gwin's concerns.

"It's ten minutes to six," our red-faced Dad said. "You boys have a few minutes to clean the fish. While you're at it, you can figure out why you couldn't tell me where the hell you were going today. And take off your stinkin' clothes on the back step." Then Dad nodded at Mr. Gwin, and the two of them walked around the corner of our house, talking in low voices.

"I'd better get home," Jack said. He cleaned the fish slime off with our garden hose and rode down the driveway.

Gramp rolled up his sleeves. "You boys go in and fetch your Mom's cutting board and butcher knife. We'll need a hammer and pliers too." We went for them, but pruney-nosed Mom refused us, stopped us at the door, handing us the tools.

Cleaning a prairie chicken or catfish was near the top of Gramp's fun list. This cat skinning occasion was no different. "The river was good to us on the ranch," he said, talking of his homesteader days. "And catfish was for birthday dinners, celebrations, and special guests."

With the pliers, Gramp latched onto the flap of cut skin behind the head and stripped the cat's skin down over its tail. Next came the gutting. Then, Gramp held the knife behind the cat's ugly head and, *"whop,"* the hammer banged the back of the butcher blade, and the head was gone to the alley cats. *"Whop"*. . . *"whop"*. . . *"whop,"* Gramp's blade and hammer marched methodically, slicing the length of the fish carcass, making perfect thick white steaks for Jim and me to wrap in butcher paper; all done in ten minutes and stamped with Gramp's blessing. Rubbing his palms together, he said, "A lot of good meat there boys."

Jim and I were stripping on the back step when Mom called out, "I've drawn a hot tub for you." We ran naked through the kitchen to the bathroom and jumped in the tub. Gramp followed. He sat on the toilet lid and prodded for more of our story. At any hint of our slowing, he asked questions to keep us talking. Plain to see that he would have enjoyed being with us. He would have liked Smoky Roy, too.

Our pork chop supper that night was a terse affair punctuated by Dad's pronouncements: "You knew better. Next time you say Horseshoe Bend, you better mean it. In the morning you tell Reed Gwin everything you know." I went to bed with my head swirling. Jim was roiled up too; I knew by his rolling about in his twin bed next to mine.

"What are we going to tell them?" I whispered.

"I told practically everything already."

"You think Roy's guilty of something? What about that secret door?"

"Maybe it ain't secret. Maybe he just forgot to show it to us."

Finally, slipping toward sleep, the acrid, sicky-sweet dumpground fragrance wafted up from my high topped shoes parked under my bed. It was a strange potion, loosing memories of the day that needed sorting through.

Next morning, Jim and I hadn't quite put down our brown-sugared oatmeal, when Jack showed. While we three culprits fidgeted about the kitchen table, Mom and Dad leaned on the countertop, close to Mom's Philco. Kaltenborn had their attention; his precise, cadenced voice marched a little faster than normal. Mom and Dad leaned ever closer, as if they wanted inside the radio. They exchanged soft mutterings, "I'll be damned" . . .

"Thank God. Sounds like she's over."

"Bill, Bill, I can't believe my ears," Mom said.

Kaltenborn talked on excitedly, throwing everything together about admirals, generals, and news about MacArthur and Hirohito. Finally, Kaltenborn signed off, and the station plugged in the Presidential March. Dad grabbed Mom and hugged her tight just as Reed Gwin walked in our back door without knocking. He punched Dad's shoulder, shook his hand, and hugged Mom. Then, he turned to us boys wearing a grin I didn't know a policeman could possess. He stood with his butt against the stove and arranged the three of us for hand shakings— Jack, Jim, and then he came to me. He happened to have my hand smothered in his huge grip as he said, "You boys would have made good soldiers someday. Looks like you'll be finding better kinds of work." Mr. Gwin exhaled then, as if getting rid of bad air.

"The Japs called it quits today, boys." Dad smiled. "All that's left is the formal surrender."

Alongside that statement, even our little un-feathered brains deciphered that, by comparison, our dumpground shenanigans were no more important than, like Mr. Stensby would say . . . "No more important than a pimple on a duck's butt." Reed Gwin had already reached the door and was halfway out before remembering, "Oh, yeah . . . boys. About your friend, Roy. Any other name for him? Smoky maybe?"

"Yes, sir, the other men out there call him "Smoky—Smoky Roy."

"Good, good. I got him pegged then, Smoky and Roy *are* the same person." Then, to Dad, Reed said, "I've only seen this Smoky Roy character in town twice, tried unsuccessfully to strike up a conversation. He's a strict loner, which makes me suspicious; but then I'm suspicious of the whole caboodle out there. That's why I'm asking these boys to stay away from their shanty-town. A nod from Dad told Reed he wouldn't need to worry about us.

With Mr. Gwin barely gone, Mom king-ed his checker. "Reed is right about that awful place, Bill. The boys must never go there."

"They damn well better not," Dad said. "Now listen, boys—and this goes for you too, Jack, because I know your dad would back me on this. From now on, *stay north of the Little Muddy Bridge!*" That part of Dad's decree, our travel restriction, was terse and solid as concrete. But then when he wrapped up with, "And wherever it is you're headed, tell us and stick to it," his voice had softened, and he allowed a faint smile. I dared to hope the second part—his punishment announcement—would be tolerable. Jim and I sat quietly waiting for the "judge's sentence" and the "bang of a gavel," but to our great and wondrous surprise, none came—a gift from Hirohito, I suppose.

Japan's formal surrender came on September 2nd, 1945. A week later we crowded into the Grande Theatre with Mom and Dad and Gram and Grampa Millhouse, and all who arrived early enough to get tickets. The main feature didn't matter: John Wayne—behind the times, commanding an aircraft carrier. We'd all come to see the newsreel showing the Japanese officers on the deck of the ship called the *MISSOURI*—special that they named the victory ship after our river. The little Japanese men marched to the surrender table where they bowed to the Americans and signed away their war.

A week later with celebrations winding down, Mr. Gwin knocked on our back door. He came at the very end of suppertime. "Bill," I heard him say from my place at the kitchen table, "I wonder if I might have a word with your sons."

"As damn many as you want, Reed," Dad gruffed, meaning Jim and I better fess up anything and everything.

"One more piece of apple pie left, Reed," Mom said. "It will be good with your coffee."

Though officer Gwin was our neighbor, and friendly in a formal sort of way, his coming to visit us had the same effect as Chief Olson's telephoning a year earlier when he banned us from the east side of Main. Reed Gwin was on to something having to do with our behavior. My heart raced uncontrollably, though I knew it shouldn't, because Jim and I hadn't been in trouble of any consequence, except our day at the out-of-bounds dumpground. Yet, Mr. Gwin wouldn't have bothered for nothing. Maybe we should know something about other kids, maybe a broken window or some stolen crab-apples. But the way officer Gwin slapped down his note pad on our big round kitchen table, I figured there was nothing simple about his visit. I sensed that our doggone dumpground fiasco had yet to pass into history.

Mom poured coffee as Reed began, "The sheriff has jurisdiction out at the dumpground; but last year when we had the string of burglaries, Chief Olson acted on a tip that the sheriff ignored. He put it on me. No uncertain terms, the Chief wants no more trouble out of the dump people."

"Like the trouble when you shot the burglar in the leg?" Dad laughed.

Reed forked in pie before answering, "Yeah, that no good bastard hid out with a couple of burglarizing brothers in their dumpground shack." I quaked a bit when I heard *"brothers,"* hoping that Dad didn't notice. Reed continued, explaining how he had to shoot the bad guy. "Damn I hate using the gun," he said. "I got a tip the burglar had been seen by the shine of a streetlight, heading east for the Scenic Highway with a gunny sack of booty. Next time he snuck back into town, I spotted him in the moonlight. He was crawling out of a window on Third Avenue. Shouldn't have tried to run on me. He's back in the pen for 20 more years. The brothers worked burglary in the Fargo-Moorhead area when they were juveniles. They served some time. They've kept their noses clean here, far as we know."

I felt better already listening to Mr. Gwin's measured reporting and without a hint of lecturing directed toward Jim and me. Besides, all of us—including Dad—had been taken up with curiosity. And as far as the heebie-jeebie brothers were concerned, well it was good that Officer Gwin had watch over them.

I'd noticed Dad's grimace and shaking head at the news of the burglar brothers. And Mom, standing by the stove, rattled her coffee cup against her saucer. Still, Mom and Dad were in no position to interrupt officer Gwin in order to scold us for mingling among grimy derelicts, who happened to be criminals. And now, as Reed Gwin began his inquiry, a pleasant feeling bubbled. I suppressed a smile, beginning to believe that my brother and I were very, very important to police work. And maybe—hopefully—our parents would think so, too.

"Now, about this Smoky fella," Reed began. "Only get to talk to the dump-ground squatters when they wander into town. Believe it or not, the judge says those decrepit shacks qualify as homes. Need a warrant to search out there, even though a few of the bums have nasty records. Still, I've got a pretty good fix on the population, all nine of 'em, except the one the boys know as Smoky Roy. The sheriff says the other squatters don't have a last name for him. I can't figure him and can't get him to talk. Seen him on south Main a couple times. I offered to buy him coffee. No go, but he was polite about it. He's a mystery: seems too civilized, almost mannerly, to be in such a predicament."

"What sort of a predicament?" Dad asked.

"Bill, you've heard the story floating around about a Montana bank robber hiding out at the dump?"

"Yah, but I didn't pay much attention."

"Well, suspicion is on him, this Smoky fella."

"A gunman?"

"No, he was too smart for that . . . dynamite, middle of the night."

"So, you have evidence tagging the guy in the dump?"

"Haven't yet. But I have some other dope on him that I can't talk about. Not yet."

Mr. Gwin directed his talk toward Mom's Great Northern calendar hanging by the telephone, then at her hands, pouring "float a pistol" coffee. Reed looked over my head and out our back window. Part of his brain arranged words, while the rest worked on the next fork in the road: "The Chief needs answers and I ain't . . . cottonpickin' bums anyway, they . . ."

Out of habit Reed jerked at his empty shirt pocket, going for a cigarette. I'd seen this before, Reed grimacing over his struggle to win the ten dollar bet with Dad on quitting smokes. They locked eyes as if trading thoughts. "Bill," Reed said, "you get around; you've got a hundred farmer friends; you bowl in two leagues. Heard any talk about this Smoky Roy character?"

"No. No, I haven't. Not him specifically. But I heard the talk about a bank robber hiding out there with a stash of cash. Probably just that, talk."

"Yeah, yeah, the whole town is taken up with it. A lot of this stuff was caused by the goddam war, Bill. Folks needed something else to talk about. Still, it's my job to follow leads. So, how about you? Anything else worth knowing?"

Dad shook his head. "Been too damn busy to listen to the yakking on Main Street. So, what do *you* think?"

"What I think, what I think." Reed sipped coffee and swiped his palm across his mouth. "Not what I think, Bill. It's what I know. The facts are few, but I have leads to keep me busy."

"Well, nothing would surprise me much," Dad said. "Bums squatting in a dumpground . . . stuck there for a reason."

"My thoughts, exactly," Reed said. "But I need something solid to get a warrant."

Mr. Gwin, turning away from Dad, looked hard at Jim and me. Jim and I shifted in straight chairs, too obviously, I thought. Reed pursed his lips, nodded at Jim, then me—like a judge, but we had no need of: "Do you swear to tell the truth, the whole . . ."

Reed Gwin exchanged glances with Dad before he began, "I think you boys might provide a clue or two about Smoky Roy. But before I go any further, I want you two to know I've already talked with Jack, got his word that my conversation with him would stay with us and his parents." Reed's brown eyes shifted from Jim to me, back to Jim, and to me again. Now I want the same deal with you two. Do I have it?"

"Yes, sir," we said in unison, me with a bit of stammer.

"Okay, I'm *counting* on you," came strong and deep, out of his barrel chest. With another glare for good measure, he opened his notepad and licked his pencil lead. At the top he printed in bold letters: SMOKY ROY—??????

Eying us, he extended his coffee cup toward Mom, "A spot more, Ruth, please, if you have it." Back at us, "So, Jack tells me Smoky Roy showed you about his shack."

"Yes, sir," Jim answered for us.

"Okay, then. I have some questions. Listen carefully. They may not seem important. Still, answer best you can."

Mr. Gwin began, posing simple questions that Jim answered, while I backed him with a "yup" or a nod of my head. Mr. Gwin's questions rolled on for 10 minutes, covering details of our time with Smoky on the river, and visiting him in his shack. After each answer Reed jotted a word or two. Nearing the end, he slowed, running out of good questions. When he went silent, I pushed my chair back, ready to escape. "Hold on, David. We're not done, not quite." I liked that Mr. Gwin said that with a blip of grin.

"You boys certain he didn't mention a last name?"

"No, sir."

"On the walls, you told me about the farm house picture. Anything else? A calendar, maybe?"

"Oh, yes, there was a calendar, I think," Jim said. "You remember, Dave?"

"Uh-huh, there was one, hanging to the side of his bookcase."

"Advertisements on it?"

"No, nothing like that."

"A picture of a business, something with a name or place?"

"Yes, there was. I remember for sure," Jim said. "It was a mountain goat."

"Oh, yeah, it was the Great Northern Railroad mountain goat, same as that one right there," I said, with a nod at Mom's calendar.

"Good, good, Davey . . . now anything else that could describe where Smoky Roy might have come from? Besides the calendar; anything else that might name a location, maybe a town?"

"Pictures. Pictures of his farm," I said.

"An Army picture too," Jim added.

"Any of those . . . I need a where," Reed Gwin urged.

We didn't answer. There wasn't an answer. Reed paused, thumb under his chin, maybe out of ideas. He started to slide his chair back, but hesitated, stroking his chin.

His question seemed out of place. To this day, I'm not sure if he had a purpose in asking, or if he simply fired a flock shot, hoping a stray pellet might hit a duck in the head: "The dog, the dog—you said he had a dog."

"Yes sir, he did. A white mongrel with three legs," Jim said.

"Two front legs and one hind," I added. "The hinder had some black along with the white."

Reed considered that, shrugged his shoulders, and pushed back from the table. Then with an afterthought: "So, what's the dog's name?"

"Malta, he called him. Funny name for a dog," Jim said.

"What?"

You'd have thought a snowball came from nowhere and blasted Mr. Gwin full in the face. "*Malta,* you said?"

"Yes sir."

I had no idea whatsoever why Mr. Gwin slapped the table over a dog's name, news that suddenly ended his interview. At the bottom of his notebook page he wrote MALTA in large letters. Then he flipped the cardboard cover to close the pad, and stood to leave. "Thank you so very much, boys. Thank you Bill, Ruth," he smiled. "We may have something here."

Chapter Eight

The Jungle

"No go there bwana."—white hunter's native tracker

After V-J Day the Muddy River guys had only Saturdays for all-day adventures. We were back in school—well, physically at least. I harbored a pocket of colored pencils for boring times, when I added more sketches to my collection of underwater scenes of perch, bass, yellow bullheads, channel cats, bluegills, sunnies, and goldies. Last school year I drew walleyes swimming among reeds in blue water Canadian lakes, and my favorite so far: a 3-foot long great northern pike. I drew my pike in different scenes: hiding in 10 foot tall jungley water weeds, then charging from his lair, and one swimming for the deep with a yellow perch clamped crossways in his dagger teeth. I can't remember a thing about school subjects from the fall of 1945. But, because I saved my drawings, I know that I worked to perfect a channel cat: a humongous steel gray one swimming through a windowless car body. I tried and tried, but I couldn't get the catfish right. My mind drifted off to the turmoil of the squatter people and the curious, unfinished story of Smoky Roy.

We talked about Smoky a lot, just Jim and I. We avoided the subject around Buck and the other guys, the best way to keep our word with Dad and Officer Gwin. Jim wouldn't forget the dumpground though. He was convinced that somehow we could get around Dad's V-J Day rule that forbade us traveling south of the Muddy River Bridge.

Summer had gone, but not its perfect weather—just a smidge cooler by mid-September, ideal for a trip to the Muddy River country. Friday came around, and still Jim and Jack hadn't proposed a destination. I was excited when Buck stepped forward with a big deal. I knew it was big, because at recess he took Jim, Jack, and me to a far corner of the playground. He lowered his bushy eyebrows. "You guys gotta promise. No one else can know. I'm takin' you to my dad and Al Stensby's secret walleye holes tomorrow. We'll leave early 'cuz we're riding clear out to the White Bridge and hiking in from there." I tossed and turned in bed that night. I had never caught a walleye. Now, with Buck's help, I relished my chance.

With the morning sun peeking over the Catwalk bluffs, we rode north up the Muddy Valley Road. What a perfect day! Buck had strapped his Dad's extra rod and reel to my handlebars. He rode beside me and talked about walleyes, how he went on five trips with his dad last summer before catching one. "They're finicky, moody, and smart. You won't catch one by accident," he said. You and I . . . we'll stop at Six Mile. It has an underwater spring in the bottom and a huge 'walleye boulder' ten feet down. Jim and Jack are in too big a hurry. They'll keep right on going, past the best fishin.'"

Buck had guessed right. We found Jim and Jack's bikes at White Bridge. They had hiked north, a moving pair of dots on the prairie.

Buck and I arrived at the riffle below Six Mile Hole, where he warned me again: "Al Stensby is crabby about his fishin' spots. I don't want you letting on you fished here." Buck lowered his voice, "We'll work our way over to that steep bank. And stay low; this is just like trout fishin'. Walleyes see your shadow, they're gone."

Buck took me crawling to the edge of the steep bank. We peeked over. "No talking," he whispered. "Move only your eyes." We peered deep into a maze of slanted light and shadows. A short cast would drop a lure at a wall of black, the "walleye boulder" that projected half-way to the water's surface and "always hides at least one big one."

"There, there . . . the white on the fins, moving . . . a walleye." I didn't spot the movement, and Buck didn't give me another chance. He pulled me back from the bank and went to work setting up the beautiful Pflueger rod and reel for me.

Buck tied on a number two black and white River Runt and clamped on a bullet weight to pull the lure deep. "Okay, Davey, crawl to the edge, but go easy. Walleyes can feel the bank shake, so don't go stompin' around. Fish the Runt slow and deep, at the bottom of the boulder. Twitch it like a hurt minnow. And don't beat the water. One cast every five minutes is plenty."

Buck left me alone and hiked upriver, leaving me to fish possibly the best walleye hole on the entire Muddy. I crawled down the bank, but didn't try casting the Pflueger, right off. "Sloppy casts will spook 'em," Buck had warned. When my heart quit racing, I started with short casts, soft as a plopping frog, I thought.

Though I was a rookie, the casting was fun. I didn't expect to catch a walleye. Nobody is expected to actually catch a walleye on his first ever trip. So just imagine my shock when the shadow coasted around the corner of the boulder. I saw a flash of an open mouth just before my rod bowed to the water surface. "I got one," I hollered as loud as I ever yelled. I knew better, but I hauled on Buck's rod with all my might. Good thing the Pflueger rod was stout, and Buck said the line was 20 pound test. Everything held. I raised my walleye from the deep, tugging him through the graveled shallows, into bright sunlight. He lightened from deep gray, to amber, finally glistening gold. I skidded my prize walleye into the skunk grass, where he thumped the ground and rattled Buck's River Runt. "Yahoo," I yelled.

Buck came running around the bend. He jumped from the high bank and dropped on his knees next to my walleye. He seemed as excited as me, if that's possible. "Wow, a dandy walleye, Eric. Pretty big for your first one, better'n three pounds. I told you, this is a great hole." I was ready to go for home right there to show off my first walleye. My walleye was ready, too. He puked up a half-rotten sucker minnow.

Buck caught the only other walleye that day, a whopper of four pounds. We talked walleyin' as we started for home. Jim and Jack swore they saw a walleye "at least 6 pounds" swirl for a rosy chub. Soon Buck's thoughts strayed from the day.

He'd seen Gram's snap-shot of Jack's huge cat and wanted to know more about the trip he'd missed. He biked along close to Jack and Jim. I closed in behind to make a tight moving pod. "Jack, your big cat, you haven't said much about him. Sure wish I'd been along . . . tell me"—

"Told you . . . twelve pounds."

"Yah, but what else, Jack? You haven't bragged him up, haven't said much."

"About what?" Jim said.

"What you caught him on, and where you went. Jack said something about Horseshoe Bend."

The laugh in Jack's voice told me his tease was on. "Yah, I guess I did say something about the Bend. We went a ways south of there," Jack said.

"How far?" Buck demanded.

"Well, I'm not supposed to say."

"What? Whadda' mean, you're not *supposed* to?"

"Just can't, that's all."

"And you aren't going to take me there," Buck gruffed, which only greased the tracks for Jack.

"Don't want to either," Jack teased. He shouldn't have.

"Gosh durn your hide, Jack. Pull over." Buck swerved left, cutting in front of Jack. They skidded to a stop, wheel-by-wheel on the edge of the road. Buck dropped his bike and straddled Jack's front wheel. He grabbed the bike's handlebars with two hands, mad—madder than I'd ever seen him.

Jim dropped his bike too, thinking he'd have to stop a fight. "Hold on, Buck, heck you can go after cats, we'll all go," Jim said. Buck, though, held tight to Jack's handlebars, his elbows locked, eyes staring into Jack's.

Earlier, I had watched the progress of the black cloud, then forgot about it. Now it snuck in from behind. The rain started softly, followed by a ground-shaking thundercrack, then a downpour. Nobody moved from our huddle on the road; there wasn't shelter within miles anyway. Besides, Buck's unfinished business wouldn't wait. "Hell or high water," as they say, Buck wanted the catfish story. His super matted hair sopped up part of the rain and shed the rest. If anything, Buck's grip on Jack's handlebars had strengthened. He demanded: "Jack, you haven't said. I heard Jim say we'll all go to your catfish hole sometime. Are you agreeing?"

Jack tucked his chin and hunkered with the rest of us, trying to make a smaller target for the incoming, stinging, nickel-sized hail. What else could Jack say? Clobbered by hail and icy rain and trapped between Buck and Jim, he said, "Sure, Buck. We'll go with Jim's plan. What are we standing here for?" Deep down he couldn't have meant what he said.

Buck gave Jack one more glare for good measure and released his bike.

Allowing himself a half grin, "Well, that's better," he said. "Jeez, I took you guys out, showed you the Six Mile hole, the Buckbrush Hole, my dad's and Mr. Stensby's favorites, an' you were sayin' you won't show me a doggone catfish hole?" Buck spoke up extra loud so's we could all get his message: "At least Big Eric will take me. He says he has a plan; ain't that right, Eric?"

"Yah, sure, but you gotta know the plan won't be simple, and no telling. It's a secret deal."

"What the hay! I know it's a secret, just like the Six Mile and Buckbrush Hole were secrets before I took you guys."

"Well, this is a different kind of secret, a bigger one. We're breakin' a huge rule by taking you, Buck. Maybe we better think how we're gonna do it." Jim threw his leg over his bike, ready to ride. "Jack and Dave will help with my plan." I understood Jim's strategy. He'd stall for time . . . figure a way to possibly squiggle out of two clashing promises.

We rode on down the Muddy Valley road. Too late to hurry; we were sogged through. Though the hail had quit, the rain drummed on. I shivered right down to my bones. I remembered one of my Dad's favorite sayings, making fun of somebody: "He ain't smart enough to come in out of the rain." That would be us, and our excuse could be that four miles north of town there wasn't a place to "come in" to. Jim rode in the middle, Jack and Buck on either side peppering him with questions, and me worrying along behind them. I heard bits and pieces, none of which seemed to settle anything.

"Dang it, Jim, we gave our word," Jack said.

"What?" Buck again, agitated, "Promised who? You guys are acting half nuts."

Jim hadn't thought of a slick enough answer to satisfy Buck. He escaped the pod and stood on his pedals, racing for town. But suddenly at the city limits sign, he slammed his brakes, sliding to a stop. We circled Jim like Indians on war ponies, Buck being the biggest Indian.

Jim scratched the back of his head and grimaced before announcing: "We'll go next Saturday. The monster cats are in the river right now; they won't be forever. Everybody can go—Big Bervie and Razzie, too."

Jack slapped himself on his forehead. "Jeez, Jim I hope you know what the heck you're doing." I caught Jim's sly wink, done so Buck couldn't see. Jack noticed, too, and his exasperation dwindled; his fun loving grin returned, along with his crazy laugh. That was enough to do Buck in, at least for the moment. He moved his bike next to Jack's, and they went to twittering like squirrels at a nut party.

My brother had ridden dangerous waves of trouble many times, but I'd never known him to be plumb stupid about it. Yet here he was, like a Jonah, rapping a whale on its snout. He decided to leave Jack guessing. At the dairy road Y he took the west fork, hollering, "Dave and I gotta get home."

Buck and Jack headed east on the left fork. Jack yelled back, "You better have 'er figured, Eric, or you and Buck can go alone."

I'd have preferred to go home glorifying my three pound walleye swinging from the stringer on my handlebar. But I couldn't ignore worries about a forbidden dumpground trip in the making. I pictured Dad delivering his V-J Day rule: "Not one foot south of the Muddy Bridge." Jim, though, ignored my worries until the intersection two blocks north of our house, where he motioned for me to slow down. We coasted side-by-side. "I've got a plan," he said. "Now, here's the deal: We're going to the Jungle next Saturday. I've got some details to work out, but we're going."

At the driveway in front of our house, Jim braked to a stop and motioned for me to pull over. "Get your throw-lines ready. We're gonna sneak across the tracks into the Jungle. We'll work our way south through the willows and the swamp. We can circle east to the channels west of the dump. Remember what I said out there at the confluence? Those backwaters are perfect for big cats, maybe jumbo bullheads, and sauger, too. And from there Buck and Bervie can cross the beaver dams to the dumpground and check on Smoky Roy. That way you and I and Jack won't violate Dad's V-J Day rule." Jim studied me . . . "Okay?"

I grimaced, picturing my dad and Reed Gwin standing shoulder to shoulder, me hunkering, while Jim explained: "Yah, we were maybe a little bit south of the Muddy River Bridge, but *mostly* west of it, and we didn't actually put a foot on the dumpground." I worked Jim's explanation back and forth; it still sounded like a big Shorty, and Dad could spot a Shorty a mile away. I wanted nothing of Jim's so-called "plan."

Jim punched me on the shoulder. "Come on, Dave. This will work."

"I don't know, Jim. I'll need to think about it."

"Nothin' to think about, Dave. Now, I'll do the talking with Mom and Dad."

"What about Jack and Buck and the other guys?"

"I'll talk to them too. They'll like my plan, guaranteed."

That night at the supper table I expected Jim to open the subject. He didn't, not the next night either. Thursday came and still nothing. When I pushed on him, Jim had a reasonable explanation. "Best not to let Dad think about the details too long," he said.

Friday had to be *the* day, for the *announcement*. But suppertime talk that night was much the same as all week. Dad didn't leave openings casual enough for Jim to slip in our Saturday plans without warning bells gonging. Besides, Dad had a couple of promising tractor deals to talk about. Better yet, he went from tractor talk to his fascination with Reed Gwin's ongoing sleuthing of the "dumpground characters."

"Reed's one smart cookie," Dad said. "He played a hunch after you boys said the bum's dog was named Malta."

"He's not really a bum, Dad. He's not like that."

"Not a bum, Jimmy? Living out there? What else would you call him? . . . Okay, maybe you're right. He might be more than a bum. He might be a crook. Reed will nail him if he's the robber."

Mom slapped the table. "Bill, for heaven's sake. This is the same man who served our boys lunch in his shack? What's this world coming to? And, why doesn't Chief Olson lock him up?"

"Ruth, first of all, the boys should have known better. And the police—they've got to have evidence. I trust Reed, though. He'll work the case. He's returning a favor to the Montana cops for helping him nail a couple of boxcar crooks who worked both sides of the state line."

Dad nodded sternly at Jim and me, "After you boys tipped him off about the dog, Reed called the Chief of Police in Malta, Montana. The guy followed up;

discovered that two summers back a fella' of Smoky Roy's description worked out there on a gypo rail crew. The crew stayed in Culbertson for a spell before moving up the line to Malta, and some other towns, including Havre, where the bank was robbed that year in September. The chief in Malta remembered a three-legged dog. Reed figures our man picked up the stray dog and named him for the town."

"Bill," Mom broke in. "Do the boys really need to know about police work and criminals?"

"To some extent they do, Ruth. They may be able to help Reed." Dad glared at Jim and me to be sure he had our attention. "The Great Northern contractor in Montana remembered a Roy somebody with a white dog; he checked his records, found a guy named Roy Clapper. So then Reed leaned on your friend, Roy. Whadda' you know? His name is Clapper. He says if Clapper's anything like the other dump squatters, he'll have a record."

Reed Gwin's news jolted me, hopefully not an obvious quiver. Jim kept his head down, gnawing on his bare drumstick.

Mom hadn't touched her food. She slapped the table twice. "Bill, our boys, how are they mixed up in . . . ? Boys, you better go to your room."

"No, no. They're all right. You boys sit right there," Dad said. "They need to know about their friend. This'll be a lesson about not taking up with derelicts from the goddam dumpground."

Watching Jim's fascination with his potatoes and gravy, I knew his turmoil, matched mine. He said not a word though, feigning no interest in Roy, as if the bum could go straight to jail for all he cared, which seemed to be very likely after the news that came next.

Dad went on about his visit with officer Gwin. Following the lead from Malta, Reed reported that Roy sent cash out of town in a money order. Old lady Severtson at the post office told him. Dad opined, "Clapper's had jobs, but not the kind that leave much of a trail." Dad passed on Reed's notion that maybe Clapper wasn't as desperate a soul as he appeared, and, "Where the hell did a guy like that get money to send out of town? What else is he hiding?"

Hiding? The word hit me like a punch in the stomach, Jim too. I saw him flinch, shaken by the same vision as mine: Roy's secret room where he hid what?—stolen bank money?

Dad's news left confusion and haunting emptiness in place of the kind stranger who we thought we knew. We'd seen how he lived. He couldn't even trust his neighbors. How could we simply abandon him in pitiful lonesomeness after we promised to come back to visit?

We went to bed that Friday night leaving Mom and Dad still in the dark about our morning's trip. Our plans, hopefully in barest detail, would come to the breakfast table.

When lights went out, Jim whispered his plan. "We'll blaze a trail through the Jungle. We'll bushwhack south and east to the channel on the west side of the dump. I talked with Jack already."

I whispered: "Jack would go back? He hated the dumpground."

"He won't have to set foot in the dump. We won't, either. I have paper and a pencil in my packsack," he whispered. "I'll write a letter for Roy; we'll have Buck take it to him. Razzie will go along. He'll be right at home dickering with Smoky on his fixed up things. And if you and I and Jack stay on the west side of the channel, then—well, we didn't get there by coming south of the Muddy Bridge. See what I mean?" I thought long and hard on that one, a weak sister explanation when, in fact, we'd be standing on the bank of the backwater, only a long slingshot across to the forbidden dump.

I fought sleep, didn't want it, wanting to be shed of worry first. "You awake," Jim?"

"Yah, barely."

"Is he really a bank robber?"

"I . . . don't think so. If he was, why didn't he buy a Cadillac and move to California? Huh? Answer that."

"Don't know."

"You worry too much."

"I guess so."

"I told the guys we'll travel light tomorrow. You carry your knapsack with our throw-lines and lunches. Jack said he'll dig enough worms for us all. He said he's done with rotten chicken and done with the dump, too. Buck, though . . . I want him to catch a big cat. We gotta help him do it."

I wasn't sold on Jim's scheme; on the other hand, just the thought of exploring the Jungle raced my heart, although here I was, tucked in, supposedly ready for sleep. Movie scenes ran wild and unstoppable: Jungle Jim, Tarzan, and South Sea island jungles. Tigers, monkeys, and parrots go silent and the skinny American marine on patrol, eyes bugged out, whispers, "It's quiet out there." And his captain says, "Yah, it's quiet—*too* quiet. I don't like it."

I think the brain's attic must have a special corner reserved for jungles. What could be better? Every jungle has its heroes who must be the wisest, strongest, and bravest to survive. I could write a whole book about jungles, but how about just one example: Tarzan, Boy, and Cheetah, his chimp—the smartest pet a kid could have—are crossing the treacherous swamp. Out of the dark, tall jungle, from all directions, come animal talkings: "ka, ka, ka, whooOOP, whooOOP, whooOOP," and, "cheeee, cheeee, cheeee"—in animal talk: "Man coming." Then the scariest, loud enough to whoosh the vines, reverberating from huge, deep lungs comes a cough and a roar: "WHOOO-UUUUAAGG."

Tarzan cups his hands around his mouth, yodeling his answer, "EEEEEWHOOOILLY-ILL-AAH-HAAH. He pats Boy on his head. "No afraid, Boy. Simba calls. Simba be friend." It wasn't the wicked black-maned lion from another movie, the one that Tarzan wrestled to the ground and sent slinking off, tail between his legs. That lion was so bad I swear I could smell his evil breath right there in the Orpheum movie house. Simba, though, was a good lion and a loyal animal friend. Furthermore, Simba saved Tarzan from the black, golden-eyed leopard. The leopard, stretched out across a limb above Tarzan's trail, licks his daggered fangs, waiting. Meanwhile, Simba walks beside Tarzan, sniffing the air. Suddenly, he moves ahead of Tarzan, blocking his path. Simba lifts his huge head and roars, shaking the tree branches, and the cowardly black leopard leaps to the ground and slinks away, while Tarzan and Boy laugh. They can't laugh for long, though, in the jungles loaded with danger.

The giant python draped over an overhead limb waits. He flicks his forked red tongue, anticipating man meat. Even vicious plants are ready. One has a red fruit in the center of its open fanged leaves. Boy reaches for the delicacy, but Tarzan grabs his arm just in time. In the movie the plant hisses.

Jungle scenes still flickered when Jim shook me awake. He had placed his BB gun and our knapsacks behind our bedroom door, ready to go.

Early morning eagerness was not advisable. We readied ourselves and scooted to the breakfast table, acting almost normal. We waited for the question, which arrived as Dad downed his last pancake. "Where you bound for?"

Jim had rehearsed the answer. He spoke decisively: "Goin' south, into the Jungle. We want to explore the country down there and maybe find some fishin' holes out in the Missouri backwaters." I poured extra syrup on my third pancake, just to keep busy.

"Who's going?"

"Buck, Jack, Razzie—and a whole bunch of guys."

"All swimmers?"

"All of us swim like fish, Dad."

"Well, don't try swimmin' in the Missouri, even the backwaters." I could have reminded Dad of his brag, how he'd swum across the Missouri when he was 14; but even Jim—the joker—knew this was a poor time to bring that up.

"Be home by six o'clock," Dad said. Best guess is that he hadn't stopped to think of the Jungle's complicated geography, that we could connive a route eastward through the swamps and willow jungles and into the territory of the dump-ground.

Dad wasn't alone in not knowing The Jungle, though it lay just across the Great Northern tracks south of town, twixt the tracks and the Big Missouri. Hardly anyone knew the few square miles of wilderness, which made the place perfect for us, rich with imaginings, jungle lore, and mystery.

We'd previously dabbled once along the Jungle's edge. We followed a primitive road that crossed the tracks by the stockyard, poked into The Jungle, but dead ended at the shore of a slough and an abandoned shack. We had yet to find a route to the heart of The Jungle. We did have a source of information, though. Al Stensby, a fishing buddy of Buck's dad, was the security manager for the Great Northern Railroad. Mr. Stensby had spent years patrolling the two miles of yards, freight buildings, grain elevators, and rail lines that bordered town on the south. And directly across the tracks were a few square miles of swampy tangles known as The Jungle.

Mr. Stensby seemed as enthralled by The Jungle as we. Earlier that summer, Jim, Buck, and I had been allowed to ride along with Stensby and Mr. Bundhund on their fishing trip to the Lindvig Hole. Mr. Bundhund said the walleyes had gone deep and sulky, so he and Al decided on bobbers and minnows. "We'll sit back and wait, perfect for your bullshitting, Al," Ernie remarked. Ernie Bundhund only had to occasionally say, "Oh yeah," or "You betcha" to keep Al Stensby blabbering.

Stensby told a story about a Hoboville bum bitten by a rabid skunk, then launched a re-telling of his bobcat story, the one Jim and I had heard second hand from Buck.

Al's cigar bobbed rhythmically as he storied. Blue smoke seemed to push his words about. "Never forget that goddam cat. My watchman was off sick that evening, and I had to fill in fer him. 'Twas closin' in toward dark, kind of spooky red clouds, and colder'n a well digger's ass . . . End 'a October, it was."

"Hold on, Al, you told me that story," Ernie Bundhund said.

"Not the whole story, Ernie. These boys gotta hear it anyhow, another lesson for them. I told 'em before, and I'm tellin' 'em again"—Stensby glared at Buck sitting on his right and Jim and me on his left—"Day or night, you boys never go past the Great Northern's "No Trespassing" signs. Just stay plumb away." He waited until we nodded, then puffed three clouds of blue smoke and continued: "Anyways, couple days before my run-in with the jungle cat, my man, Smitty, was makin' his rounds . . . told me about catching big golden eyes in his flashlight. Said it was hunkered, ready to spring, and the distance between his eyes was six inches. 'Smitty,' I says—'cougar, had to be. They follow the Missouri coming in from Montana to hunt our Jungle deer.'"

Mr. Bundhund grinned and leaned for the minnow bucket. "I'll get us some fresh minnows, Al. Go on."

"Anyways, that evening on my late inspection round, soon as I left the ice house, I wished I'd 'a brought my shotgun. Right off, a rail bum moved in the shadows, scared the beejezus outa me, cuz I was thinkin' cougar."

"I thought you said Canadian wolf last time," Mr. Bundhund laughed.

"No, that was the year before. Now just think a' what happened. If I wasn't experienced I'd of pissed my pants, maybe worse. I was just passing by the ice house. I had a funny feeling somebody or thing was watchin' me. I stopped and flashed my light around the box cars. I don't know what made me shine up to the ice house roof. Damn lucky I did. A goddam bobcat was sprawled out on the very edge of the roof, an' he was a big one, damn near big as a panther. I saw him flexin' his claws, exercisin' them, getting 'em ready fer me I guess. Never saw such mean gold eyes as his was starin' at me."

Mr. Stensby, Al, took the fat cigar from the corner of his mouth and spit into the Muddy, then went on. "I hollered and waved my arms, otherwise he woulda jumped on me . . . bobcat, lynx, whatever the hell he was."

"He'll get ya', Al. Just a matter of time," Ernie Bundhund laughed.

"Mr. Stensby, Dad says you carry your pistol on duty. So why didn't you plug him?" Buck asked, grinning his wise-guy grin.

"Think I'm crazy? I was only carrying my little .38. Ain't enough to stop a cat that big an' powerful. Besides, he didn't give me a chance. The damned cat vamoosed, jumped two stories, clean to the ground. He was across the tracks and into the Jungle in two seconds. When he hit the ground he glared my way and screeched something awful, a warnin'. He shows again I'll have my 12 gauge. He'll make me an eight foot rug."

"Al, that bobcat's getting bigger and meaner every time you tell it," Mr. Bundhund laughed.

"Maybe so, Ernie, but you never can tell about killer wildcats." With each smoke-puffed word Stensby squibbed on his cigar. "I know fer a fact bobcats or one of them wanderin' Canadian lynxes downed a buck deer in the Jungle south of the Depot. Took his jugular right out. I seen the results myself. Damn cat went right for the liver an' left perfect loins for the magpies."

In a deft move of lips and tongue, Mr. Stensby squibbed his cigar once, twice and he'd magically spun it 360 degrees. He grinned his one-sided grin allowed at the corner of his mouth, opposite his cigar. He was so pleased and practiced with his "killer cat" story, he could have told it in his sleep.

Even though Stensby complained about the Jungle, how it hid out camp squatters and rail tramps who sometimes stole from the railroad, plain to see ol' Stensby loved the mystery of the place, good fodder for his storying. Hadn't been for our fishin' trip and Stensby opening up, Jim wouldn't have known enough of the terrain to dream up his plan. Here's how he came by it—

Jim, Buck, and I were carving willow Indian whistles in Buck's garage one afternoon, when Ernie Bundhund and Al Stensby came with two stringers of walleyes from the "Nine and a Half Mile Hole." Probably their naming of the spot was likely a fib for loose-lipped kids. They went to work at Ernie's fancy cleaning station—a linoleum covered table, water spigot, gut bucket, everything. We three kids closed in to watch and listen. Always, we listened in on Mr. Stensby, because he was a funny grown man, roly-poly with his chubby boy-like face. I couldn't help thinking of him as Lou Costello. If I didn't know better, I'd say he even practiced the part. He wore a round, narrow brimmed hat and talked in short machine gun bursts like Costello. To top it off, cleaning fish with Mr. Bundhund, we were able to see him talk without his cigar, a rare occasion.

Ernie jabbed Al with an elbow. "Al, gotta remind you, no cigar. The ashes don't improve walleye."

With the cigar in the corner of his mouth Al's words dribbled and slobbered out around it, a spit-ely language. If clams could talk they'd sound like Stensby," my Grampa joked. But without the cigar, the round hole in the right hand corner of Stensby's mouth remained, from which he puffed words instead of smoke by working his right cheek and an inch of lip. If Al Stensby had nothing important to say we'd hang around anyway, just to watch his lip. And better yet, today we lucked into something mighty interesting . . . useful, exciting too.

We watched Ernie and Al chuck walleye heads, guts, and bone frames into a five gallon bucket. They piled a nice mess of fillets in a pan, which Buck ran to the house. Jim went for the gut bucket, thinking he'd dump it in the alley garbage can. He reached for the gut bucket and jumped back. "What the heck? There's a sucker in the bottom. He's still flippin.'"

"Two of 'em if you look closer," Al said. "We're gonna feed my pets. Put that bucket in my trunk. You boys can ride along."

Not even Buck was in on Al's "pet" deal, and Al wasn't talking; nor was Ernie Bundhund. We fired away: "Where we goin'?"

"What do we need to carry along?"

"What kind of pets?"

. . . and from me, "Will it take long?" thinking that we might be late for supper.

Al turned his head enough to puff stinky cigar smoke into the back seat. "You tame wild animals, you better know what you're doin'. Now when we get there, you won't see my pets if you talk or get too close."

"What pets?" I asked. Buck shrugged, so did Jim. In the middle rear view mirror, I caught Al Stensby's twinkling blue eyes and one-sided grin.

Al drove the length of Main, turned right on 2nd Street and headed west past the stockyards. At the Sand Creek Bridge he turned left on a one-track road which ducked through a narrow passageway under the roadbed of the railroad tracks. An overhead sign said:

PROPERTY OF GREAT NORTHERN RAILWAY
NO TRESPASSING

Mr. Stensby steered his black Cadillac through the passageway with only inches to spare on either side.

By then my mind was crazy with wondering what kind of fish-loving beast could be a pet. Stensby and Mr. Bundhund had a big practical joke in mind—had to be. Could be something like the "snipe hunt" that Uncle Milt had pulled on Jim and me.

The passageway ended at a T with right and left forks hugging the rail embankment. Stensby turned on the left fork, traveled a few feet, and stopped. Before us lay water, swamp, and dog-hair willows as far as we could see. "Everybody out, and stay on the road," Stensby ordered. Even Mr. Bundhund stayed with us on the road, letting on only, "You'll need to stand quiet and wait. We get lucky they'll come today."

Mr. Stensby opened the trunk, grabbed the bucket by the handle, and walked a few paces toward a south-running slough. A narrow mud beach circled the slough, which was closed in by reeds and cattails. Stensby set the bucket on the edge of the road, grabbed a stick, and rapped it on the side of the bucket. He turned toward us, holding a finger in front of his lips. Another rap on the bucket and the dangdest thing happened. A big raccoon bellied from the reeds and ran the mud beach toward Mr. Stensby. Three littler coons followed.

"That's momma and her babies," Mr. Bundhund whispered. By then the momma had skittered to the edge of the slough, not 20 feet away from Mr. Stensby. She stood up like a begging dog, and Stensby reached in his bucket and pitched gobs of fish guts and bones toward the mamma coon and her babies. Each grabbed a prize and ran to the edge of the slough to wash its food.

"Now, let's see if the big boar will come," Mr. Bundhund whispered. "Quiet now. He's the jittery one."

Stensby rapped again on his bucket and grabbed a sucker. He waited, holding the fat wiggling sucker around its middle. The reeds moved, and Al pitched the sucker as far as he could heave. The sucker splatted in the slough water, and big, fat Mr. Coon charged from the reeds and chomped down in the middle of the fish, then dropped it and batted it about in the shallows like a cat with a mouse. Finally, after the wounded sucker lay still, the coon chomped again to kill it. He picked up the ragged carcass in his tiny fingers, nibbled and washed, nibbled and washed. In all my visits to the animal park, I never saw coons or other big-toothed scavengers play with their food.

Stensby chucked the other sucker, dumped the rest of his bucket, and huffed up the slope. "There you go, boys, trained coons. They'll eat out of my hand some day. Okay, fellers, back in the car."

"Wow! That was *something,*" Jim said, as he climbed into the back seat with Buck and me. "Mr. Stensby, maybe we can help. We catch more fish than we can use. Just tell us which ones your coons like—suckers, shiners, goldies, or carp. We feed the animal park eagles, may as well feed your pet coons too and . . ."

Stensby's answer came strong and gruff. "You'll do no such thing. Under no condition do you cross to this side of the tracks without me takin' you; and that ain't likely." He shifted into reverse, then first gear, and spun his tires in the dirt going back through the passageway. He didn't quit talking all the way through town, more of a scolding, maybe thinking if we hadn't yet violated his railroad rules, we were considering doing so. I'd never heard so many gripes from a grown-up. Stensby rattled on, upset about the rail bum three years back who fell under a freight train and had his legs cut off below the knees. After that sad story Al drove slower. His voice pitched high and tinny, sounding like the third person breaking into a party line conversation. Driving slower with each complaint, Stensby's complaints dragged on: thieves breaking into boxcars, lazy watchmen he'd fired, and trespassing town kids. "Come in on the rails, goddam bums. They got a "hobotown" on railroad property in the willows. He nodded in the direction south of the stockyards, where Jelly's trail took the two of us to Hobotown. I almost let a laugh go. Stensby had a trespassing culprit in his back seat and didn't have a clue. Slowing to about five miles an hour, Stensby continued, "Move a hobo out, two more come in." Smitty says, 'No use messing with them, first really bad winter will run 'em out.'"

". . . and then I put up with Jardo Kelley and his boys. Ernie, you know what Kelley's up to now? He's runnin' his goddam scroungy rodeo stock down there. I let him have a little railroad property for his damn goat herd and some higher ground for his cabin. Now he's brought in some ringy rodeo stock too. I ain't squawked yet."

"Mighty kind of you, Al," Mr. Bundhund offered. "Jardo ain't got a pot to pee in, you know. Didn't hunt deer and rabbits, those skinny boys of his would starve."

"Guess you're right, Ernie. If I had anything of value in the Jungle, I'd kick him and his flea bag buckin' horses out. If the Northern front office found out, they'd have my ass . . . Oh, did I tell you? . . . Jardo has brahmer bulls, too. Mean bastards."

Mr. Bundhund answered in his unwavering gentle voice, the only one I'd ever heard. "I've known Kelley from way back, Al. Good man; bad luck. If it was me, I'd let sleeping dogs lie."

"Yeah, I guess you're right, Ernie. I'll let Jardo be; his boys, too, long as they stay away from our main operations. They haven't caused any trouble. But I ever catch anybody else down on railroad property . . . town kids, I'll tan their hides; then I'll turn 'em over to the sheriff."

Had Stensby glanced in his mirror, he'd have caught three sets of smirks. Heck, the three of us had snuck over the tracks just a week earlier looking for a way through the crisscross of sloughs.

Stensby's Jungle news was fascinating, but not so useful, not until his golden gift of information meant not for us boys, but Ernie Bundhund. We jabbed ribs when we heard.

Stensby parked in the alley by Bundhund's garage. "You boys pull them stinky buckets out of my trunk." Stensby handed Buck the key to his trunk; but, Al and Ernie had their windows down, and Al wasn't finished with Jungle talk. Buck and Jim and I dawdled so we could hear. "Jardo's boys . . . they've cut a secret trail, starts a half-mile east of the Depot. Smitty spotted it; says they use the trail to shortcut to school. Smitty collared them and ordered them out. Was me I'd a let 'em cross over there. Town kids, though . . . don't want 'em even *thinkin'* about crossin' over, even knowing about that trail . . . up to no good, most of 'em."

Keep in mind we learned about the Kelley boys' trail long before we'd organized a plan to trespass across the railroad. We tucked away Mr. Stensby's insider's dope, not knowing when or how we'd use it. Now, a month later and with Jim's plan before us, the time had come. The aggregate of reasons to forget about exploring the Jungle hung like a storm cloud. Regardless, I knew better than to think anyone would back out. We even added an eighth trooper, when on Saturday at 8 o'clock jump-off, Little Ergie came winging into Jack's back yard on his new bicycle, which he barely had time to break in or wreck, whichever came first. No matter. Ergie had a miraculous way of appearing for any excitement.

Our gathered-up jungle platoon was larger than for typical Muddy River trips. When the word got around, everyone wanted in. In addition to Little Ergie, we had Jim, Jack, and me—the "veterans" of the dumpground—Buck, savvy about the lay-out of the railroad, and Jack, so full of wilderness knowledge, our "bwana" guy. Big Bervie, too: mapmaker, good campfire man, and cooker, and our gofer—smiley Little Bervie, a game-for-anything kid. Razzie joined, too. He was too much fun to leave out.

We biked down 5th street and crossed Broadway, headed for the quieter, east side of the Great Northern operations, out of sight of the main station and far removed from the hubbub of the ice house, the roundhouse, and grain elevators. The better riders—Jim, Jack, Big Bervie, and Buck—rode with BB guns balanced across their handlebars. The little guys and I toted worm cans and lunch sacks in our packsacks.

We rode slowly in a pod so Buck, the commander, could be heard. "This might not be easy," he warned. "Everybody pay attention. If Big Smitty or the switchmen catch us, it's all over, cuz our's is an organized mission, not just a little mistake. The rail cops, the city cops, they work together . . . they'd probably throw us in jail. Smitty caught Jelly crossing the tracks, you know. He's workin' off his fine, shoveling sawdust in the ice house."

"Well, the cops are one thing, our old man is another," Big Bervie said. "He'd ask the cops to keep Allen and me in the jug for an extra week."

"Hey, Bervie, you're worrying over nothin'." Jim said. "Once across the tracks, how would they ever catch us in the Jungle? Huh?"

Buck raised his hand, signaling a stop. We gathered around him on his lookout spot, a crest of hill overlooking the warehouse district. "I've checked out this end of the tracks," Buck said. "They don't do many car switches here, plus . . . just look at the cover down below."

"Let's go for it then," Jim said—"nobody about except that switchman checking the line."

Buck sat tall on his bike seat and spaced his words like a U.S. Army general: "Okay men, listen up. We'll pull into the ash grove and hide our bikes. Follow me." Buck cut loose to coast, followed by his platoon. We rammed our bikes into the brushy ash grove and laid them flat in the brush, so's their chrome wouldn't shine.

"Stay down; I'll take a peek," Buck said. His head came up no higher than a hunkered badger's. He crawled forward to the rail embankment, signaling his troops to follow. Quite naturally we took on the disciplines of an army platoon, using hand signals and whispered commands. We lay in a string, heads down in the weeds, waiting for orders. We'd learned how to move unseen from the war movies. We knew the "soldier's crawl," cradling guns, wiggling butts, and snaking low. We'd used the crawl in battles with the West Side Army.

Buck waved and we crawled to the rail embankment, where we plastered our bodies against the cinders. Buck, in front, raised his head to peek. "There's a switchman up the line, and a big guy further down, might be Smitty. Everybody stay down." We waited long . . . long enough for the stupidity of our predicament to take hold.

"Aren't we supposed to have hand grenades?" Jim whispered, which set off Jack's giggling, which triggered more giggles, and whispered scoldings, and arguments. I wondered: run for my bike or stay put? Heads down, we listened for footsteps and Big Smitty's gruff voice.

"We're goin' about this all wrong, Buck," Razzie said. "We'll let Smitty see us cross. Then we'll ambush him in the Jungle and mud-ball him."

"I've got a better idea, Razzie," Jack laughed. "You go ahead. Decoy Smitty. We'll meet up with you later, assuming you ain't lost for three days."

Giggling resumed, until Buck cut us off. Loud and a little gruff, he said, "Hey men! Listen up. They've turned the other way. Bring up Little Bervie." Buck's command was whispered ear to ear, soldier to soldier. Little Bervie crawled briskly forward and tucked in tight by Buck. Buck placed his hand on the back of the kid's neck, whispering his orders, "You're first. Head down. Go fast and quiet."

Little Bervie nodded, big-eyed, acting perky as a hunting dog on scent. Buck lifted his head ever so slightly to peek up the tracks; then he pushed on Little Bervie's butt, "Git, git, git." The little guy ran low and quicker'n a striped-ass weasel. He zipped across the tracks and ducked into the swamp grass on the other side. He was dang good, not super fast, but quick and smart. He'd been recruited as a messenger carrier for the East Side Army with his older brother, who Buck sent next, followed by the rest of us in rapid succession, *"zip, zip, zip."* In scarcely a minute our squad was across, lying abreast, hidden in the swamp grass. We listened to the banging of rail cars and the "hey-yah" shouts of the switchman. The crossing had been scary, but fun. Finally, the switchman moved up the tracks to the west. We scrambled onward, slipping down a brushy bank . . . Whoa! Dead ahead, where I expected swamp, a new threat blocked our way, imposing enough to end the expedition.

"I thought you had this mapped out, Buck," Jack said. "You didn't say anything about goats."

"Yah, well Stensby didn't tell us everything, you know. What do you think, Jim?"

We milled about, wondering what to do about the plank sign in front of us attached to a barbed wire fence. The sign, hand-painted in sloppy red lettering, announced: NO TRESPASSING. On the bottom of the plank in smaller print, the warning said: THIS MEANS YOU!

"What now Eric?" Jack said.

"I'm thinkin'," Jim said.

Across the fence, the herd of nannies and their kids nibbled sparse grass. In front of them stood a pair of big muscled, long-horned billy-goats. They had us spotted and romped forward, stomping their front hooves, and shaking their shaggy heads. The big black one charged the fence, stopping inches away, slobbering. He shook his sharp horns. I didn't understand then, as I do now, about billies protecting nanny goats.

The goat pasture was closed in on both ends by slough water. To get to the willows across 50 yards of open pasture meant outrunning mean goats with their fearsome stabbing horns.

I wanted to retreat, but wasn't willing to be the first chicken. I think the rest were in the same boat, because nobody said anything worthwhile, only "son-of-a-gun," "gol-dang" and Big Bervie's customary "dag-nabbit." But I didn't anticipate my brother backing out; he'd come up with some harebrained idea. He always did. I'm forever puzzled why we fell for crazy, dangerous ideas like his battle strategy for the goats.

"Big Eric, what do you think? You want to bull-fight 'em?" Buck laughed.

"Nope, but I got a plan."

"This I gotta hear," Buck said.

"It's simple . . . we'll trick 'em. Buck you're, uh, the slowest runner. You'll stay here on this end of the pasture with Little Bervie, Dave, and Ergie. Use your BB gun on these billies to keep 'em mad at you."

"Huh? You don't think they're mad enough, Jim?"

"No, no, that's just what we need. While you keep 'em concentrated on you, I'll take Razzie and Big Bervie and Jack with me. We'll sneak to the far end of the pasture and make a run for it from there."

"What then? Me and the little guys trapped here? We're not gonna go through this fence and get gored by danged goats."

"It'll work. You'll see. After we make it, we'll divert their attention, get you guys across."

Buck shook his head. "I don't like it one bit."

Jim's part of the team, the fast guys, had sidled next to him. Jack strode about, jostling, banging shoulders, roostering, "Big Eric's right; nothin' to it, Buck. He's got a good battle plan."

"Let's go then. What are we waitin' for?" Jim said, and he took off with the fast guys, running east along the fence. The billy goats eyed them angrily, but when Buck plugged them in their rumps with BB's, they snorted and turned back to face us. The scary biggest one was jet black, his shaggy hair chock full of cock-leburs, enough to irritate him night and day. The mottled white billy glanced frequently at the black one, as if waiting for orders. They both snorted and stomped and glared beady eyes on us, shaking their sharp-horned heads, anxious to spear any trespasser dumb enough to come through the fence.

Buck grumbled, "Ain't worth it, even for a lunker catfish." Little Bervie, Ergie, and I crowded next to him, against the fence. We stared into the red eyes of our enemies. We were close enough to hear their huffing and to smell their pucky goat breaths. I thought to myself, there's no way I would try to outrun a mad billy goat, can't count on 'em to lose interest in us. The pair of billies swung their woolly heads watching Jim and his squad running fast. They pranced a few steps in their direction. Jim and the guys reached a patch of cattails on the east end of the pasture, where they ducked out of sight.

Right then I longed for the Army's precision, their field maps, and walkie-talkies. I scanned the thicket at the far end of the pasture, but saw only a blur of quick rise, then duck of a figure. "Look guys . . . " We saw one arm: Jim's, waving his red farmer handkerchief.

"This oughta be good," Buck said, cocking the lever action of his Red Ryder. He dropped to one knee, firing, cocking, and firing again. The BB's splatted goat hide, and the billies charged again and again, snorting and slobbering, so fierce that we jumped back, ready to run the other way.

Jim and his guys ran, sprinting, making it half-way across before the goats noticed. They spun, instantly charging, racing toward our guys, but only closing half the distance before Jim and his patrol dove under the far side fence. Jim, though, scooted back under the fence with his BB gun, in his hunter's stalk, advancing on the two angry goats. The goats walked stiff-legged, targeting Jim.

Jim cupped one hand and hollered across the pasture—"When they come for me, you guys run for it." Then he raised his gun and fired. With the first sting, the black goat sprung into the air kicking his heels. At the ready, Buck and I and the little guys crawled under the fence.

It all unfolded too fast, no time to think. I saw Jim racing, chased by the billies, allowed them to close within a few yards before he slid under the far side fence. Meanwhile, Buck, Little Ergie, and Little Bervie scooted through our fence. Buck lumbering away was slow, but not any slower than short-legged Little Ergie and Little Bervie. Buck and the two little guys made half the distance before the goats turned away from Jim, their lost target, and shook their horns. Heads down, charging, they came rampaging for Buck, Ergie, and Little Bervie. Buck yelled, "Go men, go!" But me?—I had a special problem. I had snagged my back pack on the wire and lost precious seconds. Untangled finally, separated from everyone, I raced—still far behind Buck's patrol. One fast glance caught a black and white blur of goats charging for me.

Arms pumping, eyes squinted for safety, I heard Jim's yell, "Faster, Davey! Come on!"

I had been in many school foot races, coming in third or fourth, sometimes last. This one I couldn't lose. Strangely, flashes of lost races seemed to lighten my legs. With seven buddies cheering, I flew for the safety of the fence. I needed to cover 30 more yards, and the goats the same distance before they would run their horns into my behind. I heard the springy "pung, pung, pung," of Red Ryder guns raining BB's on those hornet-mad, mangy goats . . . just the edge I needed. The goats with stinging butts slowed to target their tormenters, and I sprinted the last few yards, diving under the fence on my belly with shiny black horns only a goat-length behind.

"Pung, pung, pung," the goats retreated, shaking their angry heads, as the guys plugged them a few times for good measure. Then our entire squad plopped down in the willows to enjoy a few minutes of laughing and celebrating, whoopy-bragging how we fooled the nasty goats.

"Good shooting, men," I said. "You saved me."

Jim laughed, "Couldn't let them get you, Dave. You've got my lunch."

We found ourselves dead on the mark of the Kelley boys' secret trail, a dark tunnel worn through a 10 foot tall thicket of reeds. Tromping silently we followed the shadowy reed tunnel and came out the other side onto the gummy-mud shore of an east-west running slough.

The slough guarded the interior of the Jungle. We had to cross it, or turn around and face another battle with the goats to make our way home.

The slough was a remnant of the Missouri's main channel. Gramp had explained the changing nature of the river, how it carved new channels through the bottoms since the days of Lewis and Clark. The former channel before us was now an ugly, quagmire slough . . . too thick to swim and too soft to wade. Green slimy growth covered all but the open water in the middle, which shimmered with iridescent oil (mosquito control, Gramp explained later). We gawked and milled about like spooked whitetail deer. Then Jim spotted footprints."Hey, look men. Let's follow them. Maybe they go to a crossing."

Jim guessed right. Around the bend of the slough, the mud prints took us to a rickety footbridge. The "bridge" wavered inches above the slough water. "I don't know," Buck said. "I'm not sure it would hold a skinny coyote." To cross over we'd need to balance on boards supported by a series of rotting stumps and rusted oil barrels. The thin, spindly walk-boards were a random mix, some almost a foot wide, others half that. The construction seemed planned by someone with trickery in mind. He had failed to bridge the first span, and he'd chosen the skinniest board for the longest span out there in the middle, where a fallen victim could be easily lost in the stinkin' gunk-water. In a Tarzan movie beady-eyed alligators would be waiting there.

We muttered about, measuring our chances. I heard no words of confidence, but plenty of doubt: "Not worth the chance"—"The boards could be rotten"—and finally, Jack, laughing, "You go first, Jim. Then we'll decide."

"Sure, I'll go, but first we've got to find something for the first span. Spread out men. Find us a log or boards."

We hadn't gone far when Bervie hollered out, "Hey, I got it. We'll weave a willow bridge." Bervie drew his 10 inch hunting knife from a scabbard on his belt, "I'll start cutting. You guys weave 'em."

Since I knew nothing about weaving, my job was to haul Bervie's cuttings to the bridge. My job gave me time to worry. By coincidence, just last Saturday at the Orpheum's matinee, Tarzan and Boy had faced similar danger.

Tarzan, Boy, and Cheetah traveled far from their safe tree house, deep into the Pygmies' jungle. Teetering, trying to keep balanced on a narrow log across quicksand, suddenly Boy slips, plunging in, sinking, sinking to a bottomless grave, his final breath gurgling bubbles in the mud. Only a skinny disappearing finger poked from the quicksand. But Tarzan reaches deep, grabs Boy's wrist, and in a single mighty motion he pulls Boy free and flings him across the expanse of quicksand to a soft landing in the reeds. All the while, Cheetah is jumping up and down, cheering, "Chee, chee, chee, chee." Too bad, I thought, we won't have a Tarzan to rescue the unlucky one who falls into the slimy gunk, or maybe quicksand, or whatever awful stuff lay beneath the swamp water.

I suppose winning the goat battle had made us cocky. The guys were game, determined to try the slough crossing, and everyone worked hard to help with Bervie's willow bridge. Finally, Bervie weaved in his last willow and stepped back. "I declare the bridge open for business."

Jim jumped up on the bridge and bounced. "Perfect," he said. He crossed to the first board span. "Follow me, men." He took one long look. "Here goes nuthin'." Jim started slow, placing one foot carefully in line with the other like a high wire performer. Then he picked up speed, light-footing across the springy boards—I counted eight in all, covering nearly the width of a football field. From the far side Jim hollered, "Come on, it's easy."

One by one the guys lined out, bolstered by shouts of encouragement, and some teasing too: "You go in, you'll get to miss school," and "What do you want us to tell your folks?"

Ergie was the littlest; he should have gone last. But no, fearless Ergie laughed all the way across. For me, Boy's close call was too real. Besides, I was born hating muck, can't stand its slimy, slithering feel on my skin. Now, as the last and biggest chicken, I had to go. I gulped and sprung across Bervie's bridge span and made a slow, one-foot-then-the-next walk to the end of the first plank, thinking, *Seven guys made it, I can too.* And I did well, too, until I teetered in the worst possible place, on the long center span with the six inch wide board. Something moved below, and I made the mistake of stopping to look. I saw its head emerge, and my distracted mind blipped *alligator*. In an instant I knew of my silliness. The water beast was a giant yellow carp with a grapefruit-sized head. He thrust the front half of himself onto the water's oily surface, eyes bugged, gasping, as if suffocating in the guncky water. I had paid too much attention. My balance tipped his way.

Only a miraculous lurch in the opposite direction saved me. My only chance then was a go-for-broke, tight-wire run with my buddies laughing and cheering me on. My final thought as I burst onto the shore was: *How will I get home this afternoon? I can't do this again.*

"Forget the worrying," I lectured myself. "You are now entering the real Jungle, not the edge of it, but a terrific wilderness town kids have never seen . . . except for us; we're the lucky ones."

I fell in line behind the guys as they took off running a trail cut through the willows, at last making good time. We'd been gone an hour from the railroad but traveled only about a half-mile. Furthermore, the trail curved south into the sun, turning westerly, away from our destination.

The trail rode a narrow peninsula between two watercourses, where it gradually inclined out of the mucky swamp and wound its way through cottonwood saplings, wild roses, and stickery bush Jack called "grab-ass."

Suddenly we broke out of the shadowed underbrush into full sunlight and onto a grassy rise of meadow surrounded by enough water that it looked like an island, an island meadow dotted with giant cottonwoods and covered in shin tall green grass. Our patrol stopped, struck silent by the out-of-place meadow here in the middle of the Jungle.

Jim stiffened. "Oh-oh, men, look there." Jim had spotted another surprise: a tiny unpainted board shack sitting near the slough water on the north. A small window faced the meadow. I thought I caught movement there.

Since crossing the rails into this strange world, surprise had piled upon surprise: Kowabunga!—wild goats, the rotten, teetery bridge, and now a beautiful meadow with its worn shack. And stepping out of bordering willows came another surprise: a band of about 15 horses. They were uneven in size and color, like a band of Indian horses. A tall white and brown paint pranced in front, eyeballing us.

With a hand signal, Jim held us back. He slowly approached the horses, talking calmly, like Gramp had shown us. He walked calmly, reaching the paint horse, stroking his neck when "bang," the door of the shack flew open, and out came three muscled, older boys. The tallest one in front hollered, "Hey, what hell you doin' out here?" I recognized the two red-haired brothers and their black, high-topped stomper boots because I had witnessed them and their tough friend fight some boys in the junior high playground. Now they were running for us with coiled fists. "Let's go. It's the Kelleys," Jim hollered.

We sprung like spooked whitetails in hunting season and high-tailed south across the meadow with the horses running along beside us, tossing their heads, as if to say, "*Whatever game you're playing, we're playing too.*" From behind, I heard fierce yelling, "Come back here you little bastards."

Our running cluster became a string arranged according to natural foot speed. Jim took the lead. I passed Buck and Ergie, holding my own in the middle of the pack. I worried needlessly about Little Ergie and the guys in back; even the slowest of us out-distanced our pursuers, who were either lazy runners or lacked our measure of incentive. By the time we dove under the pole fence on the south end of the island meadow and plunged across the knee deep slough, the bad swear words from behind had dwindled and died.

We had won this battle, while adding a new one. The Kelley boys' command of the island would block our route home, another worry I promptly tucked away for later. For now, the mysteries of the Jungle, and big catfish lurking in the dumpground waters beckoned and hurried us.

The island's connecting peninsula widened. We ambled, big-eyed, down the narrow trail cut through doghair willows. We could see only a couple feet to either side. Nobody spoke. We were entering the heart of the Jungle, a strange world I had imagined for as long as I could remember. Dense, 10 foot tall willows closed around us, narrowing the trail. Only a ribbon of sky was visible over us. Air didn't move, but clung to us, tainting us with animal stinks left by creatures that pee on bushes, like brush coyotes, foxes, and bobcats, maybe even Montana cougars.

Jim finally broke the quiet: "Anyone know where we are?" Others chattered, nervous talk colored with braggarty—a handy tool in this darkened wilderness. Razzie offered: "We could come out here and stake out a camp."

"Yeah, live here all summer," Ergie said.

"Camp closer to the river, though," Jim said. "Snaring rabbits and fishing for cats . . . live off the land."

Wisely, Jack called a halt—"Hold up, men. This ain't right." We gathered around Jack and his hand-made map. He spread the map on the trail and positioned his Scout compass in its center. Bervie joined Jack and they swung the compass about, realigning the map, arguing. Jack prevailed. "We've gotta get off this trail. If I'm not mistaken it would take us to Jardo Kelley's cabin."

"We'll bushwhack east from here," said Jack, the bwana. I could almost hear far off jungle drums thumped by mean-eyed brown men wearing leopard skin loin cloths, and bones in their noses. They'd have spotted us the minute we stepped into the jungle. Tracking very close, camouflaged with bird feathers, they'd soundlessly float through the dark tangle of brush. Soon, little warriors would use their poison blow-guns to pick off the guys in the rear of our column. Then they'd surround our bwana leader plus two more . . . take them to their torturing tree in the village.

"Follow me," Jack said. He tomahawked the air, slicing a destination trail through the doghair willows. Parting the thick willows with our hands, like swimmer's breast strokes, took careful effort. Two of the guys—Little Bervie and Razzie—were rookie willow walkers. Because they walked too close to the guy in front, willow whips smacked them, stinging skin, leaving red welts. "Dammit, Jim, you let them willows loose on purpose," Razzie whined, as the willow whips slapped him again.

"No, no—sorry, didn't mean to," Jim said. Why then, did his denial come with a laugh?

We'd left landmarks and signs of humans far behind. In the heart of the Jungle the air was muggy and hot, even now in late September. Our Jungle safari lacked only slashing machetes and the rhythmic cutting songs of native porters.

The land sloped away, into sticky swamp mud. Questions, full of worry, rang out: "Where the heck are we?"—"Can't see a thing."

"Spread out, men," Jack directed. "Look for more daylight." Jack's advice sounded good. We pushed our way along.

From somewhere out in the willows came Little Bervie's chipper voice: "Ergie, where are you? Answer me back."

"Over here, by the beaver dam."

Ergie and Little Bervie had wandered off track. Their worried back and forth shouting seemed to echo from everywhere: "Where are you?—"Over here"—"No, come further south, keep coming."

"Hey, somebody, we're lost." Ergie's voice ghosted through the heavy air.

Big Bervie hollered back, "No, you're not. Keep calm . . ." and to us: "I'm worried about Allen. He's panicked out there." (Maybe Big Bervie saw the jungle movie where white hunters got lost and went crazy.) Finally, the rattling willows waved and here came Little Bervie smashing willows, like he flattened linebackers a few years later in eighth grade as a bruising fire-plug fullback.

After more hollering back and forth, Little Ergie found our entire expedition in a patch of sunlight, where beavers had cut and hauled away the willows. "Okay, men," Jack said, "now this time we'll stay together. Follow me." Jack led out, theoretically headed along the southeast arrow on his map.

"Little Eric, you bring up the rear," Buck hollered back.

I backed off, wary of willow whips. Suddenly, just to my right, the willows crashed and rattled; a big beast charged right at me, clattering willows. I crouched, trying to decide which way to run, or if I even could. Suddenly, in a magic flash of moment, we saw each other: me—hunkered and frozen—and the running, gargantuan buck with huge brown eyes and polished white horns, crashing, smashing willows, tucking his legs up under, flying high up and over my shoulder, and then, gone. My legs collapsed, and I plopped on my butt. "Ho. . . ly cow!" I hollered. "You guys see that?" I yelled to my entire safari, who were running hard, rushing around the curve of the faint trail, needing to know about the wild, charging beast.

"Sounded like a water buffalo," Jim said.

"He was the hugest buck you ever saw." I spread my arms as wide as they'd go: "Horns this wide, probably had 20 points. He could have gored me, but he jumped right over me."

"Kowabunga," Buck said.

"You shoulda had a spear," Jack laughed.

"No, Jack. I'm serious," I said. "That was a doggone close call."

Jim let me settle down for 10 seconds before he said, "You need to carry a big gun, Dave."

We gathered, lining out, safari-style and slogged eastward again, occasionally advised by our navigator, Big Bervie—the guy with a drawer full of self-drawn maps at home. "Everybody remember to keep the sun on your right shoulder so you don't get lost." Good advice, except that sloughs and bogs pushed us off course, forcing us to the bank of the Big Missouri. For a half-mile or so we walked easily, in single file on the river beach; then a tributary channel forced us back into the shadowy Jungle.

We were still well short of our backwater destination, when the squawkering began, sounding no different than in jungle movies where the white hunter's porters declare, "We go no more, bwana."

We squawkers targeted the planners and deciders. "Dagnabbit, Jim, the cats are gonna be under ice, time we get to that fishin' hole," Little Bervie said.

Me, too. So worried about the time, I chimed in: "How the heck will we have time to fish and still find our way home for supper?" ("And do it on an unexplored route to by-pass the mean boys on the horse island, and the horrible, dangerous bridge, and the vicious goats?" I could have added.)

"You gotta be a beaver or coon to get through this swamp," Ergie said. We could have saved our collective breath. Jim, Jack, and Buck were deaf to such talk. And Razzie? Razzie wasn't with them or against them. He was a scaredy-cat in the Jungle, clinging to Buck's side all day. Razzie had gone quiet, forgetting the braggarty stuff he used in town where he knew everything that needed knowing. And then, Big Bervie, he'd walk on broken legs without complaining.

After two hours of slogging, we emerged from the clinging jungle and walked out onto a sandbar, squinting into full, dazzling, blinding sunlight. In the South Sea war film this would be the place where the Jap Zeroes come in low over the beach, machine guns blazing.

"Yaay! We're dead on, perfect," Jim yelled. "The mouth of the Muddy is right down there a half-mile."

We faced a network of small, fingered channels and beaver dammed creeks, all gathering into a main channel. To get to the dumpground and the Muddy we'd have to find a crossing. Jim had promised that beaver dams would serve as bridges. Jim led us across the sand bar, intent on locating a "beaver bridge."

The channel was like a small, slow moving river, a jungle river surrounded with short, sapling willows, cattails, and reeds. Nervous shore birds skittered across sandbars. Raspy herons, quacking ducks, slaps of beaver tails—the place was a frenetic zoo without fences. Here came a dozen bright canvasbacks winging low over the channel, swinging right, swinging left, trying to decide which direction. As if dumbstruck, we silently watched them maneuver. Ducks just do that to people.

A quarter mile off to our right, to the south, sunlight glinted from wings as the canvasbacks banked left. The ducks disappeared around the hip of the dump hill and up the Little Muddy. Jim grabbed the moment to open his sales pitch. "Buck, you can head the expedition. I'll draw you a map showing the way. Jack and I and Dave . . . we'll fish the channel from this side. We'll give *you* guys a chance at the best catfish hole."

Buck stepped out in front of Jim, squinting into his face, "Hold it, Jim. Whadda you mean, *you guys*. You said . . ."

"I said you'll probably catch the cat of a lifetime." Jim dropped to his knees and smoothed the sand. We gathered around as he described landmarks and scratched them in the sand. Buck frowned, but dropped in the circle.

"I checked it out last time Dave and me were out here," Jim said. "You can cross there," he said, nodding at berms of logs and limbs. "The beaver have the channel dammed in three places, maybe more. Take your pick. Once you've crossed, hike along the slough here"—Jim scratched the route in the sand with a willow stick. "Follow the channel bank, but stay low. Go higher on the bank and you'll run into stinging nettles and poison ivy." Jim pointed with his stick to the south, around the looming face of the dump. "Follow the channel. You'll see it has a bit of current. If you get mixed up in the tall cattails, just find some water and follow the current. A half-mile south, you'll find the mouth of the Muddy. You'll see a trail there. It'll take you all the way up the Muddy. First, you come to a little town of squatter shacks. If it was me, I wouldn't . . ."

"The cats, Jim . . . get to it. Where's the best spot?"

"Simple, Buck," Jim said. "Like I started to tell you, follow the trail up the Muddy. You'll come to a wrecked Ford truck sitting half in the water. That's where . . ."

"Hold it, Jim," Big Bervie interrupted. "If you're the guide, why do you have to draw us the blasted map?"

"Cuz I'm not going to the dump."

"Whadda you mean, you're not going?"

"Yeah, Jim, answer that," Buck said with a punch on Jim's shoulder.

"I can't go. Neither can Jack or Dave. We, uh . . . we got into a bit of trouble last time."

"What? What kind of trouble? You're sending us into trouble?"

"No, no, not you guys. You got nothin' to worry about." Anxious to outmaneuver the worrywarts, Jim talked fast: "We didn't have permission to go to the dump last time, that's all. Officer Gwin and my dad found out. Now you guys get goin' . . . follow this route and you'll find Smoky and our secret fishin' hole." Jim looked at his timepiece, the sun—"I say you go right now. The afternoon run of big cats is due."

"Hold on," Buck said. Jim ignored him, smoothing a larger swatch of sand, where he drew symbols with his stick. "Here, these are the first squatter shacks you'll come to . . . belong to some junk dealers in a place called Trader Village. We don't know them, and they acted crazy or drunk. We didn't stop to talk with them. They'll offer things to trade or sell. Suit yourselves, but I wouldn't trust them. Further on you'll come to a kind of cave-house built in the side of the dump. That's Smoky Roy's place. He's the guy I told you about, Buck. You'll know it's him because he's friendly and pretty clean, nothing like the other cruddy bums. Roy's smart, too, and an expert fisherman. Buck, you oughta be the one to talk with him, because you've fished cats before. You guys listen to Buck; you'll catch catfish, guaranteed."

Jim fished the folded paper from his shirt pocket. "Show this note to Smoky and he'll probably take you guys to the hole by our fishin' truck."

Buck furrowed his brow. "I don't know. What do *you* think, Jack? We haven't heard much outa you."

"I . . . uh—all I can say is the "fishin' Ford" sits over the best catfish hole on the Muddy. You want a big cat—that's where I'd go."

"Well, what about the bum, Smoky? Why do we need to talk with a bum, anyways."

Jack shrugged his shoulders—"He knows his stuff, Buck, believe me. And he has good rotten chicken bait, too."

"Jack is right," Jim said. "Besides, Smoky ain't a real bum. Like I told you before, he's smart as a fox. He's built his own house, didn't spend a nickel on it. And he doesn't work for anybody but himself. How about that?—no bossy bosses."

Buck dug sand with his boot, an infectious act copied by the other deciders. Jim handed the note toward Buck; but Buck ignored him, calmly scanning the channel of water curving behind the beaver dams. "The water looks dang good right here," he said.

"Yah, and Jim still didn't tell us about the trouble he had," Bervie said.

With mutiny in the making, Jim turned to Jack. "How about if you go along, Jack. You wouldn't have to stay, just introduce the guys to Smoky Roy."

"Nope, I'm not going. I won't put one foot on the other side," Jack said. "But, Dave and I will sign the note." Jim unfolded the note, and spread it out on a drift log.

"Dear Roy," Jim had printed boldly, in pencil. "These guys are friends of ours and good fishermen. If you have the time and don't mind, please help them catch a cat like you helped us. Jim Erickson. P.S. We'll be out to visit you soon." Using Jim's stub pencil, Jack and I signed our names below the P.S. line.

"Let's go then, Buck," Razzie said.

"Yah, Buck, I guess I didn't come this far to chicken out," Big Bervie added, "and I want to see that cave-house."

During a stand-off minute, the flock of canvasbacks flashed in the sun over the mouth of the Muddy and banked sharply, racing toward us up the channel. "Ahh shit," Buck said. "Gimme the dang note." He grabbed it, tucked it away, and shouldered his pack.

The guys lined out behind Buck: Razzie, the Bervig brothers, and Little Ergie, all headed for a beaver dam crossing. They carried packsacks and walked with switching sticks. Just before they disappeared into a thicket of reeds, I said to myself, "Be danged if that isn't an African safari looking bunch. All they need are porters chanting, "Ooh, ahh . . . ooh, ahh."

Jack, Jim, and I spread out along the watercourse, throw-lines in hand, watching for imagined schools of tubby yellow bullheads and marauding cats with mouths big enough to swallow ducks.

But there are days like this when fish catching dreams turn into fishless disappointments. Today we couldn't have found snaggier water. After breaking off several hooks, Jim finally hauled out a tangle of limbs with sharpened beaver cuts. "These limbs are the beaver's winter food cache. Stew and me learned about beaver dens from his dad. When he was young, Catfish Bill trapped beaver for a living."

We gave up the snaggy place and hiked the sand spit to the Missouri. We set our lines in the big river and sprawled out along the bank . . . nothing to do but rest and wait for our buddies' return. Beyond the channel, in the eastern distance, our guys had disappeared around the shoulder of the dumpground hill, probably on the Muddy River trail by now.

The Missouri gave up nothing but little worm-stealing shiners. Finally, after we managed to beach a couple, Jack cut them into meat strips. "Perfect," he said. "Cats will take shiner meat, saugers will too, and if we're really lucky a sturgeon."

After an hour, though, shiner meat produced nothing. Our throw-line methods weren't up to the battle with the fast and powerful Big Missouri. Its racing currents tightened and vibrated our cord lines like wind humming electric wires. We added more weights, but still, our baits tumbled downriver.

Fishless fishing didn't matter so much out here in the wilderness. Like three happy muskrats, we basked on the Missouri's warm sandy bank and chomped into sticky peanut butter sandwiches. Soon we realized that we were short on drinking water. Jack's canteen leak had returned. His magic Juicy Fruit glue plug had failed, the one he bragged was a permanent fix: "Chew it slow. Don't suck all the juicy good out, work the gum into the leak hole, heat it with a wooden match, then cure it for three days. Good as new." Well, not this time.

What water remained in the bottom of Jack's canteen was barely enough for one slug apiece. Jim took off up river, looking for a "river jug" to "purify" some water, like Gramp had showed us. I remember him saying the technique was not perfect, but okay for Missouri river water "in emergencies." "The Missouri grinds away with its billion sand grits, kills the germs that way," Gramp said.

Jim returned in ten minutes with an old whiskey bottle. The drinker had corked it, allowing the bottle to float down the river, maybe as a .22 target that escaped the poor shooters. Jim pulled the cork, rinsed the bottle twice, and filled it with brown Missouri water. Then he buried the bottle upright in the cool, wet sand at the waterline to let the mud settle. "20 minutes, it'll be ready," he said. Jim waited 10 minutes, dug the bottle out, and inspected. "It's settled, not perfect, but good enough," he said. "But tip it gently, when you drink. Don't rile the bottom."

Jim slurped first, me second. It was cool and sweet, tasting slightly like willow bark. I passed the bottle to Jack. He carefully wet his lips and handed the bottle on to me.

"What's the matter, the mud coming up?"

"Nope, I'm not very thirsty," Jack said. *"Not very convincing, either,"* I could have added.

I took off my boots and socks, put a loop of my throw line around a big toe, and lay back for a nap. "A sturgeon takes that line, and you'll get a fast ride down the river," Jack teased.

"It'd be fun," I said. Easy to laugh about danger when you know how remote the chance, though the thought conjured a scary scene: both hands grasping the line to save my toe, and gulping one last breath before being pulled under by a giant sturgeon.

I had slipped into a foggy grog. Jim punched me full awake. "Look at that!" he said. "Some crazy men in an army jeep."

I jumped up and we ran down the Missouri's beach to get as close as possible. We stopped directly across the channel from the crawling jeep, near enough to see shapes of three men, but too far to make out their features.

They'd driven through a bulldozed notch up on the west rim of the dump-ground. Now they traversed the slope so slow that I wondered why the men didn't park the jeep and walk.

Though the driver found remnants of a road that circled the base of the dump, he was repeatedly forced from it to detour crushed car bodies, discarded out-houses, and unrecognizable heaped metal. The jeep bounced back and forth, working its way around the hip of the dump hill to the Muddy River side.

"They're headed for Trader Village," Jim said. "I wonder what the heck they're up to."

We hurried to our lines and pulled them in, having decided to move to the end of the peninsula where we could re-set them and watch for the curious men in the jeep. It wasn't the jeep that re-appeared, though, but, heel to heel, running hard, white headed Ergie, a step behind Little Bervie. Fast as we could, we pulled our lines, stowed them, and took off, racing parallel on our side of the channel, expecting to rendezvous with our guys at their beaver dam crossing. Jack cupped his hands and yelled; but, the droning Missouri behind us drowned out his voice, and the thick willows and cattails covered movements of Buck's safari.

On full alert, we circled by the muddy tracks the safari had left an hour earlier. Nobody showed. No movements, no yells. We hollered above the trickling waters of the beaver dam and squawking herons. Straining our ears, leaning forward, we heard a faint yell.

Jim led us onto a beaver dam for a look-see. The only part of a visible kid was Ergie's white heinie cut swathing through the cattails. "Wait for me, I'm coming," I thought I heard him say.

Over there, the length of a football field, Ergie hopped up onto the first of three connecting beaver dams, running on tricycle-hardened legs, pumping rhythmically, *cha-cha-cha-cha-cha,* as if driven by a piston engine.

Ergie tight-roped our beaver dam, mumbling, out of breath, jumbling bits of stories . . . "Police over there!—Officer Gwin and an army man, the sheriff, too."

"Come on, Ergie, get over here," Jack said. "Tell us!"

Ergie hopped from the beaver dam. He was wide-eyed and wide mouthed, as scared as I'd ever seen him. He rattled away: "Criminals and army guys over there, and the sheriff, Buck said. We . . . we hid and watched. The jeep guys had guns. They were mad, and shouting, 'Come out, come out,' and 'Hands up,' like in the movies. They rounded up some bad guys, except for one who ran off . . . that's when the sheriff man spotted Razzie and came for him. Razzie escaped around the hill. Razzie's fast, you know. We all ran. Buck said to tell you . . ."

"Hold on, Ergie," Jack said, grabbing his arm. Jack guided him to a log. "Sit here. Now slow down. What happened to our guys?"

You've never seen a quicker change. Ergie could do that: in seconds, transform from little boy to a grown kid. He drew in deep breath and hopped from the log, prancing about, gesturing, hands flying, spilling his story. The gist of it boiled down to Buck's warning for us all to stay on the west side of the channel, and "He and Bervies, and Razzie are going north across the tracks to town. He says for us to go back through the Jungle."

Jim grabbed Ergie by his wrists. "What about Smoky? He get arrested?"

"Buck said to tell you he never got a chance to talk with Smoky. We didn't know which one he was, and we didn't have time to find him."

"Okay, men," Jack said. "I've heard enough. We can't go that way. Might be bullets flyin' over there." Jack turned to face the miserable Jungle—"We'll back track, men. We've got no choice. We know what's there. We can do it." Jack was right: The Jungle, the bully boys of the horse island, the dangerous bridge, and the killer goats—none of them seemed half as important as the turmoil in the dump and our worry over Smoky Roy.

Jim began his long-striding walk, headed not for the swamps, but south and west along the Missouri. He had been thinking of a better route home. "When I went for the water jug," he shouted over his shoulder—"I saw clear sailing along the beach."

Around the bend the beach widened enough for us to travel side-by-side. Ergie's news left us wanting, like someone grabbing away your half-remaining chocolate-marshmallow milkshake. We'd taken a laborious journey to put Buck and the guys on a fabulous hole for cats, and to learn more of our friend, Smoky Roy. Ironically, we'd discovered that our best chance of knowing about Smoky probably lay at home with our policeman neighbor. Nevertheless, hurrying along the Missouri's shore, Jim prodded Ergie for more details of what he saw and heard at the dump. Ergie talked fast, short of breath from excitement . . . .

Ergie said the army man from the National Guard had driven Mr. Gwin and the sheriff right into Trader Village. Before having to run off, Ergie and the guys hid out behind some junk to watch the turmoil. "Lots of shouting and cussin' and men bangin' doors, moving fast into those shacks," Ergie said. He danced along between Jack and Jim, jabbering away. "Mr. Gwin took after a guy who tried to run away. Just before we were spotted, I saw Mr. Gwin bringing him back . . . held a gun on him."

Maybe Mr. Gwin had arrested Smoky Roy. But Ergie hadn't gotten close enough, so he couldn't describe the prisoner and, "There was a lot of hollering and commotion, and I thought maybe there would be shooting. The sheriff came chasing after us, too, but soon turned back. Buck said, 'He has his hands full with the dumpground crooks.'"

Jim was right in keeping us out of the tangles and swamps. The river left a beach as wide as a country road. We hiked a half-mile before coming up against a tributary watercourse where we struck another piece of luck. Jim captained us inland along a watercourse. A beaver dam built of new cuttings spanned a narrow neck; it was in its first season and springy-weak; nevertheless, we chanced it and jigged across—Jim in front, Ergie and me in the middle, Jack bringing up the rear, from where he teased: "If you guys fall in the quicksand, I'll toss you a jungle vine."

We rounded the watercourse and returned to easy going along the river. Dozens of blackbirds perched on shoreline snags; but, Jim and Jack didn't take time to stalk them, only aiming for miracle on-the-wing shots. Blackbird hunting took second place to navigating a route home.

"Hold up, men," Jack said. He pulled his folded map from his shirt pocket and spread it on the beach. He traced with a stick. "We go far enough west here and we'll be in position to intercept the horse island trail." Jack placed his compass in the center of his map. From his knees, he turned the compass, watching the needle. He stood up, pointing at the distant Montana-Dakota smokestack, then back to his compass. "I've got it. We're southeast of the smokestack. We'll go on until we're due south."

"Okay, Pocahontas, we'll follow you for a while," Jim said. Jack laughed and trudged on. After another mile he halted our patrol and took out his compass. This time he laid it on the flat of his palm. "All right, men, due north from here. First, we'll need to break through the flood barrier."

Along that stretch of the Missouri, flood ice had mangled the willows, logs, and snags . . . sheared, twisted, jammed, and crammed them 10 feet high. We spread out looking for beaver tunnels big enough to crawl through. "I can get across the top," Ergie said. He climbed to the top of the tangled barrier, trying to monkey his way over. Jack ordered him off. Too dangerous up there climbing slickered, broken limbs, sharp as spears.

We gathered at the lapping waters of the river. "What do you think we should . . ." Jack started. Up the shore, tree limbs cracked, and out of the flood barrier stepped a giant black brahmer bull. He was so close we heard him huffing and blowing snot.

"Nobody move," Jim whispered. If the bull saw us, he didn't let on. He waded into the Missouri, thrust his giant muzzle deep, and began guzzling. While the bull glugged a barrel of water, we froze, on full alert, ready to run. Then, in one mighty motion, the bull switched ends, blew out of the river, crashed into the "impossible" barrier, and disappeared. Jack laughed a mighty, "Whew!" We all laughed. Not the "haw, haw" kind, more the celebrating kind.

"There's our path, men," Jack said.

The odd combination of bull and beaver had torn a hole in the river barrier . . . wore a winding trail through the willows, too, which brought us to a grove of cottonwoods where the beaver had felled a few smaller trees. On the far side of the grove we found a man-cut trail, apparently the Kelleys' trail, which headed north and east, toward the horse island. Jim led out in his easy lope.

We ran around two bends of the trail, slowing to where Jim stood, his hand held high for "stop."

"Quick, take cover," Jim yelled. We heard loud yelling, and thundering hooves, and into the willows we jumped like scared rabbits. The running beasts came on so fast and hard that I felt the ground move. We hunkered on our bellies in the willows, only a body length away from the trail.

"Don't move a muscle," Jack whispered.

Here came pounding hooves, huffing animals, and loud voices I recognized. From my peeky window hole in the willows I saw them thundering toward us—first a wall-eyed, lop-eared brahmer bull. As he passed, I stared into his black saucer of an eye. His neck was as thick as an oil drum. His shoulder hump flopped back and forth. His yard wide horns and massive yellow body took up all the space the trail had to offer. Had we dawdled on the trail five seconds longer he'd have gored us and stomped us dead.

Behind the bull loped a paint horse, the same island horse that Jim had petted. Riding it bareback was the biggest of the red-haired Kelley boys. He "hee-yahed" and drove the paint in tight to the bull's butt and switched him with a willow whip. The leader boy on the paint and his buddies behind rode with elbows flared, like Tom Mix and Lash LaRue. If the Kelleys had looked sideways, they might have caught a flash of Ergie's neon hair. If not for the snorting bull, pounding hooves, and wild yelling, they'd have heard heavy breathing, too.

Fortunately, the Kelley boys "hee-yahed" down the trail, to the southwest. "Come on, men," Jim said. "They're headed for their main cabin." We lined out behind Jim, running the trail northeast toward the horse island. Jim ran at eighty percent of full speed. We pushed to keep up. I know what Jim was thinking, same as me: the tough boys could return. Besides, we were anxious to get home and hear the full story of the dumpground arrest.

If my guess was correct, Mr. Gwin would share his news with Dad, and I dared to hope the bad guy hauled out in the jeep hadn't been Smoky Roy.

We hurried the length of the island and following the path to the slough, where we took on the bridge at a respectful pace, this time without hesitant teetering. The goats cooperated, too. The billy goats stood in the far corner of the pasture, basking in the sun with their nannies. Jim and Jack put Ergie and me in front, and we raced in a four-square pack across the pasture. Funny, I was a wee disappointed when the goats didn't chase us.

"They're scared of the Empire Builder," Jack said. "I've seen deer do the same thing." I hadn't thought of that, but Jack's explanation made sense. We had made our run across the goat's pasture to the accompaniment of the streamliner's 5 o'clock whistle. The train's arrival was, well—almost perfect.

While we waited for the Empire Builder to pass, Ergie decided to pizzle on a nest of wood ants. "No, Ergie, get back," I yelled. I remembered pizzling the same kind of infested log on the ranch followed by the tickled crawling up my legs . . . then the burning hot bites. If you've had ants up your pants once, you'll never again let them get to your nuts. Unfortunately, this was Ergie's first time. He ignored me, inching forward, shoes on the edge of the nest, so he could piss-torture as many as possible. He let 'er go, and I know he was thinking, "Man, I got 'em good." Then, Ergie began frantically slapping at the crawlers in his pant legs—the scouts, looking for tender skin.

The train rolled by and seconds later we heard its brakes screech for the depot stop. With the train stopped and the coast clear, we dashed across the tracks, where Ergie leaped from the embankment, screaming. He dropped his trousers and probed under his testicuts, yelling, "AAAHHHHHHHH!" The vicious ant gripped tighter, bit deeper, willing to commit suicide for his ant hill city. Ergie plucked the warrior, flicked him to the ground, and stomped him to oblivion, while the rest of us howled with laughter.

Out of the Jungle and into the safety of the ash thicket, we discovered that Buck and his gang had made it. Their bikes were gone. We mounted our four remaining bikes and pedaled for home, riding slowly in a pack, so we could talk . . . and laugh. It was good to hear Jack's cackling giggle again. Until Ergie's "ant dance," the doggone Jungle had been holding laughs ransom.

"Tell me now, Eric," Jack laughed. "You said you had a plan for today. Remind me what the heck it was."

Jim and I parked our bikes at our back step and walked nonchalantly across the grass to Dad's garden. He and Reed Gwin stood from their tomato picking. "You boys can help," Dad said. "We're pickin' all the ripes and the half-turned yellows, boys. We've got a heavy frost coming tonight." Couldn't be more perfect, I thought. Mr. Gwin will tell Dad about the dump trouble, apprehending that bad guy.

Jim and I picked tomatoes, sharing in the filling of a half-bushel fruit basket. We worked close by Reed and Dad so's we could hear. We had evidently arrived at the tail end of Reed's story.

"Only one of 'em ran. The sheriff held the rest with his 12 gauge, while I corralled the runner. He had the goods in his shack."

Jim and I sidled closer.

"Could he be the bank robber, too?" Dad asked.

I held my breath, waiting for Reed's answer. "Have no idea," Reed said, "but we have him printed and jailed, where I can question him. I aim to find out where he's come from, his record, and what he knows about the rest of the squatters."

Dad saw that our basket was full. He nodded. "Carry that one over to Reed's porch." Jim and I hefted the basket, one on either side. We took a couple steps, staying within earshot.

". . . Don't understand the attraction of that damn place," Reed said. "The sheriff ran some boys off, while I cuffed the prisoner . . . said one of them looked like a Rasmussen kid." I felt Dad's eyes prickle the back of my neck. Jim and I hurried off, lugging our tomato basket. We returned to find the men ambling to Dad's backyard "Courtroom."

Long as I can remember, the fallen cottonwood lay in our backyard, stretching halfway across our lot. Dad had trimmed its smaller limbs and left the bigger ones stubbed for seats. The tree's bark had shed of its own accord, leaving the tree worn and bleached, remindful of an old bald man—and a wise listener. I suppose someone had felled the cottonwood before I had been born. Each year Mom would plead, "Bill, why can't we get that darned tree out of our yard?" Perhaps one reason was that he'd grown accustomed to its handiness for drinking beer with Mr. Gwin . . . and questioning Jim and me. Privately, Jim and I called it the "Courtroom." Mom called it the "Thinking Tree."

"Grab a seat, boys," Dad said. Jim and I chose our favorite stubbed branches, while Dad and Mr. Gwin skootched up onto the main trunk. They perched like warship commanders. From her kitchen window, Mom watched the developing drama. Brilliant Mom that she was, she suspected the coming inquisition. She came out with brown-bottled Grainbelt beers for the men, and stood with her back against the log to listen in.

"Where you boys been?" Dad began.

"Went to the Jungle, just like we said," Jim said. "We found a hidden trail and a sort of bridge. The willows and swamps go on for miles, and out in the middle—hard to believe—there's a beautiful grass island with a herd of horses. We got chased by some tough boys, the Kelley brothers. I don't know why; we weren't up to any trouble. We ditched them; then, we worked our way through the Jungle, went clear out to the river. Figured we'd try for cats and sauger. I know we can catch them, we just ran out of time." Jim fidgeted, needing a topic for diversion, when suddenly he hit upon a brilliant inspiration. He stood and faced our policeman neighbor. "Mr. Gwin, do you suppose those are stolen horses out there?"

Mr. Gwin stroked his chin, smiling. He glugged some Grainbelt before he answered, "Wouldn't have any idea, Jimmy . . . not in my jurisdiction anyway. And I don't know of any horses missing out of the town herds"—which brought out Dad's best belly laugh. The idea of stolen horses took his mind off in a better direction. Dad would be the one to know if there were horse thieves about, since he traveled three counties selling farm machinery and knew hundreds of country people.

Off the trail of our shenanigans—180 degrees off and three miles away from the dump, Dad opined, "Any livestock running loose down there belongs to Jardo Kelley. He's squatting on the only land across the tracks that won't flood, except maybe once in ten years it does. He lives in an old homesteader's cabin in the cottonwoods on the west end of the bottoms. He grows a little hay there." Then, for Jim and me: "You boys went out that way?"

"No, more to the south," Jim said. Also some to the east, he could have said.

"Well, still those were Jardo's horses you saw. He runs them in the willows." Dad's eyes showed end-of-day tiredness. "That ground belongs to the railroad, if you can call it ground . . . mostly swamp, and some poor pasture. Jardo's okay, hard workin', but not real smart," Dad said, for Reed's benefit. "He's stubborn enough to think he can make money on rodeo horses."

"And brahmer bulls, too," Jim interjected. "We saw a couple."

Dad and Reed went one-on-one then, enjoying easy talk, Reed asking: "So, you think Kelley's honest?"

"Honest as the day is long. Ten years ago he bought an old re-built Massey-Ferguson from me. Hasn't made many payments, and he knows a beat-up tractor's not worth repossessing. Still, he comes in when he has a five or ten spot to give me. Next time he shows up, I'm gonna call the deal square."

"Even if his boys are mean to yours?" Reed asked. Dad eyed us to see if we'd exaggerate all the way to mean. When we didn't, bit-by-bit Dad elevated the Kelley boys almost to angelhood.

"I've seen those boys scrounging around on Jardo's dirt-poor place, milking damn goats and riding broncs, broke or otherwise. Jardo's a good man. I'll bet his boys are 'alright' too; but, they were raised without a mother. They're wild and skittish like orphaned coyotes. In fact, the black haired kid *is* an orphan. He's a nephew Jardo took in. The boy's dad, Jardo's brother, was a National Guard soldier . . . killed in France. Flu took his mom. Doc Hagen says the same flu strain as we had in 1919."

"All three of the Kelley boys came through my seventh grade English class," Mom said. "They were fidgeters, hated confinement of a classroom . . . never sassed me or any teacher, though. They missed too many days of school; still they were solid "C" students."

From there talk moved on to orphans left behind by the flu epidemic of 1919. Mom fetched two more beers and one for herself. Dad grabbed her hands and pulled her up on her "Thinking Log," where now she and the men recounted war battles, epidemics, and car wrecks, all leaving dead parents and orphaned kids. "No-Dad" kids, too, described as mostly "shiftless,"or "worthless." My suspicious mind deciphered the big folks' strategy: *You boys have two parents and a policeman to look after you. You have no excuses.*

Reed slipped from the log. "I'll leave you folks. In the morning, I'll be up and gone before the rooster crows." He started home, but stopped. "Say, boys . . . your friend Rasmussen—better warn him to stay away from the dumpground. Tell him I said so."

With Reed gone, only the robins and blackbirds were interested in talking . . . plenty of thinking going on, though, because Jim and I had laid out a complicated story. Dad slid from his "Courtroom." He faced us with hands on hips. "So, Jim . . . didn't you tell me this morning that Razzie was going with you?"

"Yup. Razzie and a whole bunch of guys were in the plan."

"But Razzie didn't go?"
"He went, Dad; but, he split off in the afternoon."
"I see. So he split off to the dumpground?"
"Yah—probably shouldn't have."
"Bill, I don't think your boys should run with Razzie," Mom said.
"Nor is it a good idea for Razzie to run with *your* boys, Ruth." Dad laughed, as he always did with teasers put upon Mom. "Let's go fix some supper." Dad grinned when he said that, and I whooed out the stale air in my lungs.

Jim and I waited anxiously for more talk of law enforcement at the dumpground. It didn't happen, not that day; Jim's strategy had been too successful, taking Dad away from the subject of the dumpground. We learned little of our friend Smoky Roy Clapper, only that Reed Gwin found no criminal record in the name of Roy Clapper. On the other hand, Smoky had been in Montana working when the bank was robbed. Jim and I overheard Reed tell Dad, "Clapper says he hasn't been *hiding;* he just prefers anonymity because he's lying low until he can save money and pay back his debts."

Reed Gwin had questioned Smoky Roy Clapper regarding the latest crime by a dumpground squatter, but Jim and I weren't privy to a full explanation. Buck and Ergie and the guys helped some, even though they had four versions of what they believed they'd seen.

When all was said and done, over the next few days we learned only what our friend Smoky Roy *hadn't* done. He hadn't been arrested and he hadn't been the culprit who took Mack Nelson's cash box at his Scenic Highway coal mine, when Mack went down the shaft for a load. Nor did he steal the toolbox off the county road grader parked by Muddy River Bridge. The culprit was a rail tramp, new to the dump, who had taken up residence in an abandoned shack. Mr. Gwin told Dad that Olaf, the garbage truck driver, spotted the thief carrying the tool box, headed toward the dump. The raid we'd partially witnessed resulted in the recovery of the tools as well as Mack Nelson's cash.

On September 25th, an early snowstorm blew in from Saskatchewan, ending our easy bike rides into the Muddy River country. Jim and I decided on bird dogging for Gramp. We helped Gramp take a limit of rooster pheasants on Saturday and another Sunday. Then, two hours after school on Tuesday and Wednesday was enough time for Gramp to take another half-dozen roosters. Jim and I brushed out the birds, and Gramp busted them from the sky with his Winchester 12 gauge. On the next two Saturdays, Gramp took us to the headwaters of the Little Muddy to hunt greenhead mallards. Officially, Gramp shot them. Unofficially, Jim and I traded the gun back and forth. It was easy shooting, even for a little kid with a big gun. We belly-crawled and blasted the ducks just as they lifted from the water. Then Gramp, wearing hip boots, picked our birds from the downstream riffles. Gramp captained our bird cleaning, while he described which of a dozen game bird recipes he'd use, and which favored neighbor would get an extra bird or two.

Our hunting ended in late October, with a blizzard and early ice-up. I spent part of school time daydreaming summer memories: Stony Ford, the walleyes of Six Mile Hole, our Jungle safari, and our crazy, puzzling adventures at the dumpground. When possible, I snuck in more fish drawings, including the scary slough carp and four more versions of a monster channel cat.

I had our cat pegged at 25 pounds, tried sketching him swimming, gulping prey in his mouth: a river sucker, a duck, a weasel, and the last one—a dumpground rat. Somehow, though, I couldn't be happy with any of them. The something missing was the inspiration of another marvelous cat to look at, a real one, bigger than Jack's that the guys surely would have caught, had they not been run off before they got to our fishin' Ford. Another missing note, but worse: I hadn't a summary to Smoky Roy with the kind eyes. My memory of him, unfinished, unsettled, would sit there moldering all winter long, and for many winters thereafter.

Chapter Nine

Good Fights, Bad Fights

"If there's going to be a fight, don't wait."—Bill Erickson

"Be ready with the first punch. If there's gonna be a fight, you nail him first. Now when I finish lacing these gloves, let's see how fast that first punch comes."

At first blush Dad's advice doesn't sound like self-defense, but it was. Dad illustrated the principle with his story. "My brothers and I had to deal with an older neighbor boy with a mean streak who needed a whipping. Our dad told us all about fighting bullies on our own terms, about picking the right time. My brothers and I sparred a lot, getting ready. I happened to be the next one the bully picked on. I was ready; he wasn't. I nailed him on the bridge of the nose. He didn't see my fist coming . . . never picked on one of us again."

That was a great ending to Dad's story. Though just a tyke, I recognized the glory of a conclusion, a once-and-for-all kind of thing—a *good* fight, one with a settlement.

To prepare Jim and me for "good fights," Dad provided puffy boxing gloves for us, and a pair for himself, too. In the beginning he sparred with us on his knees. Then, at ages 6 and 5, Dad allowed Jim and me to go toe-to-toe for practice, while he stood by instructing.

Jim and I were cautioned to not go looking for fights and we didn't. Same went for our buddies. Not one of us could count more than a handful of fights in our growing up time. Our dads taught self-defense, not aggression; but, they allowed that when bullies persisted, we'd need both.

In due time, Jim and I learned that fights were about more than fisticuff skills. The outcome of a fight wasn't always simple. Win a fight, you savored it; lose, and you hurt with swallowed pride. But, while losing was hard to accept, the unfinished fight was worse. Those you worried about for a long, long time—a particularly bad sort of fight.

Most fights, better described as scraps or flare-ups, had no underlying disagreements of any account. Both parties said, in effect: "Don't ever think I'm a pushover." Jim and I had one mad fight when our boxing practice got out of hand. Fortunately, we were wearing our puffy boxing gloves.

When Stretch laid me out in third grade, the clobbering didn't measure up to a real fight. It was too one-sided. Nevertheless, I characterize it as a bad fight, definitely undecided, because I wasn't through with Stretch yet. I didn't know when or how, but there would be some kind of reckoning with Stretch. Fortunately, before that time came, I had one *good* fight under my belt. I label it *good,* not only because it was the other guy on his back with a bloody lip. I'm not bragging here.

My friend, Jimmy, was tougher than me before I clobbered him, and remained tougher after. But our fight was good. It had a conclusion.

Jimmy Schwartz and I were in fourth grade. We were school friends, but since Jimmy was a town kind of boy, excepting swimming at Harmon Pool, I didn't see him much in summers. Also, his teasing nature sometimes strained our friendship.

Jimmy was a kid who had everything: tall for his age, popular at school, a lightning fast runner, an "A" student, and mannerly in the classroom. Mom liked him for his neatness, manners, charm, and she admired his "German good looks." On rare days socked in by rain, when I dawdled about the house, she'd suggest: "Call Jimmy Schwartz. You two can find something to do."

Like our dad, Jimmy's dad had taught him self-defense. Jimmy and I laced on our boxing gloves in our back yard once, and I learned immediately of his agility and quickness. His lightning fists stung and smarted, even with oversized gloves. I didn't want a real fight with Jimmy Schwartz, and had no reason for one, not until he went too far with his teasing. Like the ornery coyote of Spring Coulee, the coyote and Jimmy were two of a kind.

On a bitter wind March morning Jim and Buck and I hiked north of Stony Ford to Spring Coulee to spear suckers. We missed the sucker run, apparently come and gone; but, we were lucky to see a teaser coyote get his comeuppance. He followed a littler coyote along the coulee ridge, nipping his heels with every step. Engaged in a significant squabble, they paid us no mind. After 10 or so foot shaking nips to his heels the little coyote wheeled, and ferociously attacked the big coyote. He chased the taunting teaser down the ridge to the Muddy River, where the not-so-tough big coyote escaped by leaping half-way across the narrows, landing in the icy water. He climbed out and shook off the ice water. With ears flattened, the bully coyote crouched and glared, making sure he was free of the attacker. Maybe thinking, *Okay, okay, I got your message, I was only teasing, you know.* The little coyote, the good fight winner, lolled his tongue and trotted off, sniffing for fat gophers. "Yah, that's the way," Jim hollered after him.

March is an unsettling time for coyotes and people in North Dakota. Winter refuses to retreat into Canada. We sometimes become snotty. On the second Saturday in March I unexpectedly needed to answer snotty with snotty.

I went off that morning to meet up with my marble partner, Jimmy Schwartz, at the Central School playground. At long last the ground was half-thawed, soft enough to dig marble pots. A dozen kids showed up with marble bags, ready to wager steelies, cat's eyes, jumbos, and puries. In the second game, Jimmy won a rare woodie. We worked as partners, alternating as player and "negotiator," arguing with opponents about "fudgies" or "no fudgies" and other hazy rules. We were doing well against a couple of poor shooters, having a great time, when here came Little Ergie. Son-of-a-gun, he rode up on a brand spankin' new red Monarch, his first-ever bike. No more borrowing his sister's girl bike. Boy-oh-boy, Ergie was proud—never saw him happier. The marble games could wait. I wanted to inspect Ergie's prize bike. He stood holding it, close enough for me to smell the new tires. "Finally saved my half of the dough," Ergie said. "What do you think of her?"

For some strange reason of his own, Jimmy reached down and twanged a spoke on Ergie's bike wheel. "Don't do that, Jimmy; you might kink it," I said.

Now I wish Ergie had laid the warning, because he was only a second grader, and Jimmy wouldn't seriously pick on a second grader; but, because it was me, Jimmy grinned and twanged another spoke. I put my hand on his shoulder, "I said don't do that, Jimmy. It's a brand new bike."

He didn't hesitate. He smiled at me, turned away, and reached for another spoke. With my mind whirring like a windmill, my cheeks turning hot, I summed up the deal: *Jimmy wants one, he needs one, there's going to be a fight.* He straightened up from twanging his third spoke with a taunting grin. He had no chance. I had already set my legs and my round-houser was on its way with every ounce of me behind it. My right fist caught him in the corner of his mouth. He went down hard, with his arms flailing, unable to catch his fall. The back of his head "thunked" on the gravel.

I stood over him, legs braced and ready. Jimmy propped to his elbows, but didn't try to get up. A trickle of blood flowed from the corner of his mouth. His eyes bugged and his mouth hung open. He shook his head and spit bloody gunk, "Why . . . why'd you hit me?"

He knew full well, and I didn't bother to answer. I grabbed my marble sack and jumped on my bike to join Ergie, who was ready, anxious to ride. Before pulling away, I checked once more to be sure the fight was over. It was. Jimmy'd regained his feet, but made no effort to come after me. His brown eyes were wet at the corners. I couldn't help myself, sad that a kid like Jimmy Schwartz could look like that. He used to be my friend, too.

Yes, I'd won a fight and proved Dad right about that first punch. Yet, I wasn't anxious to talk about it. I'd lost a friend, a kid Dad and Mom both liked. Heck, I liked him too. Still, with swollen knuckles and all, they'd have to be told. Like most things important, my fight was discussed over supper.

I told about Jimmy twanging Little Ergie's bike spokes. "Jimmy had it coming," I said.

"He sure as hell did," Dad said. "And you took him on just the way I taught you."

With everything off my chest, the whole deal was laid to rest; but then, the doggone phone rang. After Dad's "Uh-huh . . . uh-huh," and his nod at me, I suspected who it was. "For you," he said. He grinned as he handed over the phone.

"Dave, my . . . my dad's right here," Jimmy said. Jimmy's voice wasn't right for a proud kid. "Dad says one of us has to pay for my broken tooth. I'm supposed to ask you. He . . . says he'll honor your decision. Do . . . uh—do you think you should pay for it?"

"No, I don't."

I waited, expecting argument. Instead, Jimmy said in a near whisper, "That's what I thought you'd say." The phone line buzzed on . . . I was ready to hang up when Jimmy said, "Dave? . . ."

"Yah?"

"Are you sorry for what happened?"

"Yes, I am." I said that without qualms.

"Me, too," Jimmy said. "Then . . . are we still friends?"

"We're still friends, Jimmy," I said. "See ya tomorrow at school."

I couldn't say clobbering Jimmy was totally satisfying, but it did have a conclusion, a *good* kind of fight. Strong, quick, and smart—I didn't want another fight with Jimmy Schwartz. Our friendship was better now, and better for me, because he never gave me a reason to fight him again.

My next fight came just two weeks later. You might assume I'd turned cocky, thinking I could go around picking fights. But that's not what happened. I was a skinny little kid, and the opposite of cocky. But fights don't come along on a logical schedule. And I surely wasn't ready for the next one, especially another fight with Stretch Johnson.

After third grade, Stretch had become somewhat of a community project. The National Guard boxing coaches arranged challenging matches for him with older guys. Mr. Gwin and the juvenile officer kept tabs on Stretch and his roughneck buddies from the hardscrabble Flats neighborhood along the Scenic Highway. After Stretch served detention and spent the summer of 1946 without raising hell, Miss Wilkinson passed him into fourth grade—good for Stretch, bad for the rest of us fourth graders. My friends and I spent most of a nervous year staying clear of him. Then, in the spring of 1947, like a scraggly zoo bear, Stretch Johnson came out of hibernation looking for trouble.

Stretch must have been desperately agitated to instigate a fight right inside Central School. He pulled it off because his school-room dumb didn't mean he was really dumb. He found a sneaky moment on vaccination day, and made his ornery move.

Mr. Pederson came to fetch our class. "Get'n line der, all a ya'. An' not a peep outa ya, neider." Ol' Pete trooped us through the connecting hall to the junior high gym and turned us over to the beefy head nurse in her stiff, white uniform. After what came next, it's too bad Pederson hadn't stayed with us. We lined up under the watchful eyes of the boss nurse, who would administer our smallpox vaccinations. Jelly, Terry, Jake, and a passel of my friends stood in front and back of me in line. We were minding our own business, anxious to get the doggone needle job done, moving along stop and go, stop and go, toward the two nurses. We'd been poked the week before. Today we'd get the booster on top of our scabby vaccination sores.

There were about 50 of us, two classes of fourth graders. Our teachers were content to leave us with the nurses. The big one must have weighed 250. I was near the back of the line, yet I heard her sergeant's voice, "Hold still," just before she stabbed her needle. We shuffled quietly forward, docility guaranteed by dread of the needle. Kids finished with their own torture passed by us on their way to their classrooms. I thought some laid it on a little thick, whining: "Hurts way worse than the first one."

The boss nurse wielding the needle sent her assistant up the line inspecting bare arms. To Claire Ann, in front of me, she said, "Very good, nice; it's swollen, nice scab, too. You're ready."

"Well, it's real sore," Claire Ann said.

"Supposed to be, dear—means your vaccination is working," the nurse said.

She moved to me, checked my arm and continued checking a dozen kids behind me. Last in line was Stretch Johnson. He ignored the nurse, choosing instead to stare at me with his cockeyed grin.

Stretch waited until the nurse had returned to the boss nurse's table. Then he sauntered to me. I turned facing him, expecting a taunt—but nothing more—not here inside Central School.

He moved up close. "You sissies feerin' a little needle?"

"What's it to ya?" I said. He made a sour mouth, followed by a lightning belt, popping the vaccination scab on the top of my left arm. Quickly, Stretch methodically marched along the line, punching my buddies smack on their sore vaccination scabs: *Thunk*—"Ouw!"; *thunk*—"Ouw!"; *thunk*—Ouw!" Stretch nailed Jake, Jelly, Jimmy Schwartz—*thunk, thunk, thunk*. He'd whopped us quickly, expertly, and now stood grinning. We waited like brainless cows going to slaughter, trapped between Stretch and a pair of crotchety nurses holding stabbers.

Blood leaked from my hurting scab. I wanted to cry, but since I'd given up crying in second grade, I sniffed it away. *"Maybe I should try him right here,"* I thought. But why risk a broken jaw and detention too?

The big boss nurse came galumphing, on the peck. She'd heard our whiney commotion, but failed to see Stretch's sneaky poundings. She glared along the line, looking where Stretch stood, rubbing his jaw, trying for innocence. Lifting her chin above our entire line-up, she gruffed, "Any more commotion from you, and I'll send the bunch of you to Principal Wilkinson." She returned to her job. Now, I double-dreaded her needle ready to jab my throbbing arm.

"We ain't gonna take any more of him," I said loudly enough for Stretch to hear.

Jimmy moved in behind me. "We gotta fight him," he said.

"You're right, Jimmy, and it's now or never." A pod formed around me, including Claire Ann, a smart girl who always spoke up in our classroom.

"You should report him," Claire Ann said. "Fighting will get you in trouble."

Terry Flatley sidled into line between Claire Ann and me. To Claire Ann he said, "He's been reported over and over and you just saw what good it did." To me, Terry said, "Eric, if you want to whip Stretch, count me in. Johnson nailed me on my scab at recess." I wanted to cheer, because Terry was even tougher than my friend Jimmy Schwartz. Terry glared at Stretch, and whispered to me: "You tell him, I'll back you up."

I had no choice. I drew a big breath of air and walked to the end of the line. Terry followed. Stretch stood with his hands on hips, grinning. "What da hell you sissies want?" he said.

"About what you just did; you deserve a whipping," I said.

"So? Who da hell's gonna do it?"

"We are."

"Yah, so who's we?"

"A whole bunch of guys, Stretch."

"Huh! You just name the place and time."

"I'll let you know," I said.

"Back in line," the boss nurse hollered.

A few minutes later, I watched her sanitize Claire Ann's vaccination scab with alcohol, and daub her scab with the magic vaccine. "Just relax your arm, dear, only a little sting now." With a tiny needle she jabbed—*poke, poke, poke* . . . I counted five in all, bloody jabs in the scab that were to let the vaccine penetrate. Claire Ann, a tough rope climbing girl, didn't flinch, even grinned at me, meaning: *Okay, Dave, let's see you take it like that.*

Well, I have to admit I flinched on the third jab of the needle—fourth too—and each one after. Her poking went on and on, I suppose punishment for my rowdiness in her line. My "troublemaker" buddies had to endure the on-and-on poking too. When the boss nurse finished with us, we circled to the end of the line so we could watch Stretch get poked by her payback needle. He may have flinched the tiniest bit. I couldn't be sure. As he came by, he sneered, "You sissies let me know where and when."

I set fight time for 10 minutes after four on Tuesday. That allowed four days for arm healing. The place was the hidden nook in the alley behind the high school. After the dismissal bell rang, my guys and I ran the one block from Central School so we could gather and discuss strategy. But no two ideas meshed. Besides, we ran out of time. Here came Stretch in his rollicking trot on muscled bow legs. I recognized the same worn blue plaid shirt and holey Levis. How could I forget? Stretch wore the same outfit a year earlier when he nearly broke my right jaw. This year his Levis were four inches short and tight against his thighs.

Stretch sidled up, rocking his shoulders. I'd seen Ezzard Charles loosen up that way in a newsreel. Stretch danced his fists in front of my face and taunted me with his smirky grin. "You wanted this Erickson. Me aginst' you first, or I'll whup the bunch a' you at once—yer choice."

I surveyed my guys, needing time to think. Their faces didn't help—Terry, Jimmy, Jelly, and Jake Jacobs. They were as puzzled as I, not expecting Stretch's terms.

It wasn't bravery that prodded me. A brave guy wouldn't be so scared. I don't know what made me say it: "All of us at once wouldn't be fair, Stretch," I said.

"Okay, then, jus' you an' me. Come on, put 'em up."

"Don't wait," my dad had said. I advanced in my boxing crouch, wondering which surprise move to make and how to pull it off. My buddies circled around Stretch and me. Their cheers of encouragement echoed from the backside of the brick high school: "Git 'im, Dave."—"He ain't so tough." . . . and Jake: "Hit him in the belly, Eric. He's weak in the gut."

Dad's voice rehearsed in my head: *"Bend the knees, fists high, arms protect your belly and chest, keep moving, fake and jab."* Boxing lore raced and spun about in my brain. I needed to remember everything, including Stretch's technique last time when he laid me out.

Stretch danced smoothly in his crouching waltz. He circled me, shuffling: one . . . two, one . . . two. You could have put him to music. He was a discouraging sight, 30 pounds of muscle bigger than me, big enough to be an eighth grade fullback . . . and always—the confident lopsided grin. I watched, anticipating, looking for movement of his dark eyes, a twitch of muscle, a tipoff to the striking of a rattlesnake fist. *I shouldn't wait. I should take it to him; but how?*

What was he waiting for? He glided. He pranced. He swung his upper body to and fro as if he'd been doing this forever. I searched for space to plow a fist through, but Stretch held his muscled arms together, vertical barriers hiding his chest and belly. His fists were turned inward, covering his face, everything but his glowing dark eyes. He glared. "Come on, Erickson, you wanted a fight."

I bobbed and moved, matching his steps, thinking: *Okay, I'll fake; make it real, then punch hard, putting my shoulder into it. Feel the smack into his belly. He'll flinch and I'll use the moment to hit quickly, aiming for his nose.* I stared into his eyes, faked high with my right and came with my left to punish his belly. But what I got was a bouncing blow off his forearm, like hitting a rubber tire. His muscled arms didn't move, solid as fence posts. His expression didn't change. I defended, expecting the worst; but he did nothing. I came again, this time a double feint low followed by a high right hook to come in around his fists. Again he paid no price. My right fist slammed into the back of his wrist, and the hurt was all mine.

He's taunting, I know. Must be something he hasn't thought of. I gotta get past his shield of arms and fists. I unleashed a flurry, while watching for a flinch or tightening of muscle, something announcing his launch of the sledgehammer that was sure to come.

My flurry did nothing but bounce back from his big arms. Stretch circled to his right, and I followed, matching him step for step, keeping just out of his range.

"Come on," he said, "show me something." I took a step toward him, still thinking of my next strategy. I caught a flicker in his shoulder, remembering the left roundhouser that dumped me last time. But the flick of shoulder was a fake; this time his lightning right fist caught me low on the right jaw, staggering me. I pedaled backward and fell—down and dizzy, but not done.

With a ring boxer's respect, Stretch held back while I struggled to my feet. As I puzzled what to try next, here came Terry, pushing by me into the fight. Spellbound, I became part of the ring of onlookers.

Terry came wild and furious, flailing at Stretch. I suppose after watching my methodical maneuvers fail, he believed he could somehow just overwhelm Stretch. But Stretch ducked, swayed, and picked off each of Terry's blows. Then he expertly pummeled Terry in the belly. Terry doubled over, and Stretch delivered right and left hooks to his head that knocked him to the ground.

Jimmy came next. But he went down with a bloody nose even quicker than Terry with the swelling eye. "Anybody else?" Stretch taunted.

"Yeah," Jake said, but I grabbed his wrist before he could move.

"Forget it Jake," I said.

"Yeah, forget it, Jake," Stretch said. "Ya wanna fight . . . come on down to the Armory. The National Guard guys will teach ya. All you guys, you don't know nuthin."

Jake and Jelly looked at each other and shrugged. I couldn't blame them. They were the smart ones. Our little posse had run out of ammunition and ideas too.

"See ya' sissy-girls at school," Stretch said. Before leaving, he shook his head sadly. Stretch loved nothing better than a good fight, and we had failed to give him one.

We hadn't a thing to gain by announcing our humiliation of one guy beating up five of us. Jake and Jelly had to be counted, because had they been dumb enough to fight Stretch—no question—Stretch would have made short work of them.

Stretch wouldn't brag about whipping "weak sisters." Who wanted to listen to him anyhow? Still, I was naïve to think we'd keep it quiet. Terry came to school with a black eye, and Claire Ann caught him in the hallway. "What happened to you?"

He hung his head. "Stretch," was all he'd say.

Somebody else told a best friend, who told another friend, and before the day was over I heard the whole fight described back to me, only worse than it was.

The disgrace of our big defeat wasn't the end. We'd have to face Stretch again in the hallways, on the playground, anyplace he found us vulnerable.

We kept our distance from Stretch, knowing he'd still find opportunities to torment any one of us. . . . Nothing. Nothing happened. No tripping, no arm punches, or bully taunts on the playground. A week went by, still nothing. Then at recess on Friday, one-by-one, Johnson confronted each of the three of us he'd whipped, plus Jake and Jelly. As he approached me, I wouldn't let him close the distance. I'd never seen him this way, kind of squinty, biting the side of his off-kiltered lip. "Erickson," he said. "I'm invitin' ya, the others too. You oughta come over to the Armory tomorrow to watch our spring matches. Sidney and Wuff Point are comin'. Wuff Point has some goddamn tough fighters, Indian guys. You could learn a lot."

"Um, maybe . . . I'll see," I said.

"You sign up for trainin' with the Guard team; then you get free tickets for Fight Night." Stretch followed up with a mock boxing stance. I backed away; but, this time he seemed different: no wolf-eyed glare, and—if I wasn't mistaken—an honest smile.

I was curious, tempted to go and watch Stretch box, maybe see somebody give him his comeuppance. I decided instead on a walleye trip with Jim and Buck. I didn't have an open mind about competition boxing. I'd play tackle football, plenty rough, but fun. The "Fights" though . . . Gramp took Jim and me to the Armory one time to see the Fights. Even the winners were losers, bloodied and bruised and too beat up to celebrate properly.

All but Terry turned down Stretch's invite. I had to push on Terry to learn what happened. He told me about Stretch knocking down a Wolf Point fighter—down, not out, but cuckoo enough they called off the match. Terry started his lessons the next Monday evening, beginning with weight lifting, punching bag drills, and dry-run foot work in the ring. During the third week Terry sparred with a coach. The coach set him up for his first three rounder. The only guy somewhat close to Terry's weight was Stretch Johnson himself, who outweighed Terry by 20 pounds of muscle and talent.

By nature Terry had a habit of telling more than he had to. "Too honest," some would say. So Terry owned up to his match with Stretch that never came off. "The match was already on the program," Terry said. "Stretch tore it up. Then he says to the coach, 'I want somebody can give me a good fight.'" Terry made me promise to not tell anybody else from school.

"It's funny, though," Terry told me. "Stretch doesn't act as mean as before."

I had noticed a change even before Terry's story. But an even bigger surprise was to come. Stretch called me aside after school. I stood well away, waiting and wondering. He began without his scowl, "I'm goin' fishin' next Saturday. You want to go?" He said this like a perfectly normal kid.

I stalled, digging gravel with my toe, remembering the bad in him, yet seeing him different now. "Uh, maybe I can. I'll—uh—let you know tomorrow."

At the supper table, Dad didn't seem very surprised by Stretch's invite. "Well, tell me, did he ever fight dirty?"

"No, he didn't," I said.

"Did he lie to you?"

"I wouldn't talk with him unless I had to; but no, he never lied."

"Well, seems like you've got a choice. You can go fishin' with your brother or this Stretch character. From what I've heard, Stretch needs a friend. You and Jim already have friends."

"So, what should I do?"

Dad shrugged. "Up to you."

"I think you ought to go," Jim chimed in. "He's not that bad a guy."

"Well, you need to try fighting him, then."

"Are you crazy?" Jim laughed.

Jim and I could have gone on, even though we both knew the game; but, Mom came around the table and put her hand on the back of my neck. "I know of him, David . . . and all about his family too. I visited with Miss Wilkinson after your fight with him. You just be careful."

On May Day morning I rode my bike down East Broadway headed for Stretch's house. Curiosity tangled with nervousness. The Johnsons lived a half-block north off the Scenic Highway in the district known as the Flats, where the poorest of the poor lived and the toughest of the tough. Coming down the hill onto the Scenic, I spotted the broken down coal wagon. "Turn left at the coal wagon," Stretch had said. "My house is the first one past there on the right."

I bounced around the wagon corner onto a rutted dirt street, pursued by a barking mongrel. I spotted Stretch kneeling by an upturned bike in front of a shabby log house. It looked to be 100 years old, low-roofed, like a homesteader's cabin. I jammed my brakes and extended a leg, sliding sideways in my best big-shot skid. Stretch looked up from his knees. "Hey, Erickson, you made it. I need your help here. Can't go anyways 'til my mom gits home. I'm lookin' after my little brother."

Stretch's bike rested upside down. "You spin the wheel, I'll adjust the nuts," he said. With a box wrench he went to tightening one side, loosened the other, tweaking right and tweaking left. Nothing changed. His wheel wobbled and rubbed on the forks. Stretch threw down his wrench. "Goddam rim's bent. It was bent before I rode it home from Smoky's."

"Smoky's? You mean Smoky Roy?"

"Yah, he built this bike fer me. Smoky said my bike's mostly Schwinn. It'll be all Schwinn soon's he finds the parts."

I imagine I looked as ridiculous as I felt just then, dumbfounded and speechless. And here I'd planned to come off as tough, at home in a tough neighborhood. My problem was I'd never heard Stretch laugh before. He wasn't exactly the same guy I thought I knew. On top of that, throw in his apparent friendship with Smoky Roy, and—well, everything bombing at once . . . I felt like a first grader in short pants.

Stretch hoisted his stripped down bike onto its wheels. "It's good enough to ride for one day," he said.

"Where we headed?" I asked.

"Smoky's place first. Maybe he can find me a better rim. Den he'll take us fishin'."

"Holy cow! Smoky Roy. I haven't seen him since . . . " Stretch turned away at the sound of a door banging around the back.

"My mom's home," Stretch said. "Come on in."

Johnson's house appeared to be made of two log cabins joined together, ancient ones too, like the half-rotted pioneer log cabins Gramp showed me in the Badlands. The Johnson cabin-house slumped at the corners and bricks from its broken chimney littered the bare dirt front yard. A rickety outhouse stood at the rear corner.

I followed Stretch in past the plank door to discover the inside worse than the outside. The floor was made of hard packed dirt, excepting a kitchen area to the left that was planked. A wood burning stove sat against the back wall on the plank floor. Like the log walls themselves, the fibery floor planks were sawed out of cottonwood. I knew this because Grandpa Erickson showed me through the old cabin in his woods, explaining how the homesteaders sawed planks of cottonwood. That old cabin had the same musty smell as the Johnson place. Grandpa explained: "I tried cottonwood too, found out how it would swell. Nail it down and a year later it had begun to curl and creep. In a couple years it smells rank, just like this old cabin."

Stretch and I stood awkwardly in the center of the room. I found myself staring at the poorness of the place. I tried to appear nonchalant about what I saw: one large rectangular room, dim and sparsely furnished, and an open ceiling crossed by spider-webbed pole rafters. Besides the stove, the kitchen area held a dish cupboard in the corner, and an oil cloth covered table. Oh—and two paint-peeled wooden chairs.—Odd that there were only two chairs, because a mom, little brother, and a dad . . . did they eat in shifts?

The right half of the room was empty, except for two raggy stuffed chairs looking perfect for mouse nests. A small window on the west allowed a shaft of light that lit up sparkles of floating dust. That was all of any account save the little brother in a crib in the corner. He shook the slats of a crib crying: "Kenna, Kenna, I wan' out."

"Mom, I got my friend here," Stretch hollered, words to break the awkward silence. He stood with hands in his pockets, shoulders rounded, staring at a curtain at the back of the room. The curtain parted and Mrs. Johnson appeared from the attached room, I guessed the bedroom. Except for funny men's shoes and her long cotton pioneer-lady dress, she seemed like a regular mom. She looked at me with kindly dark eyes and gestured at a pot on the stove. "You drink coffee?"

"No thank you, ma'am."

We stood awkwardly in an arc of three.

"Dis here's my mom," Stretch said, "and that's my little brother over there. We call him Dillinger." Dillinger stood glaring through slats of the tall homemade crib. Dillinger . . . slats, like a kid's jail. He was only about three, yet his bare arms and torso were finely muscled.

"Did you take him to the john, Kenneth?"

"Yah, Mom, long time ago."

"And your friend's name?"

"Erickson."

Mrs. Johnson lowered her kind face on me. With smooth caramel skin, she didn't look old enough to be Stretch's mother. Her smile came mostly from her dark eyes with squinted wrinkles at the corners. "Kenneth says you're going fishing with him. Can you swim?" Her voice told of worry.

"Yes, I'm a good swimmer. I passed my swimming test."

"Kenneth can't swim," she said. "Will you, uh—your first name is? . . ."

"David."

"David, will you please look out for Kenneth?"

"Sure, I even know some lifesaving if he falls in."

Kenneth scowled. "Ain't about to fall in." He hurried over to his little brother, lifting him from his crib. Dillinger toddled after Kenneth, tugging on his pant leg, whining, "Kenna, Kenna. I wanna go too."

I was messing in Stretch's business, I knew. Yet, he and his Mom deserved to know. "Learning to swim isn't hard. I can help," I said. Stretch fidgeted, rocking from foot-to-foot.

Mrs. Johnson aimed her finger at his nose. "You ain't afraid are you, Kenneth?"

"Shi-iiit, Mom, I ain't afraid."

She bristled, "Watch you language in my house, Kenneth."

In the awkward aftermath, I was struck by their faces, two Johnson faces: the same brown almond eyes and coppery skin. Their faces were alike in everything that should matter. And his real name, Kenneth. Even though she was irritated at the moment, she spoke his name gently, like any mom should. It was then that I took a big step, surprising myself how easy it was.

"Kenneth," I said, "Harmon Park gives free lessons. You could learn to swim in no time. *"Kenneth,"* I'd said—peculiar sounding that first time; yet never again did I call him anything but Kenneth, or later on, Ken.

"Okay, Kenneth, you'll do it then," his mom said.

Kenneth backed away. "We gotta go. Gotta be at Smoky's at ten," he said.

Mrs. Johnson raised her voice, "KENNETH! I said you'll learn to swim." She was a smart mom, recognizing her boy's fib. She smiled, "Not like you have a real job out there, Kenneth. Now you wait while I fix you and David something for your lunch." She pulled a jar of peanut butter from an iceless icebox and buttered up a pair of sandwiches for us, while Kenneth and Dillinger cuffed each other like daddy bear and cub bear.

Dillinger and his Mom followed us and stood in the dirt yard littered with bottles, cans, and soggy cardboard. The mongrel with the mean bark came and sat by Kenneth's leg. With the same wan expressions as Mom and Dillinger, the mongrel watched Kenneth and me mount our bikes. Our send-off was a ho-hum deal with half-hearted goodbyes. They were a sad sight: a tired looking mom, a skinny mongrel, and a whining kid brother.

Kenneth and I waved before we turned onto the Scenic Highway, heading east. With every revolution of Kenneth's front wheel, the tire rubbed the fork like a brake. He could have walked faster and easier. But our slow one mile ride did provide time to talk. That was another surprise. In school Kenneth never talked, except when pushed hard by a teacher or readying himself for a scrap. His speech came in short bursts, propelled by swear words, same as at school.

Kenneth's house and his mom got me to thinking: Living poor made him tough-acting and fighting tough; but, at home he was still just a kid like me. On the road to the Muddy River that morning, he surprised me more. "You shoulda come to the matches. I was goddam mad at you fer not comin'. I had to go aginst Gaudreau, sumbitch left hander, everting backwards. Sumbitch knocked me down in the first round. I flattened him in the turred, though."

"So, what happened?"

"Whadda ya mean?"

"Who won?"

"Well, I won. I scored way higher. You know I ain't been beat; niver will be, eider."

That much I already knew; how proud Kenneth was, I mean. But his next remark threw me for a loop: "Would you, if you'd been there, would you have, uh . . . yelled for me?"

"Against Gaudreau?"

"Yeah, Gaudreau."

I assembled my answer without thinking, a wise guy answer, as if I was talking with my brother instead of a guy who had beat me up twice, three if I included the low-down vaccination punch. "Gaudreau's never had a squabble with me. I'd probably yell for him." Stupid of me to say that. The words just sort of spilled on their own. Quickly though, I formed a backup plan: *If Stretch—I mean Kenneth—blows at me, I can easily get away on my stripped down Hawthorne against his bent-rimmed piece of junk.*

He rode a bike length ahead of me. I pulled abreast of him, watching him warily. Kenneth pumped eight or ten times before adding, "How about in the first round when the sumbitch damn near knocked me out? Bet you would have been hollerin' for me to get up and get after him then?"

I let him stew on that for a minute, then I said, "Kenneth, tell you the truth, I hardly know Gaudreau. I know you. Might even come and watch you at the National Guard fights. If I do, I'll yell for you."

"You better or I'll whup you agin, too . . . kick your ass." Kenneth laughed, and the sound of his laughter tickled my ribs from the inside out.

Up ahead, in front of the ramp to the Muddy River Bridge, the dumpground road forked to the right, southward. We'd have to take it if, indeed, we were going to see Smoky Roy. The road fork would be the spot on the map where I'd violate Dad's rule. He called it his V-J Day Law for when he enacted it—a handy way to remember. "You boys are banned from going south of Muddy River Bridge," he'd proclaimed. But laws have a way of dying of neglect. As Kenneth and I turned off the Scenic Highway, I hoped two years was enough.

The sweet mud air drifted from the river, reminding me how the day had started—preparing my stow bag with throw-line, extra hooks, sinkers, and worm can. Wished I'd thrown in an extra line, too. "Kenneth, I didn't notice your throw-line," I said.

"Don't need a line."

"How you gonna fish?"

"You'll see. Smoky an' me got a better way." With that, he grunted and pumped hard to gain momentum for our climb up the dirt ramp to the top of the dump hill.

Topping the ramp Kenneth turned abruptly left, leaving the east escarpment to follow the same trail used by the dumpground scavenger men. I looked down the steep switchbacked trail and envied Kenneth's rubbing tire acting as an extra brake. I locked my rear wheel brake and skidded around the three switchbacks. Next we would pass the cave-house and the mean brothers.

Hah! Come out and glare at us, you bastards. I hope you do. This time I'm with a tough guy who'll clean your clocks.

Filled with a mix of curiosity and second-hand bravery, I was disappointed that the brothers either weren't at home or stayed put like rats in hiding. Or, what if they moved to town? "Find yourself some work, fellas," Gramp would say. Was it possible? I didn't think so.

Up ahead, Smoky's shack made a slight bulge in the side of the hill. From that direction a southeast breeze flowed over us, bringing new fragrance: sweet and tangy. "Smoky's cooking something good, Kenneth," I said.

"Yah, them's skipjack," Kenneth said. We walked our bikes up the rise from the river, and I spotted Smoky coming around a sort of low tin hut, "the smokin' house," Kenneth prided, as if he'd built it himself. Malta hopped on his three good legs right over to see me, sniffing my pantleg.

"Well, I'll be damned," Smoky said. "Look who's here. Malta remembers. I don't know how; you and your buddies never come to see me." I chuckled to myself. Those were exactly Gramp's words when Jim and I were supposedly too busy to stop and see *him.*

"School and everything, I never get the chance to come out here," I lied.

"Well, don't make it so long next time. Bring your brother and Jack. We need more help, don't we Kenny? Long as you're here, though, we'll put you to work." Smoky gleamed the same sparky blue-eyed smile as last time. He wore the same striped coveralls, blue workshirt, and his lucky fishin' cap—as before—too clean, out of place for a man who lives in a cave-house under the dumpground.

The smokehouse was new from last time; so was a bicycle rack made of plumber's pipes, half-full of an assortment of rescued bikes.

Smoky put his arm around my shoulder. "Let me show you my smoker. Kenny, go fetch the coffee pot. We'll have lunch right here before we go to work with the nets. Time we finish, it could be dark. Better save your sandwiches for supper," Smoky joked.

"Is it okay if I give mine to Malta?" Kenneth asked.

"Sure, one sandwich, one skipjack; you'll make him happy, hey Malta." Malta whopped legs with his wolfy tail, agreeing. I wished Smoky had sent me for the coffee. I wanted another look-see inside his mystery house.

Lunch turned out to be rescued Borrud's bread toasted in the smoker along with coffee and smoked skipjack, the same fish Gramp called "goldeyes" and the Muddy River fishers called "goldies."

We sat on a worn wooden bench by the smoker, warmed by a perfect sun. And a lucky breeze came off the Missouri today instead of from the stinking dump fires. Smoky wanted to know about school classes, answers coming entirely from me. And for Kenneth, Smoky threw in a boxing story about a first round knock-out by Joe Lewis.

Smoky rose from the bench and stretched. "Time to go to work, boys." He pulled racks from the smoker and used a spatula to collect the finished fillets. He whistled *Old Man River*; he sang part of it in a deep Negro voice. The three of us wrapped the smoked fish slabs in cotton cloth and newspapers. Then we took off to the river, with Smoky shouldering a big gear bag. "The afternoon skipjack run will be big, boys. I'll bet I saw a million skitterin' on the Missouri this morning."

The trail to the Missouri wasn't as long as I remembered, only about a city block until it entered the trader village. Only two men were in sight, the gawky Ichabod Crane character and his little silver-haired sidekick. They stood by a campfire built in the middle of the "street." As Smoky walked up to them, Icky ducked his chin and averted his eyes. His little partner, though, spoke up cheerily. "Hey, Smoky, how's fishin'?" Smoky put his hand on the little bum's shoulder. He wasn't much taller than me.

"Pearly," Smoky said, "fishin' is terrific. You need to get out of 'town' for a spell. Come along and give us a hand; I'll make it worth your while."

As if asking for permission, Pearly looked over at Icky Crane, whose eyes never left the fire. Pearly made no move to come along. "Maybe next time," he said.

On we went, sidehilling past the sewer to the mouth of the Muddy and the marvelous roll of sand separating my little river and the Mighty Mo. I'd always remember my one lonesome time there, sitting on the warm sand with the Little Muddy River by my side, gazing upon the grand Missouri and the wild and endless valley of Lewis and Clark.

Today would be my first chance to fish with a net. Smoky hadn't explained how, only that he'd set out a thing called a gill net using an old wooden boat he'd resurrected. "My boat leaks a mite," Smoky said. "I'll seal her the old-fashioned way, with sap, soon as the box elders turn it loose."

We found the rowboat tied to a snag log in the final eddy of the Little Muddy, the same place where I'd found the embarrassing "rubbers." The boat swung gently back and forth in the current. It was about ten feet long and extra fat in the middle, looked old enough to be a Lewis and Clark boat. "R. Clapper," said the black printing on the bow. "I need her for gill netting," Smoky said. "Headed for a skipjack school just off the mouth of the Muddy."

Smoky unshouldered his pack. "Here's how we'll do it: Eric, you'll be the net picker . . . uh, you're the Little Eric, aren't you?"

"Yes sir."

"Little Eric, you stay on the beach. Kenny and I will drive posts to anchor my new net. Then we'll bring the far end of my morning net in to you. I set it early, should have a few skippies by now. You drag it in and pull the fish. There's a little trick to it; I'll show you when the time comes." Smoky nodded at his pack—"Two gunnies in that pack to put our fish in. Oh, forgot to tell you. You'll use that hooker stick to snag the net."

Smoky climbed in his boat and plopped on the middle seat, commanding the oars. "Bail her out, Matey," he barked. Kenneth had apparently been the "Matey" before, picking up the funny seaman's lingo, too: "Aye, aye, Captain." He stooped to his job, bailing water with an old Folgers can.

"Ready when you are," 'Captain' Smoky said. Kenneth leaned over the bow, loosening the mooring rope from the snag. His shaky hands reminded me he couldn't swim. I worried for him.

"Smoky . . . uh, Mr. Roy, Kenneth told me he can't swim. I can go in the boat if you want."

"You had it right the first time; Smoky it is. What about it, Kenny? You want to stay on the beach with Malta?"

"Naw, I'll go with you." Kenneth's answer made sense. He'd fight anybody small or big. He'd stand up to the big river too.

"Okay," Smoky laughed. "I'll throw a rope around you if I have to."

The boat swung out of the Muddy's eddy into the swift Missouri with Smoky pulling hard on the creaking oars to hold his boat at the mouth of the Muddy. Kenneth reached wide, taking a fearsome grip on the gunnels. "Kenny, you're going to have to let loose of the boat to drive our stakes," Smoky hollered. He maneuvered the boat into position and kerplunked a junk-iron anchor into the river.

"Okay, time to drive our stakes." Kenneth kneeled in the bottom of the boat wielding the maul hammer in his right hand, steel post in the other. Though Smoky's boat swayed at anchor, close to shore, the Missouri raced past, rippling, swirling, gurgling. Ken's eyes bugged. Heck, the big river scared me too, and I was a good swimmer.

Kenneth couldn't move. Smoky leaned and grabbed him by the back of his belt. Above the river's whooshing, I heard, "Gotcha, Kenny. Go to it." Kenny though, except for jittery hands, remained frozen.

"Well, Matey," Smoky said, "looks like we better change places. I'll set the net stakes; you man the oars." Kenneth hunkered even lower; then, the two of them crawled past each other like a pair of big dogs. I viewed the scene as one-half comedy and one-half worry.

Smoky hammered the net posts into the bottom of the river, tied the gill net, and pulled the anchor. He yelled, "Starboard pull, Matey; take us upriver." Ken managed to row a jig-jagged course upriver to Smoky's morning net tied right in front of me, a throw-line cast away.

Smoky leaned out and loosed the net's tether knot. "Okay, Kenny, row for Eric there on the beach." Here they came, towing the net. I waded in to my knees, so anxious I hadn't bothered to take off my old fishin' shoes.

I knew so well the tug on my throw-line and never tired of it. But this net could catch us dozens, maybe hundreds of fish all at once. And that's exactly what happened! I stood with the "hooker stick," and Ken rowed for me, trailing the net, as wide as the boat and twice as long. The net throbbed and flashed with silvery fish. As I hooked the net, Smoky turned from his seat in the stern hollering, "Land ho." Ken stood, arms reaching high, like Joe Lewis after a knockout.

"Goddam, sumbitch, we got hundreds, Smoky."

"Sit down, Kenny. I can't fish the river for skipjack and save you at the same time."

Ken plopped on the boat seat wearing an impossible grin, one that had never been seen inside Central School. "Doggone, Smoky, this is really fun," Ken said. "What do I do now?"

"You man those oars, Kenny. We'll keep the net stretched between the boat and Eric there. We'll put him to work."

I began my goldie picking, wresting them one at a time from their gilled entanglements. They seemed identical in size and beauty—dinner plate long, and deep in the belly, like big-mouth bass. Their hundreds of dime sized scales flashed gold against the sun. Best of all, their friendly golden eyes hadn't any frantic in them. Skipjack, "goldies," don't flop much, don't live long out of water, and seem to go peacefully to fish heaven. I plucked them, filled a gunny sack, while Smoky sat in the stern of the boat, telling how he learned about smoked skipjack.

"A Canuck put me onto them. I was workin' on the rails in Montana then, barely scraping out a livin'. 'Yanks throw skipjack back or use them for fertilizer,' the Canuck said. 'Learn how to deal with the bones . . . they're fit for a king.'"

Smoky went on. "Ever since the Depression, I haven't wasted a match stick, and I never wasted another skipjack. . . . You're doin' so good in the net pickin' there, Eric, we're just gonna sit here and watch you work."

"Don't mind a bit, Smoky," I said. "If I can learn gill netting from you, I'll teach my fishin' gang. We can get a net. We'll learn fish smoking, too. We only catch skipjack by accident—Goldies, we call them. My brother and I took some home once and halfway through dinner Mom threw them out and cooked us hotdogs. 'All bone,' she said."

"I was skeptical myself, Eric. That Canuck was three sheets to the wind when he told me about smokin' them. 'You gotta brine 'em extra stout,' then 'smoke 'em long, under low heat,' he says. The bones separate out, givin' you the best eating fish there is. If I could find that Canuck, I'd buy him a bottle of Canadian whiskey, might even have a nip with him. Well, no . . . didn't mean that. I swore off drink. And I'd advise you boys to stay clear of the stuff. I haven't had a drink in—let's see . . . two years now."

Smoky had gone part way to mournful with his whiskey talk. Then he turned frisky again, rattling on, "I've almost lived on smoked skippies at times, used them for good trades too. They stick to your ribs. . . . Whoa, that's a good one," the 'good one' being a water devil whooshing around the end of the log and rocking the boat. "Change in the weather comin', mates. Lean over there, Kenny, and tie up. We'll hop ashore and give Little Eric a hand."

From his knees, Ken tied the bow rope to the snag. Then he crouched and sprung. His powerful legs vaulted him easily across the 8 or 10 feet to the sandy shore. Smoky laughed, accepting the challenge. He leaped and landed with a splat at the waterline and tumbled forward into Stretch. They steadied each other like a pair of circus bears.

Smoky clapped his hands. "Great haul, fellers. You're not great net boys yet, but you're learnin' fast. Anyway, I could never have done it without you." As if to stamp the statement, here came the opening whoosh of a whirlpool. We turned to watch. The piece of water just below Smoky's second net was about to be sucked into the 8 foot maw of a whirlpool. Had Smoky and Ken been there, their boat would have been spun and flung about, maybe overturned. The three of us stood speechless, watching the whirlpool perform.

Last summer I'd seen a belly dancer in front of a tent at the carnival. She jiggled her stuff to entice men to go inside for a dollar's worth of more. Kids were expected to go right on by, not even look. But Jelly and I looked anyway. You've gotta watch dancing floozies until it's over, whatever "over" means. Same with whirlpools: Watch until it's over. Finally the Big Missouri's whirlpool played out, and the water smoothed over. Smoky's net was still in place.

"That was a doozy," Smoky said. "But I've seen worse." He pushed Ken off balance and took up a boxing pose. "Show me your footwork, Kenny. Don't hit me, though, or I'll have to flatten you." They danced in the sand, throwing pretend jabs, bantering.

"White lightning," Kenny said. "Ya wouldn't see it comin'."

"Hard to hit thin air, Kenny," Smoky laughed.

I had been right about Smoky. He was the same kind and smart man I first met standing on the shore of the Muddy, introducing himself. From the first moment, I liked Smoky Roy. I believed in him, liked his ways, and what people gossiped about him wasn't right, couldn't be. Bank robber crap, be hanged. Like Little Gram would say, "Fiddle-faddle."

Smoky's joke about "dark before we're done" wasn't too far off. We split the skippies into two gunnies, one for Ken, one for Smoky. They lugged the gunnies and I hauled Smoky's gear sack.

In front of Smoky's house we set up an assembly line, gutting, de-heading, filleting, and rinsing. Our work lasted into the late afternoon and yielded a couple of two hundred slab sides for Smoky's brining crocks. Smoky went back and forth to his house fetching "secret potions" and spices for his crocks. "I'll be smokin' this next batch tomorrow afternoon," he said. "Using willow this time for flavor."

With reminders to "Come back real soon," Smoky helped Ken and me tie cloth wrapped packages of smoked skippies to our handlebars. We hadn't a watch among the three of us, but looking across the valley to the McKenzie County side, I noted the shade deepening along the bluff. Getting home by six o'clock would be a challenge. After Smoky's quick pry bar adjustment to spread the front fork on Ken's bastard Schwinn, we said goodbyes and took off for town.

Since Ken was a reluctant talker, I used the ride to arrange him and Smoky in my mind.

Ken was easy. After batting around excuses and reasons for him bullying me and my friends, I came to a good enough decision. The past didn't matter so much. Kenneth Johnson's ornery bulldog stuff was history—not forgotten, but tamped down. We had come to a conclusion; our three-year squabble was over. Smoky Roy?—To me a good man, but puzzling, and mostly unknown, especially for the people of Williston.

I fussed about rumoring townfolk, people not knowing Smoky Roy, who believed rumors about how he could be a bank robber hiding loot. My happy day with him on the river gill netting, cleaning his skipjack, and laughing often couldn't happen with a bank robber. A bad man wouldn't be like that. Still, who would believe me? There wasn't a doggone thing I could say that would smash the rumors. I resolved to side with trust and hope that Officer Gwin or a Montana detective would clear him for good.

Our arrival at Ken's house was disappointing, but not a surprise. Unlike coming home with Jack or Buck, there weren't neighbors in yards yelling, "How's fishin'?" or dads mowing grass—as if there were grass to mow in the Flats.

At the Johnson house, the mongrel greeted us without a tail wag, interested only in standing on his hind legs to bite Ken's package of smoked skippies, or—if I had my way—goldies. Ken leaned his bike against the house, opened the door, and yelled in, "We're home, Mom. I got fish for us."

Mrs. Johnson never came out to greet us—"Sleeping," Ken said. As for his dad, I didn't see him, never ever. Ken never mentioned him, and I didn't either, too uneasy with awkward questions.

"Gotta' go, Ken." I said. "Thanks for taking me fishin."

"See ya later," he said. "Don't forget about the Fights." As I pedaled away, I turned to wave. Ken promptly waved back, as if we'd been friends for years.

I pedaled hard for home, this time through the middle of the East Side. On the first of March, Chief Olson had lifted his East Side ban on Jim and me going there. However, Dad's six o'clock rule was still in place, always would be. I arrived 30 minutes late. I raced up the alley into our back yard. *Ah-hah!* Jim's bike wasn't there. If you're going to break rules, you need a brother who breaks them worse.

More luck: Dad was late, too. I washed up while Mom delayed dinner. At seven o'clock Dad showed, explaining, "Had a helluva time getting old Oscar to sign off on the tractor deal." Dad sat down to eat without knowing of my tardiness. Standard Saturday fried chicken, lots of it with mashed potatoes and gravy, strawberries and ice cream too—all without Jim, and Dad getting grumpier with each passing minute. "Who's he with?"

"Buck," I said. "Buck and Jim went walleye fishin'. They must have stayed for the evening bite."

"Doggone Buck has no sense either." That's how it went, conversation bouncing back and forth from here to there—never landing—all through suppertime, dish washing and drying, and into three-man rummy.

"Buck's new bike has a strong light with new batteries, Dad," I said hopefully.

"That's Buck's business," Dad said. "I'm talkin' about your numbskull brother." Inside, I smiled. Jim's tardiness had squeezed out inquiry about my whereabouts.

As things turned out, Jim's big "D" Dutch waned to little "d" Dutch when he came to the back door in the moonlight carrying his first really big walleye. Dad chewed on him, but right in the middle of the chewing he said, "Davey, go over and knock on Leiseth's door. See if you can borrow his scale."

I returned with the scale that the walleye pulled to six pounds 10 ounces. "Jeezus, what a fish!" Dad said. His unstated verdict on Jim was *innocent by extenuating circumstances.* I surmised that Jim's trophy walleye offered an excuse not to fuss. Dad was tired. What with the rush of farmer business, spring planting and all, Dad hadn't taken a day off in weeks. "I'm takin' tomorrow off," he said. "We're planting garden."

After early church we drove out to McKenzie County to "eyeball crops." We finally got around to garden planting in the heat of Sunday afternoon. Jim and I furrowed rows and Dad came behind with the seeds. Reed Gwin wandered from next door. He stood over Dad, who crawled down a row, tamping dirt. "I planted an extra row of beans for you, Reed, so you don't eat all of mine. Say, Reed, I've been meaning to ask, what's the latest on that Clapper fellow?"

"Bill, far as I know, there isn't a 'latest.'"

"Well, after you got his name, I did some checking of my own." Hearing that, I could have fainted and flopped right there. I hadn't told Dad of yesterday's whereabouts, only that I went fishin' with Kenneth Johnson.

Dad stood from his planting and dusted off. "You said the Malta cops identified a possible suspect named Clapper, that he was workin' on the rails in Montana at the time. I remembered the Clapper name from the Epping area. I checked him out. . . . Let's find some shade, and I'll tell you about it." Dad led us to seats on the cottonwood log, the "Thinking Tree."

Ever vigilant Mom came to the back stoop and hollered, "Cold beer anyone?" Dad answered by meshing his thumb with his index finger, meaning: "Perfect."

Reed twirled fingers as if directing a choir, "Okay Bill, what's the scoop?"

"Hold on Reed; first things first."

Mom came cradling three cans of Hamms beer. She handed them off and fished the "church key" from her apron pocket. "I'll go fetch us a snack to go with the beer."

Jim grabbed the "church key," claiming "dibs on opening."

After a big swill, Dad began, "Reed, I do for a fact know something you should know. Yesterday I stopped into Orville Knutsen's place out north of Epping. I'm tryin' to sell him a diesel tractor. He's farmin' three places—what he calls 'the quitters' in those rocky hills. I asked him about the name 'Clapper.' He mentioned the old Clapper place. The name has stuck to that rockpile of a farm since 1919, when a Roy Clapper broke it out of the prairie."

"So you're thinkin' he's this same Clapper?"

"Pretty sure. Orville said the Clapper he remembers just gave up, didn't even last until the Depression. The rocky ground wore out him and his work horses, and there was no money in crops anyhow. Orville was just a kid at the time, but that's what he remembers. You might want to check with Orville's dad. He's in the Bethel Lutheran Home, and he's still sharp as a tack."

"I'll do that," Reed said, "but we'll start with what you know. First question comes to mind: where did Clapper head after he gave up farming?"

"Rode the rails for a while, Orville said. Landed in Montana, and worked draft horses for gypo rail crews. Orville says he remembers postcards coming from Malta and Havre. Roy wrote that he'd found work, was happy he didn't have to take relief, and that someday he *would*—most *definitely*—pay off his debts. 'Roy was a proud man,' Orville said. He said Clapper was so good with draft horses, chances were he'd get on full time, working skunk hollows, where tractors were useless."

Listening in, it dawned on me that over time Dad had picked up some police tactics from Reed Gwin. "Thinking Tree" visits with Reed offered drama and mystery, relief from dickering with farmers promising machinery payments based on unborn rain clouds.

We listened to Dad stray off, bragging up Epping area farmers "growing 40 bushel wheat in thin soil and rock." Reed let Dad ramble until he came of his own accord to the Epping farmer named Clapper. "So, I asked Orville Knutsen to stretch his memory," Dad continued. 'What sort of a man was the Clapper out by Epping?' . . . 'Industrious,' was the first word out of Orville's mouth, and then 'ingenious and frugal.' Orville said he was a very private person, and I'm thinkin' that's one more similarity. I'm tellin' you, Reed, Orville's Clapper from Epping fits your Clapper—tinkerers, both of them. You said the dumpground guy gives new life to junk."

"In your opinion, Bill, what does all of that prove?"

"Proves nothing; but, human nature being what it is, I'd say the Montana police are on the wrong track. According to Orville, his dad had only good things to say about Roy Clapper. If your man is one and the same, he's no damn bank robber."

Reed nodded. "I'm glad to hear you say that, Bill. I don't want to spend more time on proving rumoring. The Montana authorities exported their rumor up the line to Williston. Sure, Clapper knew how to work with dynamite. So did a thousand others. When the rumor surfaced three years back, I caught up to the dumpground Clapper on South Main. Tried to interview him; he was drunker'n a lord. Still, my intuition said he was an honest man . . . lived in the dump because he's an independent cuss; that, and he couldn't stand waste. I've seen his work: cobbled together bikes and appliances. Einar Larsen says he bought a Maytag washer from him. Runs like new. . . . No, I don't expect to find incriminating evidence, nothing to put in his file that would help the Montana police, or the bank detectives. Still, if he'd talk, he might alibi good and strong—get this town off his back."

"Sure, Ruth. Thank you." Reed took a piece of smoked goldie from Mom's dish. He nibbled and smacked his lips. "Damn, that's the best smoked fish I ever ate. Where'd you find it?"

Mom smiled, always ready to do her part to settle unrest. "Davey brought it home. It's a kind of goldfish smoked by Davey's friend, Kenneth Johnson."

"Goldeyes, Mom. We call them goldies and Ken calls them skippies. We helped his old codger friend catch them in a gill net. He's an expert on smoking them."

Reed shook his head. "Kenneth Johnson, that Stretch character. He runs with the Flats roughnecks. It'll be a miracle keeping him out of reform school. Say, I hear he whipped up on you pretty good, David."

"Davey at least took him on, Reed," Dad said. "Took guts to tangle with a bigger, tougher kid like Stretch."

"*Kenneth,* Dad. Kenneth Johnson. We are kind of friends now."

"You and Stretch?" Jim said with disbelief.

"Yah, you've got to know him to understand," I said.

So far I had nicely detoured around the subject of Smoky Roy. But I couldn't end on that note. To do so would be the first stick in building a fib. I decided—what the heck! I'll just dump the cat out of the bag. I blurted: "Kenneth's friend is Smoky Roy, the Mr. Clapper you've been talking about. And I know he's no danged bank robber. He took us fishin' with a gill net . . . has a boat in the Missouri. He showed us how he smokes skipjack, sings songs, and he is a really, really nice guy."

"Well, I'll be damned," Reed said. "Your boys get around, don't they, Bill?"

Dad laughed right out loud at that, a surprise, but—then again—not. Of late, Dad had opened the gates wider on Jim and me.

"Never could keep 'em home, Reed. If I did, they'd drive their mother nuts." Dad was, by golly, proud of me. I wrestled with why for a spell. But story bits and pieces added up to a reason. Dad's stories, Grampa Millhouse's stories, Grampa Erickson, our uncles, and—for that matter, Reed Gwin—not one of them backed out on a friend, even when half the county tweedled a rumor and dog-piled on the poor guy.

Handcuffed by his dumpground predicament, Roy Clapper fought for his reputation untraditionally. He went about his business out of sight of the bigger world. From my witnessing and Jim's, kindness was Roy's highest priority. People who knew him, and they were too few, saw his selflessness and came to the right judgement. The bad rumors waned and died in the hearts of good people. Unfortunately, ill-will lingered in the heartless.

Excuses pile up quickly when I think of abandoning Smoky Roy. Jim and I and Jack are guilty on that score. We had glorious places to go where water ran clean, the air was prairie fresh, and there were no frightening people—in fact—no grown-ups, period. When we wanted grown-ups, they were convenient: parents, uncles, grandparents, and especially grandpas who offered the same kind of fun that Smoky Roy Clapper was good at.

After our day gill net fishin', I saw Smoky on the streets a few times, over a period of several years. He'd come to town to deliver refurbished things. We'd visit briefly, both of us struggling awkwardly with the sort of distance between people that comes with separation.

As for Kenneth Johnson, I conclude my three year fight with him was a *good* fight. We had a resolution, Ken and me. I discovered how wrong I had been. His orneryness at school didn't define him anymore than quills on a porcupine make a bad porky. I can't speak for Ken; but, I believe he found that punching bags or weak fighters left much to be desired. There had to be something else. I hope I helped him begin to find something more for a better life.

I'd like to say that skipjack fishing with Roy Clapper and Kenneth Johnson led to traditional friendships. That's not what happened. Boyhood friendships get battered about by circumstances and drowned out by the rest of life. When friendships don't go as they should or could, it's easy to pull a page from the book of excuses: Roy lived in the dump, Ken on the Flats. Jim and I lived in a nice little twice remodeled house on a paved street. Our friends lived in nice houses on paved streets, too, and most never found occasions to know enough of Ken; and, they didn't know enough of Smoky Roy to trust that he wasn't the bad man rumors said.

On a summer day in 1948 Ken rode to our house on his cobbled together Schwinn. He came by to show off his new red paint job. I remember the year because Dad had just brought home a brand new forest green '48 V-8 Oldsmobile. It was parked at the curb and Mr. Leiseth from next door came to see. He kicked a tire, then walked around the "Olds," with Mom and Dad, saying, "Oooh," and "Ahh, and "What a beauty!"

Ken sat on his bike waiting, while Jim and I checked out our new family automobile; then, we took time to admire Ken's spiffed up bike with a horn that went "oooghah" and made us laugh. But Jim and I didn't do enough. When Dad asked, "You boys want to go for a ride?" I dropped my bike and climbed in the back seat with my brother.

"You coming, Ken?" I asked.

"Nah, I think I'll jus' go bike ridin'," he said.

I never had to fight Ken again, not even close. Neither did my friends. Though

Ken never did much better in school, I know he did better in life. Reed Gwin said so. He made it to 8th grade before he moved to Montana.

After Kenneth Johnson whipped me I can't remember another fist fight, not for me, Jim, or our friends. Maybe the end of the Big War had something to do with the end of our fist fighting. We lost reasons for our war games, or walking around with raised hackles. We didn't need fist fights anymore, good, bad or indifferent. Roy C. Clapper didn't need his fight anymore, either. It saddens me to know that part of his world couldn't agree.

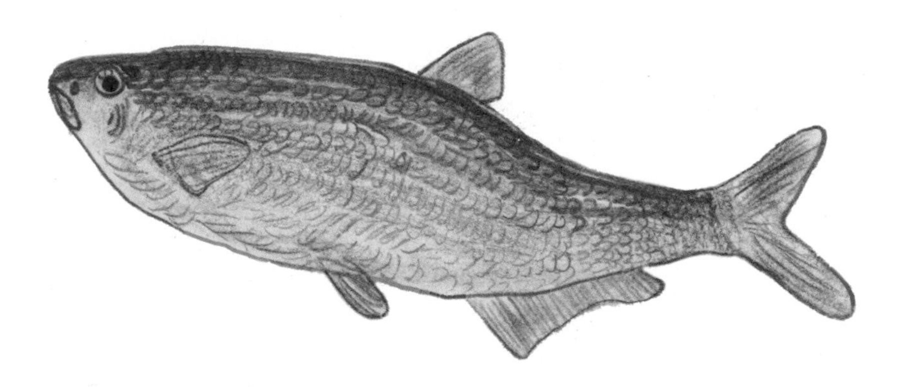

Their friendly golden eyes hadn't any frantic in them. Skipjack, "goldies," don't flop much, don't live long out of water, and seem to go peacefully to fish heaven.

Chapter 10

Train Troubles

"What are we waiting for?"—Jim Erickson
Jimmy Rasmussen— "We ain't."

Twice I had broken Dad's V-J Day rule, first with our Jungle safari and again by going to the dump with Kenneth. He didn't "lower the boom" on me because Mom sided with me, saying hopeful things about Kenneth Johnson and Roy Clapper. Buck, though, wasn't so fortunate. Word had gotten to Al Stensby and hence to Buck's dad. Buck had trespassed beyond the tracks on our Jungle adventure and had to pay with four Saturdays doing yard chores for the Bundhunds and their widow neighbor.

Buck's trouble with the Great Northern didn't start with our Jungle adventure. Like the rest of the Muddy River guys and many other gumptioned Williston kids, Buck had long been tempted by the exciting universe of the railroad. The railroad hubbub of shouting men, banging switch engines, whistles, and roaring streamliners covered a mile long strip on the south side of town. The place was a boiler pot of energy, beckoning youngsters to go see. By the time Jim and I were old enough to ride our bikes to the Great Northern Depot, the roundhouse, or the ice house, we were enthralled by the railroad . . . tempted, too. Mystery and adventure seemed to hang in the air surrounding the Great Northern.

Grampa Millhouse piqued our interest early, beginning before Jim and I were in school. Gramp opened the exciting railroad world to us with his keen books, maps, and stories. He employed the monumental empire of the Great Northern Railroad to invigorate us, and used his acquaintanceship with Mr. Stensby to finagle a tour of the Roundhouse. In the Luzon café he introduced us to brakemen and engineers. Jim and I were allowed to sit in the midst of the railroad men, drinking our creamed and sugared coffees. The men smelled of coal and oil—not so bad, not so good, either . . . but interesting—and they laughed, poked, and teased, like brothers.

On streamliner days Grampa took Jim and me to the Depot to see the famous Empire Builder highballing into town, making a quick stop on its run to the West Coast. His arrival to collect us was done with customary flair, incorporating what had become a family joke. Without knocking, Gramp would burst into our house: "Are the Riley boys ready?" Those were Gramp's teasing names for my brother and me, lifted from the radio show, "The Life of Riley." Listen for 10 minutes and you'd know Riley lived without a care in the world, like Jim and me, according to Gramp.

"I'll have the Riley boys back by supper," Gramp hollered, and off we'd go with me in the back standing on the floorboards and Jim on the seat next to Gramp.

Gramp drove Main Street headed for the Depot, window open, cussing at slow drivers. He'd pull in at the Depot's oval parking lot with its center island of green grass, a resting spot for railroad bums. Usually a bum would rise to his feet so as to become obvious. With Jim and me in tow, Gramp would walk over and greet the bum, insuring safety, so the derelict couldn't be accused of panhandling. Gramp opened the conversation by asking the man where he was from and if he'd tried to find a job. Then, based on what he heard, Gramp handed the poor guy a quarter, sometimes two. His parting words were the same: "You oughta find some work, my man." And to us, Gramp always said, "Once a man takes handouts, its hard to turn him back to work."

Gramp wasn't inclined to lecture us, though, like Mom did. Occasionally a bum would walk First Avenue West from the railroad, working housewives for handouts. Mom would hand a quickly-made sandwich out the door. When the bum man was gone, she'd admonish us: "You boys stay away from those characters. We don't know where they've come from or if they're in trouble with the law." We were plenty cautious without her warnings, though. A quick look at their stooped bodies, jittery eyes, and grimy clothes was enough. Rail tramps, bums, hobos, vagabonds, derelicts—take your choice—they were plenty scary.

Gramp employed the Empire Builder streamliner as the centerpiece of our Great Northern education. He'd take Jim by one hand, me by the other, and walk us out on the red brick tarmac to wait for the giant Empire Builder to roar in from the east at 70 miles an hour. He'd lead us to the very edge of the tracks, where we listened for the first distant sound of the Empire Builder. Jim and I argued about who heard first, until the streamliner's smooth rumble couldn't be mistaken for a freight train, a truck on the Scenic Highway, or our imaginations. Gramp allowed us to stand practically on the tracks peering east to catch the first glimpse, and hear the far whistle, before pulling us back amidst the crescendo-building, earth-shaking, silver behemoth racing in to a screeching stop. I remember trying to see more clearly the shadowed faces in the windows, envying the mysterious, privileged people who could ride a train across Montana to see the snowcapped Rocky Mountains. We never tired of our trips with Gramp to the end of South Main, rolling down the hill into the domain of the Depot. Constantly frenetic, the Depot was a busy, noisy place overrun with clanking, screeching steel, hissing steam, and—best of all—chesty conductors bellowing their melodious "All-boooorrds."

Until 1945, the pull of the Muddy River country had largely kept us unattended kids away from the territory of the Great Northern Railroad. Only a couple times did we violate the Great Northern's strict NO TRESPASSING rule prior to 1945. Norman (Jelly) Jellum was the first instigator, though I can't lay blame on him; I was prickly with curiosity about the mysteries south of the railroad tracks.

Jelly Jellum was amazingly at ease with adults. He'd talk right up to them. When he came to our house, Dad and Jelly visited about big league baseball and Williston Coyote basketball.

Among other places, Jelly learned grown-up stuff at Ed George's pool hall on

South Main. Jelly took me along once, where I saw him in action. Soon as we walked in, Mr. George directed me to a spectator's chair, a big hardwood thing with wide plank arms. "You sit right there, young man, and you can stay," he said. Jelly, though, had grown-up privileges. Mr. George took Jelly by the elbow and nodded at an older fella' holding a cue, with his butt resting against a pool table. The guy was smoking a cigarette. I think he was graduated from high school even.

Jelly came back to borrow a stick of Juicy Fruit from me. Under his breath, he said, "I beat this guy before. I'm gonna bet him two Cokes if you'll go halves with me on my bet."

"Sure, Jelly. Bet him four if you want." Jelly was my best friend. He decided on the two-Coke bet, and won handily.

Mr. Jellum had helped Jelly along, probably put a word in with Ed George, but mostly it was Jelly's doing to get permission to play in the smoky pool hall, where—at the back table—men drank beer. He and Razzie were the only young kids allowed to play. Jelly opened our back door one time yelling, "I beat Pete (Pete Ferris, pool hustler)!" If not playing pool, Jelly often sat on the sidewalk bench in front of the pool hall, befriending hobos. Before long, he was invited to their vagabond camp, *"Hobotown,"* he called it. When he asked me to go along, he'd already been there a couple of times alone.

"We'll cross the tracks when the rail crew is switching cars east of the roundhouse," Jelly explained. He led me to the granaries on west side of town. We hid out, peering up and down the tracks, watching for Mr. Stensby and Big Smitty. "We'll wait 'til that switch engine's outa sight," Jelly said. "Stensby and Smitty ride the switcher sometimes."

Signs posted right and left stated, in bold red: DANGER—NO TRESPASSING. "I didn't see the sign" would be a laughable excuse.

Jelly grabbed my arm. "Okay, let's go. We'll take cover behind the grain cars." We dashed across a rail spur and hid behind the last car in the string. I crouched behind Jelly, waiting for his next signal. "All clear," he said, and we high-tailed it, hopping the two sets of main tracks, and scooting down the embankment and into the Jungle. Jelly located a path cut through the willows, willows so thick that the only sign of anything civilized was a curl of smoke in the distance. I envisioned the smoke coming from a stovepipe in the roof of a shack. Since Jelly and I wore our winter coats that blustery March morning, I couldn't imagine anything less.

The sight of Hobotown hit me like a punch in the gut, awful sadness for pitiful men in such a decrepit place. Jelly and I stopped at the edge of the clearing, me gawking and fidgety.

Wow! Hobotown . . . as frightening as a monster movie that I don't want to watch, but I watch anyway, tempted by a little devil inside that goads: "Bet you don't have the guts." Hobo men hunched around a column of smoke in front of a jagged row of tiny shabby huts. The zoo-park animals had better shelters.

Cold March wind parted the smoke of their warming fire, revealing a super tall dark man towering in the center of seven raggy hobos. He nodded in our direction, and the gathering of hobo men closed around him. "I'll do the talking," Jelly whispered, pulling me along. The men glared at us, moving into a half-circle, maybe the beginning of a trap, I thought. One step our way and I'd run.

I didn't want to stare, but I did anyway. What kind of men could live here in the willow jungle, becoming grimier with each passing day? Their long-whiskered faces were the color of coal dust; their eyes sunk back, hard to see. They wore torn coats hanging open at the front or tied with twine, and every manner of raggy cap or scrounged hat—"thirty year hats," as Gramp would say.

Jelly stopped 20 feet from the men and their smoke-fire. I stood behind him, ready to skeedaddle. "I came to see Pearly," Jelly said. To me, Jelly whispered, "That big guy is called 'Horse.' He's their leader."

Horse ambled forward in front of the others. He was huge, pony-tailed and "an Indian," Jelly said. Including his black, domed cowboy hat, Horse stood more than six and one-half feet tall. The other decrepit men looked to him to answer. "Pearly ain't here no more," Horse gruffed. "Who be you?"

From the far side of the fire ring, a little man with long yellow-white whiskers stepped alongside Horse. The little fellow nodded at Jelly. "We seen this boy uptown. He's Pearly's friend."

"Who be the other?" Horse man asked. Shaking heads were answer enough. The hobos glared at me . . . all but one—the white-whiskered man with twinkling blue eyes . . . "Bingo," Horse called him. Bingo grinned at us and reached into the smoke and pulled out a fire-blackened coffee pot. He gestured at Jelly with the pot.

Jelly nodded, "Sure, I love coffee." Bingo flicked the "bottoms" from his own tin cup and handed it to Jelly. Then he poured black stuff as thick as engine oil.

The wind stirred, and a few flakes of snow slanted into the gathering. "Coal," Horse ordered, and a bent-backed hobo came promptly, lugging a bucketful of coal. The men hunched closer to their fire ring with hands and arms jammed within their poor coats. They looked as pitiful as mangy coyotes—nervous, hunted coyotes. Jelly would have done better to have come alone. I watched him half-heartedly sip his coffee and spit out the grits. "You're not a coffee drinker, Jelly," I said to myself, "but you're a good actor."

I tried to make myself small and unimportant. I nonchalantly studied the huts circling the clearing. They were built of domed red willow switches tied together at the top in teepee shape. Odds and ends of old boards and driftwood had been jammed into the willows. The shelters were no bigger than Gramp's Nash. Tattered canvas thrown over their tops showed poor attempts to keep out the weather. Crawley-hole openings in the huts served as entries. The huts looked about right for animals, like the flea-bit bears at the zoo park.

Jelly and I stayed well back from the hobos and their fire ring. "Without Pearly, they're not very friendly," Jelly whispered. Bingo came with his pot and another cracked enamel white cup. I held the cup and Bingo poured, showing a grin with few teeth. He went to re-filling Jelly's cup, teasing, "Wha's the matter, kid, you don' like my coffee?" Bingo didn't wait for Jelly's answer, but overtopped the cup. Jelly deftly shucked a twig from the thick coffee, flipping it over the tin lip. Bingo, with the only smile in Hobotown, announced pridefully, "Pearly's buildin' a place fer him an' me at the dump. You fellers kin come visitin'. I'll fix 'ya coffee."

All the while, I kept wary eyes on Horse, who now rocked, swaying foot-to-foot, glaring at Jelly and me. He jammed the shoulder of a gaunt, black haired hobo standing at his side. Both of them glared at us. Horse's friend had a leather thing jammed in his belt, maybe a billy-club.

I wished I hadn't come, and wondered why Jelly had visited here more than once. And maybe he wondered himself, because he abruptly handed Bingo the tin cup. "We gotta' get home," Jelly said.

Horse took a step closer, standing almost in the nearly flameless fire of coal smoke. The smoke billowed up around him, masking his face, and curled around his massive blanketed shoulders. He was an out of proportion giant, made mostly of upper body. He towered to twice Jelly's height. Horse glowered with fierce, black eyes. I handed my cup to Jelly, backed away, then turned and bee-lined for the path, thinking, *Jelly you're nuts to stay here any longer.* And he didn't. I'd waited only a couple of minutes at the railroad embankment before he came, running up the path.

"I shouldn't have brought you." Jelly said. "Horse says the new man in camp doesn't trust you. Horse says he doesn't trust the new man or you either."

Our Hobotown visit left me wide-eyed with wonder and spooked, too—well, a little spooked. I believed that at the first sign of trouble, Jelly and I could have outrun the mangy hobo men, especially their leader, the big Indian, Horse, wobbling on those stubby legs built no stouter than a goat's. I guessed Jelly and I hadn't been in any true danger. Nevertheless, our socializing with the bums was a small "t" kind of trouble, the sort of thing we wouldn't mention to parents.

Another railroad incident snared Jim and me in the summer of '45 during the peak of our war games. Our East-sider army general, an older boy named Korwin, was busy developing a new weapon to equalize the West-siders' 10 shot rubber sling Tommy guns. With his two foot steel pipe barrel and powder from firecrackers, General Korwin could rocket a lighted railway flare almost a city block. He needed supplies for his new weapon.

Korwin gathered a dozen of us troops at Headquarters, an old abandoned shack at the north end of Fifth Avenue East. "Sure, they'll easily get out of my mortar's path," Korwin said, "and then we'll advance and take over their trenches. Now I need you guys to get me as many flares as you can." That's when I joined a patrol to "appropriate" railway phosphorus flares. The flares were common, lying along the tracks, and with a little stealth, easy enough to collect without being apprehended by Mr. Stensby or Big Smitty.

Korwin's troops brought in about 20 flares that our East Side Army never employed in battle. Korwin's dad found the flares in his garage. He supervised mighty test launches of phosphorus flares on July 4th, entertaining the neighborhood.

So far, we had paid no price for railroad trespasses. But with the arrival of the troop trains, our good luck was about to end.

The first time we visited a troop train, Jim and I went with Gramp. We strung along behind a crowd of about 30 people, well-wishers handing cookies and angel food cake to soldiers hanging out open train windows. They were laughing, bantering, beer-drinking soldiers. These were coming-home-from-war men, prone to celebrate, enjoying being celebrated.

In the meantime, Razzie also knew about the troop trains, and he conjured a way to make money from them. That was typical Razzie. Like Jelly, he moved comfortably in the world of grown-ups: hanging about the pool hall, bowling alley, rail yards, and train depot, visiting with everyone.

Razzie, quick witted and fearless, harbored risky ideas. With dark, inquisitive eyes and a sparkling smile, he talked right up to grown-ups, including my dad. Still, Dad warned us: "I'm not sure Razzie knows right from wrong," and he and Mom moved off to discuss something about Razzie's dad being in trouble.

Razzie carried a pocketful of money, and didn't mind buying a candy bar for kids he knew. He'd buy penny candy and bubble gum treats to hand out randomly, not necessarily for someone he claimed as a friend, because—aside from Tommy Stahl—Razzie didn't seem to gather close friends. So, when he plotted his train scheme, he longed for a partner. After coming along to Stony Ford in the summer of 1945, Razzie began hanging around with my brother who, like Razzie, was overloaded with gumption. The two of them shared a secret. That's all I knew.

When Jim and Razzie ditched me on their bikes—last I saw headed to the south end of town—I grew more suspicious. That evening I pestered Jim about where he'd gone with Razzie. After supper he signaled me with a jerk of his head. I followed him outside and around to the back side of the cottonwood log. He whispered, "Wanna make some big money? Look at this:" Jim opened his two fistfuls.

My eyes bugged. In one palm he held four silver dollars and in the other a pile of nickels and dimes.

"Beer bottle money," he said. "Razzie and me are collecting beer bottles from the army troops. Razzie has the train schedule. If you want in on our deal, we're going back to the troop train the day after tomorrow." *Boy did I ever want in!* I figured I could earn a year's worth of allowance money in three or four days.

In advance of the day's troop train, Jim and I rode our bikes down South Main to the beer parlor up the hill from the station. "Buster's Bar," the sign over the big door said. Jim spied Razzie's purple Monarch propped against the boarded side of the saloon. We parked our bikes by Razzie's and hurried around to the front. Loud drinker talk and beer stench poured from the open door, strong enough to take a guy's breath away. We hurried past, anxious to locate Razzie and meet the troop train. Jim jerked his thumb toward the door. "We sell our bottles to Buster, nickel a bottle, dollar a case." The beer parlor stood on the hill, only a half-block from the Great Northern Station, a fortunate location in view of the task we faced. Jim and I raced down the hill looking for Razzie.

We found Razzie, ready to board the train, standing on the depot platform, where he and Jim explained the simplicity of their beer bottle business.

"Just watch what we do," Jim said. "The soldiers like us. They'll give us hundreds of bottles."

Shortly, the troop train came huffing from the east. Before the train even stopped, I heard the soldiers' rowdy celebrating. Brown-sleeved arms waved out the windows, while toasting fists swung beer bottles left and right.

The train braked to a stop, and the Negro conductor man swung open the door to a passenger car. He stood tall and proud in his spiffed blue uniform and matching shiny-billed cap. He smiled across the crowd, as if he owned the troop train.

"Let's go, men," Razzie said. We pushed through the crowd gathered to meet the troops. Razzie stepped up the steel steps and on past the conductor. The conductor paid him no mind. Like a veteran train man, Jim hopped up the steps and sauntered past the conductor. He turned back and motioned me, "Come on, come on."

By the time I caught on to the business watching Jim and Razzie in the first car, they had picked up empty cardboard cases and were half-way along the aisle with their cases almost filled.

I was stunned by the scene. Through an eye-stinging haze of cigarette smoke, I saw men in brown uniforms draped every which way across the seats. Some were asleep or maybe knocked out by beer. Others sat with their butts on the back rests and feet on the seats, laughing, and singing drunk songs. Up ahead, soldiers paraded Jim and Razzie through the car, reaching for empty bottles. "Come on, help the boys out," a soldier hollered. I picked up a cardboard case of my own and started after my buddies. And in the ensuing moments a scene unfolded that I'll never forget.

Eight or nine soldiers in a loose circle sprawled over seats or sat on the back rests. A pair of them tooted on harmonicas. The others sang a song, something about Dancing Daisy and her underpants. In the center, a tall soldier perched on the back of a leather passenger seat. He wore a different hat—not the little boat-shaped one, but a round hat with a shiny bill.

I stopped in the aisle, holding my empty case. The leader man took notice. He held up his hand for quiet, the soldiers' song dwindled, and he slid out to the aisle to stand over me. They called him "Captain." Still, he hadn't the face of a soldier, let alone captain—more like someone's older brother. Without taking his eyes from me he barked an order: "Come on men; drink up. The boy needs bottles. Here, young man, let me give you a hand," the captain said. He took my box and pushed me up the aisle, reaching right and left for bottles. I heard the tinkle of coins, too, and turned to see soldiers tossing nickels and dimes into my box along with their beer bottles. A proud time that was, where I—the littlest kid—got the greatest treatment.

By the time the captain and I left the first car and wormed through the passageway to the next one, Jim and Razzie were coming back with their cases filled. "Keep going, Davey," my brother said. "Get yourself a full case. Razzie and me will go sell ours and be back for more."

As the captain and I worked through the next car, I feared the train would start off with me aboard. My captain friend must have had a similar worry, because he stepped up our pace. Halfway through the third car, we filled my case, and the captain carried it down the steel stairs, and placed it on the red brick platform. He tipped his army hat and smiled, "Keep it up, son. With your attitude, you're gonna make something out of yourself." He turned to climb aboard, but stopped on the top step. He turned and waved, a good time for me to say something smart and polite for the help he'd given me. I waited too late; he was gone, leaving me regretful.

I picked up my heavy case of bottles and started lugging for the beer parlor. Halfway up the hill I met Jim and Razzie, running down, headed for their second round collection. Hurrying by, Jim urged me, "Hustle. Two cases, we can each get at least two cases."

I lugged and trudged up the hill fast as I could, needing two stops to rest my rubbery arms. Buster, the bartender, must have been expecting me. He met me at the door and hefted my case of bottles. "Wait here," his growly voice said. In a minute he returned and plunked a silver dollar and a pile of nickels and dimes into my open hands.

"Wow!" I said, and he smiled, saying, "I'll take all the bottles you can get."

Grinning, I pushed my money deep to the bottom of my pants pockets. Turning to run down the hill, I heard the call from the station: *"All-boooord."*

The second *"All-boooord"* came as I arrived at the platform. A big Negro conductor stood on the bottom step of the closest car, blocking my way. A case of empty bottles rested below the step on the bricks. The conductor nodded at the bottles, smiling. "The captain said these are yours."

The conductor lifted his chin to the crowd bunched in front of the station building, maybe thinking of a lingering soldier who needed to be on board. The conductor boomed out his third *"All-boooord,"* and the engineer blew his whistle, drawing it out long. I gulped. My guys were indeed still *aboard.* The train's steam brakes hissed, and the rail car connections began their domino clanks: *clank, clank, clank*—from the engine down the train to where I stood. I saw a slight turn of the iron wheels in front of me. I could scarcely breathe.

They knew better. They should have gotten off. Why weren't they off? Then, far up the line I saw Razzie jump down from a car. But Jim wasn't with him, and the train moved forward with creaking steel and banging metal. I jittered alongside, slow at first, then faster to keep pace, thinking Jim would appear on a rail car step and jump off. I trotted, and then ran to keep up. Still no brother. He was gone, headed west with the soldiers on a mighty train. Confused, scared, stunned, angry—I was all of those rolled into one.

I stared hard at the end of the caboose, heading west, becoming smaller and smaller. I hadn't noticed Razzie approaching until he was nearly at my side. He placed his case of empties on the bricks and stood with me, gazing down the empty tracks. "They'll stop soon and let him off, won't they?" I said.

"Maybe, but if I was him, I'd head for the baggage car and hide out. Heck, he might get a ride clear across Montana. Dang it, I wish I had stayed with him. I've always wanted to ride a train west to see the mountains."

Knowing what I know now, well—never doubt Razzie. Once he settled on an idea, it just kept growing.

I couldn't shake my panic. I feared for my brother and feared for me. For once, I wouldn't have an older brother to stand behind, while he tried to explain how we got into trouble.

With Razzie alongside, I lugged my booty up the hill, set the case at the door of the beer parlor, and fished the nickels and dimes from the bottom of the cardboard case. Buster came out and took my bottles and Razzie's, and paid us off. I barely noticed the silver dollar as it slid into my pocket, or the coins dropping into the other.

Razzie calmly hopped on his Monarch. Putting feet to pedals, he spoke calmly, "Let me know when you hear from Jimmy." I shook my head, angry with Razzie's unworried state.

Unlike Razzie, I wasn't ready to give up. I mounted Jim's bike. He was in trouble; somehow, I had to get his bike to him. I rode a half-block north on Main and turned west. I raced down Second Street and out of town on Highway 2. A mile out I tackled the grade headed toward four mile corner. This was the toughest ride of my life, an hour of my best stand-on-the-pedals pumping to make the long grade. At the four mile corner I had nothing left in my dead legs. Coasting around the curve, going south on Highway 85, I was finally able to rest my legs on the down-hill mile to Lewis and Clark bridge. All the while, I pictured the engineer finding Jim—hoping, hoping he'd plan a logical stop at the underpass, where the tracks passed under the highway. I allowed a faint belief he'd choose to stop and let Jim off there.

From half-mile away, I heard a train rumble, then its whistle. Could it be? Could it be? I began to believe. When the whistle came a second time, I almost cried. The train's rumble and whistle were wrong, coming west to east. I cruised to the top of the hill. Sure enough, it was a freight train chugging toward town. Just to be sure about the west-bound track, I biked to the underpass. No train and no brother. He was in double "D" Dutch, and so was I.

I turned and headed for home, swirling the day around in my brain, planning how I would tell Mom and Dad. None of it sounded worth a dang. My mind wandered, trying to escape the turmoil: *Maybe this is what Razzie feels when he talks about running away from home?*

Another hour later, circling from the alley side, using Gwin's house for cover so that Mom wouldn't see me from her kitchen window, I dropped Jim's bike in the back yard. Through the alley, to the south end of town I ran to retrieve my own bike, all the while thinking of nothing but my rehearsal, explaining how losing Jim happened. In my head, though, my dad's voice kept interrupting: "No, no, dammit, that can't be. Now start over, and calm down." Only he'd be anything but calm. He'd stand over me, red-faced, hollering loud enough to make Reed Gwin come running, "You're telling me he left town on a goddamn train?"

An hour later I had our two bikes parked at our back step. That was good. And I was home before the doomsday hour of 6 o'clock, also good. Still, I was missing a brother, the master explainer. I had never been the one who had to admit how we got into capital "T" kind of trouble, much less big double "D" Dutch.

I slunk through the back door. "Hi, Mom," I said as nonchalantly as possible. My mind worked furiously to smooth my story, to avoid trouble, though I knew better. Mom had a nose for shenanigans. She could have grilled suspects for Reed Gwin. And speaking of Officer Gwin, suddenly there he was. In a single motion, he knocked and walked through our back door, followed by—*impossibly, incredibly—my brother.*

Jim raised his eyebrows at me and flashed a quick grin. Mom locked onto Reed with her deepest frown. "What'd Jimmy do, Reed?"

"Jimmy will probably want to tell you the whole story himself, Ruth, before his dad gets home, and . . . after I tell you my part in this. Got a spot of coffee?" Without waiting for an answer, he strode to the stove. Jim used the diversion to try to disappear.

"No you don't. You get back here," Mom said. Reed grabbed a kitchen chair and held it for Mom. Then he slumped next to her in his casual after-hours manner that I had seen often in our back yard when he and Dad messed around in our garden, drinking beer, and trading stories.

Reed motioned for Jim and me to join them at Mom's round kitchen table. He tipped his police hat back. "At a quarter after three this afternoon I got a call from the sheriff's clerk," Reed started. "She said the Culbertson, Montana police called. They had a juvenile from our town named Jimmy Erickson, got him off a westbound train."

"Wha . . . wha . . . how did . . . ?"

Reed waited, but Mom couldn't put a sentence together. Reed eyed her closely, as if checking on her health, then went on.

"The county sheriff had no one to spare, asked if I could go to the state line to collect Jimmy. The Culberston chief himself drove Jimmy to the Montana state line. He told me if it wasn't for the soldiers on that train going to bat for him, the engineer would have taken your boy to the next scheduled stop; that'd be Glasgow, 120 miles out."

Mom curled into her chair, seemed about to cry.

"Train? What . . . how could this happen?"

"Now, Ruth, it ain't as bad as you might think." Reed pushed his chair back and reached for the coffee pot. He topped off his cup, looked to do the same for Mom before realizing she hadn't touched hers.

By our mutual understanding, for sitting at the table, Jim had first choice; but, he had taken the chair next to Mr. Gwin, a move that surprised me—a kid in trouble sitting next to a policeman? Then, I thought: *Hey, the two of them have just ridden 18 miles together in a squad car.* I surmised that, like so many times in our backyard, the two of them traded fishin' stories.

Mr. Gwin patted Mom on her shoulder, smiling. "Ruth, your boys used some bad judgment today, that's all." Then, he calmly reported all he knew and was kind enough to lay some blame on the railroad too. "I'll be at home if Bill wants to talk further." As he rose from our kitchen table, he cuffed Jim on the shoulder. "Your dad will back me on this: the Depot is off limits, so is the whole railroad, stem to stern. Be sure to tell your friend, Rasmussen."

Reed headed for the back door, but paused at the end of the kitchen counter, where he dropped a paper. "This release, Ruth, I'll leave it with you. Since I transported Jimmy from Montana, I'll need you and Bill to sign. It says I'm releasing him to your custody." Reed walked out, leaving my Mom breathing fast, wearing a face like a mama coon with her leg in a trap. She was in no shape to help with Dad.

Jim and I went to work on her quickly, desperate to get her shaped up before Dad came home with his temper. Jim and I worked in relays, like some pair of frantic ringsiders—trainer and manager—working furiously on a puffy faced heavyweight sagging on his corner stool: *"You're fine, Bruno, you're fine, come on."* His handlers cuff him, slap him: *Whap, whap, whap! ... "Snap out of it, Bruno. Yah, sure, it's Ezzard Charles. So what? You'll git 'im. Three more rounds, that's all."* More smelling salts—*"Come on, sniff in, shake it off."*

Like the boxer's handlers, we unloaded the gist of our story. As we talked, Jim pulled his bottle booty from his pockets, counted his coins, and silver dollars, stacking them onto the *Herald* newspaper at the corner of the countertop. Like my takings, Jim's troop tips were all in coin. "I have six silver dollars from Buster and with the little coins my two days' profit is nine dollars and eighty cents," he concluded. "Dave made some good money today too; how much, Dave?"

I stacked my coins and dollars opposite Jim's. "Two dollars, 60 cents," I said, just as the sound of Dad's car door slammed, and the three of us froze, speechless, waiting, and wondering.

The back door opened and ... Wow! His timing couldn't have been better. On the end of his first stride into the kitchen, Dad spied our bounty. "What's all this?" Dad said.

"Dave and I earned some good money," Jim said, getting his licks in fast.

"I can see that," Dad said, nodding and smiling at our coin stacks.

Mom moved over to stand in front of our display. "The boys have something to tell you, Bill."

Dad seemed not to hear. "And here I thought they were running from no-good hell to breakfast. I'll wash up, and over supper they can tell me how they earned what?—looks like about . . ."

Jim finished for him, "Twelve dollars and 40 cents between us, Dad."

Twenty minutes later Mom forked a prime cut T-bone steak onto Dad's plate. I liked that. But, she was also duty bound to report on us. She wisely let him unwind first. "Looks like we all had a good day," Dad started. "I sold a diesel TD-9 today."

"That's wonderful, Bill. Einar Swenson?"

"Yah . . . finally. He needed more tractor. The old coot's farming his neighbor's place this year, another section of wheat and summer fallow. Still the sale took a month of dickering."

"Well, your boys did some dickering, too. They earned the money honestly, but you won't like the whereabouts of their work."

"It wasn't so bad, Dad," Jim interjected.

"No, no, we were plenty safe," I said. "The soldiers took care of us."

"Soldiers? What the hell . . . *soldiers?*" Dad stiffened and sat up straight, now forced to find out why his perfect day might not be perfect.

"The troop trains, Bill— your boys were aboard collecting beer bottles. Reed Gwin knows the whole story. He can tell you."

Dad glared at Jim and then me. "Shouldn't need Reed. I'll get this story straight from the guilty parties."

"We just wanted to earn some money," Jim started.

Mom jumped in, saying that Reed didn't seem too upset, and the "train people deserve some blame too."

I was encouraged that Mom and we could talk to Dad while he chomped on his rare T-bone and licked his lips. We unfolded our story as a team. I'm proud to say that, for once, I held my own in the telling.

Jim began: "Razzie knew about the soldier train and earning beer bottle money, Dad. He brought me along twice. Then Dave wanted in"—Jim eyed me, a look I recognized, meaning: *"Jump in here, help me out."*

I told about the nice conductor man who didn't mind us getting on, and of the generous and kind soldiers.

Jim told about his accident, where he dropped his case as he was leaving to get off, then about the train departure whistle that he mistook for the freight train on the east-bound track. "The soldiers were nice guys, Dad. They replaced my broken bottles with good ones."

"Twelve dollars and 60 cents, you said?" Dad wiped his face on his napkin and pushed back from the table.

I hoped I wasn't mistaken. *Wasn't that a fleeting grin I saw?*

"That's right, Dad, twelve sixty. Pretty good huh?" Jim said.

"No, thirteen dollars, 10 cents," I said. "I forgot about the coins in my pocket."

At that, Dad couldn't keep from smiling, if only briefly. He clapped his hands, rubbed them together. He'd made a decision. He pushed his chair again, wanting room. "Now, I'll tell you what we're going to do . . . Ruth, bring me a paper and pencil. I'll need a ruler too."

Dad moved his plate aside, and arranged the paper, while we watched and wondered. Using the ruler, he drew a straight line across the paper. On the end of the line, to the left, Dad printed *Muddy River Bridge.* On the right he drew a line and labeled it Highway 2. Using his pencil he began with his mark at the Muddy Bridge. "You follow my line here on the Scenic Highway. From the bridge it goes up to Broadway, over to 2nd Street, and from there out to *Highway 2* west of town." Then he penciled broad zigzags across the top of the page above the line. Working furiously, he shaded in the zigzag section. "All of this; you see it? Everything here south of this line is no-man's land," he said. "South Main, the Depot, all of it, you boys don't set one foot there without permission, and you better have a damn good reason for asking. You got that?" His Swedish blue eyes flashed back and forth between Jim and me.

"Yah, sure," Jim said. "It probably wasn't too smart, what we did."

"Sure as hell wasn't. And you better be smarter about who you listen to. Know what I mean?"

"Razzie, yah. Razzie's a little wild sometimes," Jim said.

Dad leaned back, hands clasped behind his head and chuckled, not joke laughter, but satisfied laughter, the kind I'd heard when I stayed up late, watching him rake in poker money from his cigar-smoking friends. "Twelve dollars, you said?"

"Over thirteen," Jim said.

"Well, I hope you two learned a lesson today."

We did for sure, two of them. Number one: following Razzie's shenanigans can get a guy into trouble; and number two: if you get into big "T" Trouble or double "D" Dutch, be sure to bring home a lot of money.

Despite Razzie's instigation of our beer bottle business, Dad never blamed him for our behavior, or banned us from running with him. He wouldn't allow us to use Razzie as a handy excuse. We were in earshot, I think purposely, when he and Mom discussed our beer bottle incident: "Yeah, I know Razzie's a rascal, Ruth, but the boys knew perfectly well what they were doing was wrong, hanging around the railroad and beer parlors on South Main. Hell, I wouldn't even go there myself. As for Razzie Rasmussen, you know he doesn't have a dad at home."

Razzie came back into family talk a few days later, after Dad had time to think. "Maybe you boys can rein Rasmussen in some. Know what I mean?"

Jim shrugged, managing only: "Sure, we should do that." My brother knew Jimmy Rasmussen very well.

We had gotten to know Razzie and his running buddy, Tommy Stahl, when they tagged along on a few of our Muddy River trips. They were fun guys, game for anything, but grew other interests, and became infrequent participants in our Muddy River life. Razzie and Stahl favored town, where they earned odd job money setting pins at the Playmore Lanes and sweeping floors at the Depot. We wondered: Were Razzie and Tommy too anxious to grow up?

Though not close friends, Jim tried to fit them in, especially Razzie. Like the time Razzie stayed for supper. Dad had gone to Minot for a machine dealer's meeting and wouldn't be home until late. It was up to Mom to make Razzie feel at home. She asked him about school and teased him about girl friends. I thought that strange, because Razzie was only in seventh grade at the time, same as Jim, and Jim showed no interest in girls. At breakfast next morning when Mom and Dad visited, her talk of girls was explained . . . sort of.

"We had Jimmy Rasmussen here for supper. He's a handsome devil," Mom said of Razzie, accenting the handsome. I knew what she meant by her remark, but even in the sixth grade I had to be told which boys were handsome or homely. Clearly, though, girls agreed with my mom, since they hung around Razzie and giggled a lot. I guessed it was his penny loafers holding dimes in the slots, his twinkly dark eyes, and fancy cut *Brylcream-ed* hair, his all around slickness. He dressed like a high schooler, and carried money enough to treat girls to a movie. A few years later in high school I took a girl to a movie starring James Dean. She went absolutely crazy over the actor. *What's the big deal?* I wondered. On the skinny side, watch chain, jingling coins, a slick talker—James Dean was nothing but a blonde version of Razzie.

Even before Jim's train fiasco, we knew Razzie could be trouble. Still, hanging around with him was fun. He carried a fat leather wallet that zipped shut. With the barest hint he'd unzip his wallet and show paper money. Razzie'd spend it freely, too, on expensive things like his high powered pump-up air rifle. Jim borrowed it, shooting blackbirds from our backstep, plinking them in our garden, where they thought they were safe robbing peas. Nickel a bird, Mom paid.

I would describe Jim's friendship with Razzie as loose, but always there—different in many ways, yet bonded by something I couldn't define. Only after another train incident, a more serious one, did I figure out what Jim and Razzie had in common.

A little monster grew legs early in the winter of 1948, a crazy idea nurtured by Razzie and Tommy Stahl. Oh, they had toyed with running away to the mountains before. This time, though, they came at it with intensity, stepping up their odd job workload. It never occurred to them that the rest of the Muddy River guys had no interest in running away from home. "Anybody who comes along will need lots of money and good gear," Razzie urged, still believing others could be convinced to sign onto his crazy plan.

Razzie and Stahl had become regular pinsetters at Playmore Lanes and unofficial bosses of the other setters too. Occasionally they arranged with the manager for Jim and me to set pins when the regulars were sick or in Dutch at home. Other than those times, and talking back and forth at school, Jimmy Rasmussen and Tommy Stahl went their own ways. That is, until the winter of 1948-49, when they came storming back, as wild and unpredictable as the Arctic blizzards blasting across the Canadian prairies and into North Dakota.

Winter blew in early that year—on Armistice Day when "bluebird" weather turned to "blue whistler." Ten North Dakotans caught in the sudden storm lost their way in ground blizzards, and froze to death. Though that first storm's suddenness brought human tragedy, it wasn't the most severe one. A succession of fronts blew in from Saskatchewan, unloading snow upon snow.

Jim and I cheered the snow for a few weeks, since we socked away snow shoveling money by doing our own walks and the neighbors' up and down First Avenue West. But by Christmas time of 1948, we were weary of shoveling, and below-zero temperatures made snowballs and snow forts impossible.

Our town was all but shut down. Stuck cars, if not dug out quickly, were drifted over, leaving white blob humps up and down the streets. "Been here since 1901, and nothing comes close to this sonofabitch," Gramp declared.

Folks were wintered to the gills by January. Dad turned the calendar with as big a complaint as I'd ever heard him make. "Wouldn't mind the early start to this damn winter, if it would just subtract a couple months off the other end." His mood captured the testiness of grown-ups and youngsters alike. Everyone looked for ways to escape thinking about winter, including Razzie and Stahl, who began with extra fervor to resurrect their annual running-away-from-home fantasy.

Jim and I bumped into them on a Saturday morning in the Coast-to-Coast Hardware store. We had gone there to pick through the store's on-sale fishing lures. Razzie and Stahl's mission was not remotely similar. Here they came, scurrying down the camping aisle loaded with boxes. They had boasted at school about their stashes of after-supper and Saturday job money. Now it appeared that their money was going fast.

In the Coast-to-Coast, Razzie sidled up close and thumped on a large green box. He leaned close to us, whispering, "This is going with us to the mountains." COLEMAN, the large label read, and under that, TWO BURNER GAS STOVE.

After our meet-up in the Coast-to-Coast, Razzie and Stahl began pitching their crazy running away idea with fervor. Far as I know, only the Muddy River gang received their privileged invite. Through January and February hardly a day passed without Jim bringing home to me more details of the plan: "Just like Lewis and Clark's trip, only we'll get to the Rockies quick on the Great Northern Freight Express. Razzie and Stahl will be in the Rockies for spring. If we go along, we'll have to dig into our snow shoveling money to buy supplies."

"Jim, they're not making sense," I said. "You aren't either. Big trips can wait for summer."

"*Summer?* Heck no. Summer's forever away. Why wait for summer? Springtime in the Rockies is the best time. Just think, they've already stashed away the important stuff we need to live off the land. Razzie bought a .22 with his pin setting money, you know, for hunting down our meat. The mountains are chock full of game. And the creeks have beautiful speckled trout. Doggone, I can't wait to catch one."

"Well, that would be running away from home. I'm not going," I said.

"Wouldn't be running away if we came home for summer, would it?"

"No, but we'd still be in big, big Dutch. How can you forget about your trouble when you rode the troop train to Culbertson? And that was only 50 miles, not 500."

"Well, nothing bad happened, did it?"

I was helpless to talk sense into Jim. He was lost in his adventurer's mood, ignoring disastrous possibilities, but turning his wild imagination loose. "Lewis and Clark never had time to explore those mountains," he said. "I doubt anybody has, and we'll have a couple months to do it."

A few days later Jim went to the Coast-To-Coast on an errand for Mom and brought back a surprise with his allowance savings: a handy-dandy camper's cook kit.

Our talks grew ever stranger, but perfected too, manipulating the impossible into the possible. Jim no longer sounded like Jim, more like an Army scout. I don't know who I was, but it wasn't me. For the heck of it, I went along with Jim, fantablizing miraculous trout that Buck said "hid themselves in perfectly clear mountain water." "You fry them up crispy and eat 'em, bones and all," Buck told us. I went so far as to picture Jim's fry pan sizzling with crispered trout.

I know my brother was smitten even harder than I, because he happily lathered glory on the latest of Razzie and Stahl's secret plans. Drawbacks, though, never saw the light of day. Jim's dream and mine became ever more magnificent. Reality had been buried deep in snow. Or maybe our winter did to us what it does to bears, hibernating our brains until spring came to thaw them out.

Buck did his part by talking up his last summer's trip to the Rockies with his dad. He kept his collection of mountain pictures handy for showing. One stood out, showing Buck standing next to a waterfall with a stringer of fabulous silvery trout. Buck managed to look like a movie star, flashing his face-wide smile, head tilted just so, as if catching 10 pounds of trout was an everyday event. Maybe I was jealous? Yeah, but I still couldn't help thinking of mystical trout. I desperately yearned to see one. Buck and his trout appeared over and over in my brain and always, each night, as I was falling asleep.

Despite Buck's bragging up trout fishin' and the Rocky Mountains, he declared early—in January—that he wasn't in on the secret trip. "My dad's taking me to the Rockies again next summer. We're takin' a real train, the Empire Builder, to Glacier National Park," Buck boasted.

Besides Buck's legitimate plans to visit the mountains, the rest of the Muddy River guys were careful about offering train-hopping promises that Razzie and Stahl could glom onto. With good sense, they'd have left all of us out of their far-fetched plan. I credit the awful winter for freezing and burying good sense. Razzie and Stahl called for a meeting after school.

We gathered behind the Junior High wing, standing shin deep in a snowdrift. We shivered, in the bitter February wind. "Dadgum weather! We should have met in your clubhouse, Razzie," Big Bervie declared.

"Can't," Tommy Stahl declared. "You guys ain't club members yet."

"Come on, let's get this meetin' started," Razzie said. "Well, look who's here."

Buck came trudging through drifts, showing up out of boredom, I suppose.

"Okay, Buck, glad you could make it. As of this minute, we got Jack, Big Bervie, Big Eric, Little Eric, and Buck . . . I think. Right, Buck?"

"We didn't ask Little Ergie or Little Bervie," Tommy chipped in. "Razzie and I thought they're too young right now."

"Yah', the little guys can go next year. We'll be goin' again, I know," Razzie said. "And this year you guys are goin' for sure. But if you do chicken out, you have to promise to not say a word. Not a word, okay? It's an oath." Razzie's eyes swept the circle, satisfied with nodding heads.

Tommy glared at Buck. "And nobody can say no until we've told everything."

Buck shrugged his shoulders and went to building a snowball with spit and dry snow.

"Buck, you and the guys better be ready when the weather breaks," Razzie said.

Buck grinned, reared back and nailed the corner stop sign with his hard-packed snowball. "I'm probably not going to hop a freight any time soon . . . but I'd like to see how the rest of you pull this off."

Tommy came around in front of Buck. Angrily he said, "Buck, you ain't gonna know a thing 'til you take the oath. You can do it at the RS clubhouse. Everything said in our clubhouse is a secret."

"Hey, it's okay, Tommy," Razzie said. "Now Buck . . . all you guys, Tommy an' me are havin' a meeting at the RS clubhouse on Saturday. We got some great stuff to show you. Ain't that right, Tommy?"

"You betcha we do. An' you guys are in for a big surprise. Be there, nine o'clock. An' don't tell no-one else. You can join our club while you're there. And come in through the alley," Tommy added. "If you're late, we're marking you off the list."

"I don't want on any gol-dang list," Buck said. He turned to go, but Razzie caught him, and put his arm around Buck's wide shoulders, well—as far as he could reach.

"Awe, come on, Buck. Just come over and have a look around," Razzie said.

Saturday happened to be Valentine's Day, normally a day of pivotal expectations, when folks dared to think of spring simply because in an ordinary year water dripped from ice daggers along the eaves. But the days leading up to this Valentine's Day hadn't been encouraging, what with 20 degree days and below zero degree nights. Then, on Saturday, Valentine's Day, we awakened to the wind rattling our bedroom window.

Jim opened the blind. "Snowing pretty hard, drifting, too," he said.

I snuggled deeper, wondering—I'd never thought of this before: *Why didn't railroad lines run south? . . . Because that's where we should go.*

Jim yanked my covers. "Come on, get dressed. Let's go see what Razzie's up to."

Razzie and Stahl had started their RS club three years back. Far as I know, they and an older kid, Blackie somebody, were the only members, though others had been invited. Jim and I were candidates, but it seems every club meeting found us out on the Muddy or, in winter, playing crazy sliding basketball on an icy playground court. In desperation for something exciting to do, we tried hockey at the Harmon Park rink. Jim and I and our beginner hockey playing friends never scored a goal, only bloody lips and black eyes, badges of ice hockey glory. Still, ice hockey seemed preferable to joining a club. 4-H, Boy Scouts, all the clubs had books full of rules; probably the RS club did, too. Besides, Razzie lately smelled like real cigarettes, had to be real—nobody had reed smokes in winter. If Jim and I went home with cigarette smoke stink from their clubhouse . . . big, big trouble.

A year earlier, Jim and I had been curious enough to ask admittance to the RS clubhouse. We talked Buck into going along. The secret knock thing was ridiculous. But I liked going up the vertical wooden ladder into the Rasmussens' garage loft. That was the sort of thing French underground fighters would do. The RS clubhouse, though, had nothing going for it, in spite of Razzie's sales pitch. The place smelled of moldy dust and was so dark I couldn't identify faces. But then, a year later, came Valentine's Saturday with the blizzard howling around Rasmussens' garage. We discovered the secret RS clubhouse transformed.

We met up with Jack and Buck in the alley. As we clustered to talk, Tommy Stahl's muffled voice hollowed from a peep hole under the eaves of the garage loft. Tommy lowered his voice trying for sinister, but achieving stupid: "Wait . . . there . . . for Bervie. We'll let . . . you . . . in . . . all . . . at once."

"Hah! Big deal," Buck said. "I'll give Bervie five minutes; then, I'm goin' home to clean my .22. I'm goin' huntin' jackrabbits when the wind dies down. Who wants to go with?"

Before we could answer, Big Bervie came running down the alley. He joined us in front of the double garage door. The wood-slide lock scraped open and Tommy swung the master door just wide enough to let us in. We filed in and Tommy latched the door behind us. He wore a gray winter Canadian Mounties cap with furry cheek flaps. The cap was two sizes too big, and skewed off kilter. "Come on up," he whispered. "Razzie's got everything set."

I climbed the ladder last in line. Before I reached the top rung I heard the other guys expounding: "Man alive, you guys must be rich!"—"Holy cow, this gear is better than my dad's!"—and Bervie, "Dagnabbit, what a set-up!"

Before climbing up into the loft, I poked my head through the trap door opening. Hanging from a hook in a rafter, a white-gas lantern hissed, spreading pretty light across the loft. Razzie and Stahl sat on wooden crates, grinning. Razzie had buttoned his shirt at the neck like a store clerk. He'd pinned a home-made badge of varnished cardboard to his shirt pocket. Its inscription read, "Captain, RS Club." Tommy's badge was smaller, naming him as "Lieutenant, RS Club."

Razzie gestured with his bottle of Coke, "Go look inside."

"Hold on," Tommy said. "Before you go, you need to know we have a new rule: no smokin' in the clubhouse." As if we had to be told. None of the supposed RS candidates smoked, unless puffing on an occasional reed stogie counted.

The "inside" Razzie smiled about was a pup tent erected in the center of the loft floor. Its canvas smelled of store newness. The light from a second Coleman lantern leaked out through the tent door flap. I parted the flap and went in. *Criminy, what a sight!* There sat Buck, Jim, Jack, and Bervie, on spread-out sleeping bags.

"Toasty as a cabin in here," Jim said. He grinned, warming his hands on a Coleman stove. It had to be the one we'd seen Razzie carry out of the Coast-to-Coast.

The tent flap flew open and in came Razzie and Stahl. Tommy carried a carton of Cokes. He swept his hand around the tent like a swami, "Well, whadda ya' think? Don't we got it all?"

Tommy held the carton, and Razzie began popping the caps and handing the Cokes around. All the while, he expounded on the gear he and Tommy had collected: "All this stuff is going on the train with us." He threw his hands about, directing like a concert conductor. His brown eyes gleamed in the lantern light. "We'll set the tent up on the floor of a boxcar for the trip out. When we get to the Rockies, we'll pitch our camp in the woods."

"Back there," Razzie gestured, "is a whole case a' pork an' beans, and for dessert we got canned cherry pies. You guys think up what to bring, too. We'll need enough grub to last until we get us enough trout an' rabbits an' deer to feed us all." Razzie put his hand on my shoulder, "Step aside, Little Eric, I gotta get to the back."

Razzie stooped to the back of the tent. "Lookie here," he said. When he turned around, he held a complete fishing rod and reel, only it was stubby short. Grinning ear to ear, Razzie pulled on the rod tip and out it came, magically telescoping to five feet. "How about that?" he bragged. Back into his pile of stuff, Razzie reached and started pitching gear to us: packsacks, tin cook kits, rope coils, a hatchet, and a fold-up army shovel. . . . "Okay, Tommy, it's time to show 'em your train schedule."

Tommy hesitated . . . "You sure, Razzie? . . . They ain't signed up yet."

"Tommy, show 'em the danged schedule. They already took the oath to not tell nobody."

"Well, they better not." Tommy squatted and rubbed his hands together. With his wiry body, thin face, and intense, blue eyes, Tommy could have been rolling dice in a brick alleyway—straight out of a James Cagney movie. He ducked his head low, beginning in a whisper, as if spies lurked close by. "Okay, here's what happened. I got me a job cleaning up the Depot offices. Last Saturday morning McGinnis called me in to work. He's the boss man I work for. I was picking up the trash can when the station master came into the freight office to talk to McGinnis. I grabbed my broom and started sweeping, kept my head down, and I listened. They were talking about the new freight express schedule, which McGinnis had left on his desk. I drug out my job in the office, so's I could find out. After the station master left and Mr. McGinnis went out to go to the can, I read the schedule real quick and memorized everything important. Later I wrote it down. Catching the fast freight out of town will be a snap."

Razzie elbowed him. "Okay, okay, Tommy, now show 'em how we're gonna do it."

Tommy rolled up on his knees and poked his arm far up into a sleeping bag. He pulled out a folded paper and spread it out, holding it flat with empty Coke bottles. He reached again and brought out a leather scabbard holding a big knife with its bone handle showing. He pulled the knife out. "Look here," he said. "I got me a Bowie knife."

Tommy grinned around our circle, testing the knife's sharpness with his thumb. Then, pointing with the blade of his fancy Bowie, Tommy said, "Says right here, starting on March 1—check the dates—the freight express comes in on the third, then the seventh day, three days – four days; that's the way it goes all the next three months. And see here, I wrote the times. Every stop is scheduled for the middle of the night, pulling out again at eight AM. It's perfect. We'll sneak our stuff on in the dark when the crew is in the station drinking coffee."

"And the west-bound always reserves extra empties, not just cattle cars either," Razzie added. "See? I have the old schedule that Tommy got out of the garbage." Razzie spread a wrinkled paper and pointed: "Look, every time, at least six empties, seven, even ten. We'll have us our own private car for sure."

"Hold on! What about the warning?" Bervie pointed to a boxed-in message in the lower right corner of Tommy's treasured schedule. "WARNING," it said, in bold red.

"That? Oh, that's nothin'," Razzie said. "It just gives Stensby and his Great Northern cops something to fuss about." Within the WARNING box was written:

"CLASS A" FREIGHT
ITINERANT PASSENGER RULES STRICTLY ENFORCED

"Itinerant . . . means bums, I guess," Jack laughed. "We could land in the hoosegow with the bums."

"You're crazy, Jack," Tommy said angrily. "Bums are stupid. We ain't stupid, and we ain't gettin' caught."

The more I listened, the more I thought of Tommy as Edward G. Robinson, the gangster leader, meeting with his bad guys in a creepy warehouse.

I'd seen Tommy wearing his grandpa's old cowboy hat. His gramp in Montana had given him the bone-handled Bowie knife, too—"made from elk antler." I wanted to believe in Tommy's dream about becoming a rancher with a palomino horse. I'd pictured him galloping his long-maned palomino across the foothills toward the snow-capped Rockies.

Suddenly the fun of being in the secret clubhouse was over. I had a bad feeling in my stomach and it wasn't from two bottles of Coke. And Buck wore the biggest frown I'd ever seen. Even Jim had changed. He grimaced at me, maybe thinking what I was thinking.

Jim and I knew the freight office well, and we knew Mr. McGinnis, Tommy's *"boss man."* Gramp introduced us when we were just tykes. Occasionally, he'd pick us up an hour early so he could visit Mr. McGinnis and still have time to watch the Empire Builder come in. To visit McGinnis, Gramp would lead us across the Depot's blue-gray marble floor and circle the Great Northern mascot—the stuffed mountain goat standing proud on his pedestal. We'd go to the rear of the great room to the tall door with the milky glass. Gramp rapped his special bop-dee-bop, bop on the glass. Mr. McGinnis never hesitated, always hollered, "Come on in Rollie," knowing that only Gramp knocked that way.

Mr. McGinnis let Jim and me take turns spinning in his big wooden desk chair. He gave us Juicy Fruit gum, and writing paper to scribble on with real fountain pens. While we played at his big desk, Mr. McGinnis and Gramp sat in the visitors' chairs, drinking coffee and talking railroad talk . . . how many cattle or cars of grain were shipped, and about derailments, always a derailment somewhere between St. Paul and the Rockies.

My picture of Tommy sneaking Mr. McGinnis's freight schedule soured my attitude and I know Jim's, too. Conniving sneakers inside Mr. McGinnis's office was the final blow, the one thing needed to bring us to a reckoning. Our fantasy about a Rocky Mountain adventure was over. Shortly it would end for the other clubhouse guests, too.

Buck, it seems, wanted to let our hosts down easy: "This camp, just like you guys have it set up, would make a great camp out at Stony Ford," Buck said.

Razzie stood with hands on hips. His brown eyes reflected lantern light. "You crazy, Buck? Stony Ford, when we could camp in the Rocky Mountains? Think of it. No more school. No more Principal Wisenand, no more after school detention for any of us." He shook his head in disgust. Razzie stared around our circle, "Now, whoever's goin' raise his hand."

Nobody did and nobody spoke. Finally Tommy poked his hand up, but only as high as his ear.

Jim and Bervie thought it time to chime in with polite remarks, backing each other about how maybe just two guys would have a better chance of pulling off the trip, and: "If you change your minds, we'll help you haul your camp to Stony Ford."

Jack thought it all great entertainment, which is how he viewed 90 percent of life anyway. "Jeepers creepers, all this time I thought you guys were just blowin' smoke. I ain't so sure now."

"Well, one thing I'm sure of," Bervie said, scrambling to his feet. "I'm not getting on any confounded freight train."

"Me neither," Buck said, crossing his arms. "Good luck to anyone who goes. Super campin' stuff you guys have. And thanks for the Cokes."

Jim and I offered our own gratitudes and climbed down the ladder after the others. All of us *"chicken outs,"* in Razzie's words, gathered in the alley, past the garbage cans, out of earshot of the RS clubhouse peephole.

"I think Razzie's danged serious this time," Jim said. Buck motioned us to move. Walking in a cluster so we could hear above the wind, we headed from the alley, up 4th Avenue toward Jack's house, each competing to wedge in speculations and opinions.

Bervie again: "Just talk, that's all."

And Jack: "Yah, but they never planned it this big."

"Well, they had plenty of chances before," Jim said.

"Never been this desperate, Eric," Buck said. "They better not underestimate Al Stensby, though. They could go to jail."

Bervie walked backward, facing us, so's he could be sure we'd listen. Bervie, the book reader, was probably the smartest guy in his grade. He seemed to know how people would act before they acted. "I'll bet anyone wants to bet," he said. "It'll be big talk until the day of reckoning."

Day of reckoning! More like moment of reckoning, I thought, and it had already happened back there in the clubhouse the moment when talk turned away from the Rockies, trout fishin', and living off the land, and honed in on conniving ways to fool the railroad people—an *inside job* even, like real crooks do. I saw dismay in Bervie's face. He and his little brother, Allen, couldn't stand to be in the same room with shaded truth.

Even Tommy seemed ready to back out. Now it was all up to Razzie. For the rest of us: well, our eyes had opened wide in the clubhouse. I realized that none of us would continue dreams of springtime in the mountains for another second. And without us, Razzie's big plan would again melt with the last spring snow banks.

Through the end of February and into March hardly another word passed between Jim and me about Razzie's going-west mountain adventure. The dream soured as I faced up to hard truths, like running away meant flunking the 6th grade and making Mom cry. And Dad?—too scary to think about.

Jim and I turned attention to drudging through the rest of the school year, made tolerable by rabbit hunting on weekends. Dad helped our rabbit hunting by buying us war surplus parkas and Eskimo mukluk mittens. With Buck we hiked as far as the hills of the Catwalk, the Fox Walk, and beyond to pursue "four-bit" white jackrabbits that we sold to Dakota Hide and Fur. Dad hadn't yet granted me permission to carry a .22, but still I shared in the profits for lugging dead jacks to town.

In mid-March a soft Chinook drifted in and water trickled from snow banks. With only patchy ice to skid on, the mailman delivered on time. Our old British pastor allowed himself an encouraging smile in closing his sermon. With grumpiness narrowed to dedicated grumps, I believed addled wintertime diversions had died. But, as March wound down I was proven wrong. Jim came home from school and took me to our back alley hoop to play basketball, but—in truth—to share a secret.

"The trip is on. Razzie and Stahl are going to the mountains."

I wasn't buying that. Not in the slightest. "Ahh . . . that's just horse pucky," I said.

"No, they're serious. They said Saturday's the *third* day."

"Third day? What do you mean?"

"You remember, the *third* day, how Tommy filched the freight schedule. The Express comes in every three days, then four. The train they're taking is due on the third day, which is Saturday. And we're still invited if we want to go." Jim said that uncertainly, like maybe hopping a freight train was still possible.

"Naw. You're crazy. You can't be thinking about going, can you?"

"Got to *think* about it," Jim said. He waited, watching me fret until he was satisfied I'd taken the bait. Then he laughed; I couldn't imagine why, though Jim managed to fool me at least once a day. He put a finger on my chest. "You know what day Saturday is?"

"You just said. It's the third day on the train schedule."

"April *first,* you nitwit. Razzie and Stahl would like us to show up in the dark with our gear, ready to hop a freight car. Dang, what an April Fools joke! Ha! The joke's on them. I told them I'm goin'. Jack too, he's in on my plan. They're thinkin' we might bite on it, and Jack and I are helping them believe we will. Ha! I can hardly wait. Razzie and Stahl will be hiding back in the bushes, shivering in the dark, ready to holler, "April Fools." They'll be waitin' for nothin'. Then, when they show up at school on Monday . . . boy are we gonna have some fun."

Jim wore his special *can't wait* kind of grin leaving the house that Monday morning of April 3rd. When I met him at lunchtime on the junior high playground, his grin was gone. He took me aside.

"Believe it or not, they did it," he whispered.

"What? Who did it?"

"Razzie and Stahl. They're gone."

"What?"

"They did it. They took the freight, middle of the night, April Fools day. Jelly brought a note to my math class ordering me to go immediately to Principal Wisenand's office. Tommy's dad and mom were there. She actually cried, right there in front of everybody."

I stared in disbelief, unable to speak. After three years' crazy talk of running-away-from-home, those rascals were as believable as Elmer Fudd and Bugs. I still didn't believe they were gone.

"Who knows for sure? I said. "You know how they hate school. Maybe they're just hiding out somewhere."

"Nope, they did it all right," Jim said.

I almost choked on my own spit. I couldn't make myself believe. Finally, I came around to believing by picturing Razzie and Stahl standing with fishin' poles that pointed out over an ice-cold mountain stream, the water clear as glass.

"Wait 'til you hear the rest," Jim said. "The railroad people, the cops, and the teachers know about them hopping the freight, where they went, *the whole plan!*"

"About us too? That we knew about it, were sort of in on the plan?"

"That's exactly right. That's why I was called in. Heck, in the principal's office I felt like a criminal surrounded by cops."

Even then, in a super serious moment, Jim couldn't resist: "I thought they'd tie me to the chair," he laughed. "They have electric prods, you know."

"Come on, Jim; really . . . I want to know what happened. You had to confess everything?"

"Thought I'd have to. But I was saved, that's what. Principal Wisenand was about to call Dad in and have me own up. But then here came Miss Wilkinson with Little Stahl, Jerry from the fourth grade. Turns out Jerry helped his brother and Razzie get a two-day head start."

"So Jerry knew they were going?"

"Sure did. He's a smart little bugger. I'll bet Tommy and Razzie paid him good. Jerry backed up the fib that Tommy was at Rasmussen's house for the weekend and, on Razzie's end, visa-versa. Jerry's a gutsy kid, talking right up to two principals."

"What else did he tell them?"

"*Everything!* Everything we heard in the clubhouse. Jerry, he handed Miss Wilkinson a letter. Right off she turned to me, burning holes in me with those red eyes."

"Why you?"

"Well, I was mentioned in the letter, so Wilkinson handed the letter over to Mrs. Wisenand, 'cuz she's my principal. Wisenand stood to read it. She paused often, like a preacher, looking at her audience, especially me. She came to the part of the plan about living in the mountains 'til summer. That's where she stopped. 'James,' she said. 'You knew of this?' I didn't answer, 'cuz I didn't believe it was my job to rat on Razzie and Stahl.

"Mrs. Wisenand didn't skip over anything; read every inventory item Razzie listed in the letter. I knew it was Razzie doing the writing. He fibbed, saying I'd be coming out later to join them. And he wrote to not worry; they'd send postcards, as if that would help bail them out of trouble."

Jim held me spellbound there on the corner of the playground. He surprised me, too. Jim was normally a doer and short on explanations. "What else?" I asked, and with that Jim spun on.

"Well, Mrs. Wisenand didn't get to finish reading the letter, because Mrs. Rasmussen arrived—came in all sobby and fainty, sniffing and moaning 'Oooh,' and falling into a chair, fussing in her purse for a handkerchief. About then, Little Stahl interrupted the trial, 'er meeting, by trying to sneak out. Mr. Pederson blocked him at the doorway. 'Ware da ya' tink yer' goin'?' he said. Jim dug the gravel with his toe, laughing.

"What's so danged funny?"

"The end of Razzie's letter, what it said. Darned if that Razzie didn't pull a good one on me. While the rest of them tried to comfort Mrs. Rasmussen, Wisenand took me out to the hallway and showed me the letter. She tried looking stern and tough, but couldn't quite pull it off. She pointed at the letter, then pointed at my nose. She says, 'Read this, James.' I caught her grinning."

"Why, what's so funny?"

"The letter's closing. Razzie wrote, 'To Jim Erickson: April Fools! HA, HA, HA, HA, HA, HA. Jimmy R.'"

"Principal Wisenand tried to keep a stern face. Her job was to be tough with me. She had to question me about what Razzie meant."

"So, what did you tell her?"

"Nothing; but, I couldn't help myself: I laughed. Whew! Did that ever make her mad! . . . So how do you like that? She thought the letter was funny, but it's against the law for me to laugh? I was ready to write down everything for her, but she sent me away; said the police and Great Northern officials will be talking with me."

"Well, what's going to happen? About us, I mean—our part of the planning, and not telling."

"I've got a hunch nothing will happen to us. Miss Wilkinson set me straight. She pulled me aside at the end of the big meeting. She said, 'Tell the police everything you know. Your information could be important for the safety of Jimmy Rasmussen and Tommy Stahl.'"

After Jim's stunning news, I returned to Miss Denitch's sixth grade room that was in complete upheaval. The bell rang and a few of the most obedient girls immediately took their seats. The rest of our class milled about, mumbling, still trying to piece together the story of our rascally acquaintances, known to the principals as 'Mr. Rasmussen and Mr. Stahl.' All the while, Miss Denitch banged her chalkboard pointer and gruffed loud, "Come, come, children, take your seats." *"Children"* still—in the sixth grade—stuck in my craw, and I don't think I was the only one. We'd have minded quicker without the *children.* To be honest, though, even after she sniggered us into those hard little seats, we kept whispering . . . like children.

Not much school learning got done that day. Teachers had little chance of competing with the frenetic buzzing. At recess Jelly alerted me to the city cop car bringing Officer Gwin, Mr. Stensby, and Big Smitty. They went into our building and up the stairs to Miss Wilkinson's office. A few minutes later grumpy ol' Pederson escorted them to the junior high wing to see Mrs. Wisenand. She, in turn, brought Jim, Jack, Buck, and Big Bervie to her office for questioning. I dodged scrutiny because . . . because, little brothers are almost always innocent. Whatever I do together with Jim is my big brother's fault. Like my Gramp says, "Some things in life you can't change." What I say is: "Why would I want to change it?"

By afternoon the news of Razzie and Stahl's escapade had spread from every classroom and out the doors to the far corners of town. The mayor would have done well to call a town meeting where he could report the same story to the entire population. As it was, kids by the hundreds went home to face grilling and lectures about juvenile delinquency. Parents like ours were good at leveraging the episode of Razzie and Stahl to their parental advantage. Jim got a double dose, once with Mr. Gwin at school and another at home. We knew trouble was on its way.

In the middle of dinner, Dad daggered his questions: "You knew all about their hair-brained scheme didn't you? Didn't you know better than to hang around those two when you knew they were up to no good?" He dismissed our chicken-livered answers with: "Uh-huh" and "thought so." Dinner time talk was just a warm-up for the main feature in which both Mom and Dad double-teamed us with their lectures about trespassing on the railroad, skipping school, and—over and over—"dangerous knuckleheaded behavior."

"They could freeze to death," Dad said. "It'll drop to 20 degrees here tonight; could be 20 below up in the Rockies."

"They've got a Coleman stove, Dad," Jim said.

"Huh, a camp stove?—won't begin to heat a tent in the mountains."

Mom had heard enough. She tried to call Mrs. Rasmussen to give her comfort, tried and tried, but each time her line was busy. Jim and I went to bed plenty worried about our rascal friends. We talked long in the dark, but settled nothing, left wondering when we'd know.

Next morning we were barely out of bed and dressed when our answer came: a knock on our back door, and in walked Officer Gwin. He crossed the kitchen in three long strides, befitting his athletic six-foot-two frame. He tossed his blue police hat on the counter and reached for Mom's ever-ready coffee pot. Reed hollered at Dad, who was still in the bathroom. "They found the boys, Bill. The call came in to me late, on night shift."

In a scrambling minute our family joined Mr. Gwin around our kitchen table. Reed slurped Mom's "pistol-floating" coffee, licked his lips, spooned more sugar, stirred it in, and took another sip. *Dick Tracy, if there ever was one:* a scarred cheek and blocky head topped with stubby reddish charcoal hair. I leaned forward, so ready to hear that I wanted to blurt, *"What happened?"* But you didn't do that with Mr. Gwin without a respectful good reason, even my dad didn't.

After a minute of his policeman's careful thinking that seemed like ten minutes, Reed began his report. First, the phone call from a police chief in Montana: "The boys were in dangerous shape, folks. Half froze to death and snow blind. Plenty scared, too, as you might imagine. Lucky they got them off the box car when they did." Mr. Gwin paused to slurp coffee, giving Dad time to jump in.

"Reed, I want to know exactly the kind of trouble those two are in, and everything you know about my boys' part in this knuckleheaded deal." He said that with a glare at Jim and me that froze the air in place.

Reed responded with a wry grin, and returned to his reporting, keeping everything in order. "Jimmy Rasmussen and Tommy Stahl are in a hospital out beyond the Rockies, in a railroad town, Whitefish, Montana. And these two"—

Reed nodded at Jim and me—"were smart enough not to tag along on this fiasco. I spent hours trying to comfort the Stahl family and Mrs. Rasmussen."

Mom broke in anxiously, "Their condition. You said hospitalized? How bad are they?"

"They're lucky . . . could have been much worse. They lost a lot of body temperature. But the chief said he went back to the hospital to check on them. The boys are reviving from their deep chill. And they'll recover completely from snow blindness, the docs say. They'll be in the hospital a couple more days. They've caused a lot of trouble. But still, I can't help feeling bad for them. After all their highfalutin' plans, they never got to set foot in the mountains."

Reed had lapsed into a mood I recognized, something Jim and I had figured out long ago, when Dad mentioned: "Reed and his missuz are forever sad about their only child. Left home right out of high school . . . joined the Army." Dad speculated a secret mission, because Reed rarely mentioned his son, and even then he'd be quick to change the subject.

Because of his own empty spot, I suppose, Reed took special interest in boys. He managed to find his way to our house whenever possible to find out about our fishin' trips, to share his important street news, and to give out warnings about older boy bullies who could be dangerous.

Reed Gwin, the toughest cop our town had ever known, was also admired for coming to the rescue of many a troubled kid. He spoke of Razzie and Stahl in a softer tone, unlike his gruffness reserved for men troublemakers.

Reed talked on, at once saddened by the risks taken by two rascally boy adventurers that didn't pay off, but elated with his own good luck, a happenstance against infinitesimal odds. Reed, himself, had answered the late night call from Whitefish: "Williston Police, Lieutenant Gwin speaking," followed by . . . buzzing of telephone wires, nothing else. Then came the gravelly voice Reed had never forgotten—Jake Jablonski, Reed's partner from their rookie days on the Minneapolis police force.

"I'll be damned," Jablonski said. "Reed Gwin, you old scudder. Why don't you keep your Dakota boys in Dakota?" Ten years back the patrol mates from Minneapolis had lost track of each other.

Sitting at our kitchen table, Reed expounded, describing Jake Jablonski like a long-lost brother, "Never knew a better cop. They should have moved him right to the top of the Minneapolis department. What a coincidence to find him this way.

"I let Jake do most of the talkin' and he did a lot of it," Reed continued. "Hell, the long distance cost was on the Whitefish department anyway. Jake was taken by the boys in their pitiful condition. Said a rail bum had helped them off the freight car. Their eyes were swollen shut. Jake said they never cried, but they looked like beaten puppies. They blabbered on and on about the mountains, asking, 'Where are the mountains? Are we in the mountains?'

"Jake took them to the hospital. Then he called his wife to come and help comfort them. Good man, good man, that Jake. Those boys were damn lucky they ended up in his jurisdiction." Mr. Gwin continued, uninterrupted, holding us spellbound. In the telling he was more excited than when he told Dad about apprehending the South Main burglar, or when he fought in the Golden Gloves Nationals. My mind strayed to wondering: *Did Reed Gwin pull off a railroad adventure, or something like it, when he was a kid?*

Mr. Gwin's official version was but a start. Over the next two weeks Razzie and Stahl filled us in. The train pulled onto a siding in Havre . . . "engine trouble," a rail bum told them. The boys pulled the door shut and hid out for a day and a night before the train headed for the mountains.

Across the plains to the foothills, they perched at the open door of their box car with legs dangling, facing the glare of sun on snow. The train began ascending the steep foothills, and the boys had no way to bail off to begin their mountain adventure. They couldn't see the high mountain peaks, by now anyway. Snow blindness had set in. And like Dad predicted, the mountain temperature was below zero. Their stove was empty of gas. "We were afraid to sleep," Tommy said—"thought we'd never wake up."

Razzie and Stahl were returned with their gear to Williston in the custody of a Great Northern security agent. Tommy Stahl's parents and Mrs. Rasmussen met the train, accompanied by Officer Gwin. Reed escorted the boys to juvenile court where they became official delinquents, charged with trespassing on railroad property and being itinerant passengers. A wartime railroad regulation was in place that could have been used to enact severe punishment, but wasn't—Dad said—because of their ages, and Mr. Gwin going to bat for them.

It seems as if justice has a way of coming around. Mr. McGinnis was called to testify. He overcame objections raised by Stensby and Big Smitty, who wanted to "throw the book." And the judge accepted Reed Gwin's proposal to order Razzie and Stahl to work off a restitution fine under the direction of Mr. McGinnis. Now they'd sweep and polish the Depot floors and the baggage rooms for free.

After the boys spiffed up the Depot, McGinnis turned them over to Sorensen at the roundhouse.

"*That* Sorensen—the mean bugger?" Jim asked.

"Yup! That's him," Razzie said. "He made us degrease the engine room floor."

To me, Jim said, "Without signs of spring, Razzie and Stahl were going nuts. Now that spring is here, the poor suckers are stuck inside."

On a Saturday morning, Jim and I were riding for the south Muddy to intercept a June run of bullheads. We happened upon Razzie and Stahl headed to their non-paying railroad jobs. They had stopped at the corner to visit with Axel, the shoe salesman. "You boys, have your eyes healed?" Axel asked. Right there at the corner of Broadway and Main, Razzie and Stahl told Axel and us their hospital story, the gradual return of light through the scary shadows. Nelson, the cigar store man, and Mr. Snyder, owner of the Grande and Orpheum theatres, came along and listened in. Razzie and Stahl went on as if big folks didn't matter.

"We wuz scared spitless. We woke up in the hospital with bandaged eyes," Tommy said.

"Yeah, I figure they gave us knockout drops," Razzie added. "If not for goin' mostly blind we'd be living in the mountains right now." As he bragged, Razzie sat a little slumpy and unconvincing on his bike seat.

"It's gol-danged winter out there," Tommy added. "Snow, a couple feet, covered the prairie . . . blinding white all the way across Montana. But just when we made out the outline of mountains, the sky went gray and grayer, then dark, and I'm pretty sure the sun wasn't clear down. It was our eyelids, so puffed up we couldn't get 'em open."

"Couldn't see to get our stove lit," Razzie chipped in. "We followed the smell of gas. Doggone can had spilt."

"Yeah, and I could feel the train climb to the top of the mountains," Tommy said.

"As high as the snow clouds," Razzie added. "Never been so cold . . . must have been 20 below, an' all we could do was crawl in them cheap, no-damn-good cold sleeping bags. Tommy was right. We should have spent more money on good ones."

"No," Mr. Snyder said. He pushed past me and shook his finger at Razzie. "What you *should* have done was stay in school. You boys don't get an education, you've got nothin'."

"You had this whole damn town worried," Mr. Nelson chipped in.

"We're sorry 'bout that," Razzie said. "We didn't mean to."

Razzie and Tommy turned their bikes for the Depot. "We gotta go. Mr. McGinnis will have our necks if we're late."

Scolded daily at home and lectured downtown, Razzie and Stahl turned to—of all places—*school* for comfort. I was deeply confused. I'd never seen bad behavior so rewarded: Girls crowded around the truant lawbreakers. Guys who'd been stand-offish in the past now befriended them. Our school buzzed with talk: "Did you hear the latest about Jimmy and Tommy?" With the attention heaped upon a pair of reckless troublemakers, my black and white world was smudged gray.

In the days following the return of the runaways, my brother illustrated a popular assessment of their escapade. Jim was especially good at the telling. Driven by his own powerful itch for adventure, Jim put a glamorous slant on the outcome: "Dang, what a super train ride! And they'll never, ever forget the mountains. They had a fantastic view of them on their train ride back. We've just gotta find a way to see the Rockies ourselves."

Jimmy Rasmussen and Tommy Stahl did something incredibly stupid, dishonest, and risky. But, by golly, they did *something,* something big, while the rest of the town sat back, pummeled by a dreadful long winter, never risking adventure. And for the boys, strangely, their ill-fated trip to the mountains paid off in unexpected ways. Their close call with blindness and freezing to death sobered them. They were no longer so inclined to fight with the idea of school.

Razzie and Stahl worked off school detention by doing make-up work, good enough to pass seventh grade. By mid-August they had paid off the railroad penalty, and completed juvenile probation.

A day later, that scalawag Razzie started talk of his next adventure. "Stahl and me are raising money for a trip to the Rockies. We'll take the Empire Builder to Whitefish. Chief Jablonski promised to take us trout fishin' if we ever came back.

Ha! I'll bet he never expects us to really do it. I can't wait to see the look on his face when Tommy and me walk into his police station."

I figure a big-time Great Northern Railway shenanigan was inevitable. Jimmy Rasmussen and Tommy Stahl were not the first tempted and lured by the magnificent forces of the railroad, nor were they the last. The Great Northern was just too constant, handy, and exciting.

Each July, Barnum and Bailey's came to town, transported by—naturally—the Great Northern Railway. The circus was a big deal, but not any bigger than the railroad circus, which went on day and night. A minute seldom passed without a switch engine goosing and banging to connect rail cars, the noise clamoring to our house eight blocks north of the tracks. Switch engines, engineers' whistles, rumbling freight trains, and the roaring Empire Builder added to the noisy jumble. The racket spread up the Muddy River Valley halfway to Stony Ford.

Eight years before Razzie and Stahl hopped the freight for Montana, Gramp took Jim and me to see the Empire Builder for the first time. He held both of us by a hand and worked us through the crowd of departing and arriving passengers. Most of the men wore hats and suits and ties; ladies dressed in their best church outfits, flowery dresses, with matching hats, gloves and shoes. Everyone was full of extra energy, travel-excited, talking and laughing, waving to family and friends, all coming or going.

Gramp led us west along the red brick tarmac to the giant engine. It stood, like a true "iron horse," trembling, anxious. We stood close enough to feel its heat, uncomfortable, for it was a hot day in August. The engine spewed steam, and its iron creaked from some inside turmoil. We craned necks to glimpse the engineers moving about up in their high command. They yelled back and forth, exchanging important instructions. Suddenly one of them pulled a lever, and the giant engine roared. Gramp—still gripping our hands—did not pull us back. I was frightened and fascinated by the monster engine, dangerous . . . *stay away, dangerous . . . move closer . . . get a better look.*

Addendum: The Great Northern Railway's northern route was completed on January 6, 1893. It was the only privately funded transcontinental railroad in U.S. history. No federal land grants were used during construction. The Great Northern was founded and relentlessly promoted by industrialist and philanthropist, James J. Hill, whose company eventually built 8000 miles of track. The main line provided freight, mail, and passenger connections between St. Paul and Seattle. Branch lines connected and serviced small towns in outlying regions across the Upper Midwest. Because of his ambition and success, James Hill was known as the "Empire Builder," the name that was assigned to the Great Northern's "flagship" and mighty streamliner.

Chapter Eleven

Kowabunga! What Happened?

Though Razzie was dead serious when he said he'd return to Whitefish and the mountains, he never had a chance. He was blitzed by a girl. The rest of us laughed about how quickly Colleen corralled Razzie. Colleen was taller than Razzie and, according to my mom: "regal." She had blue-green eyes and auburn hair with a flip, like a movie queen. She laughed and talked more excitedly than Razzie—hard to believe. Razzie bought her cherry Cokes and sodas at the Castle Café.

"Razzie and Colleen practically own the back booth," Jim said.

Meantime, Tommy Stahl fell in love with his homemade motor bike. Colleen and a danged wreck of a machine stole Razzie and Stahl in the summer of 1948. Jim and I talked about their sad predicament; but we saw nothing similar coming between us and the Muddy River country. We were afflicted with a stronger strain of "River Fever." Jim and I had spent four seasons on the river, Jack and Buck five.

We'd established a "home" at Stony Ford with our rock cache, spending long summer days along the black sand beach, and Stony's fish-haven pool. But Stony Ford was only two miles out, at the near edge of our adventuring frontier. North on the Muddy was never far enough, especially for Jim, the kid born with a bright green go light, but no yellows or reds. Since he and Buck were bent on exploring north of Nine-Mile, we took up hitch-hiking. Coming or going, we never waited more than 30 minutes to get a ride. Muddy River headwaters, Metzger's Lake, Epping Dam: no problem—stick our thumbs in the air and smile. Often we were given a lift by the same farmers, like old Enoch, who thought us frivolous and told us so: "You honyauck kids ever git tared a' fishin'? You oughta larn ta 'verk.'"

After Dad, his brothers, and Grampa Erickson sold out their machine implement business, Dad got a job selling cars. So, sometimes he'd loan us an old heap from the used lot. We had no driver's licenses, but were allowed to drive country roads as long as we bought the gasoline. Perfect! Jim drove us north to Nine Mile Hole and Thirteen Mile for walleyes, and to Cow Creek to fish horny headed creek chubs using steel telescoping fly rods and white chicken feather flies.

On a September Saturday in 1950, with Jim driving a rusty-fendered Kaiser-Fraser, we were bound for the secret 14 Mile Hole, just Jim and me. Unexplainably, Jack and Buck had recently backed off from fishin', at least the kind of fishin' we had grown to love.

Jim was slow to grow up in one area of life, which I'll get around to shortly. About our buddies, Jack and Buck, Jim said, "I don't know, they're acting squirrelly."

Jim, the normally slow and deliberate driver, drove too fast that morning, steering intently to keep the bald-tired junker on the road, while he recited his litany of exciting possibilities that Jack and Buck would miss.

At age 13 Jim had become a master planner and promoter. That September morning he reveled in the mysteries of our destination: the waters of 14 Mile Hole and other nearby pools that begged for exploration. As he exuded, he worked the loose-jointed Kaiser's steering wheel. "You won't believe your eyes," he said. "The 14 Mile water is ice cold, and deep, and almost crystal clear. When the light is perfect you can see the rocks on the bottom, and if you watch carefully you can spot the white fringes on a walleye's fins. Just amazing!—and only for us to know. We can't mention 14 Mile. You can't trust anyone when it comes to five or six pound walleyes."

As usual, we planned our minnow seining for the swift channel south of Stony Ford's big pool. Jim maneuvered the narrow lane to its dead end at Stony Ford rapids.

Whadda ya know!—a car was parked there. Never had I seen a car at Stony Ford; sometimes—rarely—we spotted the pickup belonging to the cattleman who pastured the valley.

Jim pulled up behind the car before we noticed what kind of car. *What the heck?*—It was maroon, a maroon Pontiac coupe—had to be Mr. Shemorry's, the car now driven most often by Jack. *Jack at Stony? Why now?* September walleyes would be gone upriver. The bullhead bite would be mostly over. Jim switched off the Kaiser's ignition and threw his hands in the air, making a face at me, his wordless question.

Down the road embankment we went, Jim shouldering the seine and me carrying the minnow bucket. Lo and behold, there were Jack and Buck kneeling at the edge of the water tending throw lines. Both wore white short-sleeved shirts and special blue denim trousers called Levis. But why white shirts for fishin'? And collars turned up in the back? Jim tried that once and Mom promptly smoothed the collar and patted it down.

Behind Buck and Jack sat a pair of giggling girls with pony-tailed hair. They poked at a stick-wood fire. Until that very moment, I had never seen a girl at Stony Ford.

Jim and I approached and stood between the campfire and our fishin' buddies. Jim acknowledged the girls politely enough. He said, "How's fishin'?"

I chimed in with, "How ya doing?" sounding stupid. How do you talk to girls, anyway? School is one thing, but out here? We turned our back on them, not to disrespect, but this *was* Stony Ford, the "tribal ground" of our short existence on Earth, a place of ritual and easy conversation gleaned from years of shore sitting and catching bullheads. Jim tried: "Any jumbos left in here?"

"If there were, do you think we'd want you and the whole town to know?" Jack's mischievous grin, the same one I'd first seen when he was seven, had settled in for the life of him. The rest of him was molded in place too. As always, Jack spawned comic thoughts and highlighted them with infectious, cackling laughter. From his fishin' squat he popped to his feet and strutted, like an adrenaline charged rooster. He sliced the air with long arms, pontificating, "Buck and I gave up on teaching you guys to catch jumbos. We were wasting our time. We brought the girls along. They'll learn quick, way smarter than you two, right Buck?"

Buck jerked his thumb back, "Way smarter." He nodded at Jim and me. "These two dumbos are going after walleye, Jack. Jumbo bullheads take real skill. Anyone can catch walleye."

Yah, sure, I thought. *Anyone, meaning one of about a dozen who knew the river well had a reasonable chance, including Buck and his dad, the cagiest of all.* Buck rolled back onto his butt, trying to look stern and finding it impossible. His poker face broke, laughing blue eyes peered from under his wave of thick crinkly hair, famous hair—impervious to rain and wiry as a horsehair blanket.

Was it the hair, his flashing blue eyes, or his killer smile? Buck had grown to a wide-shouldered, manly six foot one, a high-schooler who walked and talked with stylish confidence. Or was it his worldly ways? I'd witnessed females young and old endearingly touch up his name: Buck becoming Bucko, and pronounced with an inflection unknown to the male mouth.

"Bucko, will you get us some more firewood please?" the pretty brunette pleaded.

"Sure. You go ahead; you can start out. There's driftwood downriver. I'll be along in a jiffy."

Turning back to us, Buck waved us away, "Don't be thinking you can fish here. We're savin' the beach for the girls."

"Better put them to tending lines, then," Jim laughed. "I see your stringers are plumb empty."

Jim hustled across the sand spit toward the long run of riffle we treasured for its rich schools of minnows. I followed, talking at his back, "What's with Buck and Jack? Are those real girlfriends?"

"Must be," was all I could get out of him. Jim's mind had already gone away to the walleyes of 14 Mile Hole.

We kicked out of our shoes and waded in. Two sweeps of our seine filled our bucket with shimmering, silvered shiners mixed with two-inch rosy fatheads, a few baby suckers and horned creek chubs. Our bucket held half water and half minnows. Jim kneeled down, thrust two hands to the bottom, and lifted the mass of a hundred or so wriggling beauties. He let them dribble through his fingers. You'd have thought our minnows were gold dust the way he spoke of them: "They're perfect. With these we can't miss."

Throughout all the years of walleye fishin', each time Jim performed his minnow ritual in exactly this way, always collecting five times what we needed, the extras getting a new home up the river. "Let's get up the road," Jim said, and he rolled up the seine, hoisting it to his shoulder. I grabbed the minnow bucket and followed Jim, leaving Stony Ford's fishy-fragrant beach. Intent on walleye-in', this time we didn't stop to jaw with Buck and Jack. The girls sat close, one on either side, with painted toenail feet dibbling at the water's edge. As we passed by, Jim delivered a parting shot: "Betcha our pair of five pound walleyes will outweigh all your bullheads put together."

"It's possible, if by some miracle you catch any," Jack said.

"I'm bettin' you don't," Buck hollered at our backs.

Their girlfriends—or whatever title was right for their dates in some current stage of romancing—had left me puzzled.

I couldn't get past the curious idea of girls at Stony Ford. There had been only one other half-hearted attempt by girls to join us there. It happened in the spring, just after ice-out. We had settled in with throw-lines. One of the guys happened to look west, toward the ridgeline. "Oh, oh, we've got company." By the size of her tall bay horse, we knew one was Yvonne Gauthier. She was followed by five other pony riders of the "Northside Girl Posse." Profiled against the skyline like Geronimo's warriors, they sat watching us. We watched them back. One of them made the first move, too far away to tell who she was. She started down the road, but thought better of it and turned away. The Posse rode off, ending the long distance meeting in a comfortable standoff, appropriate for that time in our lives. Good that they did or our *frozen nuts* swim couldn't have happened, at least not on that day.

I was handicapped by my naivety about girls, needing years more of maturation. An illuminating experience with a girl at Stony Ford was a first step to understanding.

In the spring of my freshman year in high school I dated a girl twice, first a movie, and then a dance. Before the dance, she invited me in to meet her parents. Having been tuned up by my mom, I seemed to pass muster with the girl's parents.

The next Saturday, smack in the midst of a hot bullhead run, I took a chance and invited the girl fishing. A voice in my head asked: "Would she pass muster with Stony Ford?" What a pleasant surprise! She seemed right at home, worming her own hook. She watched me, then slung an acceptable cast to the perfect line of foamy current. Minutes later she excitedly lined in a long-whiskered jumbo. She skidded him out onto the sand. He was a fat ten incher, squatty, and sassy with his little tummy nestled into the sand, beady-eying my tomboy friend. She cried out a single *"Eeeeeeeck." That,* I thought, *was a weak showing of female squeamishness.* From there on, I marveled at this good lookin' tomboy caught up in the joy of my special place, giggling in fish-slimed, muddied affection for Stony Ford. This girl was truly impressive. So that's how they do it? Let them into your territory and then . . . Who knows? *I* sure as heck didn't.

"You can't beat those little yellow bullheads up there at Stony Ford. Remember roasting them on a stick? First chance I get, I'm going back and catch a dozen."

Chapter Twelve

Work and Girls—Inevitably So

"It's time you boys learned to shave."—Grampa Rollie B. Millhouse

The double whammy of work and girls smacked the boys of Muddy River in 1950. I had just escaped seventh grade, Jim, eighth. The inevitability of girls—I mean REAL GIRLS—came upon us before we could do a thing about it. And the same goes for the new reality called work, and I don't mean paper routes, allowance chores, or occasional odd jobs. WORK fell upon us in early summer, as if eight or ten sets of parents had held a secret meeting. I picture their leader— he could have been my dad standing before the worried assemblage, "They're galavantin' from hell to breakfast. We'll stick together on this. They need tough summer jobs, every last one of them."

What little we knew of work was one of those "facts of life" things reserved for some time in the future. Without warning, the "future" took Jim and me in the summer of 1950, ending glorious summer freedom, as decisively as if a judge had banged his gavel, declaring: "Your Muddy River adventures are over." One day Jim, Buck and I were fishing rosy creek chubs with fly rods on Cow Creek, the next day all three of us were growing blisters.

Dad's decree came at early breakfast on the sixth of June. We had enjoyed less than a week of freedom from school. "Your mother has packed your suitcases," Dad announced. "The *'Boys'* need help. They've had a dry spring. They need extra hands to irrigate and keep up with everthing else."

My mind whirled. The 'Boys,' of course, were Dad's three brothers on the ranch, near the Confluence in McKenzie County. Jim and I had gone to the ranch to hoe corn a few times on weekends, and wrestled calves at branding time, but suitcases didn't sound good at all. I waited for Jim to do some powerful talking.

"Suitcases? Why do we need suitcases? We can take a change of under-shorts and go for a couple days."

"Won't do," Dad said. "The Boys want you two for the summer. You're damn lucky you have generous uncles to educate you. I told them, 'If my boys break a horse's leg or wreck a piece of equipment, just let me know what I owe.' We're leaving in five minutes. If we high-tail it, we can get to the ranch for a half-day's work. Grab your stuff." Dad pointed at the suitcases and long strided his bow legs for the door, plain to see on a mission.

Over the next hour's drive to the Erickson ranch, talk came mostly from one direction: from Dad to us, about learning to work, and how he was paid by the wagonload for pitching shocked wheat when "I was younger than you boys."

"Talked to Ernie Bundhund yesterday," Dad said. "Buck's going to work in the Massey-Ferguson shop erecting hay mowers and swathers."

"Funny, Buck didn't mention it to us," Jim said.

"Maybe Buck hadn't been told yet," Dad said.

We rode the final 20 miles of gravel roads in silence, Dad content with his decision, Jim and I stunned, bound for purgatory. We visited the ranch a couple dozen times a year and seldom saw the big folks doing anything but work. Same went for our two oldest cousins. Jim and I had never imagined ourselves in the same kind of predicament.

Until today I had always anxiously anticipated the last mile where the road drops suddenly from the prairie and winds down, following the flank of the "Road Coulee" and its greenery of chokecherry, ash, and aspen, and where sharp eyes could possibly spot the antler tine of a bedded white-tail buck. The Road Coulee was lush and beautiful, sporting bounding cottontails, chickadees, woodpeckers, sharptail grouse, and—50 years back—home to a famously tough homesteader named Pegleg. And yes, he was one-legged. Gramp told stories about "tough as nails" Pegleg choosing independence, living out here far from any town. Maneuvering on one good leg and a wooden one, Pegleg built his cabin on the steep eastern hillside in the aspens. Though his cabin eventually burned, images live on. Again, on "going to work day," I conjured Pegleg stumping a steep trail to fetch creek water, chopping firewood, and—best of all—a-horseback, his wooden leg fitting perfectly in his special leather stirrup cup.

Dad shifted his Ford V-8 into first gear to hold us back. The winding road was steep enough to pop ears, and today, added hollowed-belly to my mix of feelings.

We rounded the last bend into the bottoms, where in 1901 Great-grandpa George Millhouse had cut a clearing in the ash forest and built his homestead cabin. In 1948, a few pioneer structures remained, including an ice-house, barn, pole corrals, and the old bunkhouse. A working Delco wind generator perched on a knob 300 feet above the ranch headquarters. The Delco sent electricity down a wire to be stored in six-volt batteries housed in the old bunkhouse.

Our uncle, Frank Erickson, and his two brothers operated the expanded ranch. On the inaugural day of work for Jim and me, we drove into the "yard," where Uncle Frank was hunkered under a skittery horse named Bug Eye.

Dad stopped the Ford at a respectful distance. We shuffled over to watch Uncle Frank shoeing. To Jim and me, Dad said, "He's trimming and fitting," and to Uncle Frank's bent back, "Got two green honyaucks for you."

Uncle Frank dropped the hind foot and patted the horse on his rump. "Well, I can take some green outa them, then we'll see about the honyauck part," he laughed. He nodded in the direction of the "bunkhouse." Since the old log one "had seen better days," he directed us to the modern version, an aluminum "tear-drop" camp trailer parked against the horse corral. With his one good eye twinkling, Uncle Frank said, "Stow your bags, boys. I'll finish up here, and I'll take you out to the field. I've got corn that needs hoeing."

Dad had brought us to the ranch last Sunday to fish catfish. On our way to our catfish hole, we passed the new corn crop, a field of seedlings stretching a half-mile north from the bluff across the flats to the woods. And it all needed hoeing! I was a sick puppy, my dreams of a Muddy River summer smashed to smithereens.

That was *the* day, sixth day of June, 1948, Jim and I began 10-hour days of summer work, minus the Fourth of July and Sundays.

Every morning started the same. At first light, a rooster with a sick sense of humor hopped on the corral rail not 10 feet away and bugled into the open window of our trailer. Minutes later, from 100 yards away on his doorstep, Uncle Frank hollered loud and clear, with a laugh in his voice: "Mornin' in the swamp," meaning in 30 minutes we'd better be at his breakfast table looking chipper.

Jim and I irrigated and hoed corn, fixed fence, drove cultivators, and bucked hay bales that were nearly as heavy as we. A few times we were allowed to "cowboy." Blistered thighs and sore butts proved cowboying isn't as fun or easy as Lash Larue makes it appear.

By mid-summer the concept of work had begun to grow in us and had a decent chance of surviving. I know this, because just before falling asleep at sundown, end-of-day interchanges between Jim and me produced revelations, such as Jim's: "You know that corn field on the east that I irrigated?"

"Yah?"

"I went by there today. I *heard* it growing."

Somehow, Jim and I found energy after suppertimes to stretch our days by tending throw lines on the river, dunking in the swimmin' hole, or exploring the countryside. We were encouraged by the fact that the ranch headquarters of three family homes, shops, barns, and corrals lay smack in the middle of unpeopled bottomlands and hill country beckoning for exploration.

The ranch's settlement lay at the foot of a 300 foot east-west bluff covered with buckbrush, creeping juniper, and gnarly blue juniper. "Lewis and Clark walked those four miles across the bluff-tops on their way to the Confluence," Gramp had said on more than one occasion. Others too—uncles, neighbors, Dad—so many were driven to teach the history of the Confluence where the Yellowstone joins the Big Missouri. Jim and I resolved to someday follow the trail of Lewis and Clark to the Confluence.

Across the north of the bottoms lay a patchwork of irrigated corn, hay, and grain which gave way to bordering woods, and beyond that a lowland forest of ash, willow trees, and cottonwood. Further out, along the Missouri, red-willow jungles thicketed the river's edge, its islands, and former channels. The willows were often 12 feet tall and thick enough to confuse and lose a kid.

Jim and I used deer trails traveling the lowlands, and we stayed together. The deep woods harbored few indicators of civilization: an old logging road, and our uncles' whiteface cattle scattered throughout the woods. Their wilderness character hinting of mystery and danger lured us. A Hereford bull with a broken horn and bad temper roamed the woods, the sloughs hid quicksand, and coyotes seemed to lack customary fear of humans. We ran a deer trail one evening to get out of the woods before dark. A pair of coyotes came yipping behind, just out of sight. Reaching the open fields, we looked back to see their dark shapes. They trailed us to the ranch "yards," stopping just beyond the circle of yard lights to yip once more. "Coyotes are just curious," Uncle Dick said the following morning. *Yah, curious about the taste of a leg,* I thought.

Before our first ranch-work summer began, we knew the habits of the Big Missouri. Grampa Millhouse had educated us, talking expertly of the river, like a proud father. "The Missouri will do what it wants," he said. "When Lewis and Clark came through, the main channel was four miles north across the valley." Jim and I adopted Gramp's view of the untamable river, admirable for its wildness. The Missouri floods, carves channels, and builds new islands willy-nilly, perfect for beavers, snowshoe rabbits, and big-horned bucks. And, it sports fish of a dozen varieties. "After you figure out channel cats, you boys can try for sturgeon," Gramp advised.

The woods, swamps, and willow jungles bordering the Missouri were meant for seasonal grazing, family deer hunts, and were perfect places for exploring youngsters. Each trip into the lowland woods revealed something astounding, like the fleeting glimpse of a bobcat, or a bald eagle carrying off a rabbit. Hooves thundered, branches snapped, and the herd of wild horses slashed through the woods. Wood ants we discovered the hard way. We hiked too close to their mounds and the inch-long, black devils invaded under pant legs, biting like hell on their way to the soft skin under little nuts.

The adults in our lives had prepared Jim and me for our first summer on the ranch. Grampa Erickson and Grampa Millhouse had lived through homesteading hardships. Neither was a lecturer, but perfectly aware that grandchildren watch and learn. Five pounds of extra boot mud on a deer hunt?—Don't mention mud, just kick it away on a log. Sogged with wet snow—"Let's build us a fire, Davey."

We had taken "grampa tough" to the Muddy River, especially Jim, with his inborn tenacity. If nothing else, I was stubborn. I refused to be a "chicken" in front of Jim. Now we'd see if our Muddy River "boot camp" training would stand up to ranch work and ranch play. For starters: sunburn, blisters, sore muscles and leg cramps, poison ivy itch, and 25 mosquito bites on inventory. What to do? Ignore. At age 13, Jim claimed, "Mosquitoes used to bother me, but I'm immune to them now." There is some truth to Jim's theory, but I don't know the balance: how much truth, how much fiction. I know that before our time on the ranch, the rankness of cottonwood sap burned my nose. Now, when gone from the cottonwoods I miss their awful perfume.

Little by little our ranch work toughened Jim and me. Blisters became callouses, skin leathered, and muscles stopped their rebellion. Our adventure itches helped, too. With every opportunity we journeyed away to the bottomland ash and cottonwood forests, the slough country along the river. But the bottomlands were too vast and complicated. We'd need more summers. Yet, the bottomlands comprised only one-half of the ranch's geographical fascination, the hill country being the other half.

Exploring the hill country meant climbing the bluffs. From their tops we found it impossible to move on without a long study. From the heights we viewed the wooded valley and the winding Missouri coming out of Montana, headed east. With a telescope we could have seen the Montana-Dakota smokestack at Williston. The bluff-top became a favorite place, dependable for "Prairiefied air," as Little Gram explained: "breezes to open stuffy noses and perfectly perfumed with wildrose and buffalo grass."

From our vantage point on the bluff, Jim and I spotted the gap in the bluff, the same one discovered by Meriwether Lewis searching for the valley of the Yellowstone River. Then, 143 years later, Lewis and the Yellowstone were popular subjects around the Erickson ranch. "First chance we get, Dave, we'll hike the bluff-tops to the Confluence, just like Meriwether Lewis."

Two summers later, Jim and I took that hike to the bluff overlooking the Confluence. "Dave, if you'll take off your hat," Jim teased. "You'll look just like Sacagawea." As I look back on our boyhood journey, with Queenie, the ranch collie dog trailing along, I envision our boyhood journey as a sort of historical re-enactment without deerskin shirts, cameras, and scribes.

On one of our first visits to the ranch blufftop, Jim daydreamed a plan. "We'll build a raft and float to Williston. We'll pick up supplies in town, then float to Mandaree to visit Gramp's Indian horse trader friend." With his plan tucked away, Jim turned away from the bluff. As usual, he didn't say anything, just took off. In three easy strides he gained his traveling lope. I labored after him, trying to keep up. We headed south across the rolling prairie and descended into a network of thicketed coulees that ran in four likely directions. We tried them all. That was the night we found our way to the ranch yard by moonlight, having been long lost in the coulees.

Jim and I quickly dispelled notions of stark, featureless prairie. Over subtle rises we'd find deer trails leading us into gentle buckbrush draws that steepened, joining larger ones overgrown with chokecherries, wild purple grapes and wild plums, clustered aspen, and trickling, sweetwater springs. Before that first summer was over, we'd visited most of the coulees within five miles, including one with a spring, a rusted bucket, and the fallen logs of the Adler's homestead cabin.

There were neighbors too—Papineaus to the east, Lasseys and Meyers south, and Dobiases west. We'd occasionally see one of them on the horizon riding a tractor or horse. Sometimes we hiked or rode our horses close enough to wave.

One mid-summer day, riding four miles south to the Meyers' place, we decided to stop in to water horses and us, too. After slugging her icy well water, we sat down at Mrs. Meyers' kitchen table and feasted on her fresh glazed doughnuts from her iron stove oven. As we dunked the last of her doughnuts in malted milks, Mrs. Meyers' son, Billy, rode in on his tall black horse. We watched him tie the horse next to ours and hurry to the back door. Evidently, he'd smelled his Mom's Monarch bakery in action. "You're late, Billy," Mrs. Meyers laughed . . . "Good thing, too. These boys were starving." Neighbors received special treatment.

Though Jim and I needed seasoning to fully understand, working on the ranch could not rob freedom's spirit anointed by the Muddy River. We simply moved it to the ranch. Besides, board and room and five bucks a day made us relatively rich. Next year, packing slightly more muscle and know-how, we were paid six dollars a day, and so on, until—as college boys—we earned 12 dollars a day for

Erickson ranch work.

Our town buddies didn't fare quite so well. They all had summer jobs, Buck assembling Massey-Ferguson farm machinery and keeping the concrete floors gleaming, Big Bervie laboring in his dad's grain elevator, Jack spiffing up Pontiacs and used cars on his dad's car lot, and Jelly working with a long list of odd job customers. But the guys were too handy to spending places: the Barrel Drive-Inn, the Castle Café, movies, and especially girls who hankered to be treated. By age 14, what is the point of buying gas for your dad's car unless it's to drive up and down Main Street looking for girls, who were tooting and waving back from their dads' cars?

Though we saved more money than our Muddy River friends, Jim and I fell behind on girl education. Heck, we *started out* behind, handicapped by not having sisters or girl cousins close by. School was of no help. Serious female subjects, like *How do babies get started?* were not mentioned at school or home either. We'd heard partial explanations from savvy buddies.

I was in 6th grade and Jim in 7th when Dad believed it was *time.* The family mood was strange and uneasy. Early on a Saturday morning in October, I heard Dad talking quietly and seriously on the phone. "Yeah, that's good. I'd appreciate it," he said. "They'll be ready." When he finished, he hollered, "Jim, Dave, come here."

I didn't like the sound of that. I wished Jim and I had completed our plan to get up before dawn and bike to the nine mile bridge for walleye fishin'.

"Grampa Millhouse will be by in 30 minutes," Dad said. "He's going out to McKenzie County to sell insurance. He needs you boys to go along with him." Dad's "Needs you boys to go" meant *"you're going,"* under the circumstances, a puzzle. During the school year Mom and Dad dependably granted us Saturdays free of duties, save minor chores. Today the set-up smelled of obligation.

As Gramp opened our front door he boomed out his announcement loud enough for yard-working neighbors to hear, "Are the Riley Boys ready?" Our neighborhood was in on the tease, that boys so-named lived a completely carefree life. With his easy old horseman's stroll Gramp rollicked through our house, his grand entrance that Jim and I had known since babyhood. "Get 'em up, head 'em out," he hollered.

Today, on a Saturday, we were dismayed to see Gramp in his selling outfit—striped white shirt, gray suit, tie, and his gray fedora. He was unfit for anything fun, especially a side trip to hunt pheasants.

"Can't we hunt pheasants today, Gramp?" Jim asked.

Gramp spoke apologetically in his funny third person. "Your Grampa has a long drive to sell insurance today. No time to hunt pheasants. But, I brought the .22 in case we spot one hunkered by the road. We better get going." Mom's face confirmed her interest . . . something strange in the air.

Jim and I trooped along after Gramp, and we all piled into the front seat of his black Nash, me next to Gramp, my turn. An unlit Camel bobbed in his lips, "Big decisive Millhouse lips," Mom called them. "I get to light for you, Gramp," I said.

"It's my turn to keep the matchbook, though," Jim said (we both had matchbook collections). I held the match, and Gramp sucked to make the cigarette glow. He dropped his gear stick into first and popped his lurchy clutch. We jolted ahead down First Avenue West.

"Your Dad said you'd want to go along and keep me company," Gramp said. He motored down First Avenue West to Broadway in his usual manner, cigarette between his teeth, elbow out the window, laughing all the while at Amos and Andy on the radio—except at intersections. Every intersection, it seems, had at least one "horse's ass driver."

"McKenzie County today, boys," Gramp exulted. "The best people in the world live out there."

Gramp's radio still crackled reception when we topped Indian Hill; but, he turned it off before Amos and Andy had finished joking. Jim and I took a quick, puzzled look at each other. Gramp tipped his hat back on his head and smashed his cigarette in the ash-tray, his prelude to talking. Out of the blue came his familiar statement, the one we'd heard since toddler-hood: "Time you boys learned how . . ."—'to shave,' I silently finished for him, Gramp's well-used joke: his sideways expression about our growing up that was far ahead of reality, since neither Jim nor I grew more than peach fuzz.

As we left the city limits on Highway 85, a horse and rider crossed the highway, headed for the stockyards. The horse stumbled, enough to start Gramp on horses and ranching. "Damn flat-pastured horses. 'Don't waste a minute on one like that,' Johnny Rider said. Taught me all I know about horses." That's what I liked about country travel with Gramp. Most anything could set him off, reflecting on his old time ranching days. Stories retold got better and better, like his Montana horse-buying expedition, for example.

"Eastern Montana was wild country then, outlaw gangs from Texas and Oklahoma, horse thieves, and crooked traders." Gramp's Montana story was worth a book's worth of time.

"The Rider boys insisted Montana had a surplus of good horses. Just take your time out there, and if the deal doesn't smell right, walk away."

Gramp's Montana story lasted 20 miles. He told the story from the reservation Indian side this time, and I was convinced that Gramp, his brother, and his dad had hoodwinked the Indians, only to be just as convinced minutes later that the Indians cheated the Millhouses. Gramp chuckled, "Horse tradin', boys, just a game. True winners and losers are not easily determined. Same with the horses. We brought 60 head back, some losers; but, some turned out decent, made us some money."

"The Rider brothers made our Montana trip pay off. Three of them crossed the river to help us work the horses. Johnny ended up staying four years."

Gramp strayed off into another Rider story . . . would have been good too—about Johnny roping wild horses; but up ahead a big white-horned buck leaped the highway. The buck dashed out of the brush next to Timber Creek. "They love this crossing," Gramp said. "Time huntin' season comes, though, you won't see that big fella anywheres near a road. He'll tuck into deep brush somewhere."

"Then how would you hunt him, Gramp?" Jim asked.

"Hoodoo would find him," Gramp said. "Damn, I wish I still had a Hoodoo."

Jim pushed me against the backrest so he could talk to Gramp straight on: "Hoodoo? I thought he was just your cow pony." Jim and Gramp enjoyed bantering back and forth across my lap that way.

"Hoodoo was my greatest cow horse ever," Gramp went on, "but he was a deer hunter, too. He'd sniff out bucks for me, pick up their scent and ignore the does. He would freeze and tremble a bit under me, then blow and stare into the brush. Hell, he was better'n a huntin' dog. I'd look right between his big black ears and know a buck was hunkered tight to the ground in the brush. I'd pull the .30-30 and wait till the buck got nervous. I liked to nail him on the first jump before he got up a head of steam."

Gramp storied pridefully, pleased to be a character in the story, but reserving glory for other ranching characters, and dogs, and horses. "Wasn't another like Hoodoo in the entire ranch country of western Dakota," Gramp drove with one hand, gestured with the other. "Before I got him though, I thought he'd be too ornery and independent to be owned by anyone."

"But you broke him, Gramp?"

"Wrong word, Jimmy. If I tried, he'd a broke me. No, he had to be gentled, boys. Breaking—I never liked the sound of it. The idea is to tame a horse. First though, Hoodoo needed catching."

"You told us before, Gramp," I said.

"Not exactly, Davey. You were too little to understand, then. I told a simplified version."

Jim elbowed me, "Yah, Dave. Be quiet. I want to hear."

"Okay, the catching part . . . Hoodoo wandered up outa the wild badlands herd. I guessed him for a three year old. He'd been banged up by the old stallions down there.

"Hoodoo hung around Frank Martell's place. Frank baited him into a corral; said he escaped by jumpin' six tall rails. But then, I thought—naw, that's Frank talkin'."

Jim chimed in, "So, you didn't believe him, Gramp?"

"Not at first. Frank was a trader, liked to entertain folks. Paint couldn't dry on Martell's stories. Come a day later he might throw in different characters for the same story. Way I found the truth about Hoodoo is I loaned Johnny Rider for the Badlands roundup."

I remembered about the Riders. "Johnny? Your cowboy?"

"Better'n a cowboy, Davey. Johnny was a first-class wrangler; best horseman I ever knew. He came back from the roundup and told me he and Martell spent half a day tryin' to corner a handsome young stud, same one as broke out of Martell's corral. They named him Hoodoo for the way he shadowed in and out of the Badlands' hoodoos.

"So, how'd you get him, Gramp?"

"Comin' to that part, Jimmy, but it's a long story, maybe too long for today."

We had passed through the middle of McKenzie County, leaving behind the swath of farmland ripped apart by August hail. With crop disaster behind,

Gramp's spirits improved. "Damn, look at that wheat stubble," he said. "Bet they took forty bushel to the acre."

"Gramp, you gotta finish about Hoodoo," Jim pleaded.

"Yah, Gramp, you can't quit now," I added.

He leaned his head my way with a new cigarette in his big lips, "Give me a light, Davey." He drew hard, pulling my match fire right into the Camel. Then he blew smoke hard. That's how he smoked, not a sucker, more a blower. Gramp was a master with his cigarette. On occasion, he'd notice a wart on Jim or me. He'd glow the end white hot, like a branding iron, then burn off the wart.

East of Alexander, Gramp stopped for a cow-calf herd pushed across the highway by on old rancher and a boy, riding cow horses. "Pretty damn nimble, that one," Gramp said, as he watched the boy's horse cut around a spunky calf . . . "footwork like Hoodoo's."

"Hoodoo, yah . . . I'll shorten the story. Should be a book called 'Hoodoo.' How'd I catch him? First off, he made a mistake leavin' the Badlands. Winter turned mean and he went north after ranch feed, then went from winter fattening to mare chasing, usin' horse logic, which is none at all."

"Hold on, Gramp," Jim said. "How about horse sense you told us about?"

"Tain't the same. Horse sense keeps him from hurting himself in most circumstances. In those other circumstances, that's where horse logic comes in, and it doesn't work."

"So Hoodoo got hurt? What happened?"

"You'll see. You'll see. But not until after the catching part and after Johnny and I . . . uh, tamed him. Time you boys knew about that, too. It's a bit complicated; you gotta listen good."

Gramp eyed us seriously; we nodded, and he continued. "Martell wouldn't a minded some Badlands blood, and there it was, Hoodoo sneakin' around every night. Frank had some pretty mares open. All he had to do was turn 'em out."

"Well, why didn't he, they . . . why didn't something happen?" Jim asked. I had a fuzzy idea of what Jim was asking.

Gramp held a palm up for quiet. "Damn, what a crop of barley there." How he kept from wrecking I don't know, with eyes on everything but the road. He woofed air out as if his Hoodoo story tired him . . .

"If I was Martell? If I was Martell, I wouldn't have turned my mares out either; Hoodoo would have bred them all right, but he'd a' run 'em off into the Badlands, too. As for catching Hoodoo, Martell made his plan too obvious: six riders circling, tryin' to keep Hoodoo centered. One of his hands told me the story—said Hoodoo toyed with Martell and his men, instead of breaking out early."

We'd been on the road for an hour. Yet, for once I wasn't anxious to arrive at Gramp's destination. "How much further, Gramp?" I asked, hoping for time.

"Soon as I finish my story, we'll be there," Gramp said. "We're comin' into badlands country now." He shifted down to second as the road curved from tall grass prairie into a juniper coulee.

"Two days after Hoodoo outsmarted Martell's men, Johnny Rider spotted a big horse on the bluff above our corrals . . . couldn't have been one of ours. Ours were corralled for using and a few pastured in the bottoms. So, Johnny came to get me and my spyglass. He took the first gander. 'It's that wild ass Hoodoo hoss,' he says. While I spied on him, the horse stood stock still except for lifting his nose into the wind. Sixteen hands, coal black, and a white diamond on his forehead . . . had to be him.

"'I'm betting he'll be down here sniffing out your mares before nightfall,' Johnny said. He sez, 'Rollie, he's good horseflesh; you oughta give him a chance. Make him a trade, breedin' for his freedom.'

"I never doubted Johnny. I sez, 'Johnny, I'm makin' you the boss of this deal.' The horse was showing skitterish, but Johnny said he wouldn't be leavin' anytime soon with my mares coming in heat. Johnny was right, as usual. Over the next three-four days Hoodoo snuck around the edge of the woods, eyeballing our mares."

"But then you roped him, Gramp?"

"Jimmy, ten fine mounted horsemen together wouldn't have been able to corner Hoodoo to get a rope on him. He had either the woods or the bluffs ready at his back. We had to have a better plan. It was up to Johnny to come up with it.

"'Rollie,' he says, 'we'll get him. His weakness is his nuts. We catch him, put him with your mares, then we'll cut him.'"

Gramp gave us a looking-over, waiting. Finally, Jim volunteered: "Like Grampa Erickson casterates little bull calves, you mean?"

"Yup, you do the same to a stud horse. That is, if you don't want him kicking the hell out of your geldings and running off with your mares. So, you boys know all about baby calves and how the bull and the cow start it all?"

"Sort of, Gramp. We saw bulls get cows before," Jim said.

"Good, then you'll understand how Johnny and I outfoxed Hoodoo."

I felt left out, left behind, and I had to know, "What's casterinating got to do with it?"

"*Castrating,* Davey." Gramp grinned directly, his message meant for me. "Well, Davey, stallions have one track minds, if you know what I mean. Then they try to logic a plan for their hankering, like Hoodoo did next. I almost felt sorry for him, how horse logic failed him. But human logic is real logic, especially for fellas like Johnny Rider. There'd be nothin' to capturing Hoodoo, not after Johnny Rider explained his plan. . . . Now Davey, if you don't get this right off, Jimmy will help you."

Jim pushed me back against the seat's backrest so he could see Gramp full on. He couldn't wait. "What? What kind of plan?"

"Simple, Jimmy. We had eight mares in a big corral. A couple of them were coming in heat. You boys know about heat?"

Jim shrugged. I shrugged.

"Well, never mind about that for now," Gramp said. "I'll explain it later. Anyway, Hoodoo was lonely. He wanted some—uh, companionship with my mares. At evening time he came out of the woods and snuck around moonin'. 'Tomorrow we'll carry out the plan,' Johnny sez.

"Hoodoo was as sly as an old buck deer. I couldn't get within a quarter-mile of him on my best saddle horse. So, Johnny and I scrambled up into the bushes on the side of the bluff, stayed upwind from Hoodoo. He was all het up, pacing, agitated. Soon as he sashayed for Beehive Creek for water, we slipped down the hill and went to work. I fed the mares some fresh hay to bait them to the back of the corral, away from the gate. Johnny opened the gate and fixed it to close with a rope pulley with a bucket of rocks for weight. He buried himself in the haystack behind the corral, holding the end of a string of four lariats tied together for a gate trip. I skedaddled up the hillside and hid in the brush to watch Johnny's plan play out."

Suddenly Gramp straightened in his seat. "Goddam, will you look at that! No way to haul a horse. I can't stand to look." Ahead of us, on Highway 85, someone in a smoke-puffing old pickup pulled a two-horse trailer containing a buckskin horse. The trailer wobbled as if pulled along on a limp rope. "Get the hell over," Gramp hollered as he jerked his wheel to pass.

"Where was I? Oh yeah, Johnny and I were set up to trap Hoodoo . . . waited no mor'n five minutes, and here he came on the run, all snorty, knowing something wasn't right. I can picture him like it was yesterday, head held high, blowin', throwin' his long black mane. What a beauty, lean and muscled from runnin' the Badlands. He moved into the entrance of the open gate and pranced left, pranced right, twitching his ears. I tell you my heart was poundin' something fierce, just like waitin' for a big buck antelope to come in range. Hoodoo sniffed Johnny's pulley set-up with his chin on the ground, like a coyote checking the bait. Then he stood tall and tested the air in all directions. Finally he walked part way through the gate, pawed Johnny's lariat, and whirled around. I swear he raised his eyes to the hillside, looking for me. But one of the heated mares sashayed by Hoodoo, twitching her tail. That did it. He followed her into the back of the corral. He smelled Johnny, twisted and reared—ready to run. But he was too late, because Johnny had pulled the trip. Hoodoo ran berserk, looking to jump out; but my corral was eight rails high. We had him."

At this juncture Gramp's Nash did some bucking of its own on the steep, broken sandstone road. Around a bend and there was the green valley of the Little Missouri River. Dust spiraled up through the floorboard. Gramp choked and spit out the window. "The old timers had it right," Gramp said. "They resisted automobiles. It doesn't rain, you choke on road dust; it rains, the road's as slick as goose shit."

My mind couldn't take on everything at once, wanting the end of the Hoodoo story, but fascinated by the mazes of colored badland pinnacles and domed bluffs, even pillared hoodoos, namesake for Gramp's famous horse. Complicating further, Gramp wanted to fill us in on his customers down the road, the ranching Fredricks family. We came around the last curve where the road flattened into the valley of the Little Missouri River.

"There it is boys, the prettiest ranch privileged to exist on the Little Missouri. You're gonna like the Fredricks—salt of the earth. Too bad you'll miss their two boys. Chips said they're tending line camps."

A glint of river showed through the cottonwoods, and in a nook of upriver woods, low-roofed log buildings, corrals and livestock—all the busy-ness of a ranch operation. "Living this far out, the ranchers can't run to town for things." Gramp pointed out the necessities: a blacksmith shed, a machine shop, milking barn, horse barn, and the rocked entrance to a dirt mounded root cellar—all surrounded by corrals, both round and rectangular. Here and there about the place were dogs, cows, and horses—one led by a cowboy.

The low-built log ranch home nestled in the shade, among the cottonwoods. As Gramp pulled to a stop, a tall thin man in a pearl buttoned shirt and a sweat stained cowboy hat got up from the porch. "That's our man, Chips," Gramp said with a smile. "Let's go meet him."

After hand shakes, Mr. Chips, I mean Mr. Fredricks, motioned for Gramp to sit with him on the porch. Like spectators, a pair of oiled saddles rested on their trees next to Mr. Fredricks.

A pretty lady with a tanned face, short blond hair, and smiling brown eyes came out the door. Gramp grinned and nodded at her. "Nelly will take care of you boys, unless I miss my guess."

Nelly Fredricks took Jim and me to her kitchen and served us glazed doughnuts and coffee with cream fresh from the morning's milking. After our treats and a few niceties, I was ready to leave. I ached for the end of Gramp's Hoodoo story, and pheasant shooting. I suppose Mrs. Fredricks noticed our fidgeting. She dug us with questions, probed enough to learn of our Muddy River. She wanted more, and not out of politeness. Jim even told her our broken raft story, though we hadn't fessed up to Gramp about it. Nelly laughed easily and often, clearly liking the same things Jim and I did.

When Nelly's turn came, she told us about her secret beaver dam pool on the Little Missouri that hid catfish big enough to eat baby muskrats; and hunting mule deer bucks alone, riding out with a frying pan, coffee pot, and a bedroll behind her saddle. "The biggest deer horns out there on the barn are mine; don't let Chips tell you any different," she laughed. Nelly told of trapping coyote and bobcat and going with Chips and the sheriff to catch a rustler. Her stories, ours—we ran through an hour in nothing flat.

Jim and I were in the act of double-teaming: walleye and bullheadin' stories from the Little Muddy. That's when Gramp and Mr. Fredericks came in. Mrs. Fredericks smiled, "Rollie, bring the boys back sometime with bedrolls. They can stay in the bunkhouse and ride my horses down the Little Missouri to my catfish hole." We looked at Gramp, hoping for him to agree.

"You can have these Riley boys for good as far as I'm concerned," he said with a wink. "You ain't gonna get much work out of them though."

We gathered around Gramp's black Nash, and Gramp hugged Nelly and shook hands with Chips; signaled for us to do the same. After goodbyes and "Come back real soon," we were on our way.

Heading up the lane, Gramp took his hands from the wheel and clapped, "Chips is lining up for a big policy." I didn't understand the why or how Gramp could earn money that way.

We'd driven two hours to get to the Fredricks ranch, visited an hour, and now needed two hours to get home, plus time to pot a pheasant or two along the way. And for sure we had to hear the end of the Hoodoo story.

Wheeling the curves fast on our climb out of the bottoms, Gramp smoked a cigarette and whistled between puffs. He was in his thinking mood.

"Gramp, do you know she rides a horse after big muley bucks?"

"Be surprised if she didn't, Jimmy. She'll kill him, gut him, pack the buck in, age the meat just right, and cook the venison perfect. A ranch woman is handier than any town man. Your Gram sure is."

Gramp seemed ready to go on, but didn't. For once he trained both eyes on the road. I suspect he was thinking about his years with Gram on the ranch . . . and his years with Johnny and horses like Hoodoo.

I'm sure Jim read Gramp, same as me. "Gramp, you never finished with Hoodoo," Jim said. "How you tamed him."

"But why did you want a wild horse anyway?" I asked.

After a pause and a "*Whew*," Gramp pushed his hat back exactly as Mr. Fredricks had. "It's simple as pie, Davey. But I, myself, hadn't thought it out. It was Johnny who put me onto Hoodoo's potential. You see, for several years I'd been training colts, working my older horses, and going to horse sales, looking. But I wasn't satisfied. I wanted a horse savvy enough to push ornery cows out of the brush and agile enough to run the coulees and bluffs without breaking a leg . . . a horse that knew which move to make before I did."

"Then when Hoodoo came along, and we had him corralled, Johnny says to me, 'Rollie, we'll tame him down and see how he works cows. I'm bettin' he'll be exactly the horse you're lookin' for. His orneryness is what makes him special. He's tough and clever. He's learned by runnin' wild in the badlands.' Yessir, a dose of independence, that's what Johnny and I were looking for. 'Got the makins,' Johnny says. Johnny said it exactly that way. I remember him, just a kid, riding into the bottoms after his first roundup. He came back with the Badlands way of talking."

Gramp shifted down and tromped on the foot-feed, attacking the steep grade cutting through the rim of the broken country. A mule deer buck jumped close out of the junipers, crossing the road. "Young three point," Gramp said. "Nellie sees him, he'll be camp meat."

The road crested, topping the last of scarred sandstone and junipered draws, not yet gentle, but soon to be, enough easier that Gramp shifted up to second gear and sat back, chuckling a private joke.

"Johnny was on the money with Hoodoo. It's the same with you Riley boys. Your folks let you run wild all over town and up and down the Muddy River. As long as you stay out of trouble, it's good for you. You learn how to run without breaking a leg, if you know what I mean."

Gramp looked us over, wondering about something, his story-telling grin gone. Jim noticed and moved him along with questions.

"Gramp, how'd you break . . . I mean tame—a wild horse like Hoodoo?"

"The first part was easy," Gramp said. "We didn't do anything but watch. We let him breed two mares. Then another came in heat a month later, and he bred her, too. We got a pretty filly and two colts. The one we called Kid turned out to be your Uncle Milt's best saddle horse. The Hoodoo deal worked out just right for me . . . and for Hoodoo, too, though if he'd known what was coming next . . . well, he might've broke out an' run for the badlands."

Jim leaned past me again: "But Gramp, you don't think Hoodoo minded being captured?"

"Horses don't think that way: what if this and what if that? All I know is Hoodoo's havin' the mares settled his mind some. He learned that my ranch was not a bad place to be." . . . Gramp enjoyed a good laugh at that. "Hoodoo got his comeuppance though. After we babied him with grain, we halter broke him. Then Johnny and I tied him down and cut him. Johnny fed him alfalfa dosed with molasses and shine whiskey to keep him calm while he healed."

I pictured the knife and the poor horse, bug-eyed with fear. "Why did you have to do that, Gramp?"

. . . and Jim: "Just because Johnny said?"

"Remember what I said about running wild? Stud horses don't have enough brains to deal with females of their breed in a civilized fashion. We castrate them. Now you guys are young. But you're smart. You'll learn when it's time to chase after females of our own breed. You'll know what's right and what's wrong. Know what I mean?"

"Sure, Gramp," Jim said.

"Yah, yah, I know Gramp," I said—a half fib. I didn't know what to say. Best I could come up with was, "Yah, Gramp, guys gotta be nice to girls."

"Gramp, a big rooster, up ahead, on your side," Jim yelled. But, surprisingly, Gramp didn't even slow down.

"There'll be pheasants down the road pickin' gravel. Right now we need to finish our *talk*." By the question on Jim's face he wondered, same as me: What kind of "*talk*?" . . . the one that Gramp had been warming up for all day?

Gramp cleared his throat and shifted in his seat. Without a sideways glance, he poured forth his topic in one long fast sentence, jamming words together: "Your dad wants you to know about girls, what you should do with them and what you shouldn't, and about how they get babies . . . I don't mean girls that ain't supposed to have babies, but grown-up married women having babies and how it happens." He allowed himself a quick glimpse at Jim. Gramp waited. Jim volunteered nothing. Gramp gave me a chance, too; he leaned past Jim to look in my eyes. Finally he said, "I told your dad I thought you boys already know."

"Oh, yeah, Gramp, we know all about those things," Jim said.

"Good for you Jimmy. So, Davey—how about you?"

"Yah, me too, Gramp. I know about girls."

"Good. Thought you did all along. Okay, Davey, you hop in the back seat. The .22 is there." Gramp inhaled long, then woofed it out. He shifted down to second, "pheasant spotting speed," then tipped his hat back. "I told your dad you boys understand more than you let on; but still, we should visit some more about . . ."

"Gramp, Gramp, stop," we hollered in unison, "a rooster! a rooster!" Up ahead the rooster pheasant streaked across the road and ducked into the ditch grass.

"Right . . . here," Jim said, and Gramp eased to a gentle stop. I steadied Aunt Jeannie's pump .22 on the window frame.

The cock stretched his neck to above the sweet clover so's he could peek at us. I centered his red patched head in the peep sight and squeezed. The .22 cracked sharply, the hollow point whopped. I hopped out with Jim, and he ran for the spot, reached down and grabbed my pheasant. "Counting last year's, that's number 10 for me," I bragged.

"Might have been your best shot, too, Dave . . . no meat spoiled, dead center in the head."

Gramp held the trunk lid open and Jim handed me the bird. "He's a big old rooster, three or four years old," Gramp said. "Look at the size of those leg spurs."

"Yeah, Mr. Rooster, you're beautiful," I thought, as I tossed him in. "And I'm glad you came along when you did to end that other subject." Gramp was glad too. He stowed his suit coat and tie in a cardboard box in the trunk.

Back on the road, Gramp was his old self, waving at the occasional good driver and cussing "dilly-dallying dingbats." With musical accompaniment, Gramp could have sung a good cussing song: "You think you own the goddam road? Get the hell over. Drive it or park it."

Amongst his driving instructions, Gramp swiveled his head to the stubble fields, squinting against the slanting sunlight, looking for pheasant heads. Finally, next to Timber Creek, Jim spotted his rooster under a buffalo bush picking the orange berries, and on the slope of the coulee, a prairie chicken in a tree. He potted them both. Dang Jim, he never misses.

Gramp's insurance trip had turned much for the better. A happy trio, we were, rolling into town. At the edge of town Gramp chose Broadway and cruised over to First East, down the street to the Barrel Drive Inn, where he ordered up three root-beer floats. We slurped and talked of our day with no more mention of male-female things—horses or otherwise.

At our house, Gramp went around back with us to clean birds. He poked his head in the door and hollered: "The Riley Boys are home." His jibe at us sounded sweeter than ever, as if Gramp had handed us official papers titled: *"Renewal, Temporary Kid Licenses, 1948."* However, the nature of that day wasn't to be forgotten. We had been put on notice. Grown-up girls had to be reckoned with—but now they were a more imposing subject, and becoming more curious with each passing day.

Our "Kid Licenses" expired in 1951 when Jim and I received perfumey cards in the mail invitating us to attend the Rainbow Dance. Mine was from Karen Kline, a pretty, laughing sort of girl. But she was taller than me, a good runner, and a home run hitter. My mind buzzed with trepidation. Three days later I showed the invitation to my mom. She turned instantly angry, a surprise.

"You haven't answered this invitation?"

"No, I'm not going. I can't dance."

"You get on the phone. You're lucky to have a nice girl invite you. And you're going. You need to learn to dance. Here, take her card. Her phone number is right there in the corner."

"But I can't dance."

"I'll teach you. Gram will help. Now call Karen. If she still wants to take you, ask her about the color of her dance dress."

"Why?"

"Because you'll need to get her a corsage, and you'll want the flower to go with her dress."

"A flower?—you mean one I'd buy?"

"Yes, and with your own money. Now call her, and tell her you're sorry for waiting so long to call."

I stalled until Dad came home, but as always he backed Mom one hundred percent. I made my jittery acceptance call. Jim made his, too. And over the next week prior to the Rainbow Dance, evenings in our house were devoted to dance lessons, until Jim and I became rudimentary dancers. Well, that's a stretch. Gram and Mom managed to teach us most of the way to a thing called the two-step.

On Saturday evening Mr. Kline pulled up at the entrance to the Masonic Hall ballroom to unload his daughter—my date—and me. I knew enough to get out and hold the door for her. Like Cinderella, she extended a satin slippered foot. She leaned forward as I grabbed for her arm. Holy Moley! Her pinky-white gown slipped at her vee front showing untanned borders of milky skin, foothills skin, off limits for looking. As if she didn't care about my stolen glance, she flashed a big smile.

At the entrance to the ballroom I dropped her arm momentarily and loosened my tie knot that Dad had tightened twice. Her daddy honked his DeSoto's horn and we turned to go in—she, cool and relaxed; me, sweaty and stiff.

The ballroom's polished floors gleamed, its surrounding balcony hung with fancy colored crepe paper. The ballroom was oval shaped and larger than the Armory gym, but without the smell of old sweat. On the far end the band milled—about 10 of them—some tooting horns, others visiting. They wore Navy blue suits and red ties. By what miracle, I wondered, could I escape this place?

Jim and I and our friends hung about the tables at the edge of the floor, while the girls clustered in groups, twittering and pinning on corsages, taking no chances with jittery boy hands poking pins into embarrassing places.

A corner of my mind settled on Jack, now in high school and sometimes seen driving Main in his dad's Pontiac coupe and his white sport coat hanging on a hanger in the back. But Jack was too old for the Rainbow Dance and, and . . . where else to turn for advice? . . . Buck—had to be Buck.

I remembered Buck telling about his slick dancing cousin teaching him. Maybe he could settle my fevered mind. He was easy to find. He stood a head taller than most eighth graders. I spotted his flat, kinky top in the center of a ring of seventh and eighth grade boys. Buck reminded me of John Wayne surrounded by his captains and lieutenants. I sidled in amongst the group. We were like gray horses in a gray herd, wearing sports coats probably selected from the same sale rack at Greengard's. We'd all chosen dark ties with faint colored stripes—all except Buck, who wore a bright red tie and Navy blue sport jacket. Buck was

Buck, looking at home in a fancy outfit.

Buck lightened the mood, putting his troops at ease. "Nothing to worry about," he said. "You listen to the band and move with the beat. It's easy. Just relax." No doubt easy for him, the most self-assured, relaxed guy in town. However, he offered no dance card exchange with Karen and me, and I didn't blame him. Why would he subject his date to a kid who'd never danced with a real girl?

Karen gracefully helped me in her quest to find enough beginners to fill our card. I wanted to leave the hard ones blank, like the waltzes, schottisches, and fox-trots. Karen, though, hung tough, no deal. She and her friends were bent on filling their dance cards.

The band played a soft background tune while a beefy lady spoke into a microphone, something about the history of the Rainbow Dance and *blah, blah,* and *"how nice . . ."* I couldn't hear from the back of the ballroom, or maybe I didn't especially care to hear. My feet hurt. The oxfords that Uncle Earl gave me were the fancy kind that needed a month's wearing to take out the stiffness. I had worn them only once to Uncle Dick's wedding.

"Look up, David. There's my mom. Hi, Mom!" Karen giggled and waved toward the overhanging balcony.

Karen's mom sat amongst the crowd of parents peering down. Most were parents of girls. They sat forward, chins jutting over the rail, bald eagley, scrutinizing the klutzy boys entrusted to their daughters.

The leader and namesake of the Billy McFarlin Orchestra strolled smoothly to the front of the stage, accompanied by a drum roll. He spoke into a microphone: "Good evening ladies and gentlemen. Welcome to the Rainbow Dance. Our first number will be a Glen Miller tune, 'Moonlight Serenade.'" He smiled and bowed. As he pivoted to his players, he swooped his arms and horns magically sung in unison. The musicians' professional presence, boutonnieres and all, was just too fancy. Why were they here for a kid shuffle?

I felt her warm hand on my arm. "Are you ready to dance with me?" Karen smiled and wafted rosy perfume. She wrapped her warm hand around my clammy one, a simple thing, but then again, not simple at all—mysterious even. I suppose my four sealed layers of underarm Right Guard had been already weakened by impossible challenges bombing on me: the band-master's "gentlemen," delivered as a command; the beady-eyed parents; my worry about dancing. So when Karen squeezed my hand, my Right Guard dams burst and hot rivers of sweat rolled down my ribs and pooled above my belt.

Karen giggled, "Isn't this fun? I'm so glad you came with me." Incredible, I thought. She really likes this. She moved very close, much closer than I had expected. I gulped loud enough for her to hear. She seemed unfazed.

Concentrate, concentrate! Let's see: hand in hers, but first . . . wipe off the sweat. Now the other arm . . . which one? Oh, the right, the only one remaining. Put it around her waist. Move now, and don't look down. Step one, two, and one, two — Hey, there's Jelly over there with Ginger. Jelly looks rough. Oh oh, I shouldn't have been gawking. "Ouch," Karen said.

"Sorry," I said. "I didn't know your foot was there."

"It's *okay*," she said, smiling.

How could that be? I clomped on her and she didn't even try to get even, not even a little toe jab to my shin.

Amazingly, I discovered Karen wasn't the only one so impossibly pleasant. All the girls on my card were nice, even when I crucified the waltz. Our dance card put me up against Peggy Smitters. Ha! I mean *really* against. In the middle of the slow number she whispered warm breath in my ear: "You don't have to be so bashful. We're supposed to be right together, like this." She pulled me tight against her. She laughed at my red face, but not a real tease; extra nice actually. Furthermore, Peggy couldn't have been one of those rumored to have false ones. Son-of-a-gun, they were warm and pokey good, mysteriously so.

Before the dance was over, I learned that all of the Rainbow girls were soft, gentle, and perfumed, even the toughest ones: the Hicks girls, and Yvonne—the horse rider—and the great runner, Leah Russell. They had always been special, not too girly—smarter than that. Now they were, uh . . . *different*.

It seems that girls had us diagrammed on some kind of map, while on our side of the equation—with rare exceptions like Buck and Jack—guys were flummoxed; even the smart ones who we leaned on, let us down. Take Lars, for example.

Lars's no-nonsense Danish dad demanded that Lars learn everything precisely the first time. For instance, Lars told me that the worst butt kickin' his dad gave him was when Lars had been discovered using baling wire to fix a farm machine instead of returning to the shop to find a machine bolt. So, when Lars was taught the intricate details of farm animal reproduction—and later on—human sex stuff, he became a reliable confidant, encyclopaedically speaking. Yet, when confronted with the most benign of girl encounters, Lars turned into a red faced, stammering, Nervous Nelly. Furthermore, he danced like a wound-up tin soldier. Sadly, when watching him, I knew that Jim and I, Jelly, Stew—all of us save Buck—looked like Lars: an army of jerky tin soldiers holding warm, confident, graceful—*real* girls.

By eighth grade, I was old enough to appreciate the mystery swirling about real girls, the growing up ones. Some were so astounding that they frightened courageous guys like my brother. In his freshman year Jim came up against a dilemma. With a week left before the Freshman Frolic, all of his buddies had dates. Jim drug his feet. One logical girl choice remained: Marlene, the name he'd let slip a couple times. I was well aware of his turmoil, because the subject came up several times around our house. "Jim, you've got to call," Mom said. "You cannot call at the last minute."

"I don't know who to call; the ones I know are already taken."

"What about Marlene? You said you were going to ask her."

"I changed my mind. I'm not so sure about her."

Dad looked up from his paper reading. "Phone the girl, Jim. You get to the dance; then you can dance with them all."

"She might have a date."

"Jim, she doesn't," Mom said. "I played bridge with Maude. She says Marlene's waited two weeks for the phone to ring."

Jim fussed and grimaced while we waited. He finally gave in. "Okay then, but everybody go in the living room. This is private."

We did as he asked; but, I stood around the corner, where I could hear how he'd talk to a girl as beautiful as Marlene. She was tall and slim except right where grown-up girls aren't slim. She had skin like warm caramel, green eyes, and dark hair down past her neck. I'd seen her around Jim and the gang at the Castle Cafe. She was serene and mysterious, not giggly. In other words, fearsome. Jim wasn't the only guy intimidated; that's why Marlene didn't already have a date when Jim phoned. His call proved her scarier yet.

"Is Marlene home?" Jim spoke in a near whisper: "It's Jim Erickson."

His silence indicated a question from the other end. Finally, he fumbled out his reason for calling, "I . . . I need to, uh, ask Marlene about . . . about the Freshman Frolic."

While Jim waited, I caught myself from blurting out, "What's happening?"

Jim made throaty, chokey sounds. Then he said, "Okay . . . okay, Missuz . . . ah . . . goodbye then."

I couldn't stand the suspense and burst around the corner. Jim had replaced the receiver on the wall mount, but had forgotten to take his hand away.

"What happened?" I asked.

"I have to call back later," Jim said.

"Why?

"She was in the b-bathtub."

"You said *'bathtub?'*"After Jim answered, "Yah," he forgot to close his mouth. He looked like a bug-eyed rabbit hunkered in front of a coyote.

Marlene's Mom couldn't have known much about boys. Otherwise, she'd have known better than to tell a 14 year old boy that beautiful Marlene was in the bathtub.

Jim's Freshman Frolic with Marlene came and went as a complete mystery. "Okay," is the most Mom could get out of him, her question answered in the same manner as Jim's responding to, "How are feeling now that you've thrown up?" He had October and Buck to thank for his recovery from the Freshman Frolic.

Before daylight on Sunday, the morning after the Freshman Frolic, Buck called to share his secret. Jim shook me awake. "Buck called. Get the heck up. Walleyes are moving up into the White Bridge Hole and beyond."

"How does *he* know?"

"How do you think?—His dad said. He's a walleye master, you know. The big walleyes follow the minnow schools right up the river when the water cools. But Mr. Bundhund can't go, gotta work. Buck's taking us instead. And we've got to promise to keep his deal a secret."

This is almost too good to be true, I thought.

We surrounded the Bridge Pool, Jim, Buck, and I with casting rods, working Lazy Ikes deep, waiting for telltale soft tugs. Buck caught the first, Jim the second, each about four pounds, October gold and thick with summer fat.

"Keep pitching," Buck said, after another hour. But besides a hungry goldie that grabbed my Ike, we had no more action in the White Bridge Pool. Maybe we'd spooked the rest, or maybe they'd swum up through the chute. Anyway, Buck and Jim decided to move upriver to Six Mile.

"Don't give up here, Dave," Buck advised. "Just let 'em rest a bit."

There's walleye up there, gotta be huge,
and never been fished.

With a chilly Canadian wind swooping down the Muddy, I decided on a fire and a reed stogy, just for old times' sake. Hadn't smoked one for two or three years.

My driftwood fire roared, heat pushing me back. Then it calmed to half flame and half ember, perfect for cozying. I tucked in close and lay back listening to the rapids, hoping to catch a glimpse of the yipping coyotes hunting along the Indian trail on the bluff.

The wind swirled, pushing driftwood smoke over me. I tossed my reed stogy; no point to it now with the pleasant driftwood smoke in my nose and my wool jacket.

Summer had gone. We hadn't gotten around to rafting. The Bervigs' spare bridging planks were piled by the side of Stony Ford, waiting. Let's see . . . We could build the raft extra big. The Bervig boys would help, they loved to build. We'd float down the Muddy to the Missouri.

Naturally, it was Jim who first proposed floating the Muddy. We'd have gone, too; but, other adventures came along, crowding out a raft trip. And the girl thing got in the way. Buck had a girlfriend. And Jack wouldn't go; he was having too much fun riding his fat-tired, sooped up Doodlebug with his girlfriend behind, holding him around the waist.

I tossed sticks on my fire and untethered Jim's idea. A one-day float would take us to the mouth of the Little Muddy River. We could camp there overnight. Smoky Roy would come to our campfire. We could leave the raft with Smoky and turn right, up the Big Missouri. Jim would guide the expedition. I'd be the organizer and trip recorder, like Meriwether Lewis. Buck could part from his girlfriend for a spell. He'd have good maps. We'd go light: backpacks, .22's, throw lines . . . extra hooks, matches, and knives. That's all. Well, maybe light bedrolls. In eastern Montana we'd pool our summer money and buy an Indian packhorse from the reservation to carry our dried venison, our stash of smoked goldies, and our bedrolls. Travel right up the wooded bottoms. Let's see, 20 miles a day and we'll make the Rockies by November.

Or—or how about the other way? Yeah, with timber galore downriver from the dumpground we'll build a raft big enough for the Missouri and the Mississippi, too. Smoky Roy has all the tools needed, and lives close by, so he could help us build a perfect raft. We could put a sail on our deluxe raft; make it big enough to sleep right on board. We'll never go hungry, that's for sure. The big rivers are chock full of channel cats, flathead cats, and sauger; the bottomlands full of game. Maybe Smoky would go along. We'd heard him brag on the Mississippi.

South of South Dakota we'd run into more like us, river rat rafters, some of them Negroes with banjos and harmonicas and singin' like the dickens around campfires. Razzie and Stahl would fit right in on that trip, Jelly too.

Jeez, I should have thought of the other direction, probably the best of all. No raft needed; but, similar gear would serve. Go light, living off the land, head north to the headwaters of the Muddy. There's walleye up there, gotta be huge, and never been fished. Then, we could hike right on up into Manitoba where fishin', huntin', trappin' Canucks would help Big Bervie build an honest-to-goodness freighter canoe out of birchbark. No, build two canoes so everyone could go. Jack would sign on first. He often glorified Canada. He said, "The water's clear as air, northern pike are big enough to eat ducks, and walleyes have never seen a lure." And this would be the trip for Little Ergie. We'd never shut him down. He'd study the rivers; find one we could paddle clean to Hudson's Bay.

As the daydream faded, I heard the sandhills coming, the great birds of the north crying: "*hoowaauk, hoowaauk, hoowaauk.*" Unlike my plans, theirs were perfectly ordered: pointed sensibly south in October. I tuned my ears toward the cries, straining my eyes, and picked up the vee of cranes coming down the valley, swinging away from the hills, easterly toward White Bridge and me.

I laid out flat on my back, watching their urgent flight, celebrating their cries of joy. The giant vee of tiny flapping crosses appeared overhead, skirting the underside of puffy clouds: "*hoowaauk, hoowaauk, hoowaauk,*" each cry of each bird synchronized with its wing beat.

Never, ever would the sandhills cease their celebrations, glorying as if their urgings were meant for all of us looking up, wishing we could fly. This flock . . . before the week is over they will be in the warm south, stabbing frogs.

"Dave . . . Hurry! . . . Hurry up!" Jim's voice floated over the rapids from upriver. "Hurry, Dave! Get up here! Buck and I found the *mother lode* of walleyes" . . .

A last look at the sandhills, and I grabbed my rod and ran.

Chapter Thirteen

Transitions

Our elders had faith in the proposition that somehow—in my dad's vernacular—their youngsters would "turn out *alright*." Dad often wondered aloud about children's prospects, acknowledging fate and circumstances with his familiar greeting: "How's the world treating you?" As to how the world treated the Muddy River Boys, and how we "turned out," readers may judge for themselves. For whatever successes we have enjoyed, I credit the elders of Williston for teaching by example, granting us liberties, and watching over us from a well considered distance.

Whop!—girls. Bop!—Work. Bam!—High School. Whop whop whop!—High School Graduation, and the boys of Muddy River scattered like quail. We went off to colleges, military services, and jobs. None of us "closed the door" behind, yet life grabbed quickly and raced away with us. We heard occasional snippets of news about each other gathered by family and mutual friends: "Dale Bervig is getting his doctorate in engineering."—"Buck is in Florida now."—"Ergie's a grandfather—can you believe it?" That's life. No one is ready. Then calendars turn and I look back: "What a great and privileged boy's life, roaming the countryside, discovering, and laughing 100 times a day with rollicking, fishin' fool guys."

Gratefully, Muddy River times live. We bottled memories, aged them, sip them now, and celebrate. Until now, we have celebrated, for the most part, singly. Then my Muddy River project was born, precipitating a reunion of sorts, in which correspondence, long telephone conversations, and face-to-face meetings have brought us together. I thank my fellow characters of "The Muddy River Boys" for the honor of sharing you with readers. The following imperfect bios are brief cameos of our lives following our Muddy River times.

Allen Bervig (Little Bervie). I knew Allen's voice instantly, though I hadn't heard it for 20 years. Punctuating with laughter, expecting good news, upbeat; Allen is the same guy I remember from the huddle: "Erickson, you block the end; I'm going for a touchdown." Allen went off to North Dakota State University, graduated in economics, and entered the Army as a 2nd Lieutenant. He studied ordnance and was stationed at Fort Bragg, NC, where he and his unit trained to handle tactical nuclear warheads. After army life, Allen worked for Proctor and Gamble and International Harvester; then, he went back to grad school, entering the teaching field. He taught at the National College of Business. Allen finished his career at Williston State College, where he taught economics for 30 years. Allen and his wife, Diane, summer at their cabin on Lake Sakakawea, formerly the free running Big Missouri that is now backed up by Garrison Dam.

Dale Bervig (Big Bervie). Dale, the bridge builder—the "beaver," picked up the phone, listened, and then laughed long when he heard about *"Muddy River."* I wheedled him to learn how he earned B.S. and M.S. degrees in Mechanical Engineering from North Dakota State University and a Ph.D. in Engineering Mechanics from the University of Nebraska. Dale deftly changed the subject to the "string theory" of quantum physics, unaware that "fish guys" like me naturally shy from math and physics. I talked him into sending more career details, whereupon I learned that Dr. Dale worked with teams developing fighter aircraft for General Dynamics and designing helicopters for Bell. Dale has worked in the energy field for nuclear, coal fired, and renewable energy projects. He has six engineering patents. Following retirement, Dale founded Turvitron Energy Systems, LLC.

Ernest (Buck) Bundhund. Buck began his college career at the University of Montana and finished at the University of North Dakota with an accounting degree. He served in the U.S. Army, stationed in Japan. Buck married Louise, his high school sweetheart. Buck and Louise, with two children, moved six times as required by Buck's career with General Electric. I surmise that Buck took on the business world just as he became the master of Muddy River walleyes, never forgetting a fact, becoming *the* dependable expert. A Florida retirement, then Whitefish, Montana and the Flathead River drew Buck. No surprise—Buck is a canny trout fisherman, and forever a Muddy River Boy.

Ron Erdmann. Casey Stengel said, "They say you can't do it, but sometimes it doesn't work." Ron, "Little Ergie," personified Casey's wisdom when he followed the gang to Spring Lake, Muddy River, and home—seven miles on his tricycle. Again, when Ron asked to play both quarterback and safety, 'they' said, "It can't be done." Yet Ron excelled at both positions, sometimes playing entire 60 minute games for the North Dakota State University football team. He played four years and captained the team his senior year, all the while excelling academically. Ron was commissioned an Army 2nd Lieutentant, serving in Germany. With a degree in Physical Education, Ron taught high school P.E. and coached three high school sports. After trying his hand as a college football assistant coach, Ron married Jean, a teacher, went on to graduate school and received a degree in Educational Administration. Ron and Jean worked in public education in Minnesota. Ron finished his career in Willmar, Minnesota, where he'd been high school principal for 25 years. In retirement, Ron and Jean travel from their home in Willmar to camp and fish for walleyes. In winters they pursue salt water fish near their winter home in Port Isabel, Texas.

Norman Jellum. Forever the "shark," Jelly says he wins a few pool tournaments in Yuma, Arizona, where he and Cathy winter. He still talks rapidly and moves fast. I remember his boyhood jobs running into double figures, motivated by his driving energy and curiosity. Norm attended the University of North

Dakota, roughnecked in the Dakota oil fields, and served in the Army. He spent a career in the Postal service and retired in Bend, Oregon. I routinely receive "bragging photos" of Norm and his buddy showing off stringers of rainbow trout and kokanee salmon.

Jack Shemorry. After "hello," here came Jack's million dollar laugh. "Like the rest of you guys," Jack said: "College, army, marriage, and then the 'real test', making a living." That he made a career in the automobile business surprised no one. He worked for dealerships, before being beckoned by Pontiac Motor Division of General Motors. Traveling the West for Pontiac put Jack in touch with mountain trout steams, whereupon he became an avid fly rodder. Jack's forever fond Muddy River memories induced him to embark on his 1970 commemorative kayak trip down the length of the Little Muddy River.

Jimmy Bruegger. Long after the Muddy River Boys went their separate ways, Jimmy continued his sports reporting and box collecting, riding his "hundred thousand mile bike." He became friends with new generations of youngsters. When physical infirmities hampered his mobility, Jimmy moved to the Bethel Lutheran Home, where he became an in-house sports reporter and well-loved resident.

Kenneth Johnson. Unfortunately, Kenneth's grammar school bully-boy reputation loomed larger than his successful National Guard boxing performances. Few knew that he concealed a softer, kinder persona. He revealed his better side when he took me along to Smoky Roy's fishing operation. Then, 60 years later, after embarking on the *Muddy River Boys* project, I learned more from my boyhood friend, Terry Flatley. Terry had also been a victim of Kenneth's excellent pugilism. Terry and I were talking long, reminiscing. I told him: "Hard as it is to believe, Kenneth and I had come to an understanding," the fishing trip and all. "I'm not surprised," Terry said. "After my dad died, Kenneth pulled me aside at school. He was known as Stretch then, of course. He said, 'Sorry about your dad. I promise I'll never beat you up again.'" I believe that was Kenneth's time of awakening, when he turned a corner, headed for a better side of life. His mother with the smiling eyes believed in him . . . Smoky Roy too, and Smoky could not have been wrong. As for me: Kenneth, I hope and pray that wherever you are, the world "treated you well." And, by the way, when you clobbered Terry, I noticed a tilt of your head. You telegraphed just before you came with your left hook. If I had one more chance, I would have slipped that punch and landed one of my own. Don't laugh. At least I would have rung your bell one time.

Jim Erickson (Big Eric) and Dave Erickson (Little Eric) . . .
With summer job discipline added to school and home discipline, Muddy River parents consented to bigger adventures. We saved our money and pooled it for trips to Flin Flon, Manitoba, Swan Lake and West Glacier, Montana. We'd plan

for the last week of summer and take off in a car borrowed from a courageous dad. Our dad even loaned us his Ford V-8, though I had no driver's license, and Jim had only a beginner's permit. Buck, Jack, Big Bervie, Jim, and I rented a five dollar a day cabin on Swan Lake. We fished for trout, swam in icy water, and hiked to alpine lakes. Jack was the oldest at 18, yet we swaggered into a bar with cowboy hats pulled down over our foreheads. We were served Great Falls Select in steel cans. Fortunately, our juvenility quickly became obvious, and the bartender refused to serve us more of his skanky beer.

What a great, exhilarating time!—on our own, acting grown-up. I'm convinced we owe it to our experiences in the Little Muddy countryside that our parents allowed Montana and Manitoba trips.

After high school, lives spun faster, in every direction; "unreasonable" professors expected obedience and performance; jobs sometimes disappointed, and for all but Jim—we faced grizzly bearish boot camp instructors. Jim would gladly have taken on the military experience, too, just as he met every boyhood adventure head on.

At 14, Jim was a lithe athlete with state championship potential. Football and track coaches watched him and smiled. He was already the second fastest runner in high school and of the rare breed excelling in both sprints and distance. But then, Jim was ravaged by polio, and was left with what he calls "my bad leg." He returned from hospitals and therapy with his dauber down. Gratefully, our football coach, H. L. Pederson, an ex-marine, intervened. He befriended Jim and selected him as his team manager for football. Following football season, Coach Pederson formed a mink trapping partnership with Jim. Coach Pederson challenged Jim, mentally and physically. Jim struggled through snow and ice, using a single crutch, swinging his bad leg. By the end of the trapping season, Jim's persistence and courage paid off. He became strong enough to cover one half of the trap line. Growing up, Jim had taken on every imaginable challenge presented by vast prairies, the Missouri River swamps and jungles, and the Little Muddy River country. Until polio, he'd ventured forth with boundless curiosity and a body built for speed and endurance. After polio, with one mighty "good leg" he carried on, bolstered by his indomitable Muddy River spirit.

At 15, Jim sought everything possible, much of which the rest of us took for granted. The centerpiece for boy-girl encounters was the 10-block stretch of Main Street from the Great Northern Depot's U-turn north to Harmon Park's U-turn. Back and forth, driving Main, the separate sexes drove past each other in their father's cars, waving and flirting from open windows, and occasionally signaling to pull over to trade passengers.

"Dad, I'd like to borrow the car," Jim announced.

"Sure, Jim, but not yet, you know you . . ." Dad struggled to say what both knew: Jim's leg muscles, even in his "good" leg, weren't strong enough for driving.

"Buck will drive, Dad," Jim argued. Under those terms, Dad relented. He handed Buck the keys to his Olds, and Buck and Jim headed for Main Street.

As Buck turned the first corner, Jim said, "Pull over. I'll drive us down Main."

"Jim, you know you can't, not yet."

"I'm driving, Buck. Pull over."

Jim slid behind the wheel, and Buck was ordered down on the floorboards. "Let out some clutch, Buck, and gimme a little gas." Jim steered, shifted, tooted and waved at girls . . . and commanded his hunkered co-pilot: "More gas, Buck . . . clutch—let her out, gas, brake, hard brake. Whew!—that was close." Buck learned floorboard driving, not comfortably, but good enough to laugh about. The driving duo carried on for three months until therapy strengthened Jim's muscles.

Buck and Jim's escapades lasted through high school. After high school, Jim enrolled at Montana State and Buck the University of Montana. A year later, I followed Buck to the university, where he became my fraternity "big brother," an apt arrangement since he'd been looking after me for years anyway.

I enrolled as a tentative future geologist, made the Grizzly basketball team, and joined the fraternity social scene; yet, I was a troubled young man, my head swimming with career possibilities, but not happy with any of them. Two years later I transferred to Montana State and changed my major for the third time.

In March of 1958 I received a letter from Mom. After updating family and town news, she eased into the subject of my old friend, Roy Clapper. Mom wrote: "We know now that you and Jim were right all along. Mr. Clapper was the victim of a deadly rumor. I'm sorry to have to tell you, he died a lonely man." Mom couldn't bear to use the word murdered, choosing to let the enclosed newspaper clippings inform me.

Roy C. Clapper, born June 6, 1891 in Altoona, Pennsylvania. Died March 4, 1958, Williston, North Dakota.

Roy Clapper had been bludgeoned to death, in all likelihood, by a Phillip "Bob" Sweeney, who was concurrently implicated in the stabbing of Bert Floyd, 77, of Williston. As reported in the *Williston Herald*, "Police decided to check on Clapper's safety, long rumored to have kept a large sum of money at his shack, after Sweeney was searched and $1121.49 and a number of receipts bearing Clapper's name were taken from his pockets." In ransacking Clapper's home, the killer broke the padlock to Roy's "secret room" and found his coin collection worth about $150. The crook must have been crazy angry with disappointment, because he threw the coins far and wide.

The case against Mr. Sweeney was never pursued, evidently because his stabbing of Floyd and prior convictions were enough to lock him away for life.

Roy Clapper registered for the draft on June 5, 1917. He was inducted into the Army in Williston on March 28, 1918, and served in WW1. He returned and attempted to scratch out a living on 80 acres near Epping, North Dakota. He walked away from the farm after too many drought years and failed crops. Roy remained a bachelor, a laborer, avid fisherman, and a tinkerer. His frugality drove him to "save" broken things. He moved into the Williston dump, hacking out a living collecting and repairing. For a number of years he was paid $20 a month by the city to "look after the dump."

The county recording clerk listed his occupation as "junk dealer." The *Herald* mentioned Roy's heavy drinking, "but in recent years had stopped." Roy Clapper was interred at Riverview by Fulkerson's of Williston, undoubtedly one of many kind businesses who, in good faith, never traded in rumor.

Roy's life story, as the Muddy boys knew it, tells only of a soft spoken, friendly man who loved children and chose to live eccentrically. And well—I wish to add—in the criterion of kindness.

A few days after learning about Roy's tragic murder, I sat brooding on the "Admin" steps at Montana State. Roy's murder was just one more knock on my head during uncertain times. I had a wrecked basketball knee, through with college basketball. I needed a career path and a *FROZEN NUTS* decision. (A) Join the Navy? (B) Quit college and get a job? Or: (C) Change my major yet again? Sitting on the steps, turmoiling, I happened to be looking down the sidewalk at Lewis Hall, Natural Science Building. . . . The nickel dropped: "Natural science, that's me," I said to the empty campus.

The big campus clock said five before six, yet I found the door to Lewis Hall open. I walked in, and strolled the length of the first floor hallway, where I found empty laboratories and offices. I climbed to the second floor. Halfway down the hallway on the left, a door stood open. I peeked in. A thin, white haired man sat at his desk, surrounded by shelves holding jars of pickled fish. He had heard the ancient floor squeak and looked up. "May I help you?" Behind him was a placard, C. J. D. Brown, Ph.D, Professor of Fisheries.

"Yes, sir, I really need to talk to somebody," I said. "And I found the door to Lewis Hall open."

"Hmn, you appear to be troubled," he said. "Tell me about it." He backed his wheeled chair from his desk well and turned to face me.

"I want a college degree, sir, but I've changed my major three times, and I'm still not settled on a career path."

Dr. Brown smiled. "Sounds familiar; I had the same problem when I was your age." He nodded at a chair. "Here, sit, and tell me about yourself. First, tell me what you really *like*, not what you think you should like." As I slumped into the chair, my eyes strayed to his pickled fish. He noticed and grinned.

"This is part of my Nile River collection, and there"—he lifted his eyes to the highest shelf—"a few Amazon specimens. So, you came into Lewis Hall for a reason. Do you like biology?"

"I always have, sir, even before I knew what it was called."

"Specifically . . . can you tell me what excites you about biology?"

"Well, anything wild, especially fish. I don't know why, but I've been intrigued by fish since I caught my first yellow bullhead."

"And where was that?"

"The Little Muddy River in North Dakota."

"Interesting! I know of that little stream," Dr. Brown said. "It's more important than people know. The Little Muddy River needs a taxonomic fishery study. I may do it myself someday."

. . . Now I *really* liked the professor.

We talked of the Muddy and its spectrum of fish species, back and forth, like a couple of campfire "Joes." Then suddenly, as if he knew all he needed to know about me, Dr. Brown pointed a long bony finger. "You love fish. Perhaps you should consider making fish your subject of study. You haven't mentioned your current academic endeavor, but if you have no passion for it, I wouldn't waste another minute."

I looked at the professor with my mouth open. At least *he* was decisive. "I recommend you think on it for a spell," he said. "Assuming you have a strong interest, come in and visit again. Then visit with my graduate students. If you are still favorably inclined, come back with your transcripts. If I enroll you in my program, you'll put your heart into it." He said that as a statement and a slap on his desk. That's when I got around to introducing myself properly. As I shook his strong hand, I knew I'd be back.

Dr. Brown signed me up in fisheries and arranged transfers into required biology courses. Then he put his heart into teaching and guiding me. Aha! He was a tough and loving professor, a maker of careers, mine being one of hundreds. Dr. C. J. D. Brown, world traveled ichthyologist . . . as a senior, I earned the privilege of calling him "Brownie," though I said it to his face only after graduating in Fish and Wildlife Management, special Option: Fish Culture. Brownie came to my rescue in the winter of 1958. I became a lightfooted student and pushed my GPA above 3, whereupon Brownie began compiling a list of prospective fisheries employers, the most important one being in Idaho.

The day after graduation, my fishin' buddy, Steve, and I hiked into the Madison River's Beartrap Canyon. For ten glorious days we fished rainbows and browns, living on boiled coffee, fried potatoes, onions, and fried trout. That was as good a fishin' trip as a man can ask for. With my happy meter pegged at the top, I headed for Idaho, where my fish farming job awaited.

Brownie was right. Do what you love. For nearly 50 years, doing what I love, I've found few reasons to leave Idaho. One of those reasons is the pull of North Dakota, where once or twice a year Jim and I spend a week paling around our old "stompin' grounds," beautiful places which Jim never abandoned and knows better than anyone alive.

Jim also spent two years at Montana State, and while he was there became well acquainted with the trout of the Yellowstone, Madison, and Gallatin Rivers. But his true calling, career-wise, was selling. Jim went back to Williston. He became a crackerjack commission salesman.

Jim was born in 1937 on October 31st, significant in two ways. Our Grampa, Rollie Millhouse, was also born on October 31st, which begs questions concerning mysterious biological factors at work molding paired personalities. Secondly, Jim's Halloween spirit sports fun and shenanigans, not spooks and goblins.

Being a natural salesman of unwired ideas—like swimming the Missouri River at sundown, or selling us on the frozen nuts swim in April—Jim came easily to selling tangible things like automobiles, trucks, and oil field equipment.

As he was about to leave car and truck selling for the oil fields, his boss, the dealership owner, lamented to me, "Darn I hate to lose him."

"And why would that be?" I asked.

"Look over there," the dealer boss said. A crowd of customers and sales people surrounded Jim. He was telling a fish story, maybe for the fourth time, his tale growing each time. The boss smiled. "Jim is the reason folks come in off the street for coffee and to kick tires on my showroom autos. He's also the reason this place doesn't bore my people to death."

In 1984, Jim came to Idaho to hunt elk in the Gospel Hump Wilderness with me and four of my long time elk hunting buddies. For eight days, Jim hunted solitary, gimping out of our wall-tented "Saddle Camp" at daybreak with his walking stick and a slung rifle. During evening campfire hours, we'd spread the map, and Jim would trace his day's route. He surprised us all, trudging to the top of Confusion Mountain, where rocky cliffs, jackpine, and jungles of alpine fir "spin compasses." "Sure, I was confused," Jim said, "but I found a bull moose who wasn't. I followed him off the mountain." By our third campfire session Jim had warmed to his North Dakota story telling. Our master hunter, Kelley, primed Jim with a libation called the schlocky. From his slickered story vault, Jim pulled the one about his friend Joe Hawk, the musical Sioux. "Joe came onto Clausen's Ag television show to perform on his singing, whanging saw. The saw refused to whang, and Joe sez into Clausen's mike, 'It was 20 below last night. Shouldn't a' left da saw in da back a' my pick-up.'"

Finally, except for the camp owl, Saddle Camp fell silent. We stared into the campfire embers, buzzed on camaraderie and laughter. The full moon bathed our clearing and outlined the massive ponderosa. From its top, our camp owl hooted once more, a sort of mountain taps. Our senior sage, Ted Eastman spoke: "Jim, that was bull-shit, but *good* bull-shit. You guys should write a book." I said nothing, but had already begun preliminaries, making notes, and refreshing memories by hanging out with Jim on annual fishing and hunting trips to North Dakota.

On a frosty October morning, Jim and I drove 40 miles north to the slough country to hunt "cattail roosters." The dirt road crossed a swampy little gully holding a rivulet. On the bridge railing, in professional lettering, an official had properly designated the headwaters the "Little Muddy River." Yes, RIVER! I remembered Gramp lambasting the highway man for allowing Little Muddy *Creek* on his sign.

With six roosters in the sack and Bodie, Jim's lab, sleeping on the seat beside him, Jim turned for Williston and home. As usual, Jim chose a circuitous route to see "different country." He drove south on country roads toward the Little Muddy valley. An hour later I recognized a rim of hills topped by a pair of oil well rigs. I had to know: "Jim, isn't our old stomping grounds, the "Catwalk," on the south side of that bluff?"

Jim grinned and pointed at his jockey box. "There's an oil field map in there. Take a look." I pulled the map and unfolded it. On the map, east and a little north of Williston was a boldly printed designation: "Catwalk Oil Field." Jim had underlined it in red. I was at first stunned—our childhood shenanigans formalized on a map? Upon reflection: why not?

The following day we hunted by the Montana line on a rancher friend's property, where Jim had located a perfect combination of grain and buckbrush. Bodie and I would flush, and Jim would stand in blocking position to shoot. On the first quarter mile run, Bodie flushed three roosters for me—easy shots. We flushed two toward Jim, and he downed them both. "Great huntin' spot, Jim," I said. "I'll give you time to circle a hundred yards ahead. Bodie and I will come through—you'll get your third bird for sure. Shouldn't need more than 10 minutes; maybe we'll go to your house and watch the World Series."

"We could, but . . ." Jim turned for his pick-up. "Come on," he said. "You think this place has roosters? You won't believe your eyes when you see my hunt over by the Muddy."—Classic Jim, knowing another rooster would end our hunt early, while more country needed exploring.

An hour later, Jim walked me through beds of prickly pear on the high prairie. We followed his faint trail to a point on a 300 foot bluff overlooking the valley of the Big Missouri. All I could say was, "Wow!" We gazed over many miles of river channels, willow islands, and swamps of the river delta, where the Big Missouri meets Lake Sakakawea. The lake was formed as a result of the Garrison Dam project in the late 1950s. Directly below, Jim pointed out a channel snaking down from the north. "That's the mouth of the Little Muddy," Jim said. "It's moved three miles south since the old days."

Jim swept his walking stick across the wide valley of water and greenery. "The river country fascinates me, always will, how it cuts one place, and creates land in another." He aimed his walking stick at a long, skinny island overgrown with 10 foot willows . . . "That island, for instance."

"Looks like a hundred others," I said.

"You're right. Islands fit a pattern. Many are born the same year. They begin as naked sand and mud. Then you'll see water grass and red willow shoots poking from the sand. In time, if we live long enough, we'll see cottonwoods strong enough to hold a tree stand."

"And 200 years from now, giant cottonwoods, I suppose."

"Maybe, but you never know. Rivers, they change direction where and when they want to."

"So, Jim, why is that island special?"

"Look where it's positioned, in the channel that receives the Little Muddy, and it's made of rich Muddy River mud. The island was bare when my boy Todd was born. When Todd was three, I brought him out in my boat to fish for cats. I pulled into the island, and let Todd off to pee. He was exactly the height of the willows. When we came back a year later, he'd grown perfectly at the pace of the willows. Same deal for years four, five, and six. Todd grew with the willows." Jim fell silent, musing.

"Any special meaning to that?"

"Must be; I think the shaman would say my brave grew like the willows, powerful medicine. I'll go along with the shaman. . . . Wish I had a drum."

Me too, Jim . . . a drum, a dance, a song . . . celebrate the gifts of life on the Little Muddy River.

I never tire of looking for big fish waters. In December, 2010, I scanned the "Dakota Country" whopper list. There, second from the bottom: "Jeff Winslow, Williston . . . 12 (pounds), 8 (ounces), walleye, Little Muddy River." Laughing, I waved "Dakota Country" above my head. Little Muddy River—YES!

Gratitudes

Carolyn Erickson—my wife, editor, and passionate listener—probed, questioned, and extracted memories. I'm enormously grateful for Carolyn's eagle eyes that diagnose fractured paragraphs at a glance. I'm grateful for her radar ears that hear dissonant phrases. Most of all, I'm thankful for her love, patience, and support.

I credit the good people of Williston and Williams County, North Dakota for inspiring me, and in a round-about way challenging me: Can I be the sort of person you expected? I mention a few out of hundreds whose generosity and kindness typified the place and times. Benths, Bjellas, Bundhunds, Conlins, Coughlins, Erdmanns, Eversons, Freemans, Greengards, Gwins, Hagens, Haugens, Hickses, Hvales, Jellums, Kalils, Larsens, Leiseths, Lundbyes, Lunds, Mrs. Mehus, Nordells, Skavangers, Rawitschers, Reeps, Riders, Ritters, Schwartzes, Shemorrys, Snyders, Helga Sorensen, Stannards, Stevens, Stewarts, Treiders, Vaders, Vohses, Volneys, Williamsons, Zavalneys.

Williston's formidable teachers of the 1940s and '50s put heart and soul into teaching. Principal Lily Wilkinson, Principal Gilbertson, Miss Moe, Virgil Syverson, and others set highest standards for themselves, fellow teachers, and students. Special thanks to Coach H. L. Pederson for helping my brother, Jim. Special thanks to coach and teacher, Cliff Hendrickson, for challenging me to reach for higher goals.

I'm grateful to my friends in the Williston High School Class of 1956, many of whom reminded me, "You promised a book."

McKenzie County friends and neighbors of the Ericksons and Millhouses treated my brother and me as family: Croys, Dobiases, Jacobsons, Johnsons, Hinmans, Nygaards, Mracheks, Myers, Nelsons, Lasseys, Papineaus, Powells.

I thank the Ericksons, models of fortitude. Grandparents Frank and Ida pulled 11 children through the Great Depression and set lofty goals for the rest of us. I'm grateful for uncles Frank, Dick, and Bus and their ranch families for teaching me to work—and like it.

Grandparents Rollie and May Millhouse and Uncle Milt and Aunt Jane summoned their pioneering zest for life, infectiously so.

I'm forever grateful for my parents Bill and Ruth Erickson, who forgot our indiscretions in hours, but remembered our successes forever. They believed that success grows out of self-reliance. With courage, my parents said: "Go! We'll pray for your safe return."

I'm thankful for sons Steve and Scott, who share my enthusiasm for "The Muddy River Boys." Grandchildren, Marie, Jessica, and Morgan, assisted me in illustrating fish and the "NO TRESPASSING" sign.

The Experts: Artist Shena King created "Sandhill Cranes," "Bikes/Trikes," "Frozen Nuts," "Bobcat," and "Eagle Charm." From my crude drawings, Ken Jones illustrated maps of western North Dakota. Thanks to layout editor Daryl Hunt, advisor, planner, master "Photo-shopper," and enthusiast for "Muddy River." Appreciation to the *Williston Herald* for your diligence and fairness in covering the Roy Clapper story.

Thanks to Chuck Wilder, Books on Broadway, Williston, for advice on the commerce of bookselling.

Footnotes (1) and (2): Acknowledgement to: Gary Moulton, ed., *The Journals of the Lewis and Clark Expedition,* Volume 4 (Lincoln: University of Nebraska Press, 1987). pp 62 & 60

About the Author

At age five, the author was allowed to tag along with the boys of Muddy River. He has never recovered. From that day forward his passion and—eventually—career, included water, fish, and everything aquatic. Mr. Erickson spent 42 years as a fisheries scientist in the field of trout farming. He was part of the team that introduced biological sciences and animal husbandry expertise into the emerging aquaculture industry. David was elected President of the United States Trout Farmer's Association. He served two terms on the Idaho Water Resource Board. Mr. Erickson worked for 30 years as a biologist and Director of Technical Services for Clear Springs Foods, the world's largest and most successful producer of rainbow trout. David lives near Buhl, Idaho, on a hill overlooking the Snake River. He shares "Swede Hill" with his number one lady, Carolyn, and their two lady Labradors, Pink and Blue. David is a forever Muddy River Boy and a gonzo trout fisherman.